D1283012

THESE LIBERTIES

These

"In Bimini, on the old Spanish Main, a daughter of the island once said to me: 'Those as hunts treasure must go alone, at night, and when they finds it, they must leave a little of their blood behind them.'

"I have never heard a finer, clearer estimate of the price of wisdom. I wrote it down at once under a sea lamp, like the belated pirate I was, for the girl had given me unknowingly the latitude and longitude of a treasure—treasure more valuable than all the aptitude tests of the age."

Loren Eiseley, "The Glory and the Agony of Teaching,"
Think, October, 1962.

Liberties

CASE STUDIES
IN CIVIL RIGHTS

by
ROCCO J. TRESOLINI
Late of Lehigh University

PHILADELPHIA AND NEW YORK

J. B. LIPPINCOTT COMPANY

FOR MY MOTHER AND THE MEMORY OF MY FATHER
IMMIGRANTS TO THESE SHORES
WHOSE GREAT LOVE AND WONDER OF AMERICA
THEY PASSED ON TO THEIR SON.

"To be worthy of the American heritage, the people must live up to it. To retain it, they must shape their institutions and their thoughts for its retention. That calls for full recognition by the courts, the Congress, and most of all by the great body of the people, of the true nature of the complete Bill of Rights. They must accept, support and defend it as the bastion of the social order, the bulwark of the state, the guardian of the family and the individual. That will not put an end to political acrimony, or eliminate the extremists of Left or Right. But it will establish a climate in which no political storm can become an irresistible whirlwind."

Irving Brant, *The Bill of Rights,*
Its Origin and Meaning, Indianapolis,
The Bobbs-Merrill Co., pp. 514-515,
1965.

The background material beginning on
page 3 and ending on page 8 is reprinted,
with permission, from CONSTITUTIONAL DECISIONS
IN AMERICAN GOVERNMENT *by Professor Tresolini,*
published by The Macmillan Company,
Copyright © 1965, by Rocco J. Tresolini.

FOREWORD

Rocco Tresolini did not live to see this book published—he succumbed to a cerebral thrombosis on a cloudy day late in June of 1967. He was but 46 years old and at the very height of his career, one that encompassed all those elements that make for a truly outstanding member of an academic community: sensitive effective teacher; capable, tough-minded administrator; prolific, successful scholar. But "Rocky"—as he was known to his happy and large family and his best friends—brought another admirable quality to his life and work: that of a warm, gracious, and compassionate human being with an uncommon sense of dedication and commitment to both the private and public sector of society.

It was typical of his sense of duty that, despite feeling unwell, he turned in the manuscript of *These Liberties* just a day or two before his death. Only one chapter remained to be completed, a task commendably fulfilled by his wife, Virginia. His influence upon his profession, in his teaching as well as in his writing, will long endure. The words of his dedication in this, his last, book are a measure of the noble and fine man Rocco Tresolini was.

University of Pennsylvania

HENRY J. ABRAHAM

PREFACE

Gobitis case p.183

(For more than a decade the American people have been witnesses to a veritable revolution in civil liberties. Progress in civil liberties continues at an unprecedented pace, unmatched by any nation in any period of world history. In this revolution many organs of government, including the President and Congress, have played an important, if belated, role. But it has been the Supreme Court of the United States, that least known of our governmental institutions, which has led the way and played the decisive role. Thus "the shape of American liberty has been determined, in a major part, by the willingness of the Court to assume a place as the watchdog of constitutional liberty and by its even more recent willingness to use constitutional ambiguity as a means of extending and expanding that liberty." [1])

Yet the American people continue to be generally unaware of the importance of the Bill of Rights and other constitutional provisions dealing with individual freedom. And, ironically enough, in a lifetime few Americans ever read even one Supreme Court decision dealing with civil liberties. Many factors are responsible for this state of affairs, including the inaccessibility of the opinions to the general public and, most important, the fact that the Court still remains, in the words of a newspaper columnist writing a decade ago, "the worst reported and worst judged institution in the American system of government." [2] Much of the information that Americans receive concerning the Court's work is in the form of spot news or headlines of the sensational variety which often confuse rather than enlighten and which bring down upon the Court the most thoughtless, irresponsible, and ridiculous criticism. For an understanding of American liberties there is no substitute for reading the original Supreme Court cases themselves, for "nowhere else in the literature of the world can one

---

[1] Loren P. Beth, "The Supreme Court and American Federalism," *St. Louis University Law Review*, Vol. 10, No. 3, p. 386, 1966.

[2] Max Freedman. Quoted in Gilbert Cranberg, "What Did the Supreme Court Say?" *Saturday Review*, p. 92, April 18, 1967.

find so much thought and so much earnestness devoted to the problems of human freedom in its infinite forms." [3] And the layman will
find, to his delightful surprise, that the reading of the great civil
liberties cases is a fascinating venture.

In recent years there has been a virtual flood of materials on
civil liberties. Most of these publications, however, are of little use
to the average citizen, since they are designed principally for more
specialized or scholarly audiences. This book has been designed
specifically to meet the needs of the general reader or ordinary
citizen.

The book is based upon a widely accepted assumption that the best
way the lay reader can learn about American civil liberties is through
the case method—that is, by simply reading actual cases. There are
many reasons for this. In the first place, the case method remains one
of the best instruments for sharpening minds. It makes it possible
for the general lay reader without training in law to become personally involved in the realistic, graphic, and very human conflicts
that shape the meaning of civil liberties. This involvement is much
more useful and rewarding than listening to sermons about the importance of individual liberties or being subjected to some one else's
broad generalizations or abstractions. It enables the reader to see the
Bill of Rights for what it is—a living, dynamic, ever-changing protective shield. In short, good cases are related to real life and provide the reader with vivid examples of the difficult choices that must
be made in the conflict of values and with an awareness of the complexities inherent in many civil liberties questions. Moreover, they
are a welcome relief from the rehash provided by books and articles.
At present no up-to-date case book dealing with the most important
civil liberties questions and designed principally for lay readers is
available. A number of persons have urged over and over that such a
book be published. This book is designed to meet that need.

Though the arguments for the case method are persuasive, there
are many pitfalls along the way. These I have tried to avoid. In the
first place, there is a danger that cases appearing under selected
topical headings will be isolated from their historical period or
sequence. Most cases cannot be understood unless they are placed

---

[3] Milton R. Korwitz, *Bill of Rights Reader,* Ithaca, N.Y., Cornell University
Press, p. XIII, 1965.

in some sort of historical perspective and unless something is known
of the outside social, political, and economic forces which helped
shape the particular decision. To help overcome this difficulty, I have
introduced *each* case with a brief note describing how it evolved out
of our past history. This material has been woven into the factual
situation outlined for each case. At the same time important high-
lights in the life of the Justice rendering the opinion have also been
woven into the facts of each case in the hope that readers will be led
to view Supreme Court justices as human beings rather than as black-
robed, disembodied spirits. Also, some important historical materials
often found in the cases themselves have been retained when they
seemed useful. Moreover, the introductory materials for the *first* case
of each chapter provide general background that enables the reader
to put the ensuing cases in proper perspective and relate them to the
major topic of the chapter.

A most serious difficulty is that the general reader is simply afraid
that cases cannot be understood by the ordinary mortal. He fears
that only a person with legal training can read and understand civil
liberties cases. It is true, of course, that judges are lawyers and that
much of their work is of a highly technical nature. But the law in the
field of civil liberties is really not so mysterious or forbidding as many
people suppose. *With a little help civil liberties cases can be understood by interested lay readers.* To this end the introductory materials of Chapter I are designed to overcome technical difficulties in
reading the cases and to explain briefly the important role of the
Supreme Court in the maintenance and enlargement of American
freedoms. Also, *each* case has been carefully edited to remove all
unnecessary technical details. The facts of each case are presented
as simply and interestingly as possible before the reader is asked to
turn to the opinion itself. Throughout the book the emphasis is on
the human aspect of each case in hopes that the reader will see
clearly that cases are the very substance of life rather than dry-as-dust
legalisms—that they are brought to the Court by real people seeking answers to real problems! When terms are used that may be
unfamiliar, they are fully explained. The relevant constitutional provisions in each case are explained or analyzed to facilitate understanding. Moreover, in editing the cases the needs of the general
reader have been kept constantly in mind.

It must be emphasized that this book is much more than a mere

collection of cases in the tradition of too many casebooks, especially
those designed principally for advanced law students and containing
a great number of cases with almost no editing and with little or no
concern with the human qualities of the materials. Before the reader
is asked to peruse the case itself, all the relevant facts, ferreted out
from a host of other sources as well as from the case itself, are
presented in a readable, interesting style. In each instance the factual data have been carefully integrated with the substance of the
case. Where appropriate, each case is followed by an *Aftermath* that
reveals what happened to the principals in the case and traces the
effects of the decision.

Though by no means exhaustive in nature, the book includes cases
on all major areas of civil liberties with which American citizens
should be familiar. Particular stress has been placed on the most
recent and emerging problems familiar to any newspaper reader.
Thus the reader will find data on such varied topics as capital punishment, right to counsel and other criminal procedures, freedom of
speech and press, segregation, open housing, obscenity, loyalty oaths,
school prayers, voting rights, fair procedures for juvenile delinquents,
reapportionment, privacy, and many others.

Whenever possible, cases with the most dramatic appeal have been
selected for this book. At the same time, a determined effort has been
made to select those cases having an interesting context with which
the general reader can easily identify. Criminal cases—the most dramatic and interesting of all cases and now under wide discussion in
the United States—are presented first, so that the interest of the lay
reader will be quickly aroused and hence more easily maintained
throughout the rest of the book.

A Word of Gratitude

Without the continued enthusiasm and encouragement of a most
kindly and perceptive editor—Mr. Alex Fraser of the J. B. Lippincott
Company—this book might easily have died aborning. My longtime
colleague, Dr. Ernst B. Schulz, Professor Emeritus of Political
Science at Lehigh University, has helped me think out a number of
problems and made numerous suggestions which have improved the
book. My random discussions over the past several years with Professor Henry J. Abraham of the University of Pennsylvania and his

own most readable writings have sharpened my perception of many civil liberties issues. For this I am also deeply indebted to a host of other professional colleagues too numerous to mention here. Mr. Russell B. Barbour of the Pennsylvania Human Relations Commission has made me more acutely aware of the difficulties inherent in translating the majestic civil liberties commands of the Constitution into the everyday life of the American People, but I know no man who is more dedicated to making the dream come true. I am also indebted to Dr. Harry H. Shapiro, Professor and Chairman, Department of Political Science at Rutgers University (Camden campus), and Mr. Spencer Coxe, Executive Director of the Philadelphia branch of American Civil Liberties Union, for sharing their insights with me and my students.

Mrs. Lois R. Brown carefully typed several drafts of the manuscript over a period of time and patiently helped me in many ways during the various stages of writing and editing. This book is hers almost as much as it is mine. Mrs. Linda Dolben and Mr. William Winters, both graduate students at Lehigh, helped collect needed data for several cases discussed in the book. Over the past several years grants from the American Philosophical Society and the Lehigh University Institute of Research have made possible periods of sustained research which have enriched this work. Finally, I owe an important debt to my students of the past several year—themselves teachers for the most part—in my Teaching Civil Liberties class for their eagerness and joyful willingness to learn. They have made it all seem worthwhile.

ROCCO J. TRESOLINI

CONTENTS

Contents

I INTRODUCTION

If we fervently want to make this Nation better for those who are to follow us, we can at least abjure the hatred that consumes people, the false accusations that divide us and the bitterness that begets violence.

> Chief Justice Earl Warren at the bier of President John F. Kennedy, Washington, D.C., November 25, 1963.

In one sense freedom is always in crisis, just as beauty is, and honor and truth—all those things which man has made for himself as a garment against ever-present blasts of the barbarian spirit. Eternal vigilance is the condition not alone of liberty, but of everything which as civilized men we hold dear.

> August Heckscher, address at Kenyon College, April 4, 1957. Reprinted in New York Times *Book Review*, p. 2, April 28, 1957.

THE SUPREME COURT is more than a court. Deeply involved in the political life of the nation and in the process of deciding cases, it is making policy in some of the most controversial areas of American life. The rise of judicial power may be traced to the period following the Civil War when the Supreme Court became a virtual censor of state and federal legislation which was thought to interfere with private property rights. The legislation struck down was usually designed to aid farmers and laborers who had been badly hurt by the new industrial developments. Starting in 1898 the executive branch rose to a position of predominant leadership. Until 1937 the Supreme Court continued to invalidate social and economic legislation demanded by large segments of the American people. The climax was Franklin D. Roosevelt's abortive court-packing bill, which was designed to make sweeping changes in the federal judiciary. Since 1937 the Court has virtually abandoned its concern for the protection of property rights and the maintenance of a laissez-faire system. While in the process of relegating economics and property rights to a subordinate position the Court was involved in the creation and development of elaborate new protections of personal rights. Thus, the major trend in Supreme Court decisions since 1937 has been increased Court protection afforded to the defense and expansion of civil liberties. This can readily be seen in the decisions of the Warren Court.

With few exceptions the Warren Court has consistently defended individual freedoms. The acknowledged leaders of the civil libertarians during the first fifteen years of the Warren Court were Justices Hugo L. Black and William O. Douglas, supported by Justices William J. Brennan, Arthur J. Goldberg and his successor, Abe Fortas, and Chief Justice Warren himself. These so-called Libertarian "judicial activists" believed that the Court must play a positive role in the protection of individual freedoms. They sought generally to promote social welfare and to protect American freedom from erosion by partisan legislative bodies and executive officers. Justices Black and Douglas and their supporters thus viewed the Court as the ultimate guardian of constitutional rights. Before his retirement from the Court in 1962 Justice Felix Frankfurter headed another bloc on the Court which, on the other hand, advocated a policy of "judicial self-restraint." His supporters believed that the primary responsibility for governing lies with the people and their duly elected representatives. He was almost always supported by Justice John M. Harlan and usually by Justices Tom C. Clark, Potter Stewart and Charles E. Whittaker. Justice Harlan became the new leader of the "self-restraint" bloc.

It is the ascendancy of the judicial activists, with their concern for positively involving the Court in the affairs of the nation and protecting individual freedoms, that has gradually brought the Court to the storm center of American politics. The Court has become controversial mainly because some of its decisions have greatly disturbed powerful forces in the community. Gradually, however, the realization grew that many of the more extreme statements had been made by interested citizens who, nevertheless, had not read the Court's opinions.

In our time it is undoubtedly true that the Court has become a sort of escape valve—"maybe a scape goat." At some time or other, the Court must provide answers to such fundamental problems as segregation, reapportionment, school prayers, voting rights, the nature of obscenity, criminal procedure—problems which strike at the heart of the social and political order. It must also deal with perhaps less momentous but equally emotion-laden questions such as the use of contraceptives as a birth control measure, or whether the televising and broadcasting of a notorious trial violates a defendant's due process rights, or whether a college can deny registration to a student because of his beard and long hair. In performing this function of providing some kind of "final" answers—that is in making public policy—the Court is always embattled, as well as supported, for the cleavages are always present. Too often in recent years it has stood virtually alone in articulating the enduring principles of a democratic society and in demanding that we adhere to the rule of law which is so essential to the survival of all of us.

The task of the Court will remain that of interpreting—that is of keeping young—a Constitution, a great document which, though it is old, is never really old.

The Supreme Court's annual term runs from the first Monday in October to the following June. After adjournment special sessions may be called by the Chief Justice to consider questions of exceptional importance—but such sessions are very rare. During the first week of the term the Court usually disposes of work that has accumulated over the summer months. After that the Court divides its time between the hearing of cases and recesses. The general pattern is for the Court to hear oral argument for two weeks and then to recess for two weeks to study cases and write opinions. Decisions are usually announced at noon on Mondays following the two weeks of argument.

How Cases Are Brought to the Supreme Court

The Supreme Court will exercise the power of judicial review *only* if an actual case or controversy is presented—litigation involving a real conflict of rights and interest between contending parties. In short, the Court cannot take the initiative in declaring laws unconstitutional. It must await the action of some aggrieved litigant.

Cases are brought to the Supreme Court in accordance with the procedure established by Congress. At present, cases reach the Court by three methods: (1) by appeal; (2) by writ of certiorari; (3) by certification. The writ of error was utilized in some of the older cases in much the same way as appeal, but it was abolished for federal court usage in 1928. Relief which could be obtained in federal courts by the writ of error is now obtainable generally by appeal.

I. *Appeal*

In broad terms the word *appeal* denotes any method used to bring a case to a higher court for review. In the more technical sense used here it refers to the method of review which is a matter of right of one of the parties to an action. In other words, the higher court must hear the case when it is brought by appeal. The Supreme Court must review cases from state courts primarily in two instances: (1) where the validity of a treaty or statute of the United States is questioned and the state court has held it *invalid;* (2) where the validity of a state law has been questioned on the ground that it contravenes the Constitution, treaties, or laws of the United States and the state court *sustains* its validity.

The Supreme Court may review by appeal decisions of the Courts of Appeals when a federal statute is held unconstitutional in a suit to which the United States is a party, and when a state statute is held to be invalid as repugnant to the Constitution, treaties, or laws of the United States. Although the majority of district court decisions may be reviewed only by a court of appeals, some cases may be carried, on *appeal,* from a district court directly to the Supreme Court. Such direct appeals are allowed because some questions raised in the district court are of such importance that they need to be settled by the Supreme Court as quickly as possible.

Although review by appeal is important, it is necessary to emphasize that the right of a litigant to carry his case to the Supreme Court has been extremely limited. In 1925 Congress gave the Supreme Court almost complete power to decide what cases it would hear by allowing the Court to grant or deny petitions for writs of certiorari as it saw fit. In addition, the Supreme Court will review a case on appeal only if the justices feel that a substantial federal question has been raised.

II. *Writ of Certiorari*

(Certiorari means to be informed or to be apprised of something.) Persons who have been adversely affected by the decision of a lower court may petition for a writ of certiorari. This writ may be defined as an order to the lower court to send the entire record of the case to the higher court for review. It is granted by the Supreme Court when four justices feel that the issues raised are of sufficient public importance to merit consideration. Petitions for writs of certiorari are filed in accordance with prescribed forms, with the petitioner stating why he feels the Court should grant the writ. The opposing party also may file a brief outlining the reasons why the case should not be reviewed by the Court on certiorari. According to the Revised Rules of the Supreme Court "a review on writ of certiorari is not a matter of right, but of sound judicial discretion, and will be granted only where there are special and important reasons therefor." The Supreme Court may review on certiorari decisions of state courts when a federal question is involved and there exists no right of appeal, decisions of the Courts of Appeals, and decisions of some of the legislative courts. Only a few (less than 15 per cent) of the total number of petitions for writs of certiorari filed each year are granted by the Court.

III. *Certification*

This is a seldom used method of appeal whereby a lower court requests that the Supreme Court answer certain questions of law so that a correct decision may be made. The Supreme Court may answer the questions, after which the lower court may reach a decision in light of the answers provided; or, in instances when a Court of Appeals has certified questions, the entire record of the case may be ordered up for decision by the Supreme Court itself. This method of appeal is not within the control of the litigants, because only the lower court may determine whether or not clarifications on points of law are required. Only the Courts of Appeals and the Court of Claims may then certify questions to the Supreme Court for review.

How To Read Supreme Court Cases

Supreme Court opinions are available in a number of editions, of which the three most important are:

1. *United States Reports* (cited as U.S.). This is the official edition of Supreme Court cases, which is published by the federal government. Usually the opinions of each term of the Court can be incorporated in two or three volumes of the *Reports*. Until 1875 the reports of Supreme Court decisions were cited by the name of the reporter as follows:

1789–1800	Dallas (Dall.)	4 volumes
1801–1815	Cranch (Cr.)	9 volumes
1816–1827	Wheaton (Wheat.)	12 volumes
1828–1842	Peters (Pet.)	16 volumes
1843–1860	Howard (How.)	24 volumes
1861–1862	Black (Bl.)	2 volumes
1863–1874	Wallace (Wall.)	23 volumes
1875–1882	Otto	17 volumes

The total number of volumes cited by the name of the reporter is 107. After 1882, and beginning with Volume 108, the official reports are cited by number only.

2. *United States Supreme Court Reports, Lawyers' Edition* (cited as L. Ed.).

This edition is privately published by the Lawyers' Cooperative Publishing Company. One volume ordinarily contains all of the decisions of one term of the Court. Both the *Lawyers' Edition* and the *Supreme Court Reporter* listed below contain more detailed headnotes than the official *United States Reports*. The headnotes, which appear at the beginning of the opinion, are designed to summarize the legal contents of the case. Those which appear in the two privately published editions are prepared by editorial staffs to assist lawyers in quickly obtaining comprehensive summaries of the case law in a particular subject matter. The *Lawyers' Edition* of the Supreme Court Reports also carries excerpts from the briefs of counsel and annotations of important cases.

3. *Supreme Court Reporter* (cited as Sup. Ct.). This edition,

which is similar to the *Lawyers' Edition,* is published by West Publishing Company. It is not a complete edition, however, because it contains only Supreme Court cases decided since 1882.

In citing cases, the volume number comes first, followed by the abbreviated title of the report in which the case appears and the page number, with the date in parentheses at the end. For example, the complete citation for the important case of *Baker v. Carr,* decided in 1962, is 369 U.S. 186; 7 L.Ed. 2d 633; 82 Sup. Ct. 691 (1962). This means that the full text of the *Baker* case may be found in Volume 369 of the United States Reports at page 186, or in Volume 7 of the Lawyers' Edition 2d at page 633, or in Volume 82 of the Supreme Court Reporter at page 691. The citation for *Marbury v. Madison* is 1 Cranch 137; 2 L. Ed. 60 (1803). The case can therefore be found in Volume 1 of Cranch at page 137 or in Volume 2 of the Lawyers' Edition at page 60.

The title of each case is taken from the names of the two parties to the controversy. The name which appears first is the party bringing the action, or the *plaintiff.* The *defendant* is the other party, against whom the action is taken. He must answer the charges brought by the plaintiff. Each of the parties may be referred to as indicated in the hypothetical case that follows:

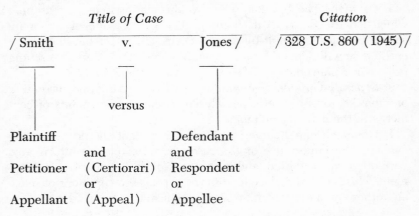

	Title of Case		*Citation*
/ Smith	v.	Jones /	/ 328 U.S. 860 (1945)/
	versus		
Plaintiff		Defendant	
and		and	
Petitioner	(Certiorari)	Respondent	
or		or	
Appellant	(Appeal)	Appellee	

These cases have been edited to eliminate technical legal matters. There is no one best way to read and analyze these cases. How this is done depends largely upon each individual's habits and methods of study. Nevertheless, an understanding of the decision, especially during the early stages, can best be acquired by following a prescribed pattern or outline which helps to bring out the essential issues of each case. It is suggested that the student read the case in its entirety at least once before attempting to use the following outline:

1. *Title and Citation.*
2. *Facts of the Case.* Here the student should make a short statement concerning the circumstances which brought about the case or controversy. The statement of facts sometimes appears in concise form at the beginning of an opinion. In other instances, the facts are found scattered throughout the case. On some occasions, the best recital of the facts is found in a dissenting opinion. Students usually obtain a better grasp of the case if the identity of the parties to the action is clearly established and if the holdings of the lower courts, if any, are understood clearly.
3. *Legal Question or Questions.* The question is revealed by the statement of facts, which should indicate the nature of the conflict of interests which the Court must resolve. The legal question is many times concisely stated by the Court.
4. *Holding.* This is the Court's answer to the question or questions presented.
5. *Opinion.* The opinion refers to the chain of legal reasoning which led the Court to its holding. The Court's line of reasoning should be outlined point by point, because an understanding of the entire case will depend largely upon how well the Court's reasoning process is followed.
6. *Separate Opinion or Opinions.* Both concurring and dissenting opinions should be carefully analyzed to show major points of conflict with the majority opinion.
7. *Comment and Evaluation.* Here the student should personally evaluate the importance of the case, show its relationship, if any, with other cases studied, and indicate its place in American government. This is also the place to criticize or praise the opinions or make any other comment that may seem significant to the student.

II INDIVIDUAL RIGHTS IN CRIMINAL CASES

[A]ll our complicated judicial apparatus yields but a human judgment, not at all sure to be correct, affecting the life of another human being. If we are at all imaginative, we will comprehend what that judgment will mean to him, and what a horror it will be if we wrongly decide against him. . . . [I]t seems to me that . . . if mankind's development has any significance against the background of eternity, then the dignity of each individual man is not an empty phrase.

> Circuit Judge Jerome Frank, dissenting
> opinion, United States v. Rubenstein, *151*
> *F. (2d) 915 (1945).*

The test of the moral quality of a civilization is its treatment of the weak and powerless.

> Judge Frank, United States v. Murphy,
> *222 F. (2d) 698 (1955).*

It is a fair summary of history to say that safeguards of liberty have frequently been forged in controversies involving not very nice people.

> Justice Felix Frankfurter, dissenting opinion, United States v. Rabinowitz, *339*
> *U.S. 56 (1950).*

Louisiana ex rel Francis v. Resweber
329 U.S. 459 (1947)

IN NOVEMBER, 1944, a popular white druggist in St. Martinville, a small Louisiana town, was found shot to death near his home. A watch and wallet containing four dollars were found missing from the dead man's clothes. Resweber, the local sheriff, and the state police doggedly followed every clue for several months in an attempt to solve the murder to no avail. But, by accident, Willie Francis, a stuttering, lanky, fifteen year old Negro boy who had grown up in St. Martinville was picked up in Texas for routine questioning. In Francis' pocket the police found the wallet of the murdered man. Willie Francis signed a written confession that he had killed and robbed the druggist. When he was brought back to St. Martinville he again confessed orally to Sheriff Resweber.

Willie Francis was brought to trial, found guilty, and sentenced to die in the electric chair. His execution was set for May 3, 1946, between the hours of noon and 3:00 p.m. Precisely at noon on May 3, Sheriff Resweber led Willie from his cell to the state's portable electric chair, which had been brought to St. Martinville the night before. Willie was strapped to the chair and a Captain Foster of the penitentiary staff was directed to throw the switch. Foster threw the switch but "for a fraction of a second, nothing happened. Then Willie jumped. He strained against the straps. He groaned."

"But even those who were witnessing their first execution knew something was wrong. Willie's body, though arched, was obviously not at the point of death. Captain Foster, all in one motion, frantically threw the switch off and then on again. Those closest to Willie heard him strain out the words, 'Let me breathe,' . . . The agonizing words spewed out from between the puffed lips. They roused Sheriff Resweber into action. He signaled to Captain Foster, who by now knew that his apparatus would not kill Willie Francis. He threw the switch back into an upright position. All in all, about two minutes had now passed since the switch had been thrown, and some of those present realized they had hardly breathed during the entire period. The hood was lifted from Willie's head, the electrodes were removed from his head and left leg, and the straps were unbuckled all around. Although obviously shaken, Willie was able to get to his feet by himself."

A reprieve from an *immediate* second attempt at execution was granted by the Governor, but the following Friday, May 10, was set as the date for execution. However, the Willie Francis story caught the imagination of the public, and pressures against another attempted execution began to build. A young Louisiana attorney, Bertrand de Blanc, took the case without pay. After the Louisiana Supreme Court, the state Board of Pardons, and the Governor refused to intervene in the case, de Blanc and other attorneys took the case to the United States Supreme Court.

Willie's lawyers argued that a second attempt to electrocute him would be a denial of "due process of law" under the Fourteenth Amendment because of the double jeopardy clause of the Fifth Amendment and the "cruel and unusual punishment provision" of the Eighth Amendment. These points need further elaboration. The Fifth Amendment provides, in part, that no person "shall be subject for the same offense to be twice put in jeopardy of life or limb." The Eighth Amendment, in addition to prohibiting excessive bail and excessive fines, provides simply that cruel and unusual punishment cannot be inflicted. However, these Fifth and Eighth Amendment provisions, like all the other first ten amendments known as the Bill of Rights, originally constituted restrictions on the federal government *alone*. The states had their own Constitutions and were originally untouched by the prohibitions of the first ten amendments. However, a broader concept of liberty and equality emerged as a result of the Civil War Amendments—the Thirteenth, Fourteenth, and Fifteenth—all designed to protect the newly freed American Negro. Gradually, the Supreme Court, in a series of important decisions held that certain provisions of the Bill of Rights as, for example, freedom of speech and press, are *fundamental* rights and hence are protected by the due process clause of the Fourteenth Amendment against *state as well as federal action*. This is why de Blanc had to use the due process clause of the Fourteenth Amendment as well as the double jeopardy and cruel and unusual punishment provisions. De Blanc also argued that a second attempt to execute Willie Francis would constitute a denial of equal protection of the laws as guaranteed to all persons by the Fourteenth Amendment.

On January 13, 1947, over two years after the murder was committed, the Supreme Court rendered its close five to four decision with Justice Reed, a conservative on civil liberties questions, writing an opinion joined by a surprising lineup of three other justices, including Justice Black. Justice Frankfurter wrote a concurring opinion while Justice Burton, also generally classified as a conservative, wrote a dissenting opinion in which he was joined by three of the most liberal men ever to sit on the Court—Justices Douglas, Murphy, and Rutledge. Justice Reed had been named to the Court by President

Roosevelt in 1938. Though an ardent New Dealer, he generally was inclined to vote against claims of individual rights.

Ex. rel. in the title of the case is an abbreviation for the Latin term ex relatione, meaning at the information of or by the relation. It is used to show that the complaining party (Willie Francis) has an interest which under existing legal procedure in Louisiana can be brought only by the attorney general or some other designated state officer. Likewise, in the case below, Willie Francis is referred to as the relator—the person bringing the action through a state officer.

MR. JUSTICE REED announced the judgment of the Court in an opinion in which THE CHIEF JUSTICE, MR. JUSTICE BLACK and MR. JUSTICE JACKSON join. . . .

First. Our minds rebel against permitting the same sovereignty to punish an accused twice for the same offense. . . . But where the accused successfully seeks review of a conviction, there is no double jeopardy upon a new trial. . . .

When an accident, with no suggestion of malevolence, prevents the consummation of a sentence, the state's subsequent course in the administration of its criminal law is not affected on that account by any requirement of due process under the Fourteenth Amendment. We find no double jeopardy here which can be said to amount to a denial of federal due process in the proposed execution.

Second. We find nothing in what took place here which amounts to cruel and unusual punishment in the constitutional sense. The case before us does not call for an examination into any punishments except that of death. . . . The traditional humanity of modern Anglo-American law forbids the infliction of unnecessary pain in the execution of the death sentence. Prohibition against the wanton infliction of pain has come into our law from the Bill of Rights of 1688. The identical words appear in our Eighth Amendment. The Fourteenth would prohibit by its due process clause execution by a state in a cruel manner.

Petitioner's suggestion is that because he once underwent the psychological strain of preparation for electrocution, now to require him to undergo this preparation again subjects him to a lingering or cruel and unusual punishment. Even the fact that petitioner has already been subjected to a current of electricity does not make his subsequent execution any more cruel in the constitutional sense than any other execution. The cruelty against which the Constitution protects a convicted man is cruelty inherent in the method of punishment, not the necessary suffering involved in any method employed to extinguish life humanely. The fact that an unforeseeable accident prevented the prompt consummation of the sentence cannot, it seems to us, add an element of cruelty to a subsequent execution. There is no purpose to inflict unnecessary pain nor any unnecessary pain involved in the proposed execution. The situation of the unfortunate victim of this accident is just as though he had suffered the identical amount of mental anguish and physical pain in any other occurrence, such as, for example, a fire in the cell block. We cannot agree that the hardship imposed upon the petitioner rises to that level of hardship denounced as denial of due process because of cruelty.

Third. The Supreme Court of Louisiana also rejected petitioner's contention that death inflicted after his prior sufferings would deny him the equal protection of the laws, guaranteed by the Fourteenth Amendment. This suggestion in so far as it differs from the due process argument is based on the idea that execution, after an attempt at execution has failed, would be a more severe punishment than is imposed upon others guilty of a like offense. That is, since others do not go through the strain of preparation for execution a second time or have not experienced a nonlethal current in a prior attempt at execution, as petitioner did, to compel petitioner to submit to execution after these prior experiences denies to him equal protection. Equal protection does not protect a prisoner against even illegal acts of officers in charge of him, much less against accidents during his detention for execution. . . . Laws cannot prevent accidents nor can a law equally protect all against them. So long as the law applies to all alike, the requirements of equal protection are met. We have no right to assume that Louisiana singled out Francis for a treatment other than that which has been or would generally be applied.

Fourth. There is a suggestion in the brief that the original trial itself was so unfair to the petitioner as to justify a reversal of the judgment of conviction and a new trial. Petitioner's claim in his brief is that he was inadequately represented by counsel. The record of the original trial presented to us shows the warrent for arrest, the indictment, the appointment of counsel and the minute entries of trial, selection of jury, verdict and sentence. There is nothing in any of these papers to show any violation of petitioner's constitutional rights. . . . Review is sought here because of a denial of due process of law that would be brought about by execution of petitioner after failure of the first effort to electrocute him. Nothing is before us upon which a ruling can be predicated as to alleged denial of federal constitutional rights during petitioner's trial. On this record, we see nothing upon which we could conclude that the constitutional rights of petitioner were infringed.

Affirmed.

[JUSTICE FRANKFURTER wrote a concurring opinion.]
MR. JUSTICE BURTON, with whom MR. JUSTICE DOUGLAS,
MR. JUSTICE MURPHY and MR. JUSTICE RUTLEDGE concur, dissenting. . . .

The capital case before us presents an instance of the violation of constitutional due process that is more clear than would be presented by many lesser punishments prohibited by the Eighth Amendment or its state counterparts. Taking human life by unnecessarily cruel means shocks the most fundamental instincts of civilized man. It should not be possible under the constitutional procedure of a self-governing people. Abhorrence of the cruelty of ancient forms of capital punishment has increased steadily until, today, some states have prohibited capital punishment altogether. It is unthinkable that any state legislature in modern times would enact a statute expressly authorizing capital punishment by repeated applications of an electric current separated by intervals of days or hours until finally death shall result. . . .

In determining whether the proposed procedure is unconstitutional, we must measure it against a lawful electrocution. The contrast is that between instantaneous death and death by installments—caused by electric shocks administered after one or more intervening periods of complete consciousness of the victim. Electrocution, when instantaneous, *can* be inflicted by a state in conformity with due process of law. . . . The Supreme Court of Louisiana has held that electrocution in the manner prescribed in its statute, is more humane than hanging. . . .

The all-important consideration is that the execution shall be so instantaneous and substantially painless that the punishment shall be reduced, as nearly as possible, to no more than that of death itself. Electrocution has been approved only in a form that eliminates suffering.

The Louisiana statute makes this clear. It provides that:

> Every sentence of death imposed in this State shall be by electrocution; that is, causing to pass through the body of the person convicted a current of electricity of sufficient intensity to cause death, and the application and continuance of such current through the body of the person convicted until such person is dead. . . .

. . . It does not provide for electrocution by interrupted or repeated applications of electric current at intervals of several days or even minutes. It does not provide for the application of electric current of an intensity less than that sufficient to cause death. It prescribes expressly and solely for the application of a current of sufficient intensity to cause death and for the *continuance* of that application until death results. Prescribing capital punishment, it should be construed strictly. There can be no implied provision for a second, third or multiple application of the current. There is no statutory or judicial precedent upholding a delayed process of electrocution. . . .

If the state officials deliberately and intentionally had placed [Willie Francis] in the electric chair five times and, each time, had applied electric current to his body in a manner not sufficient, until the final time, to kill him, such a form of torture would rival that of burning at the stake. Although the failure of the first attempt, in the present case, was unintended, the reapplication of the electric current will be intentional. How many deliberate and intentional reapplications of electric current does it take to produce a cruel, unusual and unconstitutional punishment? While five applications would be more cruel and unusual than one, the uniqueness of the present case demonstrates that, today, two separated applications are sufficiently "cruel and unusual" to be prohibited. If five attempts would be "cruel and unusual," it would be difficult to draw the line between two, three, four and five. It is not difficult, however, as we here contend, to draw the line between the one continuous application prescribed by statute and any other application of the current.

Lack of intent that the first application be less than fatal is not material. The intent of the executioner cannot lessen the torture or excuse the result. It was the statutory duty of the state officials to make sure that there was no failure. The procedure in this case contrasts with common knowledge of precautions generally taken elsewhere to insure against failure of electrocutions. The high standard of care generally taken evidences the significance properly attached to the unconditional requirement of a single continued application of the current until death results. In our view of this case, we are giving careful recognition to the law of Louisiana. Neither the Legislature nor the Supreme Court of Louisiana has expressed approval of electrocution other than by one continuous application of a lethal current. . . .

In determining whether a case of cruel and unusual punishment constitutes a violation of due process of law, each case must turn upon its particular facts. The record in this case is not limited to an instance where a prisoner was placed in the electric chair and released before being subjected to the electric current.

. . . The petition contains the unequivocal allegation that the official electrocutioner "turned on the switch and a current of electricity was caused to pass through the body of [Willie Francis], all in the presence of the official witnesses." This allegation must be read in the light of the Louisiana statute which authorized the electrocutioner to apply to the body of the relator only such an electric current as was of "sufficient intensity to cause death." On that record, denial of relief means that the proposed repeated, and at least second, application to the relator of an electric current sufficient to cause death is not, under present circumstances, a cruel and unusual punishment violative of due process of law. It exceeds any punishment prescribed by law. There is no precedent for it. What then is it, if it be not cruel, unusual and unlawful? In spite of the constitutional issue thus raised, the Supreme Court of Louisiana treated it as an executive question not subject to judicial review. We believe that if the facts are as alleged by the relator the proposed action is unconstitutional. We believe also that the Supreme Court of Louisiana should provide for the determination of the facts and then proceed in a manner not inconsistent with this opinion. . . .

The remand of this cause to the Supreme Court of Louisiana in the manner indicated would not mean that the relator necessarily is entitled to a complete release. It would mean merely that the courts of Louisiana must examine the facts, both as to the actual nature of the punishment already inflicted and that proposed to be inflicted and, if the proposed punishment amounts to a violation of due process of law under the Constitution of the United States, then the State must find some means of disposing of this case that will not violate that Constitution.

For the reasons stated, we are unable to concur in the judgment of this Court which affirms the judgment below.

Aftermath

After the Supreme Court decision, frantic efforts were made to save Willie Francis from the electric chair. But, the day before the second scheduled execution attempt, Willie asked his lawyers not to make any further efforts in his behalf. He was ready to die. He was interested to find out if he could die like a man. The next day—one year and six days after the first attempt—Willie was placed in the same portable electric chair. "It was all the same, except that this time the chair worked. The gauze on Willie's head dried up, and the burns appeared where they should have. This time the coffin could be used, and the crowd was not disappointed."

That this was an extremely difficult case to decide is shown by the close five to four vote and by the unexpected line up of justices. Justice Black is widely regarded as a "liberal" and his vote came as a surprise to many. However, it is well known that Justice Black does not like to rely on vague and undefined principles of liberty. "Finding nothing in the Constitution which specifically prohibited what had occurred, he probably could not bring himself to vote with the dissenters." The case must also have been extremely difficult for Justice Frankfurter since both he and his wife had long been bitter opponents of capital punishment. His anguish is revealed clearly by a portion of his concurring opinion: "[T]his Court must abstain from interference with State action no matter how strong one's personal feeling of revulsion against a State's insistence on its pound of flesh. . . . Strongly drawn as I am to some of the sentiments expressed by my brother Burton, I cannot rid myself of the conviction that were I to hold that Louisiana would transgress the Due Process Clause if the State were allowed, in the precise circumstances before us, to carry out the death sentence, I would be enforcing my private view rather than that consensus of society's opinion which, for purposes of due process, is the standard enjoined by the Constitution."

Finally, it is necessary to bring up-to-date Justice Burton's comment in his dissenting opinion that the death penalty is so abhorrent that some states have abolished it. Since Burton's comment in 1947, the death penalty has come under increased scrutiny and attack. For all practical purposes it is a vanishing penalty. In 1947 only six states had abolished it. Today capital punishment has been disallowed in thirteen states and a goodly number of others are seriously contemplating abolition legislation. Moreover, the use of the death penalty has decreased dramatically. In 1935 an all-time record high of 199 persons were executed in the United States, but only forty-two were executed in 1961; seven in 1965, and one in 1966. Various Gallup and other polls reveal clearly that opposition to the death penalty continues to mount. Many well known writers have argued cogently that capital punishment is ineffective and inappropriate in a modern society. The American Civil Liberties Union, an organization that has long been concerned with protecting American freedoms, argues that the imposition of the death penalty *does* constitute cruel and unusual punishment under the Eighth and Fourteenth Amendments. Finally, in a dissenting opinion in *Rudolph v. Alabama*, 375 U.S. 889 (1963), Justice Goldberg, joined by Justices Douglas and Brennan, raised a number of questions concerning the use of the death penalty for rape. In particular, Justice Goldberg wanted the Court to consider whether the Eighth and Fourteenth Amendments permit the imposition of the death penalty on a convicted rapist who has not endangered human life.

One wonders if Willie Francis' fate would have been the same if his case had arisen some twenty years later.

Chambers v. Florida
309 U.S. 227 (1940)

On Saturday, May 13, 1933, Robert Darcy, an elderly white man who operated a fish market, was robbed and beaten to death on a roadway near his home in Pompona, Florida, a small town about twelve miles from Fort Lauderdale. Within the next twenty-four hours a number of Negroes living in the area were arrested without warrants as suspects and confined in the county jail at Fort Lauderdale. Among the Negroes arrested were Isiah Chambers, Jack Williamson, Charlie Davis, and Walter Woodward—all poor, uneducated migratory farm laborers who had recently arrived in the community.

On Sunday afternoon, May 14, the four prisoners and other Negroes were questioned about the crime by the newly-elected county sheriff, a convict guard, and several other white men. The questioning and cross-questioning continued for a week without results. The four Negroes said over and over again that they had nothing to do with the crime. During this period the prisoners were not allowed to see any friends and relatives or to confer with a lawyer. They subsequently charged that during the week they were continually threatened, cursed, beaten, and tortured by the convict guard and other white men. All of this was denied by the convict guard and the other questioners. In any event, by Saturday, May 20, after a week of persistent questioning, one of the Negroes had confessed to the crime. But beginning about 3:30 P.M. on Saturday each prisoner was questioned separately on and off all night long with no rest, food or opportunity for sleep. The prisoners also later claimed that they were whipped and tortured at various intervals during the night. This was also denied by the police officers. About 2:30 A.M. one of the prisoners—Walter Woodward—"broke" and "confessed" to the crime. The state's attorney was called to the jail to hear the "confession" but he would not accept it. He told the sheriff and other police officers that they did not have enough evidence and not to call him again until the confession was more detailed! The questioning continued until 6:00 A.M. when "something worthwhile" was obtained. The state's attorney was called again. This time Williamson and Davis, as well as Woodward, confessed to the crime. Before these confessions were made no formal charges against the four Negroes had been entered. But two days after the confessions the three men along with Chambers were indicted and arraigned. Chambers' indictment rested on the confessions of the other three men. One of the prisoners later testified that after the confessions had been obtained, the county sheriff dangled a bunch of prison keys before the defendants' eyes and told them to stick to the confessions or the keys would be turned over to a crowd outside the jail waiting to lynch them.

The trial was held in the local county court. The presiding judge never issued a formal order appointing counsel for the defendants, but he did ask two local lawyers to defend them. The two lawyers did nothing. During the trial they made no inquiries and asked no questions concerning the confessions relied upon by the state to convict all of the accused. The four defendants—illiterate, terror stricken, with no knowledge whatsoever of their rights—did not know they were represented by counsel until June 17, 1933, the day they were all sentenced to death for the murder of Robert Darcy.

Death warrants for the execution of the condemned men were issued. They were about to be executed when the case went to the Florida Supreme Court for reviews as a result of the determined efforts of conscientious Negro attorneys who had been outraged by the denial of fundamental rights. During the next six years the case went to Florida's highest court four more times to no avail. The United States Supreme Court finally agreed to take the case and on Lincoln's birthday, February 12, 1940, rendered the unanimous decision below. Justice Hugo Black's majority opinion is the most celebrated of his early civil rights pronouncements and will undoubtedly stand as a classic in the cause of freedom. Black's decision came only three years after he was appointed to the Court by President Roosevelt. In 1937 Black had been roundly denounced by both liberals and conservatives when it was revealed that he had once been a member of the Ku Klux Klan for a short period of time. As an ardent New Deal Senator from Alabama, Black was completely free of the racial and religious prejudices long associated with the Klu Klux Klan. And as a member of the Supreme Court, Justice Black has ardently defended the constitutional freedoms of *all* Americans.

MR. JUSTICE BLACK delivered the opinion of the Court.

The grave question presented . . . is whether proceedings in which confessions were utilized, and which culminated in sentences of death upon four young Negro men in the State of Florida, failed to afford the safeguard of that due process of law guaranteed by the Fourteenth Amendment. . . .

The scope and operation of the Fourteenth Amendment have been fruitful sources of controversy in our constitutional history. However, in view of its historical setting and the wrongs which called it into being, the due process provision of the Fourteenth Amendment—just as that in the Fifth—had led few to doubt that it was intended to guarantee procedural standards adequate and appropriate, then and thereafter, to protect, at all times, people charged with or suspected of crime by those holding positions of power and authority. . . .

The determination to preserve an accused's right to procedural due process sprang in large part from knowledge of the historical truth that the rights and liberties of people accused of crime could not be safely entrusted to secret inquisitorial processes. The testimony of centuries, in governments of varying kinds over populations of different races and beliefs, stood as proof that physical and mental torture and coercion had brought about the tragically unjust sacrifices of some who were the noblest and most useful of their generations. The rack, the thumbscrew, the wheel, solitary confinement, protracted questioning and cross-questioning, and other ingenious forms of entrapment of the helpless or unpopular had left their wake of mutilated bodies and shattered minds along the way to the cross, the guillotine, the stake and the hangman's noose. And they who had suffered most from secret and dictatorial proceedings have almost always been the poor, the ignorant, the numerically weak, the friendless, and the powerless.

This requirement—of conforming to fundamental standards of procedure in criminal trials—was made operative against the States by the Fourteenth Amendment. Where one of several accused had limped into the trial court as a result of admitted physical mistreatment inflicted to obtain confessions upon which a jury had returned a verdict of guilty of murder, this Court recently declared, *Brown v. Mississippi* (297 U.S. 278), that "It would be difficult to conceive of methods more revolting to the sense of justice than those taken to procure the confessions of these petitioners, and the use of the confessions thus obtained as the basis for conviction and sentence was a clear denial of due process."

Here, the record develops a sharp conflict upon the issue of physical violence and mistreatment, but shows, without conflict, the dragnet methods of arrest on suspicion without warrant, and the protracted questioning and cross-questioning of these ignorant young colored tenant farmers by state officers and other white citizens, in a fourth-floor jail room, where as prisoners they were without friends, advisers, or counselors, and under circumstances calculated to break the strongest nerves and the stoutest resistance. Just as our decision in *Brown v. Mississippi* was based upon the fact that the confessions were the result of compulsion, so in the present case, the admitted practices were such as to justify the statement that "The undisputed facts showed that compulsion was applied."

For five days petitioners were subjected to interrogations culminating in Saturday's (May 20th) all-night examination. Over a period of five days they steadily refused to confess and disclaimed any guilt. The very circumstances surrounding their confinement and their questioning without any formal charges having been brought, were such as to fill petitioners with terror and frightful misgivings. Some were practically strangers in the community; three were arrested in a one-room farm tenant house which was their home; the haunting fear of mob violence was around them in an atmosphere charged with excitement and public indignation. From virtually the moment of their arrest until their eventful confessions, they never knew just when any one would be called back to the fourth-floor room, and there, surrounded by his accusers and others, interrogated by men who held their very lives—so far as these ignorant petitioners could know—in the balance. . . . To permit human lives to be forfeited upon confessions thus obtained would make of the constitutional requirement of due process of law a meaningless symbol.

We are not impressed by the argument that law enforcement methods such as those under review are necessary to uphold our laws. The Constitution proscribes such lawless means irrespective of the end. And this argument flouts the basic principle that all people must stand on an equality before the bar of justice in every American court. Today, as in ages past, we are not without tragic proof that the exalted power of some governments to punish manufactured crime dictatorially is the handmaid of tyranny. Under our constitutional system, courts stand against any winds that blow as havens of refuge for those who might otherwise suffer because they are helpless, weak, outnumbered, or because they are non-conforming victims of prejudice and public excitement. Due process of law, preserved for all by our Constitution, commands that no such practice as that disclosed by this record shall send any accused to his death. No higher duty, no more solemn responsibility, rests upon this Court, than that of translating into living law and maintaining this constitutional shield deliberately planned and inscribed for the benefit of every human being subject to our Constitution—of whatever race, creed, or persuasion. The Supreme Court of Florida was in error and its judgment is

Reversed.

[MR. JUSTICE MURPHY took no part in the consideration or decision of this case.]

Aftermath

After the Supreme Court's decision the Chambers case was returned to Florida where the trial court, as directed, threw out the confessions. This left the court with insufficient evidence for a new trial, since without the confessions the only evidence available was a bloody stick found in the yard where the defendants had lived and some testimony that they had been in the neighborhood where the crime was committed. Furthermore, each of the defendants had for years steadfastly denied any knowledge of the crime. The trial court therefore directed a verdict of not guilty against the four defendants.

But for Isiah Chambers, a very serious-minded young man who brooded a great deal while in jail, the Supreme Court's decision was indeed a hollow victory. A few years after the original trial he had been adjudged insane and confined in a Florida state hospital. The other three defendants—Jack Williamson, Charlie Davis and Walter Woodward—were released from prison. They had been in jail for almost eight years. During this period they had only one visit from a relative—Walter Woodward's sister who came from South Carolina to see the prisoners and talk with lawyers. One of the defense attorneys and a local Negro organization collected enough money to send the three men back to their original homes. They were never heard from again.

Powell v. Alabama
287 U.S. 45 (1932)

Ozie Powell was one of nine Negroes ranging in age from twelve to twenty who became defendants in a bizarre and horrifying series of courtroom dramas which involved thousands of people and resulted in protests and demonstrations throughout the world.

It all began on a freight train leaving Chattanooga, Tennessee for Alabama in March, 1931—a deep Depression month when it was not unusual for young men to hop freight trains to look for work or just to travel from town to town. A fight between a group of Negro and white boys riding the train resulted in some of the white boys being thrown off while the train was moving slowly after having stopped for water and fuel at a small depot. These boys ran back to the depot and told a railroad employee about the fight. The railroad man telegraphed ahead to Paint Rock, Alabama, that a group of Negro boys on the train had caused trouble. Two white girls—Victoria Price, who had been married twice and Ruby Bates, a single girl—were also riding on the freight train. The two girls were locally well-known as "semi-prostitutes" who were employed as mill workers at very low wages. The Negro boys were illiterate and said to have unsavory reputations. "They have been accused of various petty crimes—gambling, thieving, more or less harmful mischief in general. They are the products of ignorance, of the most wretched and extreme poverty, of dirt, disorder, and race oppression."

When the train reached Paint Rock the nine Negro boys were arrested, taken to the county seat in Scottsboro, and charged with the rape of the two white girls. From then on the "Scottsboro case" was to be headline news for more than a decade. The National Guard was called out to prevent a lynching by an enraged mob at Scottsboro and the nine Negroes were moved to Gadsen, Alabama, for safe keeping.

On April 9, after a trial lasting only one day, eight of the nine Negroes were convicted and sentenced to death. A mistrial was declared in the case of one of the youngest defendants (twelve years of age) when one member of the jury held out for life imprisonment while the other eleven insisted on the death penalty. The accused had been arrested, tried, and sentenced in an atmosphere of tense, hostile, excited public sentiment. Neither were they represented by counsel. As is noted in the case below, the trial judge had only vaguely appointed all members of the bar to represent the defendants. The Alabama Supreme Court affirmed all the convictions but one, with the chief justice writing a strong and courageous dissent on the grounds that the defendants had not been given a fair trial. (The conviction of the youngest defendant (twelve years of age) was reversed on the ground that he was a minor.) The case went to the Supreme Court on a writ of certiorari.

The opinion below represents a notable chapter in the unfolding of American liberties. It undoubtedly was Justice George Sutherland's most significant contribution to the protection of American freedom. Sutherland was appointed to the Supreme Court by President Harding and became known as a conservative who bitterly opposed Franklin D. Roosevelt and the New Deal. It has been well said of Sutherland that he was "a heretic in two important respects. He had no faith in majority rule or in the efficacy of government. The judgment for the twentieth century is against him on both counts. Therefore, his record is for us today largely irrelevant. But his career demonstrates that even the heretic has his uses. We forget this at our peril." Nothing better demonstrates the truth of this assertion than Sutherland's opinion below.

MR. JUSTICE SUTHERLAND delivered the opinion of the Court.

. . . FIRST. The record shows that immediately upon the return of the indictment defendants were arraigned and pleaded not guilty. Apparently they were not asked whether they had, or were able to employ, counsel, or wished to have counsel appointed; or whether they had friends or relatives who might assist in that regard if communicated with. . . .

It is hardly necessary to say that, the right to counsel being conceded, a defendant should be afforded a fair opportunity to secure counsel of his own choice. Not only was that not done here, but such designation of counsel as was attempted was either so indefinite or so close upon the trial as to amount to a denial of effective and substantial aid in that regard. This will be amply demonstrated by a brief review of the record.

April 6, six days after indictment, the trials began. When the first case was called, the court inquired whether the parties were ready for trial. The state's attorney replied that he was ready to proceed. No one answered for the defendants or appeared to represent or defend them. Mr. Roddy, a Tennessee lawyer not a member of the local bar, addressed the court, saying that he had not been employed, but that people who were interested had spoken to him about the case. He was asked by the court whether he intended to appear for the defendants, and answered that he would like to appear along with counsel that the court might appoint. The record then proceeds:

> The Court: If you appear for these defendants, then I will not appoint counsel; if local counsel are willing to appear and assist you under the circumstances all right, but I will not appoint them.
> Mr. Roddy: Your Honor has appointed counsel, is that correct?
> The Court: I appointed all the members of the bar for the purpose of arraigning the defendants and then of course I anticipated them to continue to help them if no counsel appears.

. . . [U]ntil the very morning of the trial no lawyer had been named or definitely designated to represent the defendants. Prior to that time, the trial judge had "appointed all the members of the bar" for the limited "purpose of arraigning the defendants." Whether they would represent the defendants thereafter if no counsel appeared in their behalf, was a matter of speculation only, or, as the judge indicated, of mere anticipation on the part of the court. Such a designation, even if made for all purposes, would, in our opinion, have fallen far short of meeting, in any proper sense, a requirement for the appointment of counsel. How many lawyers were members of the bar does not appear; but, in the very nature of things, whether many or few, they would not, thus collectively named, have been given that clear appreciation of responsibility or impressed with that individual sense of duty which should and naturally would accompany the appointment of a selected member of the bar, specifically named and assigned.

. . . [T]his action of the trial judge in respect of counsel was little more than an expansive gesture, imposing no substantial or definite obligation upon anyone. . . . [D]uring perhaps the most critical period of the proceedings against these defendants, that is to say, from the time of their arraignment until the beginning of their trial, when consultation, thorough-going investigation and preparation were vitally important, the defendants did not have the aid of counsel in any real sense, although they were as much entitled to such aid during that period as at the trial itself. . . .

. . . The prompt disposition of criminal cases is to be commended and encouraged. But in reaching that result a defendant, charged with a serious crime, must not be stripped of his right to have sufficient time to advise with counsel and prepare his defense. To do that is not to proceed promptly in the calm spirit of regulated justice but to go forward with the haste of the mob. . . .

SECOND. The Constitution of Alabama provides that in all criminal prosecutions the accused shall enjoy the right to have the assistance of counsel; and a state statute requires the court in a capital case, where the defendant is unable to employ counsel, to appoint counsel for him. The state supreme court held that these provisions had not been infringed, and with that holding we are powerless to interfere. The question, however, which it is our duty, and within our power, to decide, is whether the denial of the assistance of counsel contravenes the due process clause of the Fourteenth Amendment to the federal Constitution.

If recognition of the right of a defendant charged with a felony to have the aid of counsel depended upon the existence of a similar right at common law as it existed in England when our Constitution was adopted, there would be great difficulty in maintaining it as necessary to due process. Originally, in England, a person charged with treason or felony was denied the aid of counsel, except in respect of legal questions which the accused himself might suggest. At the same time parties in civil cases and persons accused of misdemeanors were entitled to the full assistance of counsel. After the revolution of 1688, the rule was abolished as to treason, but was otherwise steadily adhered to until 1836, when by act of Parliament the full right was granted in respect of felonies generally. . . .

An affirmation of the right to the aid of counsel in petty offenses, and its denial in the case of crimes of the gravest character, where such aid is most needed, is so outrageous and so obviously a perversion of all sense of proportion that the rule was constantly, vigorously and sometimes passionately assailed by English statesmen and lawyers. . . .

The rule was rejected by the colonies. . . .

It . . . appears that in at least twelve of the thirteen colonies the rule of the English common law, in the respect now under consideration, had been definitely rejected and the right to counsel fully recognized in all criminal prosecutions, save that in one or two instances the right was limited to capital offenses or to the more serious crimes; and this court seems to have been of the opinion that this was true in all the colonies. . . .

. . . One test which has been applied to determine whether due process of law has been accorded in given instances is to ascertain what were the settled usages and modes of proceeding under the common and statute law of England before the Declaration of Independence, subject however, to the qualification that they be shown not to have been unsuited to the civil and political conditions of our ancestors by having been followed in this country after it became a nation. . . . Plainly, as appears from the foregoing, this test, as thus qualified, has not been met in the present case. . . .

It never has been doubted by this court, or any other so far as we know, that notice and hearing are preliminary steps essential to the passing of an entorceable judgment, and that they, together with a legally competent tribunal having jurisdiction of the case, constitute basic elements of the constitutional requirement of due process of law. . . .

What, then, does a hearing include? Historically and in practice, in our own country at least, it has always included the right to the aid of counsel when desired and provided by the party asserting the right. The right to be heard would be, in many cases, of little avail if it did not comprehend the right to be heard by counsel. Even the intelligent and educated layman has small and sometimes no skill in the science of law. If charged with crime, he is incapable, generally, of determining himself whether the indictment is good or bad. He is unfamiliar with the rules of evidence. Left without the aid of counsel he may be put on trial without a proper charge, and convicted upon incompetent evidence, or evidence irrelevant to the issue or otherwise inadmissible. He lacks both the skill and knowledge adequately to prepare his defense, even though he have a perfect one. He requires the guiding hand of counsel at every step in the proceedings against him. Without it, though he be not guilty, he faces the danger of conviction because he does not know how to establish his innocence. If that be true of men of intelligence, how much more true is it of the ignorant and illiterate, or those of feeble intellect. If in any case, civil or criminal, a state or federal court were arbitrarily to refuse to hear a party by counsel, employed by and appearing for him, it reasonably may not be doubted that such a refusal would be a denial of a hearing, and, therefore, of due process in the constitutional sense. . . .

In the light of the facts . . . —the ignorance and illiteracy of the defendants, their youth, the circumstances of public hostility, the imprisonment and the close surveillance of the defendants by the military forces, the fact that their friends and families were all in other states and communication with them necessarily difficult, and above all that they stood in deadly peril of their lives—we think the failure of the trial court to give them reasonable time and opportunity to secure counsel was a clear denial of due process.

But passing that, and assuming their inability, even if opportunity had been given, to employ counsel, as the trial court evidently did assume, we are of opinion that, under the circumstances just stated, the necessity of counsel was so vital and imperative that the failure of the trial court to make an effective appointment of counsel was likewise a denial of due process within the meaning of the Fourteenth Amendment. Whether this would be so in other criminal prosecutions, or under other circumstances, we need not determine. All that it is necessary now to decide, as we do decide, is that in a capital case, where the defendant is unable to employ counsel, and is incapable adequately of making his own defense because of ignorance, feeble-mindedness, illiteracy, or the like, it is the duty of the court, whether requested or not, to assign counsel for him as a necessary requisite of due process of law; and that duty is not discharged by an assignment at such a time or under such circumstances as to preclude the giving of effective aid in the preparation and trial of the case. To hold otherwise would be to ignore the fundamental postulate, already adverted to, "that there are certain immutable principles of justice which inhere in the very idea of free government which no member of the Union may disregard." . . . In a case such as this, whatever may be the rule in other cases, the right to have counsel appointed, when necessary, is a logical corollary from the constitutional right to be heard by counsel. . . .

The judgments must be reversed and the causes remanded for further proceedings not inconsistent with this opinion.

Judgments reversed.

[MR. JUSTICE BUTLER, joined by MR. JUSTICE McREYNOLDS, wrote a dissenting opinion.]

Aftermath

Morris Ernst, a respected student of constitutional law, remarked that the Court's decision was an "empty and meaningless victory" because it decided only the right to counsel and disregarded the question of a fair trial. But the Scottsboro case was far from over. The Negro youths were tried again in Decatur, Alabama, (fifty miles from Scottsboro) where there supposedly was less open hostility. The defense was brilliantly directed by Samuel S. Leibowitz, a well-known New York criminal lawyer, who had joined with many others of every conceivable political stripe to defend the Scottsboro boys. Ruby Bates changed her testimony and denied that she had been raped. She testified that she had made up the story because Victoria Price told her that "we might have to stay in jail if we did not frame up a story after crossing a state line with men." Victoria Price refused to change her testimony, but two of the white boys who had been on the train refused to testify against what they termed innocent boys. The jury again returned a verdict of guilty but in June, 1933, the presiding judge, James E. Horton, set aside the convictions on the grounds that they were not justified by the evidence and that Victoria Price was an unreliable witness. Judge Horton's courageous act "defied an inflamed local feeling, exposed him to all manner of insinuation and abuse, and resulted in his defeat for reelection to the circuit bench the following year."

After yet another trial the case reached the Supreme Court again in *Norris v. Alabama,* 294 U.S. 587 (1935)—known as the second Scottsboro case. Here the Supreme Court again reversed the convictions on the ground that Negroes had been systematically excluded from jury service in violation of the Equal Protection Clause of the Fourteenth Amendment. After another series of trials, four of the original defendants were released in 1937; four others were again convicted of rape and a fifth on a charge of attacking an officer during a transfer between jails. Only one of the men convicted for rape was sentenced to death, but his sentence was later commuted to life imprisonment. He was later paroled as were all the others except one who escaped from prison in 1948. He was arrested as an escaped convict in Michigan, but the Governor refused to honor Alabama's warrant for his return. By June, 1950, all of the Scottsboro boys were out of prison. As the last one left prison after twenty years to take a job as a porter in Albany, New York, he remarked: "I'm not mad because the girl (Victoria Price) lied about me. If she's still living, I feel sorry for her because I don't guess she sleeps much at night."

Gideon v. Wainwright
372 U.S. 335 (1963)

Clarence Gideon was hardly the person that anyone would have picked to play a key role in a celebrated Supreme Court case. From the beginning he had all the earmarks of a born loser. At the age of fourteen he ran away from home to escape a quarrelsome home atmosphere and a step-father who could never accept him. He lived the life of a hobo until he was sent to reform school for a year. He subsequently served four separate prison terms for burglary and larceny. Each of his two marriages was a miserable failure. Lacking schooling and skills of any kind, Gideon was often without work and lived by doing odd jobs, stealing, gambling, and the good graces of a variety of welfare agencies.

In June, 1961, Gideon was arrested in Panama City, Florida, for allegedly breaking into a local poolroom in order to steal beer, coke and money. Though he was never a dangerous professional criminal, Gideon looked much like a forlorn outcast at the time of his arrest. He had all the "physical marks of a destitute life: a wrinkled, prematurely aged face, a voice and hands that trembled, a frail body, white hair." At the trial in the county court Gideon pleaded not guilty and asked the presiding judge to appoint a lawyer to represent him since he had no money to hire his own counsel. The Sixth Amendment provides that in all criminal prosecutions an accused shall have the assistance of counsel for his defense. However, the judge in declining to appoint counsel stated as follows:

> Mr. Gideon, I am sorry, but I cannot appoint counsel to repre-
> sent you in this case. Under the laws of the State of Florida,
> the only time the Court can appoint Counsel to represent a
> Defendant is when that person is charged with a capital of-
> fense. I am sorry, but I will have to deny your request to
> appoint Counsel to defend you in this case.

The presiding judge based this statement on a series of Supreme
Court decisions notably *Betts v. Brady*, discussed below, which held
that counsel was required in capital offenses but not in ordinary
criminal cases unless there were exceptional circumstances. Nevertheless, it was obvious throughout the short trial that Gideon was
handicapped by the lack of counsel both in the presentation of his
defense and in the cross-examination of state witnesses. Gideon
simply did not know enough about legal procedures to defend himself properly. As expected, the jury found him guilty and the judge
sentenced him to serve five years in the Florida State Prison.

Gideon continued to proclaim his innocence while in prison. But
he did more. He studied every aspect of his case and became a prison
"legal expert" in the process. Finally he petitioned the Florida Supreme Court for a writ of habeas corpus. The writ of habeas corpus
is a method used to determine whether or not a person is imprisoned
for a just cause. Long viewed as basic to American liberties, the writ
means literally that the body of the prisoner must be produced in
order for the court to determine at once whether or not the individual is wrongly imprisoned. The highest Florida Court denied
Gideon's petition without a hearing and he remained in jail.

But Gideon refused to give up the struggle. Writing to the United
States Supreme Court in pencil on lined sheets of paper made available by the Florida prison, he petitioned for a writ of certiorari (explained in Chapter I) asking, in effect, that the Court review his
case. Since he had no funds, Gideon also asked that he be allowed
to proceed in the manner of a pauper. A federal law allows persons
who are too poor to have their cases printed up or to pay the $100
fee for docketing a case in the Supreme Court to proceed as paupers
and thereby avoid these costs. Approximately six months after receiving his papers, the Supreme Court granted Gideon's petition for certiorari and allowed him to proceed as a pauper. Since Gideon could
not afford a lawyer, the Supreme Court appointed Abe Fortas of a
prominent Washington, D.C., law firm to represent him. A close

personal friend of President Johnson, Fortas was named to the Supreme Court in 1965 to replace Justice Arthur Goldberg, who became Ambassador to the United Nations.

Wainwright, the other party in this case, was the Director of the Division of Corrections in Florida. In delivering the majority opinion Justice Black again contributed to the enlargement of American freedoms.

MR. JUSTICE BLACK delivered the opinion of the Court.

. . . The facts upon which Betts [in *Betts v. Brady*] claimed that he had been unconstitutionally denied the right to have counsel appointed to assist him are strikingly like the facts upon which Gideon here bases his federal constitutional claim. Betts was indicted for robbery in a Maryland state court. On arraignment, he told the trial judge of his lack of funds to hire a lawyer and asked the court to appoint one for him. Betts was advised that it was not the practice in that county to appoint counsel for indigent defendants except in murder and rape cases. He then pleaded not guilty, had witnesses summoned, cross-examined the State's witnesses, examined his own, and chose not to testify himself. He was found guilty by the judge, sitting without a jury, and sentenced to eight years in prison. Like Gideon, Betts sought release by habeas corpus, alleging that he had been denied the right to assistance of counsel in violation of the Fourteenth Amendment. Betts was denied any relief, and on review this Court affirmed. It was held that a refusal to appoint counsel for an indigent defendant charged with a felony did not necessarily violate the Due Process Clause of the Fourteenth Amendment. . . . [T]he Court held that refusal to appoint counsel under the particular facts and circumstances in the *Betts* case was not so "offensive to the common and fundamental ideas of fairness" as to amount to a denial of due process. Since the facts and circumstances of the two cases are so nearly indistinguishable, we think the *Betts v. Brady* holding if left standing would require us to reject Gideon's claim that the Constitution guarantees him the assistance of counsel. Upon full reconsideration we conclude that *Betts v. Brady* should be overruled. . . .

The Sixth Amendment provides, "In all criminal prosecutions, the accused shall enjoy the right . . . to have the Assistance of Counsel for his defense." We have construed this to mean that in federal courts counsel must be provided for defendants unable to employ counsel unless the right is competently and intelligently waived. Betts argued that this right is extended to indigent defendants in state courts by the Fourteenth Amendment. In response the Court stated that, while the Sixth Amend-men laid down "no rule for the conduct laid by the Amendment upon the national courts expresses a rule so fundamental and essential to a fair trial, and so, to due process of law, that it is made obligatory upon the States by the Fourteenth Amendment." . . . In order to decide whether the Sixth Amendment's guarantee of counsel is of this fundamental nature, the Court in *Betts* set out and considered "relevant data on the subject. . . ." On the basis of this historical data the Court concluded that "appointment of counsel is not a fundamental right, essential to a fair trial." . . . It was for this reason the *Betts* Court refused to accept the contention that the Sixth Amendment's guarantee of counsel for indigent federal defendants was extended to or, in the words of that Court, "made obligatory upon the States by the Fourteenth Amendment." Plainly, had the Court concluded that appointment of counsel for an indigent criminal defendant was "a fundamental right, essential to a fair trial," it would have held that the Fourteenth Amendment requires appointment of counsel in a state court, just as the Sixth Amendment requires in a federal court.

We think the Court in *Betts* had ample precedent for acknowledging that those guarantees of the Bill of Rights which are fundamental safeguards of liberty immune from federal abridgment are equally protected against state invasion by the Due Process Clause of the Fourteenth Amendment. . . . In many cases . . . this Court has looked to the fundamental nature of original Bill of Rights guarantees to decide whether the Fourteenth Amendment makes them obligatory on the States. Explicitly recognized to be of this "fundamental nature" and therefore made immune from state invasion by the Fourteenth, or some part of it, are the First Amendment's freedoms of speech, press, religion, assembly, association, and petition for redress of grievances. For the same reason, though not always in precisely the same terminology, the Court has made obligatory on the States the Fifth Amendment's command that private property shall not be taken for public use without just compensation, the Fourth Amendment's prohibition of unreasonable searches and seizures, and the Eighth's ban on cruel and unusual punishment. . . .

We accept *Betts v. Brady's* assumption, based as it was on our prior cases, that a provision of the Bill of Rights which is "fundamental and essential to a fair trial" is made obligatory upon the States by the Fourteenth Amendment. We think the Court in *Betts* was wrong, however, in concluding that the Sixth Amendment's guarantee of counsel is not one of these fundamental rights. Ten years before *Betts v. Brady*, this Court, after full consideration of all the historical data examined in Betts, had unequivocally declared that "the right to the aid of counsel is of this fundamental character." *Powell v. Alabama.* . . . Several years later, in

1936, the Court reemphasized what it had said about the fundamental nature of the right to counsel in this language:

> We concluded that certain fundamental rights, safeguarded by the first eight amendments against federal action, were also safeguarded against state action by the Due Process Clause of the Fourteenth Amendment, and among them the fundamental right of the accused to the aid of counsel in a criminal prosecution. . . .

And again in 1938 this Court said:

> [The assistance of counsel] is one of the safeguards of the Sixth Amendment deemed necessary to insure fundamental human rights of life and liberty. . . . The Sixth Amendment stands as a constant admonition that if the constitutional safeguards it provides be lost, justice will not 'still be done.' . . .

The fact is that in deciding as it did—that "appointment of counsel is not a fundamental right, essential to a fair trial"—the Court in *Betts v. Brady* made an abrupt break with its own well-considered precedents. In returning to these old precedents, sounder we believe than the new, we but restore constitutional principles established to achieve a fair system of justice. Not only these precedents but also reason and reflection require us to recognize that in our adversary system of criminal justice, any person haled into court, who is too poor to hire a lawyer, cannot be assured a fair trial unless counsel is provided for him. This seems to us to be an obvious truth. Governments, both state and federal, quite properly spend vast sums of money to establish machinery to try defendants accused of crime. Lawyers to prosecute are everywhere deemed essential to protect the public's interest in an orderly society. Similarly, there are few defendants charged with crime, few indeed, who fail to hire the best lawyers they can get to prepare and present their defenses. That government hires lawyers to prosecute and defendants who have the money hire lawyers to defend are the strongest indications of the widespread belief that lawyers in criminal courts are necessities, not luxuries. The right of one charged with crime to counsel may not be deemed fundamental and essential to fair trials in some countries, but it is in ours. From the very beginning, our state and national constitutions and laws have laid great emphasis on procedural and substantive safeguards designed to assure fair trials before impartial tribunals in which every defendant stands equal before the law. This noble ideal cannot be realized if the poor man charged with crime has to face his accusers without a lawyer to assist him. The Court in *Betts v. Brady* departed from the sound wisdom upon which the Court's holding in *Powell v. Alabama* rested. Florida, supported by two other states, has asked that *Betts v. Brady* be left intact. Twenty-two States, as friends of the Court, argue that *Betts* was "an anachronism when handed down" and that it should now be overruled. We agree.

The judgment is reversed and the cause is remanded to the Supreme Court of Florida for further action not inconsistent with this opinion.

Reversed.

[JUSTICES DOUGLAS, CLARK and HARLAN wrote concurring opinions.]

Aftermath

The Supreme Court's decision entitled Gideon to another trial. His case came up again in the same courtroom but this time a local attorney was appointed to represent him. During the trial Gideon's attorney presented evidence which indicated that the state's star witness against Gideon may have committed the crime himself. This time the jury found Gideon not guilty. After nearly two years in the Florida prison, Gideon was again a free man. Moreover, his case had an immediate impact on other Florida prisoners. More than half of the eight thousand prisoners in Florida had been convicted without the benefit of counsel. On the basis of the Gideon case their convictions were obviously illegal. To date nearly six thousand prisoners have petitioned for new trials and over one thousand have already won their freedom.

Escobedo v. Illinois
378 U.S. 478 (1964)

Danny Escobedo was a scrawny, twenty-two year old high school drop-out and laborer when he was picked up for questioning in connection with the slaying of his sister's husband. A product of the Chicago slums, Escobedo was extremely fond of his sister, but he hated her husband who often beat his wife and who was once arrested for stabbing her more than a dozen times.

On the night of January 19, 1960, the husband was shot in the back as he arrived home. No gun was found and there were no witnesses to the crime. Escobedo was picked up eleven days after the shooting and questioned along with his sister and two youthful friends. The police suspected that this group had plotted the husband's killing. Escobedo was brought to police headquarters with his hands manacled behind his back and told by one of the arresting officers that one of his friends had named him as the killer of his sister's husband. The questioning continued for fourteen and one half hours. During the later stages of interrogation a "friendly" officer who knew Escobedo's family informed the accused that he and his sister could go home if he made a full statement. Thereupon, Escobedo said that his friend, and not he, had fired the fatal shots. He thereby indirectly confessed complicity in the crime. He later made additional statements which further implicated him in the murder plot. Throughout this period of interrogation, Escobedo was not advised by the police of his right to remain silent. The police also denied repeated requests by Escobedo to see his lawyer who was at the police station during the interrogation. At the same time, Escobedo's attorney made several attempts to see his clients but was refused permission by the police.

Though Escobedo later recanted his incriminatnig statements, he was convicted of first degree murder and sentenced to twenty years imprisonment. His friend, who had supposedly fired the shots, drew a life sentence. The Illinois Supreme Court first reversed the conviction on the ground that the confession was involuntary and therefore inadmissible. However, on rehearing the case the Illinois court affirmed the conviction. Ably represented by court appointed counsel, Escobedo then took his case to the Supreme Court on a writ of certiorari.

Justice Arthur Goldberg's opinion reveals clearly his alignment with the liberal bloc on the Court which is determined to protect individual liberties. Appointed to the Court by President Kennedy, Justice Goldberg was persuaded by President Johnson to leave after less than three years service to become Ambassador to the United Nations. It is interesting to note that the dissenting opinion was written by Justice Byron R. White, the other Kennedy appointee, who has been much less attracted to the "activist" role of the Court. It has been stated that if a member of the American Civil Liberties Union were asked how he regarded President Kennedy's appointments to the Court, he probably would answer that "Goldberg was a good man, but White has been a disappointment."

MR. JUSTICE GOLDBERG delivered the opinion of the Court.

The critical question in this case is whether, under the circumstances, the refusal by the police to honor petitioner's request to consult with his lawyer during the course of an interrogation constitutes a denial of "the

Assistance of Counsel" in violation of the Sixth Amendment to the Constitution as "made obligatory upon the States by the Fourteenth Amendment," *Gideon v. Wainwright*. . . . and thereby renders inadmissible in a state criminal trial any incriminating statement elicited by the police during the interrogation. . . .

In *Massiah v. United States,* 377 U.S. 201, this Court observed that "a Constitution which guarantees a defendant the aid of counsel at . . . trial could surely vouchsafe no less to an indicted defendant under interrogation by the police in a completely extrajudicial proceeding. Anything less . . . might deny a defendant 'effective representation by counsel at the only stage when legal aid and advice would help him.' " . . .

The interrogation here was conducted before petitioner was formally indicted. But in the context of this case, that fact should make no difference. When petitioner requested, and was denied, an opportunity to consult with his lawyer, the investigation had ceased to be a general investigation of "an unsolved crime." . . . Petitioner had become the accused, and the purpose of the interrogation was to "get him" to confess his guilt despite his constitutional right not to do so. At the time of his arrest and throughout the course of the interrogation, the police told petitioner that they had convincing evidence that he had fired the fatal shots. Without informing him of his absolute right to remain silent in the face of this accusation, the police urged him to make a statement. . . . Petitioner, a layman, was undoubtedly unaware that under Illinois law an admission of "mere" complicity in the murder plot was legally as damaging as an admission of firing of the fatal shots. . . . The "guiding hand of counsel" was essential to advise petitioner of his rights in this delicate situation. . . . This was the "stage when legal aid and advice" were most critical to petitioner. . . . What happened at this interrogation could certainly "affect the whole trial," . . . since rights "may be as irretrievably lost, if not then and there asserted, as they are when an accused represented by counsel waives a right for strategic purposes." . . . It would exalt form over substance to make the right to counsel, under these circumstances, depend on whether at the time of the interrogation, the authorities had secured a formal indictment. Petitioner had, for all practical purposes, already been charged with murder. . . .

In *Gideon v. Wainwright* we held that every person accused of a crime, whether state or federal, is entitled to a lawyer at trial. The rule sought by the State here, however, would make the trial no more than an appeal from the interrogation; and the "right to use counsel at the formal trial [would be] a very hollow thing [if], for all practical purposes, the conviction is already assured by pretrial examination." . . .

It is argued that if the right to counsel is afforded prior to indictment, the number of confessions obtained by the police will diminish significantly, because most confessions are obtained during the period between arrest and indictment, and "any lawyer worth his salt will tell the suspect in no uncertain terms to make no statement to police under any circumstances." . . . This argument, of course, cuts two ways. The fact that many confessions are obtained during this period points up its critical nature as a "stage when legal aid and advice" are surely needed. . . . The right to counsel would indeed be hollow if it began at a period when few confessions were obtained. There is necessarily a direct relationship between the importance of a stage to the police in their quest for a confession and the criticalness of that stage to the accused in his need for legal advice. Our Constitution, unlike some others, strikes the balance in favor of the right of the accused to be advised by his lawyer of his privilege against self-incrimination. . . .

We have learned the lesson of history, ancient and modern, that a system of criminal law enforcement which comes to depend on the "confession" will, in the long run, be less reliable and more subject to abuses than a system which depends on extrinsic evidence, independently secured through skillful investigation. . . . This Court also has recognized that "history amply shows that confessions have often been extorted to save law enforcement officials the trouble and effort of obtaining valid and independent evidence. . . ."

We have also learned the companion lesson of history that no system of criminal justice can, or should, survive if it comes to depend for its continued effectiveness on the citizens' abdication through unawareness of their constitutional rights. No system worth preserving should have to *fear* that if an accused is permitted to consult with a lawyer, he will become aware of, and exercise, these rights. If the exercise of constitutional rights will thwart the effectiveness of a system of law enforcement, then there is something very wrong with that system.

We hold, therefore, that where, as here, the investigation is no longer a general inquiry into an unsolved crime but has begun to focus on a particular suspect, the suspect has been taken into police custody, the police carry out a process of interrogations that lends itself to eliciting incriminating statements, the suspect has requested and been denied an opportunity to consult with his lawyer, and the police have not effectively warned him of his absolute constitutional right to remain silent, the accused has been denied "the Assistance of Counsel" in violation of the Sixth Amendment to the Constitution as "made obligatory upon the States by the Fourteenth Amendment," *Gideon v. Wainwright*. . . . and that no statement elicited by the police during the interrogation may be used against him at a criminal trial. . . .

Nothing we have said today affects the powers of the police to investigate "an unsolved crime," . . . by gathering information from witnesses and by other "proper investigative efforts." . . . We hold only that when the process shifts from investigatory to accusatory—when its focus is on the accused and its purpose is to elicit a confession—our adversary system begins to operate, and, under the circumstances here, the accused must be permitted to consult with his lawyer.

The judgment of the Illinois Supreme Court is reversed and the case remanded for proceedings not inconsistent with this opinion.

Reversed and remanded. . . .

MR. JUSTICE WHITE, with whom MR. JUSTICE CLARK and MR. JUSTICE STEWART join, dissenting.

In *Massiah v. United States* the Court held that as of the date of the indictment the prosecution is disentitled to secure admissions from the accused. The Court now moves that date back to the time when the prosecution begins to "focus" on the accused. . . . The Court holds that once the accused becomes a suspect and, presumably, is arrested, any admission made to the police thereafter is inadmissible in evidence unless the accused has waived his right to counsel. The decision is thus another major step in the direction of the goal which the Court seemingly has in mind—to bar from evidence all admissions obtained from an individual suspected of crime, whether involuntarily made or not. . . .

The right to counsel now not only entitles the accused to counsel's advice and aid in preparing for trial but stands as an impenetrable barrier to any interrogation once the accused has become a suspect. From that very moment apparently his right to counsel attaches, a rule wholly unworkable and impossible to administer unless police cars are equipped with public defenders and undercover agents and police informants have defense counsel at their side. I would not abandon the Court's prior cases defining with some care and analysis the circumstances requiring the presence or aid of counsel and substitute the amorphous and wholly unworkable principle that counsel is constitutionally required whenever he would or could be helpful. . . .

Today's decision cannot be squared with other provisions of the Constitution which, in my view, define the system of criminal justice this Court is empowered to administer. The Fourth Amendment permits upon probable cause even compulsory searches of the suspect and his possessions and the use of the fruits of the search at trial, all in the absence of counsel. The Fifth Amendment and state constitutional provisions authorize, indeed require, inquisitorial grand jury proceedings at which a potential defendant, in the absence of counsel, is shielded against no more than compulsory incrimination. . . . A grand jury witness, who may be a suspect, is interrogated and his answers, at least until today, are admissible in evidence at trial. And these provisions have been thought of as constitutional safeguards to persons suspected of an offense. Furthermore, until now, the Constitution has permitted the accused to be fingerprinted and to be identified in a line-up or in the courtroom itself.

The Court chooses to ignore these matters and to rely on the virtues and morality of a system of criminal law enforcement which does not depend on the "confession." No such judgment is to be found in the Constitution. It might be appropriate for a legislature to provide that a suspect should not be consulted during a criminal investigation; that an accused should never be called before a grand jury to answer, even if he wants to, what may well be incriminating questions; and that no person, whether he be a suspect, guilty criminal or innocent bystander, should be put to the ordeal of responding to orderly noncompulsory inquiry by the State. But this is not the system our Constitution requires. The only "inquisitions" the Constitution forbids are those which compel incrimination. Escobedo's statements were not compelled and the Court does not hold that they were.

This new American judge's rule, which is to be applied in both federal and state courts, is perhaps thought to be a necessary safeguard against the possibility of extorted confessions. To this extent it reflects a deep-seated distrust of law enforcement officers everywhere, unsupported by relevant data or current material based upon our own experience. Obviously law enforcement officers can make mistakes and exceed their authority, as today's decision shows that even judges can do, but I have somewhat more faith than the Court evidently has in the ability and desire of prosecuters and of the power of the appellate courts to discern and correct such violations of the law.

The Court may be concerned with a narrower matter: the unknowing defendant who responds to police questioning because he mistakenly believes that he must and that his admissions will not be used against him. But this worry hardly calls for the broadside the Court has now fired. The failure to inform an accused that he need not answer and that his answers may be used against him is very relevant indeed to whether the disclosures are compelled. Cases in this Court, to say the least, have never placed a premium on ignorance of constitutional rights. If an accused is told he must answer and did not know better, it would be very doubtful that the resulting admissions could be used against him. When the accused has not been informed of his rights at all the Court characteristically and properly looks very closely at the surrounding circumstances. . . . I would continue to do so. But in this case Danny Escobedo knew full well that he need not answer and knew full well that his lawyer had advised him not to answer.

I do not suggest for a moment that law enforcement will be destroyed by the rule announced today. The need for peace and order is too insistent for that. But it will be crippled and its task made a great deal more difficult, all in my opinion, for unsound, unstated reasons, which can find no home in any of the provisions of the Constitution.

[JUSTICES HARLAN and STEWART also wrote brief separate dissenting opinions.]

Aftermath

The Chicago Police Department revamped its treatment of accused citizens after the *Escobedo* decision. An order was issued by the Superintendent admonishing the police to:

1. Permit each prisoner to communicate with his attorney and a member of his family.
2. Never use force or coercion in seeking confessions.
3. Respect the right of the accused to refuse to give testimony against himself.
4. Never engage in the use of derogatory terms such as *nigger, boy, spic, wop, kike, chink, shine, dago, polack, bohunk,* etc.

As for Escobedo, he was released from prison and returned to Chicago where he has been arrested three times—for illegal possession of a pistol, for selling barbiturates, and for suspected burglary of a restaurant. Escobedo's friend is still in prison under a life sentence. Meanwhile, his sister's new husband was shot to death by a gunman from a passing car. The police have yet to locate the killer.

Malloy v. Hogan
378 U.S. 1 (1964)

William Malloy, a fifty-two year old small-time gambler, was arrested in a raid in Hartford, Connecticut, and pleaded guilty to pool-selling, an offense defined as "occupying and keeping a building containing gambling apparatus." He was sentenced to one year in jail and fined $500, but was released after serving three months of his sentence and placed on probation for two years. While on probation Malloy was summoned to appear before a referee appointed by a county court to investigate gambling and other criminal activities in the area. However, he refused to answer virtually all the questions put to him relating to the circumstances surrounding his arrest and conviction on the ground that any response would tend to incriminate him. He was cited for contempt by the county court and sent to prison until he was willing to answer the questions. His application for a writ of habeas corpus was denied by the county court. The Connecticut Supreme Court of Errors (the state's highest court) affirmed. Malloy then brought the case to the Supreme Court on a writ of certiorari.

The concern here is with that portion of the Fifth Amendment which provides that an accused person shall not "be compelled in any criminal case to be a witness against himself." Since this action began in a state court, Malloy argued that the Fifth Amendment provision is made applicable to him through the Fourteenth Amendment. Though the privilege against self-incrimination has come under sharp attack in recent years, it still stands, in the words of Justice William O. Douglas, as "one of the great landmarks of man's struggle to be free from tyranny, to be decent and civilized. It is our way of escape from the use of torture. It protects man against any forces of the Inquisition. It is part of our respect for the dignity of man."

Justice William J. Brennan's opinion provides a good example of his activist concern for civil liberties. Named to the Court by President Eisenhower in 1956, few observers expected Brennan to join the civil-libertarian bloc on the Court. A Democrat born of poor Irish-Catholic immigrants, Brennan worked his way through college and served on the New Jersey Supreme Court before his elevation to the highest court. Justice Harlan's dissenting opinion again demonstrates the narrower, self-restraint conception of the Court's function.

MR. JUSTICE BRENNAN delivered the opinion of the Court.

In this case we are asked to reconsider prior decisions holding that the privilege against self-incrimination is not safeguarded against state action by the Fourteenth Amendment, *Twining v. New Jersey,* . . . *Adamson v. California.* . . .

The Court has not hesitated to re-examine past decisions according the Fourteenth Amendment a less central role in the preservation of basic liberties than that which was contemplated by its Framers when they added the Amendment to our constitutional scheme. Thus, although the Court as late as 1922 said that "neither the Fourteenth Amendment nor any other provision of the Constitution of the United States imposes upon the States any restrictions about 'freedom of speech.' . . ." . . . three years later *Gitlow v. New York* . . . initiated a series of decisions which today holds immune from state invasion every First Amendment protection for the cherished rights of mind and spirit—the freedoms of speech, press, religion, assembly, association, and petition for redress of grievances.

Similarly, *Palko v. Connecticut* . . . decided in 1938, suggested that the rights secured by the Fourth Amendment, were not protected against state action. . . . In 1961, however, the Court held that in the light of later decisions, it was taken as settled that ". . . the Fourth Amendment's right of privacy has been declared enforceable against the States through the Due Process Clause of the Fourteenth. . . ." *Mapp v. Ohio.* . . . Again, although the Court held in 1942 that in a state prosecution for a non-capital offense, "appointment of counsel is not a fundamental right," *Betts v. Brady* . . . only last Term this decision was re-examined and it was held that provision of counsel in all criminal cases was "a fundamental right essential to a fair trial," and thus was made obligatory on the States by the Fourteenth Amendment. *Gideon v. Wainwright.* . . .

We hold today that the Fifth Amendment's exception from compulsory self-incrimination is also protected by the Fourteenth Amendment against abridgment by the States. Decisions of the Court since *Twining* and *Adamson* have departed from the contrary view expressed in those cases. . . .

The marked shift to the federal standard in state cases began with *Lisenba v. California,* 314 U.S. 219, where the Court spoke of accused's "free choice to admit, to deny, or to refuse to answer." . . . The shift reflects recognition that the American system of criminal prosecution is accusatorial, not inquisitorial, and that the Fifth Amendment privilege is its essential mainstay. . . . Governments, state and federal, are thus constitutionally compelled to establish guilt by evidence independently and freely secured, and may not by coercion prove a charge against an accused out of his own mouth. Since the Fourteenth Amendment prohibits the States from inducing a person to confess through "sympathy falsely aroused," . . . or other like inducement far short of "compulsion by torture," . . . it follows *a fortiori* that it also forbids the States to resort to imprisonment, as here, to compel him to answer questions that might incriminate him. The Fourteenth Amendment secures against state invasion the same privilege that the Fifth Amendment guarantees against federal infringement—the right of a person to remain silent unless he chooses to speak in the unfettered exercise of his own will, and to suffer no penalty . . . for such silence.

This conclusion is fortified by our recent decision in *Mapp v. Ohio* . . . which had held "that in a prosecution in a state court for a state crime the Fourteenth Amendment does not forbid the admission of evidence obtained by an unreasonable search and seizure." . . . *Mapp* held that the Fifth Amendment privilege against self-incrimination implemented the Fourth Amendment in such cases, and that the two guarantees of personal security conjoined in the Fourteenth Amendment to make the exclusionary rule obligatory upon the States. . . .

The respondent State of Connecticut concedes in its brief that under our decisions, particularly those involving coerced confessions, "the accusatorial system has become a fundamental part of the fabric of our society and, hence, is enforceable against the States." The State urges, however, that the availability of the federal privilege to a witness in a state inquiry is to be determined according to a less stringent standard than is applicable in a federal proceeding. We disagree. We have held that the guarantees of the First Amendment, . . . the prohibition of unreasonable searches and seizures of the Fourth Amendment, . . . and the right to counsel guaranteed by the Sixth Amendment, . . . are all to be enforced against the States under the Fourteenth Amendment according to the same standards that protect those personal rights against federal encroachment. In the coerced confession cases, involving the policies of the privilege itself, there has been no suggestion that a confession might be considered coerced if used in a federal but not a state tribunal. The Court thus has rejected the notion that the Fourteenth Amendment applies to the states only a "watered-down, subjective version of the Bill of Rights." . . . What is accorded is a privilege of refusing to incriminate one's self, and the feared prosecution may be by either federal or state authorities. *Murphy v. Waterfront Comm'n.* . . . It would be incongruous to have different standards determine the validity of a claim of privilege based on the same feared prosecution, depending on whether the claim was asserted in a state or federal court. Therefore, the same standards must determine whether an accused's silence in either a federal or state proceeding is justified.

We turn to the petitioner's claim that the State of Connecticut denied him the protection of his federal privilege. It must be considered irrelevant that the petitioner was a witness in a statutory inquiry and not a defendant in a criminal prosecution, for it has long been settled that the privilege protects witnesses in similar federal inquiries. . . . We recently elaborated the content of the federal standard: . . .

> The privilege afforded not only extends to answers that would in themselves support a conviction . . . but likewise embraces those

which would furnish a link in the chain of evidence needed to prosecute . . . if the witness, upon interposing his claim, were required to prove the hazard . . . he would be compelled to surrender the very protection which the privilege is designed to guarantee. To sustain the privilege, it need only be evident from the implication of the question, in the setting in which it is asked, that a responsive answer to the question or an explanation of why it cannot be answered might be dangerous because injurious disclosure would result. . . .

The State of Connecticut argues that the Connecticut courts properly applied the federal standards to the facts of this case. . . .

The conclusions of the Court of Errors, tested by the federal standard, fails to take sufficient account of the setting in which the questions were asked. The interrogation was part of a wide-ranging inquiry into crime, including gambling, in Hartford. It was admitted on behalf of the State at oral argument— . . . that the State desired to elicit from the petitioner the identity of the person who ran the pool-selling operation in connection with which he had been arrested in 1959. It was apparent that petitioner might apprehend that if this person were still engaged in unlawful activity, disclosure of his name might furnish a link in a chain of evidence sufficient to connect the petitioner with a more recent crime for which he might still be prosecuted. . . .

We conclude, therefore, that as to each of the questions, it was "evident from the implication of the question, in the setting in which it [was] asked, that a responsive answer to the question or an explanation of why it [could not] be answered might be dangerous because injurious disclosure could result." . . .

Reversed.

[JUSTICE DOUGLAS joined the opinion of the Court but adhered to his view that the Fourteenth Amendment incorporates the entire Bill of Rights.]

MR. JUSTICE HARLAN, whom MR. JUSTICE CLARK joins, dissenting.

The Court's undiscriminating approach to the Due Process Clause carries serious implications for the sound working of our federal system in the field of criminal law.

The Court concludes, almost without discussion, that "the same standards must determine whether an accused's silence in either a federal or state proceeding is justified." . . . About all that the Court offers in explanation of this conclusion is the observation that it would be "incongruous" if different standards governed the assertion of a privilege to remain silent in state and federal tribunals. Such "incongruity," however, is at the heart of our federal system. The powers and responsibilities of the state and federal governments are not congruent; under our Constitution, they are not intended to be. Why should it be thought, as an *a priori* matter, that limitations on the investigative power of the States are in all respects identical with limitations on the investigative power of the Federal Government? This certainly does not follow from the fact that we deal here with constitutional requirements; for the provisions of the Constitution which are construed are different. . . .

"The States under our federal system have the principal responsibility for defining and prosecuting crimes." The Court endangers this allocation of responsibility for the prevention of crime when it applies to the States doctrines developed in the context of federal law enforcement, without any attention to the special problems which the States as a group or particular States may face. If the power of the States to deal with local crime is unduly restricted, the likely consequence is a shift of responsibility in this area to the Federal Government, with its vastly greater resources. Such a shift, if it occurs, may in the end serve to weaken the very liberties which the Fourteenth Amendment safeguards by bringing us closer to the monolithic society which our federalism rejects. Equally dangerous to our liberties is the alternative of watering down protections against the Federal Government embodied in the Bill of Rights so as not unduly to restrict the powers of the States. . . .

Rather than insisting, almost by rote, that the Connecticut court, in considering the petitioner's claim of privilege, was required to apply the "federal standard," the Court should have fulfilled its responsibility under the Due Process Clause by inquiring whether the proceedings below met the demands of fundamental fairness which due process embodies. Such an approach may not satisfy those who see in the Fourteenth Amendment a set of easily applied "absolutes" which can afford a haven from unsettling doubt. It is, however, truer to the spirit which requires this Court constantly to re-examine fundamental principles and at the same time enjoins it from reading its own preferences into the Constitution.

The Connecticut Supreme Court of Errors gave full and careful consideration to the petitioner's claim that he would incriminate himself if he answered the questions put to him. . . .

I do not understand how anyone could read the opinion of the Connecticut court and conclude that the state law which was the basis of its decision or the decision itself was lacking in fundamental fairness. The truth of the matter is that under any standard—state or federal—the commitment for contempt was proper. . . . The Court's reference to a federal standard is, to put it bluntly, simply an excuse for the Court to substitute its own superficial assessment of the facts and state law for the careful and better informed conclusions of the state court. No one who scans the two opinions with an objective eye will, I think, reach any other conclusion.

I would affirm.

[JUSTICE WHITE, joined by JUSTICE STEWART, also dissented, but on much narrower grounds. Although he apparently agreed that the Fifth Amendment privilege against self-incrimination applies to the states, he felt that the privilege was improperly invoked in this particular case.]

Miranda v. Arizona
384 U.S. 436 (1966)

The Miranda case is one of four decided together involving similar convictions for robbery, kidnapping, rape and murder. In each case the convictions were based on confessions but none of the defendants had been advised of his right to consult with an attorney prior to the confessions. Moreover, in three of the cases the defendants had not been warned of their right to remain silent. The procedural facts of the Miranda case are typical.

In 1963 an eighteen-year old girl was kidnapped and forcibly raped near Phoenix, Arizona, after being threatened with a knife. Ten days later the police arrested Ernesto Arthur Miranda, a twenty-three year old indigent and one-time truck driver who had not gone beyond the ninth grade. At the police station the girl identified Miranda as the one who had kidnapped and raped her. Two officers then took the suspect to a separate room and began questioning him about the crime. Within two hours Miranda orally confessed and wrote out a brief statement describing the crime. No force, threats or promises were used by the police, but Miranda was not advised that he had a right to consult with a lawyer. Neither was he advised of his right to remain silent. Miranda's confession was admitted as evidence at his trial over the objections of his defense counsel. He was found guilty and sentenced to prison for twenty to thirty years. The Supreme Court of Arizona affirmed the conviction emphasizing that Miranda had not specifically requested counsel. The Supreme Court then granted certiorari.

The Miranda decision was a logical consequence of the holdings in *Gideon, Escobedo,* and *Malloy* and other cases. The Court's task was made infinitely easier particularly because of the Malloy holding that the privilege against self-incrimination is safeguarded *against state action* by the Fourteenth Amendment. Though the Malloy case is discussed only briefly in the decision below, it was an essential step on the way to the Court's holding.

Chief Justice Earl Warren's opinion illustrates well his deep commitment to the protection and expansion of individual liberties. Since he was named to the Court by President Eisenhower in 1953, Warren has, with few exceptions, led the Court to an increasingly libertarian position on questions of American freedoms. His historic opinions in the school segregation cases, discussed in the next chapter, will long be remembered as landmarks in the struggle for freedom and liberty. The son of a railroad worker, Warren was Governor of California and Republican vice-presidential candidate on the ticket headed by Thomas E. Dewey in 1948, before being moved to the Court. Former President Harry Truman often praised Warren and once remarked that "Warren is really a Democrat, but doesn't know it."

Justice John Marshall Harlan's dissenting opinion reveals well his deep commitment to the belief that the Court must leave primary responsibility for protecting individual liberties to the people and other organs of society. It is interesting to note that Harlan was also named to the Court by President Eisenhower.

MR. CHIEF JUSTICE WARREN delivered the opinion of the Court.

The cases before us raise questions which go to the roots of our concepts of American criminal jurisprudence: the restraints society must observe consistent with the Federal Constitution in prosecuting individuals for crime. More specifically, we deal with the admissibility of statements obtained from an individual who is subjected to custodial police interrogation and the necessity for procedures which assure that the individual is accorded his privilege under the Fifth Amendment to the Constitution not to be compelled to incriminate himself.

We dealt with certain phases of this problem recently in *Escobedo v. Illinois.* . . .

We start here, as we did in Escobedo, with the premise that our holding is not an innovation in our jurisprudence, but is an application of principles long recognized and applied in other settings. We have undertaken a thorough re-examination of the Escobedo decision and the principles it announced, and we reaffirm it. That case was but an explication of basic rights that are enshrined in our Constitution—that "No person

. . . shall be compelled in any criminal case to be a witness against himself," and that "the accused shall . . . have the Assistance of Counsel"— rights which were put in jeopardy in that case through official over-bearing. These precious rights were fixed in our Constitution only after centuries of persecution and struggle. And in the words of Chief Justice Marshall, they were secured "for ages to come and . . . designed to approach immortality as nearly as human institutions can approach it." . . .

It was necessary in Escobedo, as here, to insure that what was proclaimed in the Constitution had not become but a "form of words," . . . in the hands of government officials. And it is in this spirit, consistent with our role as judges that we adhere to the principles of Escobedo today. . . .

An understanding of the nature and setting of in-custody interrogation is essential to our decisions today. The difficulty in depicting what transpires at such interrogations stems from the fact that in this country they have largely taken place incommunicado. From extensive factual studies undertaken in the early 1930's, including the famous Wickersham Report to Congress by a Presidential Commission, it is clear that police violence and the "third degree" flourished at that time. In a series of cases decided by this Court long after these studies, the police resorted to physical brutality—beatings, hanging, whipping—and to sustained and protracted questioning incommunicado in order to extort confessions. The 1961 Commission on Civil Rights found much evidence to indicate that "some policemen still resort to physical force to obtain confessions." . . . The use of physical brutality and violence is not, unfortunately, relegated to the past or to any part of the country. . . .

The examples given above are undoubtedly the exception now, but they are sufficiently widespread to be the object of concern. Unless a proper limitation upon custodial interrogation is achieved—such as these decisions will advance—there can be no assurance that practices of this nature will be eradicated in the foreseeable future. . . .

[T]he modern practice of in-custody interrogation is psychologically rather than physically oriented. As we have stated before, "Since *Chambers v. Florida* . . . this Court has recognized that coercion can be mental as well as physical, and that the blood of the accused is not the only hallmark of an unconstitutional inquisition." . . . Interrogation still takes place in privacy. . . .

To be alone with the subject is essential to prevent distraction and to deprive him of any outside support. The aura of confidence in his guilt undermines his will to resist. He merely confirms the preconceived story the police seem to have him describe. Patience and persistence, at times relentless questioning, are employed. To obtain a confession, the interrogator must "patiently maneuver himself or his quarry into a position from which the desired object may be obtained." When normal procedures fail to produce the needed result, the police may resort to deceptive stratagems such as giving false legal advice. It is important to keep the subject off balance, for example, by trading on his insecurity about himself or his surroundings. The police then persuade, trick, or cajole him out of exercising his constitutional rights.

Even without employing brutality, the "third degree" or the specific stratagems described above, the very fact of custodial interrogation exacts a heavy toll on individual liberty and trades on the weakness of individuals. . . .

In the cases before us today, given this background, we concern ourselves primarily with this interrogation atmosphere and the evils it can bring. . . .

In these cases, we might not find the defendants' statements to have been involuntary in traditional terms. Our concern for adequate safeguards to protect precious Fifth Amendment rights is, of course, not lessened in the slightest. In each of the cases, the defendant was thrust into an unfamiliar atmosphere and run through menacing police interrogation procedures. . . . [T]he records do not evince overt physical coercion or patented psychological ploys. The fact remains that in none of these cases did the officers undertake to afford appropriate safeguards at the outset of the interrogation to insure that the statements were truly the product of free choice. . . .

It is obvious that such an interrogation environment is created for no purpose other than to subjugate the individual to the will of his examiner. This atmosphere carries its own badge of intimidation. To be sure, this is not physical intimidation, but it is equally destructive of human dignity. The current practice of incommunicado interrogation is at odds with one of our Nation's most cherished principles—that the individual may not be compelled to incriminate himself. Unless adequate protective devices are employed to dispel the compulsion inherent in custodial surroundings, no statement obtained from the defendant can truly be the product of his free choice.

From the foregoing, we can readily perceive an intimate connection between the privilege against self-incrimination and police custodial questioning. . . .

We sometimes forget how long it has taken to establish the privilege against self-incrimination, the sources from which it came and the fervor with which it was defended. Its roots go back into ancient time. . . .

[T]he constitutional foundation underlying the privilege is the respect a government—state or federal—must accord to the dignity and integrity of its citizens. To maintain a "fair state-individual balance," to require the government "to shoulder the entire load," . . . to respect the inviolability of the human personality our accusatory system of criminal justice demands that the government seeking to punish an individual produce the evidence against him by its own independent labors, rather than by the cruel, simple expedient of compelling it from his own mouth. . . .

The question in these cases is whether the privilege is fully applicable during a period of custodial interrogation. . . . We are satisfied that all the principles embodied in the privilege apply to informal compulsion exerted by law-enforcement officers during in-custody questioning. An individual swept from familiar surroundings into police custody, surrounded by antagonistic forces, and subjected to the techniques of persuasion described above cannot be otherwise than under compulsion to speak. As a practical matter, the compulsion to speak in the isolated setting of the police station may well be greater than in courts or other official investigations, where there are often impartial observers to guard against intimidation or trickery. . . .

This question, in fact, could have been taken as settled in federal courts almost seventy years ago, when, in *Bram v. United States*, 168 U.S. 532, 542 (1897), this Court held:

"In criminal trials, in the courts of the United States, wherever a question arises whether a confession is incompetent because not voluntary, the issue is controlled by that portion of the Fifth Amendment . . . commanding that no person 'shall be compelled in any criminal case to be a witness against himself.' " . . .

Our decision in *Malloy v. Hogan*, 378 U.S. 1 (1964), necessitates an examination of the scope of the privilege in state cases as well. In *Malloy*, we squarely held the privilege applicable to the States, and held that the substantive standards underlying the privilege applied with full force to state court proceedings. . . .

It is impossible for us to foresee the potential alternative for protecting the privilege which might be devised by Congress or the States in the exercise of their creative rule-making capacities. Therefore we cannot say that the Constitution necessarily requires adherence to any particular solution for the inherent compulsions of the interrogation process as it is presently conducted. Our decision in no way creates a constitutional straitjacket which will handicap sound efforts at reform, nor is it intended to have this effect. We encourage Congress and the States to continue their laudable search for increasingly effective ways of protecting the rights of the individual while promoting efficient enforcement of our criminal laws. However, unless we are shown other procedures which are at least as effective in apprising accused persons of their right of silence and in assuring a continuous opportunity to exercise it, the following safeguards must be observed. . . .

At the outset, if a person in custody is to be subjected to interrogation, he must first be informed in clear and unequivocal terms that he has the right to remain silent. For those unaware of the privilege, the warning is needed simply to make them aware of it—the threshold requirement for an intelligent decision as to its exercise. More important, such a warning is an absolute prerequisite in overcoming the inherent pressures of the interrogation atmosphere. It is not just the subnormal or woefully ignorant who succumb to an interrogator's imprecations, whether implied or expressly stated, that the interrogation will continue until a confession is obtained or that silence in the face of accusation is itself damning and will bode ill when presented to a jury. Further, the warning will show the individual that his interrogators are prepared to recognize his privilege should he choose to exercise it.

The Fifth Amendment privilege is so fundamental to our system of constitutional rule and the expedient of giving an adequate warning as to the availability of the privilege so simple, we will not pause to inquire in individual cases whether the defendant was aware of his rights without a warning being given. Assessments of the knowledge the defendant possessed, based on information as to his age, education, intelligence, or prior contact with authorities, can never be more than speculation; a warning is a clear-cut fact. More important, whatever the background of the person interrogated, a warning at the time of the interrogation is indispensable to overcome its pressures and to insure that the individual knows he is free to exercise the privilege at that point in time.

The warning of the right to remain silent must be accompanied by the explanation that anything said can and will be used against the individual in court. This warning is needed in order to make him aware not only of the privilege, but also of the consequences of forgoing it. It is only through an awareness of these consequences that there can be any assurance of real understanding and intelligent exercise of the privilege. Moreover, this warning may serve to make the individual more acutely aware that he is faced with a phase of the adversary system—that he is not in the presence of persons acting solely in his interest.

The circumstances surrounding in-custody interrogation can operate very quickly to overbear the will of one merely made aware of his privilege by his interrogators. Therefore, the right to have counsel present at the interrogation is indispensable to the protection of the Fifth Amendment privilege under the system we delineate today. Our aim is to assure that the individual's right to choose between silence and speech remains unfettered throughout the interrogation process. A once-stated warning, delivered by those who will conduct the interrogation, cannot itself suffice to that end among those who most require knowledge of their rights. A mere warning given by the interrogators is not alone sufficient to accomplish that end. . . . Thus, the need for counsel to protect the Fifth Amendment privilege comprehends not merely a right to consult with counsel prior to questioning, but also to have counsel present during any questioning if the defendant so desires.

The presence of counsel at the interrogation may serve several significant subsidiary functions as well. If the accused decides to talk to his interrogators, the assistance of counsel can mitigate the dangers of untrustworthiness. With a lawyer present the likelihood that the police will practice coercion is reduced, and if coercion is nevertheless exercised the lawyer can testify to it in court. The presence of a lawyer can also help to guarantee that the accused gives a fully accurate statement to the police and that the statement is rightly reported by the prosecution at trial. . . .

An individual need not make a pre-interrogation request for a lawyer. While such request affirmatively secures his right to have one, his failure to ask for a lawyer does not constitute a waiver. No effective waiver of the right to counsel during interrogation can be recognized unless specifically made after the warnings we here delineate have been given. The accused who does not know his rights and therefore does not make a request may be the person who most needs counsel. . . .

Accordingly we hold that an individual held for interrogation must be clearly informed that he has the right to consult with a lawyer and to have a lawyer with him during interrogation under the system for protecting the privilege we delineate today. As with the warnings of the right to remain silent and that anything stated can be used in evidence against him, this warning is an absolute prerequisite to interrogation. No amount of circumstantial evidence that the person may have been aware of this right will suffice to stand in its stead. Only through such a warning is there ascertainable assurance that the accused was aware of this right.

If an individual indicates that he wishes the assistance of counsel before any interrogation occurs, the authorities cannot rationally ignore or deny his request on the basis that the individual does not have or cannot afford a retained attorney. The financial ability of the individual has no relationship to the scope of the rights involved here. The privilege against self-incrimination secured by the Constitution applies to all individuals. The need for counsel in order to protect the privilege exists for the indigent as well as the affluent. In fact, were we to limit these constitutional rights to those who can retain an attorney, our decisions today would be of little significance. The cases before us as well as the vast majority of confession cases with which we have dealt in the past involve those unable to retain counsel. While authorities are not required to relieve the accused of his poverty, they have the obligation not to take advantage of indigence in the administration of justice. . . .

In order fully to apprise a person interrogated of the extent of his rights under this system then, it is necessary to warn him not only that he has the right to consult with an attorney, but also that if he is indigent a lawyer will be appointed to represent him. Without this additional warning, the admonition of the right to consult with counsel would often be understood as meaning only that he can consult with a lawyer if he has one or has the funds to obtain one. The warning of a right to counsel would be hollow if not couched in terms that would convey to the indigent—the person most often subjected to interrogation—the knowledge that he too has a right to have counsel present. As with the warnings of the right to remain silent and of the general right to counsel only by effective and express explanation to the indigent of this right can there be assurance that he was truly in a position to exercise it.

Once warnings have been given, the subsequent procedure is clear. If the individual indicates in any manner, at any time prior to or during questioning, that he wishes to remain silent, the interrogation must cease. At this point he has shown that he intends to exercise his Fifth Amendment privilege; any statement taken after the person invokes his privilege cannot be other than the product of compulsion, subtle or otherwise. Without the right to cut off questioning, the setting of in-custody interrogation operates on the individual to overcome free choice in producing a statement after the privilege has been once invoked. If the individual states that he wants an attorney, the interrogation must cease until an attorney is present. At that time, the individual must have an opportunity to confer with the attorney and to have him present during any subsequent questioning. If the individual cannot obtain an attorney and he indicates that he wants one before speaking to police, they must respect his decision to remain silent.

This does not mean, as some have suggested, that each police station must have a "station house lawyer" present at all times to advise prisoners. It does mean, however, that if police propose to interrogate a person they must make known to him that he is entitled to a lawyer and that if he cannot afford one, a lawyer will be provided for him prior to any interrogation. If authorities conclude that they will not provide counsel during a reasonable period of time in which investigation in the field is carried out, they may do so without violating the person's Fifth Amendment privilege so long as they do not question him during that time.

If the interrogation continues without the presence of an attorney and a statement is taken, a heavy burden rests on the Government to demonstrate that the defendant knowingly and intelligently waived his privilege against self-incrimination and his right to retained or appointed counsel. . . .

An express statement that the individual is willing to make a statement and does not want an attorney followed closely by a statement could constitute a waiver. But a valid waiver will not be presumed simply from the silence of the accused after warnings are given or simply from the fact that a confession was in fact eventually obtained. . . .

Moreover, where in-custody interrogation is involved, there is no room for the contention that the privilege is waived if the individual answers some questions or gives some information on his own prior to invoking his right to remain silent when interrogated.

Whatever the testimony of the authorities as to waiver of rights by an accused, the fact of lengthy interrogation or incommunicado incarceration before a statement is made is strong evidence that the accused did not validly waive his rights. In these circumstances the fact that the individual eventually made a statement is consistent with the conclusion that the compelling influence of the interrogation finally forced him to do so. It is inconsistent with any notion of a voluntary relinquishment of the privilege. Moreover, any evidence that the accused was threatened, tricked, or cajoled into a waiver will, of course, show that the defendant did not voluntarily waive his privilege. The requirement of warnings and waiver of rights is a fundamental with respect to the Fifth Amendment privilege and not simply a preliminary ritual to existing methods of interrogation.

The warnings required and the waiver necessary in accordance with our opinion today are, in the absence of a fully effective equivalent, prerequisites to the admissibility of any statement made by a defendant. No distinction can be drawn between statements which are direct confessions and statements which amount to "admissions" of part or all of an offense. The privilege against self-incrimination protects the individual from being compelled to incriminate himself in any manner; it does not distinguish degrees of incrimination. . . .

The principles announced today deal with the protection which must be given to the privilege against self-incrimination when the individual is first subjected to police interrogation while in custody at the station or otherwise deprived of his freedom of action in any way. It is at this point that our adversary system of criminal proceedings commences, distinguishing itself at the outset from the inquisitorial system recognized in some countries. Under the system of warnings we delineate today or under any other system which may be devised and found effective, the safeguards to be erected about the privilege must come into play at this point.

Our decision is not intended to hamper the traditional function of police officers in investigating crime. . . . When an individual is in custody on probable cause, the police may, of course, seek out evidence in the field to be used at trial against him. Such investigation may include inquiry of persons not under restraint. General on-the-scene questioning as to facts surrounding a crime or other general questioning of citizens in the fact-finding process is not affected by our holding. It is an act of responsible citizenship for individuals to give whatever information they may have to aid in law enforcement. In such situations the compelling atmosphere inherent in the process of in-custody interrogation is not necessarily present.

In dealing with statements obtained through interrogation, we do not purport to find all confessions inadmissible. Confessions remain a proper element in law enforcement. Any statement given freely and voluntarily without any compelling influences is, of course, admissible in evidence. The fundamental import of the privilege while an individual is in custody is not whether he is allowed to talk to the police without the benefit of warnings and counsel, but whether he can be interrogated. There is no requirement that police stop a person who enters a police station and states that he wishes to confess to a crime, or a person who calls the police to offer a confession or any other statement he desires to make. Volunteered statements of any kind are not barred by the Fifth Amendment and their admissibility is not affected by our holding today.

To summarize, we hold that when an individual is taken into custody or otherwise deprived of his freedom by the authorities and is subjected to questioning, the privilege against self-incrimination is jeopardized. Procedural safeguards must be employed to protect the privilege, and unless other fully effective means are adopted to notify the person of his right of silence and to assure that the exercise of the right will be scrupulously honored, the following measures are required. He must be warned prior to any questioning that he has the right to remain silent, that anything he says can be used against him in a court of law, that he has the right to the presence of an attorney, and that if he cannot afford an attorney one will be appointed for him prior to any questioning if he so desires. Opportunity to exercise these rights must be afforded to him throughout the interrogation. After such warnings have been given, and such opportunity afforded him, the individual may knowingly and intelligently waive these rights and agree to answer questions or make a statement. But unless and until such warnings and waiver are demonstrated by the prosecution at trial, no evidence obtained as a result of interrogation can be used against him. . . .

In announcing these principles, we are not unmindful of the burdens which law enforcement officials must bear, often under trying circumstances. We also fully recognize the obligation of all citizens to aid in enforcing the criminal laws. This Court, while protecting individual rights, has always given ample latitude to law enforcement agencies in the legitimate exercise of their duties. The limits we have placed on the interrogation process should not constitute an undue interference with a proper system of law enforcement. . . .

MR. JUSTICE HARLAN, whom MR. JUSTICE STEWART and MR. JUSTICE WHITE join, dissenting.

I believe the decision of the Court represents poor constitutional law and entails harmful consequences for the country at large. How serious these consequences may prove to be only time can tell. . . .

At the outset, it is well to note exactly what is required by the Court's new constitutional code of rules for confessions. The foremost requirement, upon which later admissibility of a confession depends, is that a four-fold warning be given to a person in custody before he is questioned: namely, that he has a right to remain silent, that anything he says may be used against him, that he has a right to have present an attorney during the questioning, and that if indigent he has a right to a lawyer without charge. To forego these rights, some affirmative statement of rejection is seemingly required, and threats, tricks, or cajolings to obtain this waiver are forbidden. If before or during questioning the suspect seeks to invoke his right to remain silent, interrogation must be forgone or cease; a request for counsel brings about the same result until a lawyer is procured. . . .

While the fine points of this scheme are far less clear than the Court admits, the tenor is quite apparent. The new rules are not designed to guard against police brutality or other unmistakably banned forms of coercion. Those who use third-degree tactics and deny them in court are equally able and destined to lie as skillfully about warnings and waivers. Rather, the thrust of the new rules is to negate all pressures, to reinforce the nervous or ignorant suspect, and ultimately to discourage any confession at all. The aim in short is toward "voluntariness" in a utopian sense, or to view it from a different angle, voluntariness with a vengeance.

To incorporate this notion into the Constitution requires a strained reading of history and precedent and a disregard of the very pragmatic concerns that alone may on occasion justify such strains. I believe that reasoned examination will show that the Due Process Clauses provide an adequate tool for coping with confessions and that, even if the Fifth Amendment privilege against self-incrimination be invoked, its precedents taken as a whole do not sustain the present rules. Viewed as a choice based on pure policy, these new rules prove to be a highly debatable if not one-sided appraisal of the competing interests, imposed over widespread objection, at the very time when judicial restraint is most called for by the circumstances. . . .

Legal history has been stretched before to satisfy deep needs of society. In this instance, however, the Court has not and cannot make the powerful showing that its new rules are plainly desirable in the context of our society, something which is surely demanded before those rules are engrafted onto the Constitution and imposed on every State and county in the land.

Without at all subscribing to the generally black picture of police conduct painted by the Court, I think it must be frankly recognized at the outset that police questioning allowable under due process precedents may inherently entail some pressure on the suspect and may seek advantage in his ignorance or weaknesses. The atmosphere and questioning techniques, proper and fair though they be, can in themselves exert a tug on the suspect to confess, and in this light "[t]o speak of any confessions of crime made after arrest as being 'voluntary' or 'uncoerced' is somewhat inaccurate, although traditional. A confession is wholly and incontestably voluntary only if a guilty person gives himself up to the law and becomes his own accuser." . . . Until today, the role of the Constitution has been only to sift out *undue* pressure, not to assure spontaneous confessions.

The Court's new rules aim to offset these minor pressures and disadvantages intrinsic to any kind of police interrogation. The rules do not serve due process interests in preventing blatant coercion since . . . they do nothing to contain the policeman who is prepared to lie from the start. . . .

What the Court largely ignores is that its rules impair, if they will not eventually serve wholly to frustrate, an instrument of law enforcement that has long and quite reasonably been thought worth the price paid for it. There can be little doubt that the Court's new code would markedly decrease the number of confessions. To warn the suspect that he may remain silent and remind him that his confession may be used in court are minor obstructions. To require also an express waiver by the suspect and an end to questioning whenever he demurs must heavily handicap questioning. And to suggest or provide counsel for the suspect simply invites the end of the interrogation. . . .

[T]he Court is taking a real risk with society's welfare in imposing its new regime on the country. The social costs of crime are too great to call the new rules anything but a hazardous experimentation.

While passing over the costs and risks of its experiment, the Court portrays the evils of normal police questioning in terms which I think are exaggerated. Albeit stringently confined by the due process standards interrogation is no doubt often inconvenient and unpleasant for the suspect. However, it is no less so for a man to be arrested and jailed, to have his house searched, or to stand trial in court, yet all this may properly happen to the most innocent given probable cause, a warrant, or an indictment. Society has always paid a stiff price for law and order, and peaceful interrogation is not one of the dark moments of the law. . . .

There is now in progress in this country a massive re-examination of criminal law enforcement procedures on a scale never before witnessed. . . .

[T]he practical effect of the decision made today must inevitably be to handicap seriously sound efforts at reform, not least by removing options necessary to a just compromise of competing interests. Of course legislative reform is rarely speedy or unanimous, though this Court has been more patient in the past. But the legislative reforms when they came would have the vast advantage of empirical data and comprehensive study, they would allow experimentation and use of solutions not open to the courts, and they would restore the initiative in criminal law reform to those reforms where it truly belongs. . . .

Nothing in the letter or the spirit of the Constitution or in the precedents squares with the heavy handed and one-sided action that is so precipitously taken by the Court in the name of fulfilling its constitutional responsibilities. The foray which the Court takes today brings to mind the wise and farsighted words of Mr. Justice Jackson in *Douglas v. Jeannette*, 319 U.S. 157 . . . "This Court is forever adding new stories to the temples of constitutional law, and the temples have a way of collapsing when one story too many is added."

MR. JUSTICE WHITE, with whom MR. JUSTICE HARLAN and MR. JUSTICE STEWART join, dissenting. . . .

The proposition that the privilege against self-incrimination forbids in-custody interrogation without the warnings specified in the majority opinion and without a clear waiver of counsel has no significant support in the history of the privilege or in the language of the Fifth Amendment. . . .

That the Court's holding today is neither compelled nor even strongly suggested by the language of the Fifth Amendment, is at odds with American and English legal history, and involves a departure from a long line of precedent does not prove either that the Court has exceeded its powers or that the Court is wrong or unwise in its present reinterpretation of the Fifth Amendment. It does, however, underscore the obvious—that the Court has not discovered or found the law in making today's decision, nor has it derived it from some irrefutable sources; what it has done is to make new law and new public policy in much the same way that it has in the course of interpreting other great clauses of the Constitution. This is what the Court historically has done. Indeed, it is what it must do and will continue to do until and unless there is some fundamental change in the constitutional distribution of governmental powers.

But if the Court is here and now to announce new and fundamental policy to govern certain aspects of our affairs, it is wholly legitimate to examine the mode of this or any other constitutional decision in this Court and to inquire into the advisability of its end product in terms of the long-range interest of the country. At the very least the Court's text and reasoning should withstand analysis and be a fair exposition of the constitutional provision which its opinion interprets. Decisions like these cannot rest alone on syllogism, metaphysics or some ill-defined notions of natural justice, although each will perhaps play its part. In proceeding to such constructions as it now announces, the Court should also duly consider all the factors and interests bearing upon the cases, at least insofar as the relevant materials are available; and if the necessary considerations are not treated in the record or obtainable from some other reliable source, the Court should not proceed to formulate fundamental policies based on speculation alone. . . .

[F]or all the Court's expounding on the menacing atmosphere of police interrogation procedures it has failed to supply any foundation for the conclusions it draws or the measures it adopts. . . .

There is, in my view, every reason to believe that a good many criminal defendants, who otherwise would have been convicted on what this Court has previously thought to be the most satisfactory kind of evidence, will now, under this new version of the Fifth Amendment, either not be tried at all or acquitted if the State's evidence, minus the confession, is put to the test of litigation.

I have no desire whatsoever to share the responsibility for any such impact on the present criminal process.

[JUSTICE CLARK wrote a separate opinion dissenting in three of the cases (including *Miranda v. Arizona*) and concurring in one.]

AFTERMATH

A week after the Miranda decision the Court held in *Johnson v. New Jersey*, 384 U.S. 719, that both the Miranda and Escobedo rulings did not apply retroactively. That is the two decisions apply only to cases in which trials began *after* the dates of the opinions. The Court declared that "retroactive application of Escobedo and Miranda would seriously disrupt the administration of our criminal laws. It would require the retrial or release of numerous prisoners found guilty by trustworthy evidence in conformity with previously announced constitutional standards."

Coming on the heels of the Court's opinions in *Gideon v. Wainwright* and *Escobedo v. Illinois,* the Miranda decision provoked bitter controversy and launched a national dialogue on the issue of criminal confessions. The same deep divisions apparent on the Court were revealed in the heated debates that bitterly divided judges, lawyers, scholars and law enforcement officials. Many accused the Court of "coddling criminals" and "handcuffing the police" but it is now apparent that police departments throughout the country have learned to live with the Miranda decision without any decline in successful prosecutions. It has been well written that "if we acknowledge the educational role of the Court, then the majority in *Miranda* comes out on the better side of the argument. That the Court is ahead of popular currents is hardly an accusation of misconduct. Indeed, it is when the Court ceases to educate and lead that the quality of our civilization is in danger."

As for Miranda himself, he was not as fortunate as Danny Escobedo. After the Court's decision he remained in jail under another sentence of twenty to twenty-five years for robbery. As this is written Miranda faces another trial on the rape charge on the basis of new evidence obtained from other women who had been accosted and nearly raped by him.

Estes v. Texas
381 U.S. 532 (1965)

Billie Sol Estes, a much publicized financial "wizard" who had made a fortune in various questionable dealings with a number of private individuals as well as government officials, was indicted by a grand jury in Texas for inducing farmers to buy non-existent ammonia-fertilizer tanks. Because of the massive pre-trial publicity, Estes' counsel made a motion to exclude all television and news cameras from the courtroom during the trial. The pre-trial hearing, held to consider the defense motion, was telecast "live" and photographers were permitted to take pictures in the courtroom which was overflowing with spectators, cameramen and reporters. The hearing was undoubtedly considerably disrupted by the crowd. The *New York Times* described the scene as follows:

> A television motor van, big as an intercontinental bus, was parked outside the courthouse and the second floor courtroom was a forest of equipment. Two television cameras had been set up inside the bar and four marked cameras were aligned just outside the gates. A microphone stuck its twelve-inch snout inside the jury box, now occupied by an overflow of reporters from the press table, and three microphones confronted Judge Dunagon (presiding judge) on his bench. Cable and wires snaked over the floor.

The motion to bar television and news cameras from the trial was denied but the scene at the trial was much different from the one at the hearing because of certain restrictions placed on the news media by the presiding judge. "Live" telecasting and radio broadcasting of the *entire* proceeding was not permitted. Only the opening and closing arguments of the state's counsel and the returning of the verdict by the jury were telecast "live." Only noiseless cameras were permitted in the courtroom. Flood lights and flash cameras were prohibited. The number of cameramen and photographers in the courtroom at any given time was limited and they were restricted to an area at the back of the courtroom, where a booth had been constructed for their use.

The trial lasted only three and a half days. Estes was found guilty and sentenced to an eight year prison term. (He was already in a federal prison (Leavenworth) serving a fifteen year sentence imposed by a federal court for mail fraud and conspiracy.) The conviction was affirmed by the highest state court. Estes then brought the case to the Supreme Court on a writ of certiorari.

Justice Tom C. Clark's opinion is an unusually clear exposition of the problems raised by the use of television in court proceedings.

Moreover, the case demonstrates well how misleading it is to attach permanent "liberal" or "conservative" labels on Supreme Court justices. Long regarded as the most consistent conservative on the Warren Court, Clark was supported by three dedicated liberals—Chief Justice Warren himself, Justices Goldberg and Douglas—and by conservative Justice Harlan. In his dissenting opinion Justice Stewart was joined not only by Justice White but also by Justices Black and Brennan who usually were found on the same side as Warren, Goldberg and Douglas. Cases like *Estes,* where two extremely important constitutional values are in conflict—in this instance a fair trial versus a free press—are bound to produce unusual line-ups simply because the choice for each individual justice is far from easy. *Both* values need to be preserved, but the Court must make the agonizing choice of one over the other in a particular situation.

Before his elevation to the Court by President Truman in 1949, Justice Clark had been an important figure in Democratic party circles and had served as Attorney General of the United States.

MR. JUSTICE CLARK delivered the opinion of the Court.

The question presented here is whether the petitioner . . . was deprived of his right under the Fourteenth Amendment to due process by the televising and broadcasting of his trial. . . .

We start with the proposition that it is a "public trial" that the Sixth Amendment guarantees to the "accused." The purpose of the requirement of a public trial was to guarantee that the accused would be fairly dealt with and not unjustly condemned. History had proven that secret tribunals were effective instruments of oppression. . . . It is said, however, that the freedoms granted in the First Amendment extend a right to the news media to televise from the courtroom, and that to refuse to honor this privilege is to discriminate between the newspapers and television. This is a misconception of the rights of the press.

The free press has been a mighty catalyst in awakening public interest in governmental affairs, exposing corruption among public officers and employees, and generally informing the citizenry of public events and occurrences, including court proceedings. While maximum freedom must be allowed the press in carrying on this important function in a democratic society, its exercise must necessarily be subject to the maintenance of absolute fairness in the judicial process. . . .

Court proceedings are held for the solemn purpose of endeavoring to ascertain the truth, which is the *sine qua non* of a fair trial. Over the centuries Anglo-American courts have devised careful safeguards by rule and otherwise to protect and facilitate the performance of this high function. As a result, at this time those safeguards do not permit the televising and photographing of a criminal trial, save in two States and there only under restrictions. The federal courts prohibit it by specific rule. This is weighty evidence that our concepts of a fair trial do not tolerate such an indulgence. We have always held that the atmosphere essential to the preservation of a fair trial—the most fundamental of all freedoms—must be maintained at all costs. Our approach has been through rules, contempt proceedings, and reversal of convictions obtained under unfair conditions. Here the remedy is clear and certain of application and it is our duty to continue to enforce the principles that from time immemorial have proven efficacious and necessary to a fair trial. . . .

The State contends that the televising of portions of a criminal trial does not constitute a denial of due process. Its position is that because no prejudice has been shown by the petitioner as resulting from the televising, it is permissible; that claims of "distractions" during the trial due to the physical presence of the television are wholly unfounded; and that psychological considerations are for psychologists, not courts, because they are purely hypothetical. It argues further that the public has a right to know what goes on in the courts; that the court has no power to "suppress, edit, or censor events which transpire in proceedings before it;" . . . and that the televising of criminal trials would be enlightening to the public and promote greater respect for the courts.

At the outset the notion should be dispelled that telecasting is dangerous because it is new. It is true that our empirical knowledge of its full effect on the public, the jury or the participants in a trial, including the judge, witnesses and lawyers, is limited. However, the nub of the question is not its newness but, as Mr. Justice Douglas says, "the insidious influences which it puts to work in the administration of justice." . . .

It is true that the public has the right to be informed as to what occurs in its courts, but reporters of all media, including television, are always present if they wish to be and are plainly free to report whatever occurs in open court through their respective media. . . .

The State, however, says that the use of television in the instant case was "without injustice to the person immediately concerned," basing its position on the fact that the petitioner has established no isolatable prejudice and that this must be shown in order to invalidate a conviction in these circumstances. The State points too broadly in this contention, for this Court itself has found instances in which a showing of actual prejudice is not a prerequisite to reversal. This is such a case. It is true that in most cases involving claims of due process deprivations we require a showing of identifiable prejudice to the accused. Nevertheless, at times a procedure employed by the State involves such a probability that prejudice will result that it is deemed inherently lacking in due process. . . .

Forty-eight of our States and the Federal Rules have deemed the use of television improper in the courtroom. This fact is most telling in buttressing our conclusion that any change in procedure which would permit its use would be inconsistent with our concepts of due process in this field. . . .

As has been said, the chief function of our judicial machinery is to ascertain the truth. The use of television, however, cannot be said to contribute materially to this objective. Rather its use amounts to the injection of an irrelevant factor into court proceedings. In addition experience teaches that there are numerous situations in which it might cause actual unfairness—some so subtle as to defy detection by the accused or control by the judge. We enumerate some in summary:

1. The potential impact of television on the jurors is perhaps of the greatest significance. They are the nerve center of the fact-finding process. It is true that in States like Texas where they are required to be sequestered in trials of this nature the jurors will probably not see any of the proceedings as televised from the courtroom. But the inquiry cannot end there. From the moment the trial judge announces that a case will be televised it becomes a *cause célèbre*. The whole community, including prospective jurors, becomes interested in all the morbid details surrounding it. The approaching trial immediately assumes an important status in the public press and the accused is highly publicized along with the offense with which he is charged. Every juror carries with him into the jury box these solemn facts and thus increases the chance of prejudice that is present in every criminal case. And we must remember that realistically it is only the notorious trial which will be broadcast, because of the necessity for paid sponsorship. The conscious or unconscious effect that this may have on the juror's judgment cannot be evaluated, but experience indicates that it is not only possible but highly probable that it will have a direct bearing on his vote as to guilt or innocence. Where pretrial publicity of all kinds has created intense public feeling which is aggravated by the telecasting or picturing of the trial the televised jurors cannot help but feel the pressures of knowing that friends and neighbors have their eyes upon them. If the community be hostile to an accused, a televised juror, realizing that he must return to neighbors who saw the trial themselves, may well be led "not to hold the balance nice, clear and true between the State and the accused. . . ."

Moreover, while it is practically impossible to assess the effect of television on jury attentiveness, those of us who know juries realize the problem of jury "distraction." The State argues this is *de minimis* since the physical disturbances have been eliminated. But we know that distractions are not caused solely by the physical presence of the camera and its telltale red lights. It is the awareness of the fact of telecasting that is felt by the juror throughout the trial. We are all self-conscious and uneasy when being televised. Human nature being what it is, not only a juror's eyes but his mind will often be on that fact rather than on the witness stand.

Furthermore, in many States the jurors serving in the trial may see the broadcasts of the trial proceedings. Admittedly, the Texas sequestration rule would prevent this occurring there. In other States following no such practice jurors would return home and turn on the TV, if only to see how they appeared upon it. They would also be subjected to re-enactment and emphasis of the selected parts of the proceedings which the requirements of the broadcasters determined would be telecast and would be subconsciously influenced the more by that testimony. Moreover, they would be subjected to the broadest commentary and criticism and perhaps the well-meant advice of friends, relatives and inquiring strangers who recognized them on the streets.

Finally, new trials plainly would be jeopardized in that potential jurors will often have seen and heard the original trial when it was telecast. Yet viewers may later be called upon to sit in the jury box during the new trial. These very dangers are illustrated in this case where the court, due to the defendant's objections, permitted only the State's opening and closing arguments to be broadcast with sound to the public.

2. The quality of the testimony in criminal trials will often be impaired. The impact upon a witness of the knowledge that he is being viewed by a vast audience is simply incalculable. Some may be demoralized and frightened, some cocky and given to overstatement; memories may falter, as with anyone speaking publicly, and accuracy of statement may be severely undermined. Embarrassment may impede the search for the truth, as may a natural tendency toward over-dramatization. Furthermore, inquisitive strangers and "cranks" might approach witnesses on the street with jibes, advice or demands for explanation of testimony. There is little wonder that the defendant cannot "prove" the existence of such factors. Yet we all know from experience that they exist.

In addition, the invocation of the rule against witnesses is frustrated. In most instances witnesses would be able to go to their homes and view broadcasts of the day's trial proceedings, notwithstanding the fact that they had been admonished not to do so. They could view and hear the testimony of preceding witnesses, and so shape their own testimony as to make its impact crucial. And even in the absence of sound, the influences of such viewing on the attitude of the witness toward testifying, his frame of mind upon taking the stand or his apprehension of withering cross-examination defy objective assessment. Indeed, the mere fact that the trial is to be televised might render witnesses reluctant to appear and thereby impede the trial as well as the discovery of the truth.

While some of the dangers mentioned above are present as well in newspaper coverage of any important trial, the circumstances and extraneous influences intruding upon the solemn decorum of court procedure in the televised trial are far more serious than in cases involving only newspaper coverage.

3. A major aspect of the problem is the additional responsibilities the presence of television places on the trial judge. His job is to make certain that the accused receives a fair trial. This most difficult task requires his undivided attention. Still when television comes into the courtroom he must also supervise it. In this trial, for example, the judge on several different occasions—aside from the two days of pretrial—was obliged to have a hearing or enter an order made necessary solely because of the presence of television. Thus, where telecasting is restricted as it was here, and as even the State concedes it must be, his task is made much more difficult and exacting. And, as happened here, such rulings may unfortunately militate against the fairness of the trial. In addition, laying physical interruptions aside, there is the ever-present distraction that the mere awareness of television's presence prompts. Judges are human beings also and are subject to the same psychological reactions as laymen. Telecasting is particularly bad where the judge is elected, as is the case in all save a half dozen of our States. The telecasting of a trial becomes a political weapon, which along with other distractions inherent in broadcasting, diverts his attention from the task at hand—the fair trial of the accused.

But this is not all. There is the initial decision that must be made as to whether the use of television will be permitted. This is perhaps an even more crucial consideration. Our judges are high-minded men and women. But it is difficult to remain oblivious to the pressures that the news media can bring to bear on them both directly and through the shaping of public opinion. Moreover, where one judge in a district or even in a State permits telecasting, the requirement that the others do the same is almost mandatory. Especially is this true where the judge is selected at the ballot box.

4. Finally, we cannot ignore the impact of courtroom television on the defendant. Its presence is a form of mental—if not physical—harassment, resembling a police line-up or the third degree. The inevitable close-ups of his gestures and expressions during the ordeal of his trial might well

transgress his personal sensibilities, his dignity, and his ability to concentrate on the proceedings before him—sometimes the difference between life and death—dispassionately, freely and without the distraction of wide public surveillance. A defendant on trial for a specific crime is entitled to his day in court, not in a stadium, or a city or nationwide arena. The heightened public clamor resulting from radio and television coverage will inevitably result in prejudice. Trial by television is, therefore, foreign to our system. Furthermore, telecasting may also deprive an accused of effective counsel. The distractions, intrusions into confidential attorney-client relationships and the temptation offered by television to play to the public audience might often have a direct effect not only upon the lawyers, but the judge, the jury and the witnesses. . . .

The television camera is a powerful weapon. Intentionally or inadvertently it can destroy an accused and his case in the eyes of the public. While our telecasters are honorable men, they too are human. The necessity for sponsorship weighs heavily in favor of the televising of only notorious cases, such as this one, and invariably focuses the beam of the lens upon the unpopular or infamous accused. Such a selection is necessary in order to obtain a sponsor willing to pay a sufficient fee to cover the costs and return a profit. We have already examined the ways in which public sentiment can affect the trial participants. To the extent that television shapes that sentiment, it can strip the accused of a fair trial.

The Senate would dispose of all these observations with the simple statement that they are for psychologists because they are purely hypothetical. But we cannot afford the luxury of saying that, because these factors are difficult of ascertainment in particular cases, they must be ignored. Nor are they "purely hypothetical." . . . They are real enough to have convinced the Judicial Conference of the United States, this Court and the Congress that television should be barred in federal trials by the Federal Rules of Criminal Procedure; in addition they have persuaded all but two of our States to prohibit television in the courtroom. They are effects that may, and in some combination almost certainly will, exist in any case in which television is injected into the trial process.

It is said that the ever-advancing techniques of public communication and the adjustment of the public to its presence may bring about a change in the effect of telecasting upon the fairness of criminal trials. But we are not dealing here with future developments in the field of electronics. Our judgment cannot be rested on the hypothesis of tomorrow but must take the facts as they are presented today.

The judgment is therefore

Reversed.

[CHIEF JUSTICE WARREN, joined by JUSTICES DOUGLAS and GOLDBERG, wrote a separate concurring opinion. JUSTICE HARLAN also wrote a separate concurring opinion.]

MR. JUSTICE STEWART, whom MR. JUSTICE BLACK, MR. JUSTICE BRENNAN, and MR. JUSTICE WHITE join, dissenting.

I cannot agree with the Court's decision that the circumstances of this trial led to a denial of the petitioner's Fourteenth Amendment rights. I think that the introduction of television into a courtroom is, at least in the present state of the art, an extremely unwise policy. It invites many constitutional risks, and it detracts from the inherent dignity of a courtroom. But I am unable to escalate this personal view into a *per se* constitutional rule. And I am unable to find, on the specific record of this case, that the circumstances attending the limited televising of the petitioner's trial resulted in the denial of any right guaranteed to him by the United States Constitution. . . .

We deal here with matters subject to continuous and unforeseeable change—the techniques of public communication. In an area where all the variables may be modified tomorrow, I cannot at this time rest my determination on hypothetical possibilities not present in the record of this case. There is no claim here based upon any right guaranteed by the First Amendment. But it is important to remember that we move in an area touching the realm of free communication, and for that reason, if for no other, I would be wary of imposing any *per se* rule which, in the light of future technology, might serve to stifle or abridge true First Amendment rights. . . .

It is obvious that the introduction of television and news cameras into a criminal trial invites many serious constitutional hazards. The very presence of photographers and television cameramen plying their trade in a courtroom might be so completely and thoroughly disruptive and distracting as to make a fair trial impossible. . . .

What ultimately emerges from this record, therefore, is one bald question—whether the Fourteenth Amendment of the United States Constitution prohibits all television cameras from a state courtroom whenever a criminal trial is in progress. In the light of this record and what we now know about the impact of television on a criminal trial, I can find no such prohibition in the Fourteenth Amendment or in any other provision of the Constitution. If what occurred did not deprive the petitioner of his constitutional right to a fair trial, then the fact that the public could view the proceeding on television has no constitutional significance. The Constitution does not make us arbiters of the image that a televised state criminal trial projects to the public.

While no First Amendment claim is made in this case, there are intimations in the opinions filed by my Brethren in the majority which strike me as disturbingly alien to the First and Fourteenth Amendments' guarantees against federal or state interference with the free communication of information and ideas. The suggestion that there are limits upon the public's right to know what goes on in the courts causes me deep concern. The idea of imposing upon any medium of communications the burden of justifying its presence is contrary to where I had always thought the presumption must lie in the area of First Amendment freedoms. . . . Where there is no disruption of the "essential requirement of the fair and orderly administration of justice," "[f]reedom of discussion should be given the widest range." . . .

I do not think that the Constitution denies to the State or to individual trial judges all discretion to conduct criminal trials with television cameras present, no matter how unobtrusive the cameras may be. I cannot say at this time that it is impossible to have a constitutional trial whenever any part of the proceedings is televised or recorded on television film. I cannot now hold that the Constitution absolutely bars television cameras from every criminal courtroom, even if they have no impact upon the jury, no effect upon any witness, and no influence upon the conduct of the judge.

For these reasons I would affirm the judgment.

[Though joining this dissenting opinion, JUSTICES WHITE and BRENNAN also wrote brief separate dissenting opinions.]

Sheppard v. Maxwell
384 U.S. 333 (1966)

Though the facts and circumstances were quite different, *Sheppard v. Maxwell*, like the *Estes* case, posed a similar conflict of constitutional values—how to reconcile freedom of the press with the necessity for fair trials by impartial juries. The key figure in this sensational case was Dr. Samuel Sheppard, a prominent Cleveland osteopathic physician, tried for the murder of his wife in a "carnival atmosphere" which is fully described in the opinion below. Many additional details concerning the crime are also provided in Justice Clark's opinion.

Sheppard was convicted of the murder and sentenced to life imprisonment. A divided Ohio Supreme Court sustained the conviction and, in 1956, the United States Supreme Court denied certiorari in a brief opinion written by Justice Frankfurter. After nearly ten years in prison and a dozen appeals, Sheppard brought a suit for a writ of habeas corpus in a federal district court, asking that he be released from prison on the ground that he had been denied a fair trial in violation of the Due Process Clause of the Fourteenth Amendment. In an eighty-six page decision the district court freed Sheppard ruling that his constitutional rights had been violated in a trial which "fell far below the minimum requirements of due process." A federal court of appeals reversed the district court by a close two to one vote but allowed Sheppard to remain free on bond while the case was brought to the Supreme Court on a writ of certiorari. Maxwell was the warden of the Ohio penitentiary in Columbus where Sheppard had been serving his sentence.

Through the years of appeals and petitions which finally led to the Supreme Court decision below, a series of events conspired to keep the Sheppard case in the public eye. Shortly after the trial Sheppard's mother committed suicide and his father died soon thereafter. The combined efforts of Sheppard's two brothers, who were also doctors, and other members of the family to secure his release were widely publicized. Paul Holmes, a Chicago newsman, wrote a controversial best-selling book entitled *The Sheppard Murder Case* which purported to show that Sheppard was innocent. Finally, Sheppard's prison correspondence and subsequent marriage to an attractive German divorcee also helped to keep the case in the headlines.

MR. JUSTICE CLARK delivered the opinion of the Court. . . .

Marilyn Sheppard, petitioner's pregnant wife, was bludgeoned to death in the upstairs bedroom of their lakeshore home in Bay Village, Ohio, a suburb of Cleveland. On the day of the tragedy, July 4, 1954, Sheppard pieced together for several local officials the following story: He and his wife had entertained neighborhood friends, the Aderns, on the previous evening at their home. After dinner they watched television in the living room. Sheppard became drowsy and dozed off to sleep on a couch. Later, Marilyn partially awoke him saying that she was going to bed. The next thing he remembered was hearing his wife cry out in the early morning hours. He hurried upstairs and in the dim light from the hall saw a "form" standing next to his wife's bed. As he struggled with the "form" he was struck on the back of the neck and rendered unconscious. On regaining his senses he found himself on the floor next to his wife's bed. He raised up, looked at her, took her pulse and "felt that she was gone." He then went to his son's room and found him unmolested. Hearing a noise he hurried downstairs. He saw a "form" running out the door and pursued it to the lake shore. He grappled with it on the beach and lost consciousness. Upon his recovery he was laying face down with the lower portion of his body in the water. He returned to his home, checked the pulse on his wife's neck, and "determined or thought that she was gone." He then went downstairs and called a neighbor, Mayor Houk of Bay Village. The Mayor and his wife came over at once, found Sheppard slumped in an easy chair downstairs and asked, "What happened?" Sheppard replied: "I don't know but somebody ought to try to do something for Marilyn." Mrs. Houk immediately went up to the bedroom. The Mayor told Sheppard, "Get hold of yourself. Can you tell me what happened?" Sheppard then related the above-outlined events. . . .

From the outset officials focused suspicion on Sheppard. After a search of the house and premises on the morning of the tragedy, Dr. Gerber, the Coroner, is reported—and it is undenied—to have told his men, "Well, it is evident the doctor did this, so let's go get the confession out of him." He proceeded to interrogate and examine Sheppard while the latter was under sedation in his hospital room. On the same occasion, the Coroner was given the clothes Sheppard wore at the time of the tragedy together with the personal items in them. Later that afternoon Chief Eaton and two Cleveland police officers interrogated Sheppard at some length, confronting him with evidence and demanding explanations. Asked by Officer Shotke to take a lie detector test, Sheppard said he would if it were reliable. Shotke replied that it was "infallible" and "you might as well tell us all about it now." Still later in the same afternoon a physician sent by the Coroner was permitted to make a detailed examination of Sheppard. Until the Coroner's inquest on July 22, at which time he was subpoenaed, Sheppard made himself available for frequent and extended questioning without the presence of an attorney.

On July 7, the day of Marilyn Sheppard's funeral, a newspaper story appeared in which Assistant County Attorney Mahon—later the chief prosecutor of Sheppard—sharply criticized the refusals of the Sheppard family to permit his immediate questioning. From there on headline stories repeatedly stressed Sheppard's lack of cooperation with the police and other officials. Under the headline "Testify Now In Death, Bay Doctor Is Ordered," one story described a visit by Coroner Gerber and four police officers to the hospital on July 8. When Sheppard insisted that his lawyer be present, the Coroner wrote out a subpoena and served it on him. Sheppard then agreed to submit to questioning without counsel and the subpoena was torn up. The officers questioned him for several hours. On July 9, Sheppard, at the request of the Coroner, re-enacted the tragedy at his home before the Coroner, police officers, and a group of newsmen, who apparently were invited by the Coroner. The home was locked so that Sheppard was obliged to wait outside until the Coroner arrived. Sheppard's performance was reported in detail by the news media along with photographs. The newspapers also played up Sheppard's refusal to take a lie detector test and "the protective ring" thrown up by his family. Front-page newspaper headlines announced on the same day that "Doctor Balks At Lie Test; Retells Story." A column opposite that story contained an "exclusive" interview with Sheppard headlined: " 'Loved My Wife, She Loved Me,' Sheppard Tells News Reporters." The next day, another headline story disclosed that Sheppard had "again late yesterday refused to take a lie detector test" and quoted an Assistant County Attorney as saying that "at the end of a nine-hour questioning of Dr. Sheppard, I felt he was now ruling [a test] out completely." But subsequent newspaper articles reported that the Coroner was still pushing Sheppard for a lie detector test. More stories appeared when Sheppard would not allow authorities to inject him with "truth serum."

On the 20th, the "editorial artillery" opened fire with a front-page charge that somebody is "getting away with murder." The editorial attributed the ineptness of the investigation to "friendships, relationships, hired lawyers, a husband who ought to have been subjected instantly to the same third degree to which any person under similar circumstances is subjected. . . ." The following day, July 21, another page-one editorial was headed: "Why No Inquest? Do It Now, Dr. Gerber." The Coroner called an inquest the same day and subpoenaed Sheppard. It was staged the next day in a school gymnasium; the Coroner presided with the County Prosecutor as his advisor and two detectives as bailiffs. In the front of the room was a long table occupied by reporters, television and radio personnel, and broadcasting equipment. The hearing was broadcast with live microphones placed at the Coroner's seat and the witness stand. A swarm of reporters and photographers attended. Sheppard was brought into the room by police who searched him in full view of several hundred spectators. Sheppard's counsel were present during the three-day inquest but were not permitted to participate. When Sheppard's chief counsel attempted to place some documents in the record, he was forcibly ejected from the room by the Coroner, who received cheers, hugs, and kisses from ladies in the audience. Sheppard was questioned for five and one-half hours about his actions on the night of the murder, his married life, and a love affair with Susan Hayes. At the end of the hearing the Coroner announced that he "could" order Sheppard held for the grand jury, but did not do so.

Throughout this period the newspapers emphasized evidence that tended to incriminate Sheppard and pointed out discrepancies in his statements to authorities. At the same time, Sheppard made many public statements to the press and wrote feature articles asserting his innocence. During the inquest on July 26, a headline in large type stated: "Kerr [Captain of the Cleveland Police] Urges Sheppard's Arrest." In the story, Detective McArthur "disclosed that scientific tests at the Sheppard home have definitely established that the killer washed off a trail of blood from the murder bedroom to the downstairs section," a circumstance casting doubt on Sheppard's accounts of the murder. No such evidence was produced at trial. The newspapers also delved into Sheppard's personal life. Articles stressed his extra-marital love affairs as a motive for the crime. The newspapers portrayed Sheppard as a Lothario, fully explored his relationship with Susan Hayes, and named a number of other women who were allegedly involved with him. The testimony at trial never showed that Sheppard had any illicit relationships besides the one with Susan Hayes.

On July 28, an editorial entitled "Why Don't Police Quiz Top Suspect" demanded that Sheppard be taken to police headquarters. It described him in the following language:

> Now proved under oath to be a liar, still free to go about his business, shielded by his family, protected by a smart lawyer who has made monkeys of the police and authorities, carrying a gun part of the time, left free to do whatever he pleases. . . .

A front-page editorial on July 30 asked: "Why Isn't Sam Sheppard In Jail?" It was later titled "Quit Stalling—Bring Him In." After calling Sheppard "the most unusual murder suspect ever seen around these parts" the article said that "[e]xcept for some superficial questioning during Coroner Sam Gerber's inquest he has been scot-free of any official grilling. . . ." It asserted that he was "surrounded by an iron curtain of protection [and] concealment."

That night at 10 o'clock Sheppard was arrested at his father's home on a charge of murder. He was taken to the Bay Village City Hall where hundreds of people, newscasters, photographers and reporters were awaiting his arrival. He was immediately arraigned—having been denied a temporary delay to secure the presence of counsel—bound over to the grand jury.

The publicity then grew in intensity until his indictment on August 17. . . . On August 18, an article appeared under the headline "Dr. Sam Writes His Own Story." And reproduced across the entire front page was a portion of the typed statement signed by Sheppard: "I am not guilty of the murder of my wife, Marilyn. How could I, who have been trained to help people and devote my life to saving life, commit such a terrible and revolting crime?" . . .

With this background the case came on for trial two weeks before the November general election at which the chief prosecutor was a candidate for municipal judge and the presiding judge, Judge Blythin, was a candidate to succeed himself. Twenty-five days before the case was set, a list of 75 veniremen were called as prospective jurors. This list, including the addresses of each venireman, was published in all three Cleveland newspapers. As a consequence, anonymous letters and telephone calls, as well as calls from friends, regarding the impending prosecution were received by all of the prospective jurors. The selection of the jury began on October 18, 1954.

The courtroom in which the trial was held measured 26 by 48 feet. A long temporary table was set up inside the bar, in back of the single counsel table. It ran the width of the courtroom, parallel to the bar railing, with one end less than three feet from the jury box. Approximately 20 representatives of newspapers and wire services were assigned seats at this table by the court. Behind the bar railing there were four rows of benches. These seats were likewise assigned by the court for the entire trial. The first row was occupied by representatives of television and radio stations, and the second and third rows by reporters from out-of-town newspapers and magazines. One side of the last row, which accommodated 14 people, was assigned to Sheppard's family and the other to Marilyn's. The public was permitted to fill vacancies in this row on special passes only. Representatives of the news media also used all the rooms on the courtroom floor, including the room where cases were ordinarily called and assigned for trial. Private telephone lines and telegraphic equipment were installed in these rooms so that reports from the trial could be speeded to the papers. Station WSRS was permitted to set up broadcasting facilities on the third floor of the courthouse next door to the jury room, where the jury rested during recesses in the trial and deliberated. Newscasts were made from this room throughout the trial, and while the jury reached its verdict.

On the sidewalk and steps in front of the courthouse, television and newsreel cameras were occasionally used to take motion pictures of the participants in the trial, including the jury and the judge. Indeed, one television broadcast carried a staged interview of the judge as he entered the courthouse. In the corridors outside the courtroom there was a host of photographers and television personnel with flash cameras. This group photographed the prospective jurors during selection of the jury. After the trial opened, the witnesses, counsel, and jurors were photographed and televised whenever they entered or left the courtroom. Sheppard was brought to the courtroom about 10 minutes before each session began; he was surrounded by reporters and extensively photographed for the newspapers and television. A rule of court prohibited picture-taking in the courtroom during the actual sessions of the court, but no restraints were put on photographers during recesses, which were taken once each morning and afternoon, with a longer period for lunch.

All of these arrangements with the news media and their massive coverage of the trial continued during the entire nine weeks of the trial. The courtroom remained crowded to capacity with representatives of news media. Their movement in and out of the courtroom often caused so much confusion that, despite the loud speaker system installed in the courtroom, it was difficult for the witnesses and counsel to be heard. Furthermore, the reporters clustered within the bar of the small courtroom made confidential talk among Sheppard and his counsel almost impossible during the proceedings. They frequently had to leave the courtroom to obtain privacy. And many times when counsel wished to raise a point with the judge out of the hearing of the jury it was necessary to move to the judge's chambers. Even then, news media representatives so packed the judge's anteroom that counsel could hardly return from the chambers to the courtroom. The reporters vied with each other to find out what counsel and the judge had discussed, and often these matters later appeared in newspapers accessible to the jury.

The daily record of the proceedings was made available to the newspapers and the testimony of each witness was printed *verbatim* in the local editions, along with objections of counsel, and rulings by the judge. Pictures of Sheppard, the judge, counsel, pertinent witnesses, and the jury often accompanied the daily newspaper and television accounts. At times the newspapers published photographs of exhibits introduced at the trial, and the rooms of Sheppard's house were featured along with relevant testimony.

The jurors themselves were constantly exposed to the news media. Every juror, except one, testified to reading about the case in the Cleveland papers or to having heard broadcasts about it. Seven of the 12 jurors who rendered the verdict had one or more Cleveland papers delivered in their home; the remaining jurors were not interrogated on the point. Nor were there questions as to radios or television sets in the talesmen's homes, but we must assume that most of them owned such conveniences. As the selection of the jury progressed, individual pictures of prospective members appeared daily. During the trial, pictures of the jury appeared over 40 times in the Cleveland papers alone. The court permitted photographers to take pictures of the jury in the box, and individual pictures of the members in the jury room. One newspaper ran pictures of the jurors at the Sheppard home when they went there to view the scene of the murder. Another paper featured the home life of an alternate juror. The day before the verdict was rendered—while the jurors were at lunch and sequestered by two bailiffs—the jury was separated into two groups to pose for photographs which appeared in the newspapers. . . .

We now reach the conduct of the trial. While the intense publicity continued unabated, it is sufficient to relate only the more flagrant episodes:

1. On October 9, 1954, nine days before the case went to trial, an editorial in one of the newspapers criticized defense counsel's random poll of people on the streets as to their opinion of Sheppard's guilt or innocence in an effort to use the resulting statistics to show the necessity for change of venue. The article said the survey "smacks of mass jury tampering," called on defense counsel to drop it, and stated that the bar association should do something about it. It characterized the poll as "non-judicial, non-legal, and nonsense." The article was called to the attention of the court but no action was taken.

2. On the second day of *voir dire* examination a debate was staged and broadcast live over WHK radio. The participants, newspaper reporters, accused Sheppard's counsel of throwing roadblocks in the way of the prosecution and asserted that Sheppard conceded his guilt by hiring a prominent criminal lawyer. Sheppard's counsel objected to this broadcast and requested a continuance, but the judge denied the motion. When counsel asked the court to give some protection from such events, the judge replied that "WHK doesn't have much coverage," and that "[a]fter all, we are not trying this case by radio or in newspapers or any other means. We confine ourselves seriously to it in this courtroom and do the very best we can."

3. While the jury was being selected, a two-inch headline asked: "But Who Will Speak for Marilyn?" The front-page story spoke of the "perfect face" of the accused. "Study that face as long as you want. Never will you get from it a hint of what might be the answer. . . ." The two brothers of the accused were described as "Prosperous, poised. His two sisters-in-law. Smart, chic, well-groomed. His elderly father. Courtly, reserved. A perfect type for the patriarch of a staunch clan." The author then noted Marilyn Sheppard was "still off stage," and that she was an only child whose mother died when she was very young and whose father had no interest in the case. But the author—through quotes from Detective Chief James McArthur—assured readers that the prosecution's exhibits would speak for Marilyn. "Her story," McArthur stated, "will come into this courtroom through our witnesses." The article ends:

> Then you realize how what and who is missing from the perfect setting will be supplied.
> How in the Big Case justice will be done.

Justice to Sam Sheppard.
And to Marilyn Sheppard.

4. As has been mentioned, the jury viewed the scene of the murder on the first day of the trial. Hundreds of reporters, cameramen and onlookers were there, and one representative of the news media was permitted to accompany the jury while they inspected the Sheppard home. The time of the jury's visit was revealed so far in advance that one of the newspapers was able to rent a helicopter and fly over the house taking pictures of the jurors on their tour.

5. On November 19, a Cleveland police officer gave testimony that tended to contradict details in the written statement Sheppard made to the Cleveland police. Two days later, in a broadcast heard over Station WHK in Cleveland, Robert Considine likened Sheppard to a perjurer and compared the episode to Alger Hiss' confrontation with Whittaker Chambers. Though defense counsel asked the judge to question the jury to ascertain how many heard the broadcast, the court refused to do so. The judge also overruled the motion for continuance based on the same ground, saying:

> Well, I don't know, we can't stop people, in any event, listening to it. It is a matter of free speech, and the court can't control everybody. . . . We are not going to harass the jury every morning. . . . It is getting to the point where if we do it every morning, we are suspecting the jury. I have confidence in this jury. . . .

6. On November 24, a story appeared under an eight-column headline: "Sam Called A 'Jekyll-Hyde' By Marilyn, Cousin To Testify." It related that Marilyn had recently told friends that Sheppard was a "Dr. Jekyll and Mr. Hyde" character. No such testimony was ever produced at the trial. The story went on to announce: "The prosecution has a 'bombshell witness' on tap who will testify to Dr. Sam's display of fiery temper—countering the defense claim that the defendant is a gentle physician with an even disposition." Defense counsel made motions for change of venue, continuance and mistrial, but they were denied. No action was taken by the court.

7. When the trial was in its seventh week, Walter Winchell broadcasted over WXEL television and WJW radio that Carole Beasley, who was under arrest in New York City for robbery, had stated that, as Sheppard's mistress, she had borne him a child. The defense asked that the jury be queried on the broadcast. Two jurors admitted in open court that they had heard it. The judge asked each: "Would that have any effect upon your judgment?" Both replied, "No." This was accepted by the judge as sufficient; he merely asked the jury to "pay no attention whatever to that

type of scavenging . . . Let's confine ourselves to this courtroom, if you please." . . .

8. On December 9, while Sheppard was on the witness stand he testified that he had been mistreated by Cleveland detectives after his arrest. Although he was at the trial, Captain Kerr of the Homicide Bureau issued a press statement denying Sheppard's allegations which appeared under the headline: " 'Bare-faced Liar,' Kerr Says of Sam." Captain Kerr never appeared as a witness at the trial.

9. After the case was submitted to the jury, it was sequestered for its deliberations, which took five days and four nights. After the verdict, defense counsel ascertained that the jurors had been allowed to make telephone calls to their homes every day while they were sequestered at the hotel. Although the telephones had been removed from the jurors' rooms, the jurors were permitted to use the phones in the bailiff's rooms. The calls were placed by the jurors themselves; no record was kept of the jurors who made calls, the telephone numbers, or the parties called. The bailiffs sat in the room where they could hear only the jurors' end of the conversation. The court had not instructed the bailiffs to prevent such calls. . . .

The principle that justice cannot survive behind walls of silence has long been reflected in the "Anglo-American distrust for secret trials." . . . A responsible press has always been regarded as the handmaiden of effective judicial administration, especially in the criminal field. Its function in this regard is documented by an impressive record of service over several centuries. The press does not simply publish information about trials but guards against the miscarriage of justice by subjecting the police, prosecutors, and judicial processes to extensive public scrutiny and criticism. This Court has, therefore, been unwilling to place any direct limitations on the freedom traditionally exercised by the news media for "[w]hat transpires in the court room is public property." . . .

But the Court has also pointed out that "[l]egal trials are not like elections, to be won through the use of the meeting-hall, the radio, and the newspaper." . . . And the Court has insisted that no one be punished for a crime without "a charge fairly made and fairly tried in a public tribunal free of prejudice, passion, excitement, and tyrannical power." . . . "Freedom of discussion should be given the widest range compatible with the essential requirement of the fair and orderly administration of justice." . . . But it must not be allowed to divert the trial from the "very purpose of a court system . . . to adjudicate controversies, both criminal and civil, in the calmness and solemnity of the courtroom according to legal procedures." . . . Among these "legal procedures" is the requirement that the jury's verdict be based on evidence received in open court, not from out-side sources. . . .

Only last Term in *Estes v. Texas,* we set aside a conviction despite the absence of any showing of prejudice. We said there:

> It is true that in most cases involving claims of due process de-privations we require a showing of identifiable prejudice to the accused. Nevertheless, at times a procedure employed by the State involves such a probability that prejudice will result that it is deemed inherently lacking in due process. . . .

It is clear that the totality of circumstances in this case also warrant such an approach. Unlike Estes, Sheppard was not granted a change of venue to a locale away from where the publicity originated; nor was his jury sequestered. The Estes jury saw none of the television broadcasts from the courtroom. On the contrary, the Sheppard jurors were subjected to newspaper, radio and television coverage of the trial while not taking part in the proceedings. They were allowed to go their separate ways outside of the courtroom, without adequate directions not to read or listen to anything concerning the case. The judge's "admonitions" at the begin-ning of the trial are representative:

> I would suggest to you and caution you that you do not read any newspapers during the progress of this trial, that you do not listen to radio comments nor watch or listen to television comments, inso-far as this case is concerned. You will feel very much better as the trial proceeds. . . . I am sure that we shall all feel very much better if we do not indulge in any newspaper reading or listening to any comments whatever about the matter while the case is in progress. After it is all over, you can read it all to your heart's content. . . .

At intervals during the trial, the judge simply repeated his "suggestions" and "requests" that the jury not expose themselves to comment upon the case. Moreover, the jurors were thrust into the role of celebrities by the judge's failure to insulate them from reporters and photographers. . . . The numerous pictures of the jurors, with their addresses, which appeared in the newspapers before and during the trial itself exposed them to ex-pressions of opinion from both cranks and friends. The fact that anony-mous letters had been received by prospective jurors should have made the judge aware that this publicity seriously threatened the jurors' pri-vacy. . . .

Sheppard stood indicted for the murder of his wife; the State was de-manding the death penalty. For months the virulent publicity about Sheppard and the murder had made the case notorious. Charges and countercharges were aired in the news media besides those for which Sheppard was called to trial. . . .

While we cannot say that Sheppard was denied due process by the judge's refusal to take precautions against the influence of pretrial publicity alone, the court's later rulings must be considered against the setting in which the trial was held. In light of this background, we believe that the arrangements made by the judge with the news media caused Sheppard to be deprived of that "judicial serenity and calm to which [he] was entitled." . . . The fact is that bedlam reigned at the courthouse during the trial and newsmen took over practically the entire courtroom, hounding most of the participants in the trial, especially Sheppard. At a temporary table within a few feet of the jury box and counsel table sat some 20 reporters staring at Sheppard and taking notes. The erection of a press table for reporters inside the bar is unprecedented. The bar of the court is reserved for counsel, providing them a safe place in which to keep papers and exhibits, and to confer privately with client and co-counsel. It is designed to protect the witness and the jury from any distractions, intrusions or influences, and to permit bench discussions of the judge's rulings away from the hearing of the public and the jury. Having assigned almost all of the available seats in the courtroom to the news media the judge lost his ability to supervise that environment. The movement of the reporters in and out of the courtroom caused frequent confusion and disruption of the trial. And the record reveals constant commotion within the bar. Moreover, the judge gave the throng of newsmen gathered in the corridors of the courthouse absolute free rein. Participants in the trial, including the jury, were forced to run a gantlet of reporters and photographers each time they entered or left the courtroom. The total lack of consideration for the privacy of the jury was demonstrated by the assignment to a broadcasting station of space next to the jury room on the floor above the courtroom, as well as the fact that jurors were allowed to make telephone calls during their five-day deliberation. . . .

Much of the material printed or broadcast during the trial was never heard from the witness stand, such as the charges that Sheppard had purposely impeded the murder investigation and must be guilty since he had hired a prominent criminal lawyer; that Sheppard was a perjurer; that he had sexual relations with numerous women; that his slain wife had characterized him as a "Jekyll-Hyde"; that he was "a bare-faced liar" because of his testimony as to police treatment; and, finally, that a woman convict claimed Sheppard to be the father of her illegitimate child. As the trial progressed, the newspapers summarized and interpreted the evidence, devoting particular attention to the material that incriminated Sheppard, and often drew unwarranted inferences from testimony. At one point, a front-page picture of Mrs. Sheppard's blood-stained pillow was published after being "doctored" to show more clearly an alleged imprint of a surgical instrument.

Nor is there doubt that this deluge of publicity reached at least some of the jury. On the only occasion that the jury was queried, two jurors admitted in open court to hearing the highly inflammatory charge that a prison inmate claimed Sheppard as the father of her illegitimate child. Despite the extent and nature of the publicity to which the jury was exposed during trial, the judge refused defense counsel's other requests that the jury be asked whether they had read or heard specific prejudicial comment about the case, including the incidents we have previously summarized. In these circumstances, we can assume that some of this material reached members of the jury. . . .

The court's fundamental error is compounded by the holding that it lacked power to control the publicity about the trial. From the very inception of the proceedings the judge announced that neither he nor anyone else could restrict prejudicial new accounts. . . .

The carnival atmosphere at trial could easily have been avoided since the courtroom and courthouse premises are subject to the control of the court. . . . [T]he presence of the press at judicial proceedings must be limited when it is apparent that the accused might otherwise be prejudiced or disadvantaged. Bearing in mind the massive pretrial publicity, the judge should have adopted stricter rules governing the use of the courtroom by newsmen, as Sheppard's counsel requested. The number of reporters in the courtroom itself could have been limited at the first sign that their presence would disrupt the trial. They certainly should not have been placed inside the bar. Furthermore, the judge should have more closely regulated the conduct of newsmen in the courtroom. For instance, the judge belatedly asked them not to handle and photograph trial exhibits laying on the counsel table during recesses.

Secondly, the court should have insulated the witnesses. All of the newspapers and radio stations apparently interviewed prospective witnesses at will, and in many instances disclosed their testimony. A typical example was the publication of numerous statements by Susan Hayes, before her appearance in court, regarding her love affair with Sheppard. Although the witnesses were barred from the courtroom during the trial the full *verbatim* testimony was available to them in the press. This completely nullified the judge's imposition of the rule. . . .

Thirdly, the court should have made some effort to control the release of leads, information, and gossip to the press by police officers, witnesses, and the counsel for both sides. Much of the information thus disclosed was inaccurate, leading to groundless rumors and confusion. . . .

[T]he judge should have at least warned the newspapers to check the accuracy of their accounts. And it is obvious that the judge should have further sought to alleviate this problem by imposing control over the statements made to the news media by counsel, witnesses, and especially the Coroner and police officers. The prosecution repeatedly made evidence available to the news media which was never offered in the trial. Much of the "evidence" disseminated in this fashion was clearly inadmissible. The exclusion of such evidence in court is rendered meaningless when a news media makes it available to the public. . . .

From the cases coming here we note that unfair and prejudicial news comment on pending trials has become increasingly prevalent. Due process requires that the accused receive a trial by an impartial jury free from outside influences. Given the pervasiveness of modern communications and the difficulty of effacing prejudicial publicity from the minds of the jurors, the trial courts must take strong measures to ensure that the balance is never weighed against the accused. And appellate tribunals have the duty to make an independent evaluation of the circumstances. Of course, there is nothing that proscribes the press from reporting events that transpire in the courtroom. But where there is a reasonable likelihood that prejudicial news prior to trial will prevent a fair trial, the judge should continue the case until the threat abates, or transfer it to another county not so permeated with publicity. In addition, sequestration of the jury was something the judge should have raised . . . with counsel. If publicity during the proceedings threatens the fairness of the trial, a new trial should be ordered. But we must remember that reversals are but palliatives; the cure lies in those remedial measures that will prevent the prejudice at its inception. The courts must take such steps by rule and regulation that will protect their processes from prejudicial outside interferences. Neither prosecutors, counsel for defense, the accused, witnesses, court staff nor enforcement officers coming under the jurisdiction of the court should be permitted to frustrate its function. Collaboration between counsel and the press as to information affecting the fairness of a criminal trial is not only subject to regulation, but is highly censurable and worthy of disciplinary measures.

Since the state trial judge did not fulfill his duty to protect Sheppard from the inherently prejudicial publicity which saturated the community and to control disruptive influences in the courtroom, we must reverse the denial of the habeas petition. The case is remanded to the District Court with instructions to issue the writ and order that Sheppard be released from custody unless the State puts him to its charges again within a reasonable time. . . .

MR. JUSTICE BLACK dissents [without a written opinion].

AFTERMATH

After some hesitation the State of Ohio decided to try Sheppard again for the murder of his wife. The trial began on October 24, 1966—more than twelve years after the first trial. But this time it was all very different. An obviously less biased judge presided. The "Roman Holiday" atmosphere of the first trial was nowhere in evidence. Sheppard's new lawyer who had been on the case for five years was widely regarded as a brilliant adversary in the court room. New expert witnesses weakened the prosecutor's case against Sheppard. In the end the jury came in with a verdict of *not guilty* and Sheppard was a free man again. Shortly after the trial his personal account of his long ordeal was published—*Endure and Conquer, My Twelve-Year Fight for Vindication,* World Publishing Co., 1966.

Michael V. DiSalle, former Governor of Ohio who is strongly opposed to the death penalty, has argued persuasively that the Sheppard case supports his contentions that trial by newspaper may result in the unreasoned imposition of the death penalty and that the penalty itself is reserved almost exclusively for the poor, illiterate, weak and friendless. Said DiSalle: "The lesson of l'affaire Sheppard . . . could not be clearer. Guilty or not, Dr. Sam was certainly tried by the newspapers before he appeared in court, and even before he was arrested. . . . The Cleveland papers left themselves wide open by usurping the role of police, prosecutor, and jury. . . . The campaign to prejudice a man, who under the sacrosanct principle of our common law is presumed innocent until proven guilty before a jury of his peers, was continued after the trial had begun. . . . In such an atmosphere, the kind that fosters the death penalty and beats down reason, only the skill of highly paid counsel could have brought about a second-degree verdict. (Sheppard could have been found guilty of first-degree murder—premeditated and not committed in the heat of passion or in the course of a quarrel—and sentenced to death rather than life imprisonment.) Given the same set of circumstances, what would the verdict have been had the accused been a penniless Negro artisan defended by a court-appointed attorney? Without the backing of a well-to-do family, would anyone, after ten years, have raised the issue of constitutional rights? I don't even wonder." (Michael V. DiSalle, with Lawrence G. Blochman, *The Power of*

Life or Death, Random House, 1965, pp. 197-198.) This book appeared *before* the Supreme Court's decision reproduced above was announced.

Thompson v. Louisville
362 U.S. 199 (1960)

For over thirty years Sam Thompson, a forty-six year old Negro handyman who lived alone in a small house in the suburbs of Louisville, Kentucky, had done odd jobs for various families in the community. Though his income was meager, it was sufficient to meet his needs.

One Saturday evening Thompson went into the Liberty End Cafe which sold food and beer. When he had been there about half an hour, two city police officers came in on a routine check and saw Thompson shuffling his feet on the floor to the rhythm of jukebox music. One of the officers walked up to Thompson and asked him what he was doing in the cafe. Thompson replied that he was waiting for a bus. The officer thereupon informed Thompson that he was under arrest for loitering and took him outside. After going outside, the officers testified that Thompson "argued with us back and forth and so then we placed a disorderly conduct charge on him." Thompson, who had a record of fifty-four previous arrests on minor charges, was then brought to trial for loitering and disorderly conduct in the Louisville police court.

A family for whom Thompson worked felt that the police had been harassing him so they persuaded Louis Lusky, a distinguished lawyer with a deep interest in civil liberties, to take the case. As revealed in the opinion below, the manager of the cafe testified at the trial that Thompson frequently patronized the cafe and that he was welcome there. He also testified that no objection had been raised to Thompson's "shuffling" on the day of his arrest. His conduct had not been boisterous or offensive to anyone. The judge, nevertheless, found Thompson guilty on both charges of loitering and disorderly conduct and fined him ten dollars on each count. Since police court fines of less than twenty dollars on a single charge cannot be appealed to a higher court in Kentucky, Thompson brought his case *directly* to the Supreme Court on a writ of certiorari after a stay of the judgments against him was granted by the Kentucky courts. Before the Supreme Court Louis Lusky argued that Thompson's conviction deprived him of liberty and property without due process of law in violation of the Fourteenth Amendment. In the oral argument before the Court, the case was given twice the amount of time that was originally allotted. In his opinion Justice Black spoke for a unanimous Court.

MR. JUSTICE BLACK delivered the opinion of the Court.

. . . The ultimate question presented to us is whether the charges against petitioner were so totally devoid of evidentiary support as to render his conviction unconstitutional under the Due Process Clause of the Fourteenth Amendment. Decision of this question turns not on the sufficiency of the evidence, but on whether this conviction rests upon any evidence at all.

. . . [I]f there is no support for these convictions in the record they are void as denials of due process. The pertinent portion of the city ordinance under which petitioner was convicted of loitering reads as follows:

> It shall be unlawful for any person . . . , without visible means of support, or who cannot give a satisfactory account of himself, . . . to sleep, lie, loaf, or trespass in or about any premises, building or other structure in the City of Louisville, without first having obtained the consent of the owner or controller of said premises, structure, or building; . . .

In addition to the fact that petitioner proved he had "visible means of support," the prosecutor at trial said "This is a loitering charge here. There is no charge of no visible means of support." Moreover, there is no suggestion that petitioner was sleeping, lying or trespassing in or about this cafe. Accordingly he could only have been convicted for being unable to give a satisfactory account of himself while loitering in the cafe, without the consent of the manager. Under the words of the ordinance itself, if the evidence fails to prove all three elements of this loitering charge, the conviction is not supported by evidence, in which event it does not comport with due process of law. The record is entirely lacking in evidence to support any of the charges.

Here, petitioner spent about half an hour on a Saturday evening in January in a public cafe which sold food and beer to the public. When asked to account for his presence there, he said he was waiting for a bus. The city concedes that there is no law making it an offense for a person in such a cafe to "dance," "shuffle" or "pat" his feet in time to music. The undisputed testimony of the manager, who did not know whether petitioner had bought macaroni and beer or not but who did see the patting, shuffling or dancing, was that petitioner was welcome there. The manager testified that he did not, at any time during petitioner's stay in the cafe, object to anything petitioner was doing and that he never saw petitioner do anything that would cause any objection. Surely this is implied consent, which the city admitted in oral argument satisfies the ordinance. The arresting officer admitted that there was nothing in any way "vulgar" about what he called petitioner's "ordinary dance," whatever relevance, if any, vulgarity might have to a charge of loitering. There simply is no semblance of evidence from which any person could reasonably infer that petitioner could not give a satisfactory account of himself or that he was loitering or loafing there (in the ordinary sense of the words) without "the consent of the owner or controller" of the cafe.

Petitioner's conviction for disorderly conduct was under Section 85-8 of the city ordinance which, without definition, provides that "whoever shall be found guilty of disorderly conduct in the City of Louisville shall be fined. . . ." etc. The only evidence of "disorderly conduct" was the single statement of the policeman that after petitioner was arrested and taken out of the cafe he was very argumentative. There is no testimony that petitioner raised his voice, used offensive language, resisted the officers or engaged in any conduct of any kind likely in any way to adversely affect the good order and tranquillity of the City of Louisville. The only information the record contains on what the petitioner was "argumentative" about is his statement that he asked the officers "what they arrested me for." We assume, for we are justified in assuming, that merely "arguing" with a policeman is not, because it could not be, "disorderly conduct" as a matter of the substantive law of Kentucky. . . . Moreover, Kentucky law itself seems to provide that if a man wrongfully arrested fails to object to the arresting officer, he waives any right to complain later that the arrest was unlawful. . . .

Thus we find no evidence whatever in the record to support these convictions. Just as "Conviction upon a charge not made would be sheer denial of due process," so is it a violation of due process to convict and punish a man without evidence of his guilt.

The judgments are reversed and the cause is remanded to the Police Court of the City of Louisville for proceedings not inconsistent with this opinion.

Reversed and remanded.

AFTERMATH

On the surface Sam Thompson's case seemed unimportant when it was decided largely because the twenty dollar fine seemed so trivial. Seldom do cases involving so small a penalty reach the Court. In fact, the Court had not reviewed a case carrying such a small fine since 1886 when a case involving a ten dollar fine was decided. Yet, it is out of this combination of seemingly trivial circumstances that the Court sometimes has the opportunity to enumerate important principles. And the Thompson case did announce an important and new constitutional doctrine: conviction and punishment without proof or evidence of guilt violates due process of law. This principle became an important precedent in the key sit-in demonstration cases where the Court held that the demonstrators' convictions for breach of the peace deprived them of due process of law since there was no evidence of their guilt.

Moreover, though it is true that without the help of an established family and a distinguished attorney, Sam Thompson never could have taken his case to the Supreme Court, the fact remains that a Court busy with a host of agonizing problems *did* review the conviction of a penniless Negro handyman with almost no status in our society. The case demonstrates well the fact that "an active ingredient in the workings of one branch of the most powerful government on earth is compassion. Compassion for the fate of solitary people, of desperate, lonely, untutored and disturbed people. Compassion for human life regardless of its extrinsic worth." Is it not possible that this concern may well be America's most enduring gift to the world?

In re Gault
387 U.S. 1 (1967)

The first juvenile court was created in Chicago, Illinois, in 1899 and served as a model which was quickly followed by almost every state. By 1967 there were some three thousand juvenile courts in the United States; but, surprisingly enough, the Supreme Court had considered the legality of juvenile court procedures in only one relatively minor case coming from the District of Columbia in March, 1966. The *Gault* case is a landmark on the question of procedural protections required for children in juvenile courts. As one writer aptly remarked shortly after the Court agreed to hear the *Gault* case, "a Children's Hour has come to the Supreme Court of the United States. It has been a long time coming."

The term *in re* in the unusual title of the *Gault* case means "in the matter of" or "concerning." This method is used to entitle a case instead of the usual way when there are no real adversary parties but simply some object concerning which judicial action is to be taken as, for example, the distribution of a bankrupt's estate. It is also used, as in this case, to designate a proceeding where a party makes an application on his own behalf or for a minor child. As noted below, an application was made in this case for a writ of *habeas corpus* designed to direct the jailer to bring Gault before a court so that it could determine if there had been a just cause for his imprisonment.

Gerald Gault, a fifteen-year old boy, was arrested by the Sheriff of Gila County, Arizona, and taken to the local detention home as the result of a verbal complaint made by a housewife accusing Gerald and one of his friends of making lewd and indecent remarks to her over the telephone. The remarks said to be made to her were of the "imitatingly, offensive, adolescent, sex variety." At the time Gerald was picked up by the sheriff both his mother and father were at work. The parents did not receive any written notice of the charges against Gerald. The only written notice granted them was the date set for Gerald's second hearing before a juvenile court judge. Neither were the parents or their son advised of any right to counsel or of the boy's right to remain silent. No transcript was kept of the proceedings before the juvenile court. The complaining housewife at no time appeared at the two hearings held by the juvenile judge. In fact, the judge did not speak with her on any occasion regarding the alleged offense. It was not clear at the initial hearing whether or not Gerald Gault had actually made any obscene remarks over the telephone. His mother contended that he had only dialed the neighboring housewife's number and that his companion had made the indecent remarks. The probation officer maintained that Gerald had admitted making the remarks. At the conclusion of the brief hearing the judge remarked that "he would think about it."

Gerald was taken back to the detention home but released three days later. His parents were notified that a second hearing would be held in another three days at an appointed hour. At the second hearing there again was some dispute as to whether Gerald had actually made the lewd remarks over the telephone. Nevertheless, at the conclusion of the informal hearing the judge declared Gerald to be a "delinquent child" and sentenced him to six years in the State Industrial School. If Gerald had been an adult, the maximum penalty for the alleged offense was a $50 fine and two months imprisonment. No appeal is permitted by Arizona law in juvenile cases, but Gerald's parents filed a petition for a writ of *habeas corpus* with the Arizona Supreme Court which referred the petition to a lower state court. The court refused to issue the writ of *habeas corpus* and the Arizona Supreme Court later affirmed. Gerald's parents then brought the case to the Supreme Court on appeal.

Justice Abe Fortas who, as noted above, won fame as Gideon's counsel in the well known case of *Gideon v. Wainwright,* was President Johnson's first appointee to the Supreme Court. A Johnson friend for thirty years and member of the White House "inner circle," Fortas had long served as the President's unofficial legal advisor, confidant and business consultant. A hard working graduate of the Yale Law School, Fortas taught at Yale and then went to work for the federal government under his ex-Yale law professor, William O. Douglas, who was Chairman of the Securities and Exchange Commission before being moved to the Supreme Court. Eventually Fortas became Under Secretary of the Interior but left government service to launch a highly successful and prestigious Washington, D.C., law firm. As indicated by his Gault opinion, Fortas is likely to join the liberal, activist bloc on the Court.

MR. JUSTICE FORTAS delivered the opinion of the Court. . . .

From the inception of the juvenile court system, wide differences have been tolerated—indeed insisted upon—between the procedural rights accorded to adults and those of juveniles. In practically all jurisdictions, there are rights granted to adults which are withheld from juveniles. . . .

The history and theory underlying this development are well-known, but a recapitulation is necessary for purposes of this opinion. The juvenile court movement began in this country at the end of the last century. From the juvenile court statute adopted in Illinois in 1899, the system has spread to every State in the Union, the District of Columbia, and Puerto Rico. The constitutionality of juvenile court laws has been sustained in over 40 jurisdictions against a variety of attacks.

The early reformers were appalled by adult procedures and penalties, and by the fact that children could be given long sentences and mixed in jails with hardened criminals. They were profoundly convinced that society's duty to the child could not be confined by the concept of justice alone. They believed that society's role was not to ascertain whether the child was "guilty" or "innocent," but "What is he, how has he become what he is, and what had best be done in his interest and in the interest of the state to save him from a downward career." The child—essentially good, as they saw it—was to be made "to feel that he is the object of [the State's] care and solicitude," not that he was under arrest or on trial. The rules of criminal procedure were therefore altogether inapplicable. The apparent rigidities, technicalities, and harshness which they observed in both substantive and procedural criminal law were therefore to be discarded. The idea of crime and punishment was to be abandoned. The child was to be "treated" and "rehabilitated" and the procedures, from apprehension through institutionalization, were to be "clinical" rather than punitive.

These results were to be achieved, without coming to conceptual and constitutional grief, by insisting that the proceedings were not adversary, but that the State was proceeding as *parens patriae* [substitute governmental parents]. The Latin phrase proved to be a great help to those who sought to rationalize the exclusion of juveniles from the constitutional scheme; but its meaning is murky and its historic credentials are of dubious relevance. The phrase was taken from chancery practice, where, however, it was used to describe the power of the State to act *in loco parentis* [in place of a parent] for the purpose of protecting the property interests and the person of the child. But there is no trace of the doctrine in the history of criminal jurisprudence. At common law, children under seven were considered incapable of possessing criminal intent. Beyond that age, they were subjected to arrest, trial, and in theory to punishment like adult offenders. In these old days, the State was not deemed to have authority to accord them fewer procedural rights than adults.

The right of the State, as *parens patriae,* to deny to the child procedural rights available to his elders was elaborated by the assertion that a child, unlike an adult, has a right "not to liberty but to custody." He can be made to attorn to his parents, to go to school, etc. If his parents default in effectively performing their custodial functions—that is, if the child is "delinquent"—the state may intervene. In doing so, it does not deprive the child of any rights, because he has none. It merely provides the "custody" to which the child is entitled. On this basis, proceedings involving juveniles were described as "civil" not "criminal" and therefore not subject to the requirements which restrict the state when it seeks to deprive a person of his liberty.

Accordingly, the highest motives and most enlightened impulses led to a peculiar system for juveniles, unknown to our law in any comparable context. The constitutional and theoretical basis for this peculiar system is—to say the least—debatable. And in practice, . . . the results have not been entirely satisfactory. Juvenile court history has again demonstrated that unbridled discretion, however benevolently motivated, is frequently a poor substitute for principle and procedure. . . . The absence of substantive standards has not necessarily meant that children receive careful, compassionate, individualized treatment. The absence of procedural rules based upon constitutional principle has not always produced fair, efficient, and effective procedures. Departures from established principles of due process have frequently resulted not in enlightened procedure, but in arbitrariness. . . .

Failure to observe the fundamental requirements of due process has resulted in instances, which might have been avoided, of unfairness to individuals and inadequate or inaccurate findings of fact and unfortunate prescriptions of remedy. Due process of law is the primary and indispensable foundation of individual freedom. It is the basic and essential term in the social compact which defines the rights of the individual and delimits the powers which the State may exercise. As Mr. Justice Frankfurter has said: "The history of American freedom is, in no small measure, the history of procedure." But in addition, the procedural rules which have been fashioned from the generality of due process are our best instruments for the distillation and evaluation of essential facts from the conflicting welter of data that life and our adversary methods present. It is these instruments of due process which enhance the possibility that truth will emerge from the confrontation of opposing versions and conflicting data. "Procedure is to law what 'scientific method' is to science."

It is claimed that juveniles obtain benefits from the special procedures applicable to them which more than offset the disadvantages of denial of the substance of normal due process. As we shall discuss, the observance of due process standards, intelligently and not ruthlessly administered, will not compel the States to abandon or displace any of the substantive benefits of the juvenile process. But it is important, we think, that the claimed benefits of the juvenile process should be candidly appraised. Neither sentiment nor folklore should cause us to shut our eyes, for example, to such startling findings as that reported in an exceptionally reliable study of repeaters or recidivism conducted by the Stanford Research Institute for the President's Commission on Crime in the District of Columbia. This Commission's Report states:

> In fiscal 1966 approximately 66 percent of the 16- and 17-year-old juveniles referred to the court by the Youth Aid Division had been before the court previously. In 1965, 56 percent of those in the Receiving Home were repeaters. The SRI study revealed that 61 percent of the sample Juvenile Court referrals in 1965 had been previously referred at least once and that 42 percent had been re-referred at least twice before. . . .

Certainly, these figures and the high crime rates among juveniles . . . could not lead us to conclude that the absence of constitutional protections reduces crime, or that the juvenile system, functioning free of constitutional inhibitions as it has largely done, is effective to reduce crime or rehabilitate offenders. We do not mean by this to denigrate the juvenile court process or to suggest that there are not aspects of the juvenile system relating to offenders which are valuable. But the features of the juvenile system which its proponents have asserted are of unique benefit will not be impaired by constitutional domestication. For example, the commendable principles relating to the processing and treatment of juveniles separately from adults are in no way involved or affected by the procedural issues under discussion. Further, we are told that one of the important benefits of the special juvenile court procedures is that they avoid classifying the juvenile as a "criminal." The juvenile offender is now classed as a "delinquent." There is, of course, no reason why this should not continue. It is disconcerting, however, that this term has come to involve only slightly less stigma than the term "criminal" applied to adults. It is also emphasized that in practically all jurisdictions, statutes provide that an adjudication of the child as a delinquent shall not operate as a civil disability or disqualify him for civil service appointment. There is no reason why the application of due process requirements should interfere with such provisions. . . .

[T]he summary procedures of juvenile courts are sometimes defended by a statement that it is the law's policy "to hide youthful errors from the full gaze of the public and bury them in the graveyard of the forgotten past." This claim of secrecy, however, is more rhetoric than reality. Disclosure of court records is discretionary with the judge in most jurisdictions. Statutory restrictions almost invariably apply only to the court records, and even as to those the evidence is that many courts routinely furnish information to the FBI and the military, and on request to government agencies and even to private employers. Of more importance are police records. In most States the police keep a complete file of juvenile "police contacts" and have complete discretion as to disclosure of juvenile records. Police departments receive requests for information from the FBI and other law-enforcement agencies, the Armed Forces, and social service agencies, and most of them generally comply. Private employers word their application forms to produce information concerning juvenile arrests and court proceedings, and in some jurisdictions information concerning juvenile police contacts is furnished private employers as well as government agencies.

In any event, there is no reason why, consistently with due process, a State cannot continue, if it deems it appropriate, to provide and to improve provision for the confidentiality of records of police contacts and court action relating to juveniles.

. . . Further, it is urged that the juvenile benefits from informal proceedings in the court. The early conception of the juvenile court proceeding was one in which a fatherly judge touched the heart and conscience of the erring youth by talking over his problems, by paternal advice and admonition, and in which, in extreme situations, benevolent and wise institutions of the State provided guidance and help "to save him from a downward career." Then, as now, goodwill and compassion were admirably prevalent. But recent studies have, with surprising unanimity, entered sharp dissent as to the validity of this gentle conception. They suggest that the appearance as well as the actuality of fairness, impartiality and orderliness—in short, the essentials of due process may be a more impressive and more therapeutic attitude so far as the juvenile is concerned. . . .

Ultimately, however, we confront the reality of that portion of the juvenile court process with which we deal in this case. A boy is charged with misconduct. The boy is committed to an institution where he may be restrained of liberty for years. It is of no constitutional consequence—and of limited practical meaning—that the institution to which he is committed is called an Industrial School. The fact of the matter is that, however euphemistic the title, a "receiving home" or an "industrial school" for juveniles is an institution of confinement in which the child is incarcerated for a greater or lesser time. His world becomes "a building with whitewashed walls, regimented routine and institutional laws. . . ." Instead of mother and father and sisters and brothers and friends and classmates, his world is peopled by guards, custodians, state employees, and "delinquents" confined with him for anything from waywardness to rape and homicide.

In view of this, it would be extraordinary if our Constitution did not require the procedural regularity and the exercise of care implied in the phrase "due process." Under our Constitution, the condition of being a boy does not justify a kangaroo court. The traditional ideas of juvenile court procedure, indeed, contemplated that time would be available and care would be used to establish precisely what the juvenile did and why he did it—was it a prank of adolescence or a brutal act threatening serious consequences to himself or society unless corrected? Under traditional notions, one would assume that in a case like that of Gerald Gault, where the juvenile appears to have a home, a working mother and father, and an older brother, the Juvenile Judge would have made a careful inquiry and judgment as to the possibility that the boy could be disciplined and dealt with at home, despite his previous transgressions. . . .

The essential difference between Gerald's case and a normal criminal case is that safeguards available to adults were discarded in Gerald's case.

The summary procedure as well as the long commitment were possible because Gerald was 15 years of age instead of over 18.

If Gerald had been over 18, he would not have been subject to Juvenile Court proceedings. For the particular offense immediately involved, the maximum punishment would have been a fine of $5 to $50, or imprisonment in jail for not more than two months. Instead, he was committed to custody for a maximum of six years. If he had been over 18 and had committed an offense to which such a sentence might apply, he would have been entitled to substantial rights under the Constitution of the United States as well as under Arizona's laws and constitution. The United States Constitution would guarantee him rights and protections with respect to arrest, search and seizure, and pretrial interrogation. It would assure him of specific notice of the charges and adequate time to decide his course of action and to prepare his defense. He would be entitled to clear advice that he could be represented by counsel, and, at least if a felony were involved, the State would be required to provide counsel if his parents were unable to afford it. If the court acted on the basis of his confession, careful procedures would be required to assure its voluntariness. If the case went to trial, confrontation and opportunity for cross-examination would be guaranteed. So wide a gulf between the State's treatment of the adult and of the child requires a bridge sturdier than mere verbiage, and reasons more persuasive than cliche can provide. . . .

We now turn to the specific issues which are presented to us in the present case. . . .

Notice of Charges

. . . We cannot agree with the court's [Supreme Court of Arizona] conclusion that adequate notice was given in this case. Notice, to comply with due process requirements, must be given sufficiently in advance of scheduled court proceedings so that reasonable opportunity to prepare will be afforded, and it must "set forth the alleged misconduct with particularity." It is obvious, as we have discussed above, that no purpose of shielding the child from the public stigma of knowledge of his having been taken into custody and scheduled for hearing is served by the procedure approved by the court below. The "initial hearing" in the present case was a hearing on the merits. Notice at that time is not timely; and even if there were a conceivable purpose served by the deferral proposed by the court below, it would have to yield to the requirements that the child and his parents or guardian be notified, in writing, of the specific charge or factual allegations to be considered at the hearing, and that such written notice be given at the earliest practicable time, and in any event sufficiently in advance of the hearing to permit preparation. Due process of law requires notice of the sort we have described—that is, notice which would be deemed constitutionally adequate in a civil or criminal proceeding. It does not allow a hearing to be held in which a youth's freedom and his parents' right to his custody are at stake without giving them timely notice, in advance of the hearing, of the specific issues that they must meet. Nor, in the circumstances of this case, can it reasonably be said that the requirement of notice was waived. . . .

RIGHT TO COUNSEL

. . . A proceeding where the issue is whether the child will be found to be "delinquent" and subjected to the loss of his liberty for years is comparable in seriousness to a felony prosecution. The juvenile needs the assistance of counsel to cope with problems of law, to make skilled inquiry into the facts, to insist upon regularity of the proceedings, and to ascertain whether he has a defense and to prepare and submit it. The child "requires the guiding hand of counsel at every step in the proceedings against him. . . ."

During the last decade, court decisions, experts and legislatures have demonstrated increasing recognition of this view. In at least one-third of the States, statutes now provide for the right of representation by retained counsel in juvenile delinquency proceedings, notice of the right of assignment of counsel, or a combination of these. In other States, court rules have similar provisions.

The President's Crime Commission has recently recommended that in order to assure "procedural justice for the child," it is necessary that "Counsel . . . be appointed as a matter of course wherever coercive action is a possibility, without requiring any affirmative choice by child or parent." . . .

We conclude that the Due Process Clause of the Fourteenth Amendment requires that in respect of proceedings to determine delinquency which may result in commitment to an institution in which the juvenile's freedom is curtailed, the child and his parent must be notified of the child's right to be represented by counsel retained by them, or if they are unable to afford counsel, that counsel will be appointed to represent the child.

At the habeas corpus proceeding, Mrs. Gault testified that she knew that she could have appeared with counsel at the juvenile hearing. This knowledge is not a waiver of the right to counsel which she and her juvenile son had, as we have defined it. They had a right expressly to be advised that they might retain counsel and to be confronted with the need for specific consideration of whether they did or did not choose to waive the right. If they were unable to afford to employ counsel, they were entitled in view of the seriousness of the charge and the potential commitment, to appointed counsel, unless they chose waiver. Mrs. Gault's knowledge that she could employ counsel is not an "intentional relinquishment or abandonment" of a fully known right. . . .

CONFRONTATION, SELF-INCRIMINATION, CROSS-EXAMINATION

. . . It would indeed be surprising if the privilege against self-incrimination were available to hardened criminals but not to children. The language of the Fifth Amendment, applicable to the States by operation of the Fourteenth Amendment, is unequivocal and without exception. . . .

Against the application to juveniles of the right to silence, it is argued that juvenile proceedings are "civil" and not "criminal," and therefore the privilege should not apply. It is true that the statement of the privilege in the Fifth Amendment, which is applicable to the States by reason of the Fourteenth Amendment, is that no person "shall be compelled in any *criminal case* to be a witness against himself." However, it is clear that the availability of the privilege does not turn upon the type of proceeding in which its protection is invoked, but upon the nature of the statement or admission and the exposure which it invites. The privilege may, for example, be claimed in a civil or administrative proceeding, if the statement is or may be inculpatory.

It would be entirely unrealistic to carve out of the Fifth Amendment all statements by juveniles on the ground that these cannot lead to "criminal" involvement. In the first place, juvenile proceedings to determine "delinquency," which may lead to commitment to a state institution, must be regarded as "criminal" for purposes of the privilege against self-incrimination. To hold otherwise would be to disregard substance because of the feeble enticement of the "civil" label-of-convenience which has been attached to juvenile proceedings. Indeed, in over half of the States, there is not even assurance that the juvenile will be kept in separate institutions, apart from adult "criminals." In those States juveniles may be placed in or transferred to adult penal institutions after having been found "delinquent" by a juvenile court. For this purpose, at least, commitment is a deprivation of liberty. It is incarceration against one's will, whether it is called "criminal" or "civil." And our Constitution guarantees that no person shall be "compelled" to be witness against himself when he is threatened with deprivation of his liberty—a command which this Court has broadly applied and generously implemented in accordance with the teaching of the history of the privilege and its great office in mankind's battle for freedom.

In addition, apart from the equivalence for this purpose of exposure to commitment as a juvenile delinquent and exposure to imprisonment as an adult offender, the fact of the matter is that there is little or no assurance in Arizona, as in most if not all of the States, that a juvenile apprehended and interrogated by the police or even by juvenile court itself will remain outside of the reach of adult courts as a consequence of the offense for which he has been taken into custody. In Arizona, as in other States, provision is made for juvenile courts to relinquish or waive jurisdiction to the ordinary criminal courts. . . .

We conclude that the constitutional privilege against self-incrimination is applicable in the case of juveniles as it is with respect to adults. We appreciate that special problems may arise with respect to waiver of the privilege by or on behalf of children, and that there may well be some differences in technique—but not in principle—depending upon the age of the child and the presence and competence of parents. The participation of counsel will, of course, assist the police, juvenile courts and appellate tribunals in administering the privilege. If counsel is not present for some permissible reason when an admission is obtained, the greatest care must be taken to assure that the admission was voluntary, in the sense not only that it has not been coerced or suggested, but also that it is not the product of ignorance of rights or of adolescent fantasy, fright or despair. . . .

Absent a valid confession adequate to support the determination of the Juvenile Court, confrontation and sworn testimony by witnesses available for cross-examination were essential for a finding of "delinquency" and an order committing Gerald to a state institution for a maximum of six years. . . . We now hold that, absent a valid confession, a determination of delinquency and an order of commitment to a state institution cannot be sustained in the absence of sworn testimony subjected to the opportunity for cross-examination in accordance with our law and constitutional requirements. . . .

APPELLATE REVIEW AND TRANSCRIPT OF PROCEEDINGS

. . . This Court has not held that a State is required by the Federal Constitution "to provide appellate courts or a right to appellate review at all." In view of the fact that we must reverse the Supreme Court of Arizona's affirmance of the dismissal of the writ of habeas corpus for other reasons, we need not rule on this question in the present case or upon the failure to provide a transcript or recording of the hearings—or, indeed, the failure of the juvenile court judge to state the grounds for his conclusion. . . . As the present case illustrates, the consequences of failure to provide an appeal, to record the proceedings, or to make findings or state the grounds for the juvenile court's conclusion may be to throw a burden upon the machinery for habeas corpus, to saddle the reviewing process with the burden of attempting to reconstruct a record, and to impose upon the juvenile judge the unseemly duty of testifying under cross-examination as to the events that transpired in the hearings before him.

For the reasons stated, the judgment of the Supreme Court of Arizona is reversed and the cause remanded for further proceedings not inconsistent with this opinion.

[Concurring opinions were written by JUSTICES BLACK and WHITE. JUSTICE HARLAN wrote a separate opinion concurring in part and dissenting in part.]

MR. JUSTICE STEWART, dissenting.

The Court today uses an obscure Arizona case as a vehicle to impose upon thousands of juvenile courts throughout the Nation restrictions that the Constitution made applicable to adversary criminal trials. I believe the Court's decision is wholly unsound as a matter of constitutional law, and sadly unwise as a matter of judicial policy.

Juvenile proceedings are not criminal trials. They are not civil trials. They are simply not adversary proceedings. Whether treating with a delinquent child, a neglected child, a defective child, or a dependent child, a juvenile proceeding's whole purpose and mission is the very opposite of the mission and purpose of a prosecution in a criminal court. The object of the one is correction of a condition. The object of the other is conviction and punishment for a criminal act.

In the last 70 years many dedicated men and women have devoted their professional lives to the enlightened task of bringing us out of the dark world of Charles Dickens in meeting our responsibilities to the child in our society. The result has been the creation in this century of a system of juvenile and family courts in each of the 50 States. There can be no denying that in many areas the performance of these agencies has fallen disappointingly short of the hopes and dreams of the courageous pioneers who first conceived them. For a variety of reasons, the reality has sometimes not even approached the ideal, and much remains to be accomplished in the administration of public juvenile and family agencies—in personnel, in planning, in financing, perhaps in the formulation of wholly new approaches.

I possess neither the specialized experience nor the expert knowledge to predict with any certainty where may lie the brightest hope for progress in dealing with the serious problems of juvenile delinquency. But I am certain that the answer does not lie in the Court's opinion in this case, which serves to convert a juvenile proceeding into a criminal prosecution.

The inflexible restrictions that the Constitution so wisely made applicable to adversary criminal trials have no inevitable place in the proceedings of those public social agencies known as juvenile or family courts. And to impose the Court's long catalog of requirements upon juvenile proceedings in every area of the country is to invite a long step backwards into the Nineteenth Century. In that era there were no juvenile proceedings, and a child was tried in a conventional criminal court with all the restrictions of a conventional criminal trial. So it was that a 12-year-old boy named James Guild was tried in New Jersey for killing Catherine Beakes. A jury found him guilty of murder, and he was sentenced to death by hanging. The sentence was executed. It was all very constitutional.

A state in all its dealings must, of course, accord every person due process of law. And due process may require that some of the same restrictions which the Constitution has placed upon criminal trials must be imposed upon juvenile proceedings. For example, I suppose that all would agree that a brutally coerced confession could not constitutionally be considered in a juvenile court hearing. But it surely does not follow that the testimonial privilege against self-incrimination is applicable in all juvenile proceedings. Similarly, due process clearly requires timely notice of the purpose and scope of any proceedings affecting the relationship of parent and child. . . . But it certainly does not follow that notice of a juvenile hearing must be framed with all the technical niceties of a criminal indictment. . . .

I would dismiss the appeal.

III EQUAL RIGHTS OF AMERICAN NEGROES

We are confronted primarily with a moral issue. It is as old as the scriptures and is as clear as the American Constitution. The heart of the question is whether all Americans are to be afforded equal rights and equal opportunities; whether we are going to treat our fellow Americans as we want to be treated. If an American, because his skin is dark, cannot eat lunch in a restaurant open to the public; if he cannot send his children to the best public school available; if he cannot vote for the public officials who represent him; if, in short, he cannot enjoy the full and free life which all of us want, then who among us would be content to have the color of his skin changed and stand in his place? Who among us would then be content with the counsels of patience and delay?

> *President John F. Kennedy, address to the Nation requesting what became the Civil Rights Act of 1964, June 11, 1963.*

The Supreme Court of the United States does not deserve all credit for the nation's new march toward the color-blind society, but what it has done in the last third of a century since the close of the Civil War has helped mightily. Certainly it broke the log jam of law and precedent without which little or nothing could have been done. It would take blindness of another sort and of great dimensions to conceal the fact that much remains to be done. But there is hope now where there was once despair; there is faith now where there was once doubt and cynicism.

There is Tomorrow Bright Before Us.

> *Loren Miller, The Petitioners, the Story of the Supreme Court of the United States and the Negro, N.Y., Pantheon Books, p. 433, 1966.*

Plessy v. Ferguson
163 U.S. 537 (1896)

AT THE END OF the Civil War it seemed that American Negroes had finally won their freedom. The Thirteenth, Fourteenth and Fifteenth Amendments adopted at the close of the war were designed to make the newly-won freedoms secure. The Thirteenth Amendment prohibited slavery and involuntary servitude except as a punishment for crime. The Fourteenth Amendment defined citizenship; provided that no state was to abridge the privileges and immunities of citizens of the United States; forbade states to deprive persons of life, liberty, or property without due process of law; and forbade the states to deny anyone the equal protection of the laws. The Fourteenth Amendment also provided for a method of reduced representation in Congress as a punishment for states which denied the right to vote to adult male citizens. The Fifteenth Amendment stated that the right to vote could not be denied on the ground of race, color, or previous condition of servitude.

But the Negro never achieved full equality. Even as the Civil War Amendments were being adopted the South began to fight bitterly to turn back the tide running toward full emancipation of the Negro. Many factors were involved in the virtual repudiation of the bright promises of the post-Civil War period. Northern liberals lost interest and gradually abandoned the cause of Negro freedom. The removal of federal troops from the South in 1877 was a signal that Negroes could expect little further help from the federal government. In the *Civil Rights Cases,* 109 U.S. 3 (1883), the Supreme Court denied Congress the power to protect Negroes when it declared unconstitutional the Civil Rights Act of 1875, designed to forbid discrimination in places of public accommodation as in our own time. Many southern publications saw in racism an avenue to power while southern conservatives viewed anti-Negro politics as an instrument to direct poor-white farmers from Populist causes, such as regulation of wealth and control of financial institutions which threatened conservative interests.

Gradually American Negroes were relegated to a position of complete inferiority not very different from their pre-Civil War slave status. This was accomplished, in part, by a host of state laws and local ordinances, enacted after 1887, that separated whites and Negroes in every possible area of activity. At issue in this case was one such Louisiana statute enacted in 1890 requiring railroads to provide "separate but equal" accommodations for white and colored passengers.

On June 2, 1892, Homer Adolph Plessy, who was one-eighth Negro and appeared to be white, boarded the East Louisiana Railroad in New Orleans bound for Covington, Louisiana, and took a vacant seat in a coach reserved for white persons. The conductor ordered Plessy to move to a coach for colored passengers, but he refused. With the aid of a police officer, Plessy was thereupon forcibly ejected from the train, locked up in the New Orleans jail, and taken before a Judge Ferguson to answer a charge of violating the Louisiana law. In affirming Plessy's conviction, the Supreme Court of Louisiana upheld the state statute. Plessy then took the case to the Supreme Court on a writ of error (an older form of appeal which was abolished for federal court usage in 1928) arguing that Louisiana's segregation law was unconstitutional as a denial of the Thirteenth Amendment and the equal protection clause of the Fourteenth Amendment.

Justice Henry B. Brown's majority opinion reflected the prevailing climate of opinion concerning the place of Negroes in American society in the 1890's and accepted without question the then fashionable sociological assumptions concerning the superiority of the white race. Surprisingly enough, Brown was a native of Massachusetts who had settled in Michigan and gone to the Supreme Court after fifteen years' experience as a federal judge in Detroit. Brown's opinion is characterized by facile generalizations and obvious insensitivity to the plight of the Southern Negro. But it is Justice John Marshall's solitary dissenting opinion which has stood the test of time! That opinion is now a classic in the literature of American civil liberties. Harlan saw clearly Brown's attempt to write white supremacy into law with this now widely quoted assertion: "But in view of the Constitution, in the eye of the law, there is in this country no superior, dominant ruling class of citizens. There is no caste here. Our Constitution is color-blind, and neither knows nor tolerates classes among citizens." Born in Kentucky and a former slave owner himself, Harlan first opposed abolition but later became a leading champion of Negro rights. Harlan had fought with the Union forces during the Civil War, and became a leading figure in Lincoln's Republican Party before his appointment to the Court in 1877.

MR. JUSTICE BROWN delivered the opinion of the Court.

The constitutionality of this act is attacked upon the ground that it conflicts both with the Thirteenth Amendment of the Constitution, abolishing slavery, and the Fourteenth Amendment, which prohibits certain restrictive legislation on the part of the States.

1. That it does not conflict with the Thirteenth Amendment, which abolished slavery and involuntary servitude, except as a punishment for crime, is too clear for argument. . . .

A statute which implies merely a legal distinction between the white and colored races—a distinction which is founded in the color of the two races, and which must always exist so long as white men are distinguished from the other race by color—has no tendency to destroy the legal equality of the two races, or reestablish a state of involuntary servitude. . . .

2. By the Fourteenth Amendment, all persons born or naturalized in the United States, and subject to the jurisdiction thereof, are made citizens of the United States and of the State wherein they reside; and the States are forbidden from making or enforcing any law which shall abridge the privileges or immunities of citizens of the United States, or shall deprive any person of life, liberty, or property without due process of law, or deny to any person within their jurisdiction the equal protection of the laws. . . .

The object of the amendment was undoubtedly to enforce the absolute equality of the two races before the law, but in the nature of things it could not have been intended to abolish distinctions based upon color, or to enforce social, as distinguished from political equality, or a commingling of the two races upon terms unsatisfactory to either. Laws permitting, and even requiring, their separation in places where they are liable to be brought into contact do not necessarily imply the inferiority of either race to the other, and have been generally, if not universally, recognized as within the competency of the state legislatures in the exercise of their police power. The most common instance of this is connected with the establishment of separate schools for white and colored children, which has been held to be a valid exercise of the legislative power even by courts of States where the political rights of the colored race have been longest and most earnestly enforced. . . .

[T]he case reduces itself to the question whether the statute of Louisiana is a reasonable regulation, and with respect to this there must necessarily be a large discretion on the part of the legislature. In determining the question of reasonableness it is at liberty to act with reference to the established usages, customs, and traditions of the people, and with a view to the promotion of their comfort, and the preservation of the public peace and good order. Gauged by this standard, we cannot say that a law which authorizes or even requires the separation of the two races in public conveyances is unreasonable, or more obnoxious to the Fourteenth Amendment than the acts of Congress requiring separate schools for colored children in the District of Columbia, the constitutionality of which does not seem to have been questioned, or the corresponding act of state legislatures.

We consider the underlying fallacy of the plaintiff's argument to consist in the assumption that the enforced separation of the two races stamps the colored race with a badge of inferiority. If this be so, it is not by reason of anything found in the act, but solely because the colored race chooses to put that construction upon it. The argument necessarily assumes that if, as has been more than once the case, and is not unlikely to be so again, the colored race should become the dominant power in the state legislature, and should enact a law in precisely similar terms, it would thereby relegate the white race to an inferior position. We imagine that the white race, at least, would not acquiesce in this assumption. The argument also assumes that social prejudices may be overcome by legislation, and that equal rights cannot be secured to the Negro except by an enforced commingling of the two races. We cannot accept this proposition. If the two races are to meet upon terms of social equality, it must be the result of natural affinities, a mutual appreciation of each other's merits, and a voluntary consent of individuals. . . . Legislation is powerless to eradicate racial instincts or to abolish distinctions based upon physical differences, and the attempt to do so can only result in accentuating the difficulties of the present situation. If the civil and political rights of both races be equal one cannot be inferior to the other socially, the Constitution of the United States cannot put them upon the same plane.
. . . The judgment of the court below is, therefore,

Affirmed.

MR. JUSTICE HARLAN, dissenting:

. . . It was said in argument that the statute of Louisiana does not discriminate against either race, but prescribes a rule applicable alike to white and colored citizens. But this argument does not meet the difficulty. Everyone knows that the statute in question had its origin in the purpose, not so much to exclude white persons from railroad cars occupied by blacks, as to exclude colored people from coaches occupied by or assigned to white persons. Railroad corporations of Louisiana did not make discrimination among whites in the matter of accommodation for travellers. The thing to accomplish was, under the guise of giving equal accommodation for whites and blacks, to compel the latter to keep to themselves while travelling in railroad passenger coaches. No one would be so wanting in candor as to assert the contrary. The fundamental objection, therefore, to

the statute is that it interferes with the personal freedom of citizens. . . .
If a white man and a black man choose to occupy the same public con-
veyance on a public highway, it is their right to do so, and no government, proceeding alone on grounds of race, can prevent it without
infringing the personal liberty of each.

. . . The white race deems itself to be the dominant race in this country.
And so it is, in prestige, in achievements, in education, in wealth, and in
power. So, I doubt not, it will continue to be for all time, if it remains
true to its great heritage and holds fast to the principles of constitutional
liberty. But in view of the Constitution, in the eye of the law, there is in
this country no superior, dominant, ruling class of citizens. There is no
caste here. Our Constitution is color-blind, and neither knows nor tolerates classes among citizens. In respect of civil rights, all citizens are
equal before the law. The humblest is the peer of the most powerful. The
law regards man as man, and takes no account of his surroundings or of
his color when his civil rights as guaranteed by the supreme law of the
land are involved. It is, therefore, to be regretted that this high tribunal,
the final expositor of the fundamental law of the land, has reached the
conclusion that it is competent for a state to regulate the enjoyment by
citizens of their civil rights solely upon the basis of race.

. . . The sure guarantee of the peace and security of each race is the
clear, distinct, unconditional recognition by our governments, National
and State, of every right that inheres in civil freedom, and of the equality
before the law of all citizens of the United States without regard to race.
State enactments regulating the enjoyment of civil rights upon the basis of
race, and cunningly devised to defeat legitimate results of the war, under
the pretence of recognizing equality of rights, can have no other result
than to render permanent peace impossible, and to keep alive a conflict of
races, the continuance of which must do harm to all concerned. . . .

The arbitrary separation of citizens, on the basis of race, while they are
on a public highway, is a badge of servitude wholly inconsistent with the
civil freedom and the equality before the law established by the Constitution. It cannot be justified upon any legal grounds.

If evils will result from the commingling of the two races upon public
highways established for the benefit of all, they will be infinitely less than
those that will surely come from state legislation regulating the enjoyment
of civil rights upon the basis of race. We boast of the freedom by our
people above all other peoples. But it is difficult to reconcile that boast
with a state of the law which, practically, puts the brand of servitude and
degradation upon a large class of our fellow-citizens, our equals before the
law. The thin disguise of "equal" accommodations for passengers in rail-

road coaches will not mislead anyone, nor atone for the wrong this day done. . . .

I am of the opinion that the statute of Louisiana is inconsistent with the personal liberty of citizens, white and black, in that State, and hostile to both the spirit and letter of the Constitution of the United States. . . .

For the reasons stated, I am constrained to withhold my assent from the opinion and judgment of the majority.

[MR. JUSTICE BREWER did not hear the argument or participate in the decision of this case.]

Aftermath

It has been well written that "one cannot help thinking that Harlan was a better sociologist than his colleagues, a better Southerner than the irreconcilables." Yet the fact remains that Brown's majority opinion had put the Court's stamp of approval on a developing system of segregation which was now bound to spread and deepen. In the years following the Plessy ruling racial segregation became deeply entrenched as a way of life. Negroes were segregated in trains, buses, steamboats, schools, hospitals, and every conceivable place of amusement. Drinking fountains, stairways, elevators, doorways, waiting rooms, parks, toilets, pay windows, and even churches were all made separate for whites and Negroes. Some communities went to ridiculous ends. New Orleans, for example, segregated white and Negro prostitutes. In Atlanta, Georgia, Negroes and whites were not allowed to visit the local zoo at the same time. In effect, a separate world designed "to keep the Negro in his place" and insure white supremacy was created.

In case after case the "separate but equal" doctrine was followed but not reexamined. Actually, the equal part of the doctrine had no real meaning, for the Supreme Court refused to look beyond lower court holdings to find if the segregated facilities for Negroes were in fact equal to those provided for whites. As a result many Negro accommodations were said to be equal when everyone knew that they were decidedly inferior. President Truman's Committee on Civil Rights remarked aptly in 1947 that the separate but equal doctrine "is one of the outstanding myths of American history for it is almost always true that while indeed separate, these facilities are far from equal. Throughout the segregated public institutions, Negroes have been denied an equal share of tax supported services and facilities."

But gradually, "as the twentieth century wore on, the forces opposed to racism and segregation gathered strength." Novelists such
as Lillian Smith, herself a Southerner, wrote of the evils of segregation. Some church leaders and educators, both North and South,
began to openly question the philosophical and intellectual justifica-
tions for segregation. Beginning in 1938, the Supreme Court became
much more strict about the equality requirements for Negro facilities. By 1950, the Court had made it clear that the "separate but
equal" principle could not be applied in practice in higher education.
The defeat of Nazi Germany and its cult of racial superiority deprived the doctrine of Negro inferiority of its intellectual justification.
And as the horrible Nazi crimes against the Jewish people were
unmasked, Americans became increasingly aware of the dangers
inherent in theories of racial supremacy. Negroes acquired greater
political rights in many urban centers of the North, such as New
York, Philadelphia, and Chicago, where they held the balance of
power in close elections. At the same time increasing numbers of
Negroes were voting in the Southern states where industrialization
and unionization after World War II created new job opportunities
for Negroes as well as whites. The armed forces slowly but surely
eliminated segregation. Some places of amusement began to be desegregated. Negro baseball players joined the major leagues. Hence,
by mid-century the Plessy rule was under severe attack. Time and
the course of events seemed to be vindicating Harlan's lonely stand.
The stage was now set for the Court's historic decision in *Brown v.
Board of Education.*

Brown v. Board of Education
347 U.S. 483 (1954)

Linda Carol Brown, an eight year old Negro girl whose father,
Oliver Brown, was assistant pastor of a church in Topeka, Kansas,
lived only four blocks from the Sumner Elementary School. But
Linda had to attend a segregated school twenty-one blocks from her
home simply because Kansas laws permitted cities like Topeka with
more than fifteen thousand inhabitants to segregate Negro and white
pupils in the public elementary schools. Moreover, to get to her
school Linda had to cross a dangerous railroad bridge and wait for

an overcrowded school bus which was often late. Ironically enough, Topeka was not a city plagued with flaming hatred of the Negro and the Browns lived in a white neighborhood where Linda spent much of her time playing with white children. But the Browns were anxious to give their child the best possible education and they did not want Linda to grow up in a segregated school environment. Oliver Brown and the parents of twelve other Negro children therefore asked that their children be admitted to the all-white Sumner School which was much closer to home, but the principal refused them admission. Thereupon Brown and the other parents filed a suit in a federal district court against the Topeka Board of Education contending that refusal to admit the Negro children to the all-white school was a denial of the "equal protection clause" of the Fourteenth Amendment. Thus was born the most important case of the Twentieth Century.

The federal district court was sympathetic to the Negro cause and even agreed that segregation in public schools had a detrimental effect on Negro children but it felt bound by the decision in *Plessy v. Ferguson* and therefore refused to declare segregation unconstitutional. Oliver Brown then took the case directly to the Supreme Court. Meanwhile cases involving school segregation from three other states—Delaware, Virginia, South Carolina—and the District of Columbia had been winding their way to the Court and arrived at about the same time as the Brown case. Since they all raised the same basic issue, the state cases were consolidated under *Brown v. Board of Education.* However, since the equal protection clause of the Fourteenth Amendment is a restriction that applies only to the states, the case from the District of Columbia was rested on the due process clause of the Fifth Amendment which is applicable to the federal government, and entitled *Bolling v. Sharpe,* 349 U.S. 294 (1955). The reasoning in the *Bolling* case is, nevertheless, the same as the one in *Brown v. Board of Education.*

Before the Supreme Court the arguments against segregation were presented by Thurgood Marshall, counsel for the National Association for the Advancement of Colored People, an organization which had directed the five cases through the courts and which had previously won many legal battles for American Negroes. The states relied primarily on *Plessy v. Ferguson,* in arguing for continued segregation in the public schools.

It fell to Chief Justice Earl Warren to write the historic decision in *Brown v. Board of Education* during his first year on the Court. To future generations of Americans Warren will undoubtedly be best remembered as the author of this great landmark in the history of American liberties.

MR. CHIEF JUSTICE WARREN delivered the opinion of the Court.

. . . The plaintiffs contend that segregated public schools are not "equal" and cannot be made "equal," and that hence they are deprived of the equal protection of the laws. Because of the obvious importance of the question presented, the Court took jurisdiction. Argument was heard in the 1952 Term, and reargument was heard this Term (1953-'54) on certain questions propounded by the Court.

Reargument was largely devoted to the circumstances surrounding the adoption of the Fourteenth Amendment in 1868. It covered exhaustively consideration of the Amendment in Congress, ratification by the states, then existing practices in racial segregation, and the view of the proponents and opponents of the Amendment. This discussion and our own investigation convince us that, although these sources cast some light, it is not enough to resolve the problem with which we are faced. At best, they are inconclusive. The most avid proponents of the postwar Amendments undoubtedly intended them to remove all legal distinctions among "all persons born or naturalized in the United States." Their opponents, just as certainly, were antagonistic to both the letter and the spirit of the Amendments and wished them to have the most limited effect. What others in Congress and the state legislatures had in mind cannot be determined with any degree of certainty.

An additional reason for the inclusive nature of the Amendment's history, with respect to segregated schools, is the status of public education at that time. In the South, the movement toward free common schools, supported by general taxation, had not yet taken hold. Education of white children was largely in the hands of private groups. Education of Negroes was almost non-existent, and practically all of the race were illiterate. In fact, any education of Negroes was forbidden by law in some states. Today, in contrast, many Negroes have achieved outstanding success in the arts and sciences as well as in the business and professional world. It is true that public education had already advanced further in the North, but the effect of the Amendment on northern states was generally ignored in the congressional debates. Even in the North, the conditions of public education did not approximate those existing today. The curriculum was usually rudimentary; ungraded schools were common in rural areas; the school term was but three months a year in many states; and compulsory school attendance was virtually unknown. As a consequence, it is not surprising that there should be so little in the history of the Fourteenth Amendment relating to its intended effect on public education.

In the first cases in this Court construing the Fourteenth Amendment, decided shortly after its adoption, the Court interpreted it as proscribing all state-imposed discriminations against the Negro race. The doctrine of "separate but equal" did not make its appearance in this Court until 1896 in the case of *Plessy v. Ferguson* . . . involving not education but transportation. American courts have since labored with the doctrine for over half a century. In this Court, there have been six cases involving the "separate but equal" doctrine in the field of public education. . . . In none of these cases was it necessary to reexamine the doctrine to grant relief to the Negro plaintiff. And in *Sweatt v. Painter,* 339 U.S. 629, the Court expressly reserved decision on the question whether *Plessy v. Ferguson* should be held inapplicable to public education.

In the instant cases, that question is directly presented. Here, unlike *Sweatt v. Painter,* there are findings below that the Negro and white schools involved have been equalized, or are being equalized, with respect to buildings, curricula, qualifications and salaries of teachers, and other "tangible" factors. Our decision, therefore, cannot turn on merely a comparison of these tangible factors in the Negro and white schools involved in each of the cases. We must look instead to the effect of segregation itself on public education.

In approaching this problem, we cannot turn the clock back to 1868 when the Amendment was adopted, or even to 1896 when *Plessy v. Ferguson* was written. We must consider public education in the light of its full development and its present place in American life throughout the Nation. Only in this way can it be determined if segregation in public schools deprives these plaintiffs of the equal protection of the laws.

Today, education is perhaps the most important function of state and local governments. Compulsory school-attendance laws and the great expenditures for education both demonstrate our recognition of the importance of education to our democratic society. It is required in the performance of our most basic public responsibilities, even service in the armed forces. It is the very foundation of good citizenship. Today it is a principal instrument in awakening the child to cultural values, in preparing him for later professional training, and in helping him to adjust normally to his environment. In these days, it is doubtful that any child may reasonably be expected to succeed in life if he is denied the opportunity of an education. Such an opportunity, where the state has undertaken to provide it, is a right which must be made available to all on equal terms.

We come then to the question presented: Does segregation of children in public schools solely on the basis of race, even though the physical facilities and other "tangible" factors may be equal, deprive the children of the minority group of equal educational opportunities? We believe that it does.

In *Sweatt v. Painter* . . . in finding that a segregated law school for Negroes could not provide them equal educational opportunities, this Court relied in large part on "those qualities which are incapable of objective measurement but which make for greatness in a law school." In *McLaurin v. Oklahoma State Regents*, 329 U.S. 637, the Court, in requiring that a Negro admitted to a white graduate school be treated like all other students, again resorted to intangible considerations: ". . . his ability to study, to engage in discussions and exchange views with other students, and, in general, to learn his profession." Such considerations apply with added force to children in grade and high schools. To separate them from others of similar age and qualifications solely because of their race generates a feeling of inferiority as to their status in the community that may affect their hearts and minds in a way unlikely ever to be undone. The effect of this separation on their educational opportunities was well stated by a finding in the Kansas case by a court which nevertheless felt compelled to rule against the Negro plaintiffs:

> Segregation of white and colored children in public schools has a detrimental effect upon the colored children. The impact is greater when it has the sanction of the law; for the policy of separating the races is usually interpreted as denoting the inferiority of the Negro group. A sense of inferiority affects the motivation of a child to learn. Segregation with the sanction of law, therefore, has a tendency to retard the educational and mental development of Negro children and to deprive them of some of the benefits they would receive in a racially integrated school system.

Whatever may have been the extent of psychological knowledge at the time of *Plessy v. Ferguson*, this finding is amply supported by modern authority. Any language in *Plessy v. Ferguson* contrary to this finding is rejected.

We conclude that in the field of public education the doctrine of "separate but equal" has no place. Separate educational facilities are inherently unequal. Therefore, we hold that the plaintiffs and others similarly situated for whom the actions have been brought are, by reason of the segregation complained of, deprived of the equal protection of the laws guaranteed by the Fourteenth Amendment. This disposition makes unnecessary any discussion whether such segregation also violates the Due Process Clause of the Fourteenth Amendment.

Because these are class actions, because of the wide applicability of this decision, and because of the great variety of local conditions, the formulation of decrees in these cases presents problems of considerable complexity. On reargument, the consideration of appropriate relief was necessarily subordinated to the primary question—the constitutionality of segregation in public education. We have now announced that such segregation is a denial of the equal protection of the laws. In order that we may have the full assistance of the parties in formulating decrees, the cases will be restored to the docket, and the parties are requested to present further argument. . . . The Attorney General of the United States is again invited to participate. The Attorneys General of the states requiring or permitting segregation in public education will also be permitted to appear as *amici curiae* [friends of the Court who give advice on matters pending before it] upon request to do so by September 15, 1954, and submission of briefs by October 1, 1954.

It is so ordered.

AFTERMATH

Even before the Court's ruling the Topeka Board of Education ended segregation in the public schools and Linda Brown started junior high school in the fall of 1955 in an integrated school. Before completing high school Linda moved with her family to Springfield, Missouri, where she attended another integrated school, graduated, won a scholarship, and went on to college. But the case to which Linda Brown gave her name had deep repercussions far beyond her personal life and started a virtual revolution in American race relations.

After the decision, the Court heard further arguments on how it could be enforced and in May, 1955, ruled that school districts must end segregation under the supervision of federal district courts "with all deliberate speed." Segregation was quickly abandoned in four non-southern states—Arizona, Wyoming, New Mexico and Kansas. Immediate action was taken to desegregate public schools in the District of Columbia and in some communities in the border states of Virginia, Missouri, Delaware and Maryland. Other states took important steps toward compliance with the Court's order. But there was also great resistance particularly in the states of the deep South—Alabama, Georgia, Louisiana and Mississippi—where the ratio of Negroes to whites is higher than in the South as a whole. There has been some arrogant defiance of the law by public officials as

illustrated clearly by the next two cases of *Cooper v. Aaron* and
Griffin v. School Board of Prince Edward County. Nevertheless, the
direction of events is unmistakable. Segregation will eventually be
ended in the United States simply because "there is no stopping
place between the granting of a few rights and full citizenship. Once
the first Negro was educated, once slavery was abolished, America
made her choice. Negroes will demand and secure the same rights
as other citizens. No other Americans have asked for more than this,
or settled long for less."

The Brown decision was instrumental in clearing the way for the
movement of American Negroes toward full equality. With it school
segregation as a symbol of white supremacy began to crumble.
Though the Brown case did not *directly* overrule *Plessy v. Ferguson,*
it made it crystal clear that segregation in areas other than public
education could not be maintained. Using the Brown case as precedent the courts soon ended segregation in public parks, theatres,
court rooms, public beaches, depots, buses and golf courses. Moreover, the Brown case enabled American Negroes to fight for their
freedom through peaceful sit-ins, demonstrations, and exercise of
their voting rights. It further alerted Americans of good will both
North and South of the evils of segregation and racial hatred and
helped launch a moral crusade of wide appeal. The decision changed
behavior patterns of large segments of the American public and
eventually compelled both Congress and the President to at last come
to grips with the problem of the place of twenty million Negroes in
American life and society—a monumental problem which had been
too long ignored.

The Brown decision finally vindicated Justice Harlan's classic dissent in *Plessy v. Ferguson.* A *New York Times* editorial a few days
after the Brown decision (May 23, 1954) paid proper tribute to
Justice Harlan as follows: "It is fifty-eight years since the Supreme
Court, with Justice Harlan dissenting, established the doctrine of
'separate but equal' provision for the white and Negro races on interstate carriers. It is forty-three years since John Marshall Harlan
passed from this earth. Now the words he used in his lonely dissent
. . . have become in effect by last Monday's unanimous decision of
the Supreme Court a part of the law of the land. . . . Last Monday's
case dealt solely with segregation in the schools, but there was not
one word in Chief Justice Warren's opinion that was inconsistent

with the earlier views of Justice Harlan. This is an instance in which the voice crying in the wilderness finally becomes the expression of a people's will and in which justice overtakes and thrusts aside a timorous expediency."

Cooper v. Aaron
359 U.S. 1 (1958)

The almost unbelievable difficulties encountered in enforcing the Brown decision in some parts of the country are revealed well by the course of events in Little Rock, Arkansas, where *Cooper v. Aaron* originated. It was a well-known fact that desegregation of the public schools in many parts of the country could not be accomplished without the help and leadership of both Congress and the President. But though President Eisenhower moved quickly to end segregation in the District of Columbia, he refused to place the enormous power and prestige of his office behind the Brown decision. In fact, all his wavering statements were so cautious and conservative that at no time as President did he publicly support the decision, and he never stated that he intended to support the law. He, therefore, never provided the moral leadership necessary to help persuade Southerners and many others to accept the Court's decision. At the same time, a hard core of Southern senators and representatives successfully blocked the few, half-hearted attempts made by Congress to provide leadership and help for a host of beleaguered judges and school officials who were trying desperately to enforce the Brown decision. This state of affairs was bound to produce the conditions which ultimately ended in a dramatic showdown between state and federal authorities in Little Rock.

With the support of the state legislature, Arkansas' Governor Orval E. Faubus, a political opportunist under severe pressure from extreme segregationists, ordered the Arkansas National Guard to bar nine Negro teen-age students (six girls and three boys) from previously all-white Central High School in Little Rock in naked defiance of a federal court. President Eisenhower was belatedly forced to act. He sent a thousand tough paratroopers into Little Rock and federalized the National Guard, thus removing it from Governor Faubus' command. It marked the first time that federal troops had been sent into the South to compel equal treatment of American Negroes since Reconstruction days. The fascinating facts leading to the Supreme

Court's decision in a special term in August, 1958, are set forth in more detail in the case.

In an unusual show of solidarity which emphasized the seriousness of the issue, each member of the Court was listed as author of the opinion. Cooper was one of the members of the Little Rock School Board who sought to postpone the desegregation plans because of extreme public hostility brought about by the irresponsible behavior of Governor Faubus and the state legislature. Aaron was one of the nine colored pupils seeking admission to Central High School.

Opinion of the Court by THE CHIEF JUSTICE, MR. JUSTICE BLACK, MR. JUSTICE FRANKFURTER, MR. JUSTICE DOUGLAS, MR. JUSTICE BURTON, MR. JUSTICE CLARK, MR. JUSTICE HARLAN, MR. JUSTICE BRENNAN, AND MR. JUSTICE WHITTAKER:

. . . On May 17, 1954, this Court decided that enforced racial segregation in the public schools of a State is a denial of the equal protection of the laws enjoined by the Fourteenth Amendment. *Brown v. Board of Education.* . . . The Court postponed, pending further argument, formulation of a decree to effectuate this decision. That decree was rendered May 31, 1955. . . . In the formulation of that decree the Court recognized that good faith compliance with the principles declared in *Brown* might in some situations "call for elimination of a variety of obstacles in making the transition to school systems operated in accordance with the constitutional principles set forth in our May 17, 1954, decision." . . .

It was made plain that delay in any guise in order to deny the constitutional rights of Negro children could not be countenanced, and that only a prompt start, diligently and earnestly pursued, to eliminate racial segregation from the public schools could constitute good faith compliance. State authorities were thus bound to devote every effort toward initiating desegregation and bring about the elimination of racial discrimination in the public school system.

On May 20, 1954, three days after the first *Brown* opinion, the Little Rock District School Board adopted, and on May 23, 1954, made public a statement of policy entitled "Supreme Court Decision—Segregation in Public Schools." In this statement the Board recognized that

It is our responsibility to comply with Federal Constitutional Requirements and we intend to do so when the Supreme Court of the United States outlines the method to be followed.

Thereafter the Board undertook studies of the administrative problems confronting the transition to a desegregated public school system at Little Rock. It instructed the Superintendent of Schools to prepare a plan for desegregation, and approved such a plan on May 24, 1955, seven days before the second *Brown* opinion. The plan provided for desegregation at the senior high school level (grades 10 through 12) as the first stage. Desegregation at the junior high and elementary levels was to follow. It was contemplated that desegregation at the high school level would commence in the fall of 1957, and the expectation was that complete desegregation of the school system would be accomplished by 1963. Following the adoption of this plan, the Superintendent of Schools discussed it with a large number of citizen groups in the city. As a result of these discussions, the Board reached the conclusion that "a large majority of the residents" of Little Rock were "of the belief . . . that the Plan, although objectionable in principle," from the point of view of those supporting segregated schools, "was still the best for the interests of all pupils in the District." . . .

While the School Board was thus going forward with its preparation for desegregating the Little Rock school system, other state authorities, in contrast, were actively pursuing a program designed to perpetuate in Arkansas the system of racial segregation which this Court had held violated the Fourteenth Amendment. First came, in November 1956, an amendment to the State Constitution flatly commanding the Arkansas General Assembly to oppose "in every Constitutional manner the unconstitutional desegregation decisions of May 17, 1954, and May 31, 1955 of the United States Supreme Court." . . . Pursuant to this state constitutional command, a law relieving school children from compulsory attendance at racially mixed schools . . . and a law establishing a State Sovereignty Commission . . . were enacted by the General Assembly in February 1957.

The School Board and the Superintendent of Schools nevertheless continued with preparations to carry out the first stage of the desegregation program. Nine Negro children were scheduled for admission in September 1957 to Central High School which has more than 2,000 students. Various administrative measures, designed to assure the smooth transition of this first stage of desegregation, were undertaken.

On September 2, 1957, the day before these Negro students were to enter Central High, the school authorities were met with drastic opposing action on the part of the Governor of Arkansas who dispatched units of the Arkansas National Guard to the Central High School grounds, and placed the school "off limits" to colored students. As found by the District Court in subsequent proceedings, the Governor's action had not been requested by the school authorities, and was entirely unheralded. The findings were these:

Up to this time (September 2), no crowds had gathered about Central High School and no acts of violence or threats of violence in connection with the carrying out of the plan had occurred. Nevertheless, out of an abundance of caution, the school authorities had frequently conferred with the Mayor and Chief of Police of Little Rock about taking appropriate steps by the Little Rock police to prevent any possible disturbances or acts of violence in connection with the attendance of the nine colored students at Central High School. The Mayor considered that the Little Rock police force could adequately cope with any incidents which might arise at the opening of school. The Mayor, the Chief of Police, and the school authorities made no request to the Governor or any representative of his for State assistance in maintaining peace and order at Central High School. Neither the Governor nor any other official of the State government consulted with the Little Rock authorities about whether the Little Rock police were prepared to cope with any incidents which might arise at the school, about any need for State assistance in maintaining peace and order, or about stationing the Arkansas National Guard at Central High School. . . .

The Board's petition for postponement in this proceeding states: "The effect of that action (of the Governor) was to harden the core of opposition to the Plan and cause many persons who theretofore had reluctantly accepted the Plan to believe that there was some power in the State of Arkansas which, when exerted, could nullify the Federal law and permit the disobedience of the decree of this (District) Court, and from that date hostility to the Plan was increased and criticism of the officials of the (School) District has become more bitter and unrestrained." The Governor's action caused the School Board to request the Negro students on September 2 not to attend the high school "until the legal dilemma was solved." The next day, September 3, 1957, the Board petitioned the District Court for instructions, and the court, after a hearing, found that the Board's request of the Negro students to stay away from the high school had been made because of the stationing of the military guards by the state authorities. The court determined that this was not a reason for departing from the approved plan, and ordered the School Board and Superintendent to proceed with it.

On the morning of the next day, September 4, 1957, the Negro children attempted to enter the high school but, as the District Court later found, units of the Arkansas National Guard "acting pursuant to the Governor's order, stood shoulder to shoulder at the school grounds and thereby forcibly prevented the nine Negro students . . . from entering," as they continued to do every school day during the following three weeks. . . .

That same day, September 4, 1957, the United States Attorney for the Eastern District of Arkansas was requested by the District Court to begin an immediate investigation in order to fix responsibility for the interference with the orderly implementation of the District Court's direction to carry out the desegregation program. Three days later, September 7, the District Court denied a petition of the School Board and the Superintendent of Schools for an order temporarily suspending continuance of the program.

Upon completion of the United States Attorney's investigation, he and the Attorney General of the United States, at the District Court's request, entered the proceedings and filed a petition on behalf of the United States, as *amicus curiae* (friends of the court), to enjoin the Governor of Arkansas and officers of the Arkansas National Guard from further attempts to prevent obedience to the court's order. After hearings on the petition, the District Court found that the School Board's plan had been obstructed by the Governor through the use of National Guard troops, and granted a preliminary injunction on September 20, 1957, enjoining the Governor and the officers of the Guard from preventing the attendance of Negro children at Central High School, and from otherwise obstructing or interfering with the orders of the court in connection with the plan. . . . The National Guard was then withdrawn from the school.

The next school day was Monday, September 23, 1957. The Negro children entered the high school that morning under the protection of the Little Rock Police Department and members of the Arkansas State Police. But the officers caused the children to be removed from the school during the morning because they had difficulty controlling a large and demonstrating crowd which had gathered at the high school. . . . On September 25, however, the President of the United States dispatched federal troops to Central High School and admission of the Negro students to the school was thereby effected. Regular army troops continued at the high school until November 27, 1957. They were then replaced by federalized National Guardsmen who remained throughout the balance of the school year. Eight of the Negro students remained in attendance at the school throughout the school year.

We come now to the aspect of the proceedings presently before us. On February 20, 1958, the School Board and the Superintendent of Schools filed a petition in the District Court seeking a postponement of their program for desegregation. Their position in essence was that because of extreme public hostility, which they stated had been engendered largely by the official attitudes and actions of the Governor and the Legislature, the maintenance of a sound educational program at Central High School, with the Negro students in attendance, would be impossible. The Board therefore proposed that the Negro students already admitted to the school be withdrawn and sent to segregated schools, and that all further steps to carry out the Board's desegregation program be postponed for a period later suggested by the Board to be two and one-half years.

After the hearing the District Court granted the relief requested by the Board. Among other things the court found that the past year at Central High School had been attended by conditions of "chaos, bedlam, and turmoil"; that there were "repeated incidents of more or less serious violence directed against the Negro students and their property"; that there was "tension and unrest among the school administrators, the class-room teachers, the pupils, and the latter's parents, which inevitably had an adverse effect upon the educational program"; that a school official was threatened with violence; that a "serious financial burden" had been cast on the School District; that the education of the students had suffered "and under existing conditions will continue to suffer"; that the Board would continue to need "military assistance or its equivalent"; that the local police department would not be able "to detail enough men to afford the necessary protection"; and that the situation was "intolerable."

. . . The District Court's judgment was dated June 20, 1958. The Negro respondents appealed to the Court of Appeals for the Eighth Circuit and also sought there a stay of the District Court's judgment. . . . The Court of Appeals did not act on the petition for a stay but on August 18, 1958, after convening in special session on August 4 and hearing the appeal, reversed the District Court. . . . On August 21, 1958, the Court of Appeals stayed its mandate to permit the School Board to petition this Court for Certiorari. . . .

In affirming the judgment of the Court of Appeals which reversed the District Court we have accepted without reservation the position of the School Board, the Superintendent of Schools, and their counsel that they displayed entire good faith in the conduct of these proceedings and in dealing with the unfortunate and distressing sequence of events which has been outlined. We likewise have accepted the findings of the District Court as to the conditions at Central High School during the 1957-1958 school year, and also the findings that the educational progress of all the students, white and colored, of that school has suffered and will continue to suffer if the conditions which prevailed last year are permitted to continue.

The significance of these findings, however, is to be considered in light of the fact, indisputably revealed by the record before us, that the conditions they depict are directly traceable to the actions of legislators and executive officials of the State of Arkansas, taken in their official capacities, which reflect their own determination to resist this Court's decision in the

Brown case and which have brought about violent resistance to that decision in Arkansas. In its petition for certiorari filed in this Court, the School Board itself describes the situation in this language: "The legislative, executive, and judicial departments of the state government opposed the desegregation of Little Rock schools by enacting laws, calling out troops, making statements vilifying federal law and federal courts, and failing to utilize state law enforcement agencies and judicial processes to maintain public peace."

One may well sympathize with the position of the Board in the face of the frustrating conditions which have confronted it, but, regardless of the Board's good faith, the actions of the other state agencies responsible for those conditions compel us to reject the Board's legal position. Had Central High School been under the direct management of the State itself, it could hardly be suggested that those immediately in charge of the school should be heard to assert their own good faith as a legal excuse for delay in implementing the constitutional rights of these respondents, when vindication of those rights was rendered difficult or impossible by the actions of other state officials. The situation here is in no different posture because the members of the School Board and the Superintendent of Schools are local officials; from the point of view of the Fourteenth Amendment, they stand in this litigation as the agents of the State.

The constitutional rights of respondents are not to be sacrificed or yielded to the violence and disorder which have followed upon the actions of the Governor and Legislature. . . . [L]aw and order are not here to be preserved by depriving the Negro children of their constitutional rights. The record before us clearly establishes that the growth of the Board's difficulties to a magnitude beyond its unaided power to control is the product of state action. Those difficulties, as counsel for the Board forthrightly conceded on the oral argument in this Court, can also be brought under control by state action.

The controlling legal principles are plain. The command of the Fourteenth Amendment is that no "State" shall deny to any person within its jurisdiction the equal protection of the laws. "A State acts by its legislative, its executive, or its judicial authorities. It can act in no other way. The constitutional provision, therefore, must mean that no agency of the State, or of the officers or agents by whom its powers are exerted, shall deny to any person within its jurisdiction the equal protection of the laws. Whoever, by virtue of public position under a State government . . . denies or takes away the equal protection of the laws, violates the constitutional inhibition; and as he acts in the name and for the State, and is clothed with the State's power, his act is that of the State. This must be so, or the constitutional prohibition has no meaning." . . . In short, the constitutional rights of children not to be discriminated against in school admission on grounds of race or color declared by this Court in the *Brown* case can neither be nullified openly and directly by state legislators or state executive or judicial officers, nor nullified indirectly by them through evasive schemes for segregation whether attempted "ingeniously or ingenuously."

   . . . What has been said, in the light of the facts developed, is enough to dispose of the case. However, we should answer the premise of the actions of the Governor and Legislature that they are not bound by our holding in the *Brown* case. It is necessary only to recall some basic constitutional propositions which are settled doctrine.

   Article VI of the Constitution makes the Constitution the "supreme Law of the Land." In 1803, Chief Justice Marshall, speaking for a unanimous court, referring to the Constitution as "the fundamental and paramount law of the nation," declared in the notable case of *Marbury v. Madison,* 1 Cranch 137, . . . that "It is emphatically the province and duty of the judicial department to say what the law is." This decision declared the basic principle that the federal judiciary is supreme in the exposition of the law of the Constitution, and that principle has ever since been respected by this Court and the Country as a permanent and indispensable feature of our constitutional system. It follows that the interpretation of the Fourteenth Amendment enunciated by this Court in the *Brown* case is the supreme law of the land, and Art. VI of the Constitution makes it of binding effect on the States "any Thing in the Constitution or Laws of any State to the Contrary notwithstanding." Every state legislator and executive and judicial officer is solemnly committed by oath taken pursuant to Art. VI §3 "to support this Constitution." . . .

   No state legislator or executive or judicial officer can war against the Constitution without violating his undertaking to support it. Chief Justice Marshall spoke for a unanimous Court in saying that: "If the legislatures of the several states may, at will, annul the judgments of the courts of the United States, and destroy the rights acquired under those judgments, the constitution itself becomes a solemn mockery. . . ." . . . A Governor who asserts a power to nullify a federal court order is similarly restrained. If he had such power, said Chief Justice Hughes, in 1932, also for a unanimous Court, "it is manifest that the fiat of a state Governor, and not the Constitution of the United States, would be the supreme law of the land; that the restrictions of the Federal Constitution upon the exercise of state power would be but impotent phrases. . . ."

   It is, of course, quite true that the responsibility for public education is primarily the concern of the States, but it is equally true that such responsibilities, like all other state activity, must be exercised consistently with federal constitutional requirements as they apply to state action. The Constitution created a government dedicated to equal justice under law. The Fourteenth Amendment embodied and emphasized that ideal. State support of segregated schools through any arrangement, management, funds, or property cannot be squared with the Amendment's command that no State shall deny to any person within its jurisdiction the equal protection of the laws. . . . The basic decision in *Brown* was unanimously reached by this Court only after the case had been briefed and twice argued and the issues had been given the most serious consideration. Since the first *Brown* opinion three new Justices have come to the Court. They are at one with the Justices still on the Court who participated in the basic decision as to its correctness, and that decision is now unanimously reaffirmed. The principles announced in that decision and the obedience of the States to them, according to the command of the Constitution, are indispensable for the protection of the freedoms guaranteed by our fundamental charter for all of us. Our constitutional ideal justice under law is thus made a living truth.

Aftermath

Eight of the Negro students returned to Central High School after the Court's decision and later graduated, some with honors. Little more than token integration was achieved in Little Rock immediately after the decision, but by the middle sixties desegregation was moving at an accelerated pace.

Cooper v. Aaron contains some of the strongest language on the subject of race relations and reveals well the impatience of the justices with those who would defy the federal courts. The Court had now made it crystal clear that there would be no turning back from the *Brown* decision. There would be other tragic acts of defiance in other places, but there would no longer be any doubt of the outcome.

Writing in 1958, Harry S. Ashmore, executive editor of the *Arkansas Gazette,* remarked well that Little Rock was not an isolated event but an episode in "an unfolding drama of social change. . . . For Little Rock was simply the temporary focus of a great, continuing and unresolved American dilemma which touches upon fundamental concepts of morality, of social change, and of law."

Griffin v. County School Board of Prince Edward County
377 U.S. 218 (1964)

Ten years after the Court's decision in *Brown v. Board of Education* only 10 per cent of the South's Negro students were attending integrated classes. In a few areas resistance was so great that local officials were willing to abandon public education completely rather than comply with the Court's order to integrate the schools. The most extreme and perhaps the most tragic example was that of rural Prince Edward County, located about sixty miles southwest of Richmond, Virginia. Of the 30,000 people in the county about half are Negroes. After an involved series of federal court decisions, Prince Edward County was ordered to begin integrating its schools in September, 1959. Instead, the county closed down its entire public school system. At the same time, the state legislature, in a special massive resistance session, repealed the compulsory school attendance law. Schools for white children were then set up in Prince Edward County by a private foundation financed by tuition grants and tax credits, and classes were held in churches, lodges, and other places. No schools were provided for the 1,700 Negro children of the county. In fact, these children had virtually no schooling for four years! As a result, illiteracy among Negroes in the county shot up from 3 to 23 per cent, and volunteer teachers from outside the state who conducted summer "catch up" courses found ten-year-olds who had to be started at the kindergarten level.

In the summer of 1963 President Kennedy stated at a press conference that there were only four places in the world where children did not have the right to attend school: North Vietnam, Cambodia, North Korea and Prince Edward County. The President then said that "something has *got* to be done about Prince Edward County." Spurred on by the President's remark and the intervention of the Department of Justice, a group of interested persons set up the Prince Edward Free School Association designed to provide schooling for the Negroes of the county and supported with funds from private foundations and individual contributions. Thus, in effect, two "private" school systems were set up although the Free School Association made it clear that white children were welcome. A few white parents did send their children to the Free School. (The story of the opening of the Free School and the difficulties encountered has been told in a readable book: *Bound for Freedom, an Educator's Adventures in Prince Edward County, Virginia,* by Neil V. Sullivan with Thomas LaSalle Maynard and Carol Lynn Yellin, Little, Brown and Co., 1965. Mr. Sullivan was the first superintendent of the Free School.)

In the meantime the Negro community continued to fight for a desegregated public school system. The Griffin case was actually, under a new name, one of the four original state cases that had come before the Court in *Brown v. Board of Education.* But in the intervening years it is clear from the recital above that Prince Edward County had not budged an inch. In 1962 a federal district court held that Prince Edward's public schools could not be kept closed to avoid desegregation. The Court of Appeals reversed the decision on a narrow technical ground. In granting certiorari the Supreme Court noted the long delay since its decision in the *Brown* case. The opinion below was delivered on May 25, 1964—ten years and eight days after the *Brown* decision. Griffin was one of the Negro children seeking admission to the public schools.

MR. JUSTICE BLACK delivered the opinion of the Court. . . .

[W]e agree with the District Court that, under the circumstances here, closing the Prince Edward County Schools while public schools in all the other counties of Virginia were being maintained, denied the petitioners and the class of Negro students they represent, the equal protection of the laws guaranteed by the Fourteenth Amendment. . . .

Since 1959, all Virginia counties have had the benefits of public schools but one: Prince Edward. . . .

Virginia law, as here applied, unquestionably treats the school children of Prince Edward differently from the way it treats the school children of all other Virginia counties. Prince Edward children must go to a private school or none at all; all the other Virginia children can go to public schools. Closing Prince Edward's schools bears more heavily on Negro children in Prince Edward County since white children there have accredited private schools which they can attend, while colored children until very recently have had no available private schools, and even the school they now attend is a temporary expedient. Apart from this expedient, the result is that Prince Edward County school children, if they go to school in their own county, must go to racially segregated schools which, although designated as private, are beneficiaries of county and state support.

A State, of course, has a wide discretion in deciding whether laws shall operate statewide or shall operate only in certain counties, the legislature "having in mind the needs and desires of each." . . . A State may wish to suggest, . . . that there are reasons why one county ought not to be treated like another. . . . But the record in the present case could not be clearer that Prince Edward's public schools were closed and private schools operated in their place with state and county assistance, for one reason, and one reason only: to ensure, through measures taken by the county and the State, that white and colored children in Prince Edward County would not, under any circumstances, go to the same school. Whatever nonracial grounds might support a State's allowing a county to abandon public schools, the object must be a constitutional one, and grounds of race and opposition to desegregation do not qualify as constitutional. . . .

Accordingly, we agree with the District Court that closing the Prince Edward schools and meanwhile contributing to the support of the private segregated white schools that took their place denied petitioners the equal protection of the laws. . . .

The District Court enjoined the county officials from paying county tuition grants or giving tax exemptions and from processing applications for state tuition grants so long as the county's public schools remained closed. We have no doubt of the power of the court to give this relief to enforce the discontinuance of the county's racially discriminatory practices. It has long been established that actions against a county can be maintained in United States courts in order to vindicate federally guaranteed rights. . . . The injunction against paying tuition grants and giving tax credits while public schools remain closed is appropriate and necessary since those grants and tax credits have been essential parts of the county's program, successful thus far, to deprive petitioners of the same advantages of a public school education enjoyed by children in every other part of Virginia. For the same reasons the District Court may, if necessary to prevent further racial discrimination, require the Supervisors to exercise the power that is theirs to levy taxes to raise funds adequate to reopen, operate, and maintain without racial discrimination a public school system in Prince Edward County like that operated in other counties in Virginia.

The District Court held that "the public schools of Prince Edward County may not be closed to avoid the effect of the law of the land as interpreted by the Supreme Court, while the Commonwealth of Virginia permits other public schools to remain open at the expense of the taxpayers." . . . At the same time the court gave notice that it would later consider an order to accomplish this purpose if the public schools were not reopened by September 7, 1962. That day has long passed, and the schools are still closed. On remand, therefore, the court may find it necessary to consider further such an order. An order of this kind is within the court's power if required to assure these petitioners that their constitutional rights will no longer be denied them. The time for mere "deliberate speed" has run out, and that phrase can no longer justify denying these Prince Edward County School children their constitutional rights to an education equal to that afforded by the public schools in the other parts of Virginia.

The judgment of the Court of Appeals is reversed, the judgment of the District Court is affirmed, and the cause is remanded to the District Court with directions to enter a decree which will guarantee that these petitioners will get the kind of education that is given in the State's public schools. And, if it becomes necessary to add new parties to accomplish this end, the District Court is free to do so.

It is so ordered.

MR. JUSTICE CLARK and MR. JUSTICE HARLAN disagree with the holding that the federal courts are empowered to order the reopening of the public schools in Prince Edward County, but otherwise join in the Court's opinion.

AFTERMATH

In accordance with the Supreme Court's ruling, the district court ordered Prince Edward County officials to appropriate funds for a desegregated school system to be opened by the beginning of the 1964 fall term. However, only a handful of white students showed up for classes in the desegregated schools in September, 1964. Most white parents kept their children in the private schools. Today there still exists in Prince Edward County "a sort of unwritten understanding that the reopened public schools would be almost wholly Negro." And though some progress has been made in Prince Edward County as the result of the *Griffin* case, the struggle still goes on simply because judicial decrees in themselves are not enough. "Judges can do much to speed desegregation, but they need political support from the White House, the State House, or the City Hall. Unless they have this backing they will not, perhaps cannot, desegregate the schools. This is the lesson of Prince Edward."

A whole "generation of children in Prince Edward County will always carry the scars of the conflict that closed their schools. But perhaps even they will disregard the cost if their children are permitted to share the American dream."

Heart of Atlanta Motel v. United States
379 U.S. 241 (1964)

For nearly ten years after its decision in *Brown v. Board of Education* the Supreme Court stood virtually alone in articulating the principles of freedom and equality with little or no support from the President or Congress. But finally President Kennedy undertook to arouse the national conscience in support of the Court by calling for civil rights legislation in a message to Congress. After the death of President Kennedy, President Johnson vigorously espoused the course of civil rights legislation and Congress responded with the Civil Rights Act of 1964—the most comprehensive attack on race discrimination in American history. The Act was passed with the overwhelming support of both Republicans and Democrats in both the House and Senate. It undertook generally to prevent discrimination in voting, places of public accommodation, federally supported programs and employment. It has been well said that the Civil Rights Act of 1964 was "a great achievement motivated by a bad conscience on the part of white men. If Negroes had been treated like other human beings from the time of emancipation, their equal rights would not now require spelling out. But we have at least shown that the self-correcting machinery of democracy still works."

The first and most controversial section of the Act to be legally challenged was Title II which prohibited discrimination in hotels, motels, inns, restaurants, cafeterias, movie houses and other public places. A very different Supreme Court of another era had declared a similar public accommodation law (Civil Rights Act of 1875) enacted by the Reconstruction Congress unconstitutional in the *Civil Rights Case*, 109 U.S. 3 (1883). The 1964 Act was challenged by Moreton Rolleston, Jr., a bitter Alabama segregationist, who owned and operated the Heart of Atlanta Motel which had long followed a practice of refusing to rent rooms to Negroes. Three-fourths of the motel's guests were transient interstate travelers. After the passage of the 1964 Act, Rolleston announced that he would continue to allow only white persons to use the motel, and brought suit in a federal district court to prevent the enforcement of the public accommodations section of the law. But the district ruled that Title II was constitutional and enjoined Rolleston for refusing to accommodate Negro guests for racial reasons. The case then went quickly to the Supreme Court on direct appeal.

MR. JUSTICE CLARK delivered the opinion of the Court.

The sole question is . . . the constitutionality of the Civil Rights Act of 1964. . . . The legislative history of the Act indicates that Congress based the Act on §5 and the Equal Protection Clause of the Fourteenth Amendment as well as its power to regulate interstate commerce under Art. I, §8, cl. 3 of the Constitution.

The Senate Commerce Committee made it quite clear that the fundamental object of Title II was to vindicate "the deprivation of personal dignity that surely accompanies denials of equal access to public establishments." At the same time, however, it noted that such an objective has been and could be readily "by congressional action based on the commerce power of the Constitution." Our study of the legislative record, made in the light of prior cases, has brought us to the conclusion that Congress possessed ample power in this regard, and we have therefore not considered the other grounds relied upon. This is not to say that the remaining authority upon which it acted was not adequate, a question upon which we do not pass, but merely that since the commerce power is sufficient for our decision here we have considered it alone. . . .

In light of our ground for decision, it might be well at the outset to discuss the Civil Rights Cases which declared provisions of the Civil Rights Act of 1875 unconstitutional. We think that decision inapposite, and without precedential value in determining the constitutionality of the present Act. Unlike Title II of the present legislation, the 1875 Act broadly proscribed discrimination in "inns, public conveyances on land or water, theaters, and other public places of amusement," without limiting the categories of affected businesses to those impinging upon interstate commerce. In contrast, the applicability of Title II is carefully limited to enterprises having a direct and substantial relation to the interstate flow of goods and people, except where state action is involved. Further, the fact that certain kinds of businesses may not in 1875 have been sufficiently involved in interstate commerce to warrant bringing them within the ambit of the commerce power is not necessarily dispositive of the same question today. Our populace had not reached its present mobility, nor were facilities, goods and services circulating as readily in interstate commerce as they are today. Although the principles which we apply today are those first formulated by Chief Justice Marshall in *Gibbons v. Ogden,* the conditions of transportation and commerce have changed dramatically, and we must apply those principles to the present state of commerce. The sheer increase in volume of interstate traffic alone would give discriminatory practices which inhibit travel a far larger impact upon the nation's commerce than such practices had in the economy of another day. Finally, there is language in the *Civil Rights Cases* which indicates that the Court did not fully consider whether the 1875 Act could be sustained as an exercise of the commerce power. . . . Since the commerce power was not relied on by the Government and was without support in the record it is understandable that the Court narrowed its inquiry and excluded the Commerce Clause as a possible source of power. In any event, it is clear that such a limitation renders the opinion devoid of authority for the proposition that the Commerce Clause give no power to Congress to regulate discriminatory practices now found substantially to affect interstate commerce. We, therefore, conclude that the *Civil Rights Cases* have no relevance to the basis of decision here where the Act not only explicitly relies upon the commerce power, but the record is filled with testimony of obstructions and restraints resulting from the discriminations found to be existing. We now pass to that phase of the case. . . .

While the Act as adopted carried no congressional findings the record of its passage through each house is replete with evidence of the burdens that discrimination by race or color places upon interstate Commerce. . . . This testimony included the fact that our people have become increasingly mobile with millions of all races traveling from State to State; that Negroes in particular have been the subject of discrimination in transient accommodations, having to travel great distances to secure the same; that often they have been unable to obtain accommodations and have had to call upon friends to put them up overnight; and that these conditions had become so acute as to require the listing of available lodging for Negroes in a special guidebook which was itself "dramatic testimony of the difficulties" Negroes encounter in travel. These exclusionary practices were found to be nationwide, the Under Secretary of Commerce testifying that there is "no question that this discrimination in the North still exists to a large degree" and in the West and Midwest as well. This testimony indicated a qualitative as well as quantitative effect on interstate travel by Negroes. The former was the obvious impairment of the Negro traveler's pleasure and convenience that resulted when he continually was uncertain of finding lodging. As for the latter, there was evidence that this uncertainty stemming from racial discrimination had the effect of discouraging travel on the part of a substantial portion of the Negro community. This was the conclusion not only of the Under Secretary of Commerce but also of the Administrator of the Federal Aviation Agency who wrote the Chairman of the Senate Commerce Committee that it was his "belief that air commerce is adversely affected by the denial to a substantial segment of the traveling public of adequate and desegregated public accommodations." We shall not burden this opinion with further details since the voluminous testimony presents overwhelming evidence that discrimination by hotels and motels impedes interstate travel. . . .

The power of Congress to deal with these obstructions depends on the meaning of the Commerce Clause. . . . [The Court then spells out the meaning of the Commerce Clause beginning with *Gibbons v. Ogden* and citing a number of the leading Commerce Clause Cases.]

It is said that the operation of the motel here is of a purely local character. But, assuming this to be true, "if it is interstate commerce that feels the pinch, it does not matter how local the operation that applies the squeeze." . . . As Chief Justice Stone put it in *United States v. Darby,* . . .

> The power of Congress over interstate commerce is not confined to the regulation of commerce among the states. It extends to those activities intrastate which so affect interstate commerce or the exercise of the power of Congress over it as to make regulation of them appropriate means to the attainment of a legitimate end, the exercise of the granted power of Congress to regulate interstate commerce. . . .

Thus the power of Congress to promote interstate commerce also includes the power to regulate the local incidents thereof, including local activities in both the States of origin and destination, which might have a substantial and harmful effect upon that commerce. . . . Congress may—as it has—prohibit racial discrimination by motels serving travelers, however "local" their operations may appear.

Nor does the Act deprive appellant of liberty or property under the Fifth Amendment. The commerce power invoked here by the Congress is a specific and plenary one authorized by the Constitution itself. The only questions are: (1) whether Congress had a rational basis for finding that racial discrimination by motels affected commerce, and (2) if it had such a basis, whether the means it selected to eliminate that evil are reasonable and appropriate. If they are, appellant has no "right" to select its guests as it sees fit, free from governmental regulation.

There is nothing novel about such legislation. Thirty-two States now have it on their books either by statute or executive order and many cities provide such regulation. Some of these Acts go back four-score years. It has been repeatedly held by this Court that such laws do not violate the Due Process Clause of the Fourteenth Amendment. . . .

It is doubtful if in the long run appellant will suffer economic loss as a result of the Act. Experience is to the contrary where discrimination is completely obliterated as to all public accommodations. But whether this be true or not is of no consequence since this Court has specifically held that the fact that a "member of the class which is regulated may suffer economic losses not shared by others . . . has never been a barrier" to such legislation. . . . Likewise in a long line of cases this Court has rejected the claim that the prohibition of racial discrimination in public accommodations interferes with personal liberty. . . . Neither do we find any merit in the claim that the Act is a taking of property without just compensation. The cases are to the contrary. . . .

We find no merit in the remainder of appellant's contentions, including that of "involuntary servitude." As we have seen, 32 States prohibit racial discrimination in public accommodations. These laws but codify the common-law inn-keeper rule which long predated the Thirteenth Amendment. It is difficult to believe that the Amendment was intended to abrogate this principle. . . .

We, therefore, conclude that the action of the Congress in the adoption of the Act as applied here to a motel which concededly serves interstate travelers is within the power granted it by the Commerce Clause of the Constitution, as interpreted by this Court for 140 years. It may be argued that Congress could have pursued other methods to eliminate the obstructions it found in interstate commerce caused by racial discrimination. But this is a matter of policy that rests entirely with the Congress not with the courts. How obstructions in commerce may be removed—what means are to be employed—is within the sound and exclusive discretion of the Congress. It is subject only to one *caveat*—that the means chosen by it must be reasonably adapted to the end permitted by the Constitution. We cannot say that its choice here was not so adapted. The Constitution requires no more. . . .

MR. JUSTICE DOUGLAS, concurring.

Though I join the Court's opinion, I am somewhat reluctant here, as I was in *Edwards v. California* to rest solely on the Commerce Clause. My reluctance is not due to any conviction that Congress lacks power to regulate commerce in the interests of human rights. It is rather my belief that the right of people to be free of state action that discriminates against them because of race, like the "right to persons to move freely from State to State" . . . "occupies a more protected position in our constitutional system than does the movement of cattle, fruit, steel and coal across state lines." . . .

Hence I would prefer to rest on the assertion of legislative power contained in §5 of the Fourteenth Amendment which states: "The Congress shall have power to enforce, by appropriate legislation, the provisions of this article"—a power which the Court concedes was exercised at least in part in this Act.

A decision based on the Fourteenth Amendment would have a more settling effect, making unnecessary litigation over whether a particular restaurant or inn within the commerce definitions of the Act or whether a particular customer is an interstate traveler. Under my construction, the Act would apply to all customers in all the enumerated places of public accommodation. And that construction would put an end to all obstructionist strategies and finally close one door on a bitter chapter in American history. . . .

Thus while I agree with the Court that Congress in fashioning the present Act used the Commerce Clause to regulate racial segregation, it also used (and properly so) some of its power under §5 of the Fourteenth Amendment.

I repeat what I said earlier, that our decision should be based on the Fourteenth Amendment, thereby putting an end to all obstructionist strategies and allowing every person—whatever his race, creed, or color— to patronize all places of public accommodation without discrimination whether he travels interstate or intrastate.

[Concurring opinions were also written by JUSTICES BLACK and GOLDBERG.]

AFTERMATH

In the companion case of *Katzenbach v. McClung*, 379 U.S. 294, decided the same day, the Court upheld, again unanimously, the application of Title II to an Alabama restaurant known as Ollie's Barbecue catering to virtually only local customers. However, a substantial portion of the food served by the restaurant came from outside the state.

On the afternoon (Monday, December 14, 1964) of the decisions President Johnson issued this statement: "The Civil Rights Act of 1964 was proposed by two Presidents. It was overwhelmingly approved by Congress and now the constitutionality of the public accommodations section has been upheld by unanimous vote of the Supreme Court. The nation has spoken with a single voice on the question of equal rights and opportunity. I have been heartened by the spirit with which the people of the South have accepted this act even though many of them were opposed to its passage. There already has been encouraging and widespread compliance with the act during the five months it has been law. Now that the Supreme Court has also ruled, I think we all join in the hope and the resolution that this kind of reasonable and responsible acceptance of law will continue and increase."

The three branches of the federal government had at last come together to lay the legal foundations for the freedom of twenty million American Negroes.

Neil Reitman et al., v. Lincoln W. Mulkey et al.
387 U.S. 369 (1967)

Racial discrimination in housing was fought by the Supreme Court as early as 1917. The Court ruled in *Buchanan v. Warley,* 245 U.S. 60 (1917), that the Fourteenth Amendment is violated by municipal residential-segregation ordinances. Since this ruling made it legally impossible to prevent Negroes from moving into white neighborhoods, private agreements, known as restrictive covenants, whereby property owners agree not to sell or lease their property to Negroes or others, came to be widely used. The Court upheld the use of restrictive covenants in *Corrigan v. Buckley,* 271 U.S. 323 (1926), declaring that the Fourteenth Amendment restricts state action only, and not that of private individuals. However, in *Shelley v. Kraemer,* 334 U.S. 1 (1948) the Court held that enforcement of these private agreements by state courts would violate the equal protection clause of the Fourteenth Amendment. In *Hurd v. Hodge,* 334 U.S. 24 (1948), the Court made a similar ruling regarding the District of Columbia. Lawsuits followed but the Court ruled in *Barrows v. Jackson,* 346 U.S. 249 (1953) that damage suits brought against those who broke those agreements could not be upheld by the states.

Extreme dissatisfaction on the part of those who wanted freedom to sell or lease restrictively resulted in California in the passage of "Proposition 14," an amendment to the California constitution proposed in the form of an initiative for the purpose of repealing fair housing legislation previously passed by the Legislature. As Article I, Section 26 of the state constitution this amendment provided that property owners were free to sell or rent to whomever they chose. They were equally free not to sell. This was equivalent to state-sanctioned discrimination, charged those, often Negroes, who were frustrated in their quest of housing under this provision, and therefore a violation of the Fourteenth Amendment.

Mr. and Mrs. Neil Reitman sued apartment owner Lincoln Mulkey, declaring he had refused to rent them an apartment because they were Negroes, basing their action on violation of California's anti-discrimination statutes. A California trial court entered summary judgment against the Reitmans on the ground that the anti-discrimination statute had been rendered null and void by the new amendment. The Supreme Court of California reversed the judgment against the Reitmans, stating that Article I, Section 26 is unconstitutional as it denies the equal protection of the laws guaranteed by the Fourteenth Amendment. The case then went to the United States Supreme Court on a writ of certiorari.

MR. JUSTICE WHITE delivered the opinion of the Court.

The question here is whether Art. I, Sec. 26 of the California Constitution denies "to any person . . . the equal protection of the laws" within the meaning of the Fourteenth Amendment of the Constitution of the United States. Section 26 of Art. I, an initiated measure submitted to the people as Proposition 14 in a statewide ballot in 1964, provides in part as follows:

> Neither the State nor any subdivision or agency thereof shall deny, limit or abridge, directly or indirectly, the right of any person, who is willing or desires to sell, lease or rent any part or all of his real property, to decline to sell, lease or rent such property to such person or persons as he, in his absolute discretion, chooses.

. . . The California Supreme Court . . . held that Art. I, Sec. 26 was invalid as denying the equal protection of the laws guaranteed by the Fourteenth Amendment . . .

We affirm the judgment of the California Supreme Court. We first turn to the opinion of that court, which quite properly undertook to examine the constitutionality of Sec. 26 in terms of its "immediate objective," its "ultimate impact" and its "historical context and conditions existing prior to its enactment."

First, the court considered whether Sec. 26 was concerned at all with private discriminations in residential housing. This involved a review of past efforts by the California Legislature to regulate such discriminatons. The Unruh Act, Civil Code Sections 51-52, on which respondents based their cases, was passed in 1959. The Hawkins Act, formerly Health & Saf.

Code Sections 35700-35741, followed and prohibited discriminations in publicly assisted housing. In 1961, the legislature enacted proscriptions against restrictive covenants. Finally, in 1963, came the Rumford Fair Housing Act, Health & Saf. Code Sections 35700-35744 superseding the Hawkins Act and prohibiting racial discriminations in the sale or rental of any private dwelling containing more than four units. That act was enforceable by the State Fair Employment Practice Commission.

It was against this background that Proposition 14 was enacted. Its immediate design and intent, the California court said, was "to overturn state laws that bore on the right of private sellers and lessors to discriminate," the Unruh and Rumford Acts, and "to forestall future state action that might circumscribe this right." This aim was successfully achieved: the adoption of Proposition 14 "generally nullifies both the Rumford and Unruh Acts as they apply to the housing market," and establishes "a purported constitutional right to privately discriminate on grounds which admittedly would be unavailable under the Fourteenth Amendment should state action be involved."

Second, the court conceded that the State was permitted a neutral position with respect to private racial discriminations and that the State was not bound by the Federal Constitution to forbid them. But, because a significant state involvement in private discriminations could amount to unconstitutional state action, *Burton v. Wilmington Parking Authority,* 365 U.S. 715, . . . the court deemed it necessary to determine whether Proposition 14 invalidly involved the State in racial discrimination in the housing market. Its conclusion was that it did.

To reach this result, the state court examined certain prior decisions in this Court in which discriminatory state action was identified. . . . It concluded that a prohibited state involvement could be found "even where the State can be charged only with encouraging, rather than commanding, discrimination. . . ." Also of particular interest to the court was Mr. Justice Stewart's concurrence in *Burton* . . . , where it was said that the Delaware courts had construed an existing Delaware statute as "authorizing" racial discrimination in restaurants and that the statute was therefore invalid. To the California court "the instant case presents an undeniably analogous situation" wherein the State had taken affirmative action designed to make private discriminations legally possible. Section 26 was said to have changed the situation from one in which discriminatory practices were restricted "to one where it is encouraged . . ."; Section 26 was legislative action "which authorized private discrimination" and made the State "at least a partner in the instant act of discrimination. . . ." The court could "conceive of no other purpose for an application of Sec. 26 aside from authorizing the perpetration of a purported private discrimination. . . ." The judgment of the California court was that Sec. 26 unconstitutionally involves the State in racial discriminations and is therefore invalid under the Fourteenth Amendment.

There is no sound reason for rejecting this judgment. Petitioners contend that the California court has misconstrued the Fourteenth Amendment since the repeal of any statute prohibiting racial discrimination, which is constitutionally permissible, may be said to "authorize" and "encourage" discrimination because it makes legally permissible that which was formerly proscribed. But as we understand the California court, it did not posit a constitutional violation on the mere repeal of the Unruh and Rumford Acts. It did not read either our cases or the Fourteenth Amendment as establishing an automatic constitutional barrier to the repeal of an existing law prohibiting racial discrimination in housing; nor did the court rule that a State may never put in statutory form an existing policy of neutrality with respect to private discriminations. What the court below did was first to reject the notion that the State was required to have a statute prohibiting racial discriminations in housing. Second, it held the purpose and intent of Sec. 26 was to authorize private racial discriminations in the housing market, to repeal the Unruh and Rumford Acts and to create a constitutional right to discriminate on racial grounds in the sale and leasing of real property. Hence, the court dealt with Sec. 26 as though it expressly authorized and constitutionalized the private right to discriminate. Third, the court assessed the ultimate impact of Sec. 26 in the California environment and concluded that the section would encourage and significantly involve the State in private racial discrimination contrary to the Fourteenth Amendment.

The California court could very reasonably conclude that Sec. 26 would and did have wider impact than a mere repeal of existing statutes. Section 26 mentioned neither the Unruh nor Rumford Acts in so many words. Instead, it announced the constitutional right of any person to decline to sell or lease his real property to anyone to whom he did not desire to sell or lease. Unruh and Rumford were thereby *pro tanto* repealed. But the section struck more deeply and more widely. Private discriminations in housing were now not only free from Rumford and Unruh but they also enjoyed a far different status than was true before the passage of those statutes. The right to discriminate, including the right to discriminate on racial grounds, was now embodied in the State's basic charter, immune from legislative, executive, or judicial regulation at any level of the state government. Those practicing racial discriminations need no longer rely solely on their personal choice. They could now invoke express constitutional authority, free from censure or interference of any kind from official sources. All individuals, partnerships, corporations and other legal entities, as well as their agents and representatives, could now discriminate with respect to their residential real property, which is defined as any interest in real property of any kind or quality, "irrespective of how obtained or financed," and seemingly irrespective of the relationship of the State to such interests in real property. Only the State is excluded with respect to property owned by it.

This Court has never attempted the "impossible task" of formulating an infallible test for determining whether the State "in any of its manifestations" has become significantly involved in private discriminations. "Only by sifting the facts and weighing the circumstances" on a case-to-case basis can a "non-obvious involvement of the State be attributed its true significance." *Burton*. . . . Here the California court, armed as it was with the knowledge of the facts and circumstances concerning the passage and potential impact of Sec. 26, and familiar with the milieu in which that provision would operate, has determined that the provision would involve the State in private racial discriminations to an unconstitutional degree. We accept this holding of the California court.

Affirmed.

MR. JUSTICE DOUGLAS, concurring.

While I join the opinion of the Court, I add a word to indicate the dimensions of our problem.

. . . We deal here with a problem in the realm of zoning, similar to the one we had in *Shelley v. Kraemer,* 334 U.S. 1, . . . where we struck down restrictive covenants.

Those covenants are one device whereby a neighborhood is kept "white" or "Caucasian" as the dominant interests desire. Proposition 14 in the setting of our modern housing problem is only another device of the same character.

Real estate brokers and mortgage lenders are largely dedicated to the maintenance of segregated communities. Realtors commonly believe it is unethical to sell or rent to a Negro in a predominantly or all-white neighborhood, and mortgage lenders throw their weight alongside segregated communities, rejecting applications by a member of a minority group who tries to break the white phalanx save and unless the neighborhood is in process of conversion into a mixed or a Negro community. . . .

The builders join in the same scheme . . . [We are told by the Commission on Civil Rights]: "In short, as the Commission on Race and Housing has concluded, 'it is the real estate brokers, builders, and mortgage finance institutions, which translate prejudice into discriminatory action.' Thus, at every level of the private housing market members of minority groups meet mutually reinforcing and often unbreakable barriers of rejection."

Proposition 14 is a form of sophisticated discrimination whereby the people of California harness the energies of private groups to do indirectly what they cannot under our decisions allow their government to do.

Zoning is a state and municipal function. . . . When the State leaves that function to private agencies or institutions who are licensees and who practice racial discrimination and zone our cities into white and black belts or white and black ghettoes, it suffers a governmental function to be performed under private auspices in a way the State itself may not act. . . .

Leaving the zoning function to groups who practice racial discrimination and are licensed by the States constitutes state action in the narrowest sense in which *Shelley v. Kraemer,* supra, can be construed. . . .

Under California law no person may "engage in the business, act in the capacity of, advertise or assume to act as a real estate broker or a real estate salesman within this State without first obtaining a real estate license." West Calif Code Ann Sec 10130. These licensees are designated to serve the public. Their licenses are not restricted, and could not be restricted, to effectuate a policy of segregation. That would be state action that is barred by the Fourteenth Amendment. There is no difference, as I see it, between a State authorizing a licensee to practice racial discrimination and a State, without any express authorization of that kind nevertheless launching and countenancing the operation of a licensing system in an environment where the whole weight of the system is on the side of discrimination. In the latter situation the State is impliedly sanctioning what it may not do specifically.

If we were in a domain exclusively private, we would have different problems. But urban housing is in the public domain as evidenced not only by the zoning problems presented but by the vast schemes of public financing with which the States and the Nation have been extensively involved in recent years. Urban housing is clearly marked with the public interest. Urban housing, like restaurants, inns, and carriers . . . , or like telephone companies, drugstores, or hospitals, is affected with a public interest in the historical and classical sense. . . .

Since the real estate brokerage business is one that can be and is state regulated and since it is state licensed, it must be dedicated, like the telephone companies and the carriers and the hotels and motels, to the requirements of service to all without discrimination—a standard that in its modern setting is conditioned by the demands of the Equal Protection Clause of the Fourteenth Amendment.

And to those who say that Proposition 14 represents the will of the people of California, one can only reply:

"Wherever the real power in a Government lies, there is the danger of oppression. In our Governments the real power lies in the majority of the Community, and the invasion of private rights is *chiefly* to be apprehended, not from acts of Government contrary to the sense of its constituents, but from acts in which the Government is the mere instrument of the major number of the Constituents. This is a truth of great importance, but not yet sufficiently attended to. . . ." V Writings of James Madison (Hunt ed 1904), p. 272.

MR. JUSTICE HARLAN, whom MR. JUSTICE BLACK, MR. JUSTICE CLARK, and MR. JUSTICE STEWART join, dissenting.

I consider that this decision, which cuts deeply into state political processes, is supported neither by anything "found" by the Supreme Court of California nor by any of our past cases decided under the Fourteenth Amendment. In my view today's holding, salutary as its result may appear at first blush, may in the long run actually serve to handicap progress in the extremely difficult field of racial concerns. I must respectfully dissent.

I am wholly at loss to understand how this straight forward effectuation of a change in the California constitution can be deemed a violation of the Fourteenth Amendment, thus rendering Sec. 26 void and petitioners' refusal to rent their property to respondents, because of their race, illegal under prior state law.

The Equal Protection Clause of the Fourteenth Amendment, which forbids a State to use its authority to foster discrimination based on such factors as race . . . does not undertake to control purely personal prejudices and predilections, and individuals acting on their own are left free to discriminate on racial grounds if they are so minded, *The Civil Rights Cases,* 109 U.S. 3 . . . By the same token, the Fourteenth Amendment does not require of States the passage of laws preventing such private discrimination, although it does not of course disable them from enacting such legislation if they wish.

. . . [A]ll that has happened is that California has effected a *pro tanto* repeal of its prior statutes forbidding private discrimination. This runs no more afoul of the Fourteenth Amendment than would have California's failure to pass any such antidiscrimination statutes in the first instance. . . .

I.

The Court attempts to fit Sec. 26 within the coverage of the Equal Protection Clause by characterizing it as in effect an affirmative call to residents of California to discriminate. The main difficulty with this viewpoint is that it depends upon a characterization of Sec. 26 that cannot fairly be made. The provision is neutral on its face, and it is only by in effect asserting that this requirement of passive official neutrality is camouflage that the Court is able to reach its conclusion. In depicting the provision as tantamount to active state encouragement of discrimination the Court essentially relies on the fact that the California Supreme Court so concluded . . .

. . . [T]here is no supporting fact in the record for this characterization. Moreover, the grounds which prompt legislators or state voters to repeal a law do not determine its constitutional validity. That question is decided by what the law does, not by what those who voted for it wanted it to do, and it must not be forgotten that the Fourteenth Amendment does not compel a State to put or keep any particular law about race on its books. The Amendment forbids only a State to pass or keep in effect laws discriminating on account of race. California has not done this.

A state enactment, particularly one that is simply permissive of private decision-making rather than coercive and one that has been adopted in this most democratic of processes, should not be struck down by the judiciary under the Equal Protection Clause without persuasive evidence of an invidious purpose or effect. The only "factual" matter relied on by the majority of the California Supreme Court was the context in which Proposition 14 was adopted, namely that several strong antidiscrimination acts had been passed by the legislature and opposed by many of those who successfully led the movement for adoption of Proposition 14 by popular referendum. These circumstances, and these alone, the California court held, made Sec. 26 unlawful under this Court's cases interpreting the Equal Protection Clause. . . .

II.

. . . The core of the Court's opinion is that Sec. 26 is offensive to the Fourteenth Amendment because it effectively *encourages* private discrimination. By focusing on "encouragement" the Court, I fear, is forging a slippery and unfortunate criterion by which to measure the constitutionality of a statute simply permissive in purpose and effect, and inoffensive on its face. . . .

A moment of thought will reveal the far-reaching possibilities of the Court's new doctrine, which I am sure the Court does not intend. Every act of private discrimination is either forbidden by state law or permitted by it. There can be little doubt that such permissiveness—whether by express constitutional or statutory provision, or implict in the common law— to some extent "encourages" those who wish to discriminate to do so. Under this theory "state action" in the form of laws that do nothing more than passively permit private discrimination could be said to tinge all private discrimination with the taint of unconstitutional state encouragement.

This type of alleged state involvement, simply evincing a refusal to involve itself at all, is of course very different from that illustrated in such cases as *Lombard, Peterson, Evans, and Burton,* supra, where the Court found active involvement of state agencies and officials in specific acts of discrimination. It is also quite different from cases in which a state enactment could be said to have the obvious purpose of fostering discrimination. *Anderson v. Martin,* 375 U.S. 399. . . . I believe the state action required to bring the Fourteenth Amendment into operation must be affirmative and purposeful, actively fostering discrimination. Only in such a case is ostensibly "private" action more properly labeled "official." I do not believe that the mere enactment of Sec. 26, on the showing made here, falls within this class of cases.

III.

I think that this decision is not only constitutionally unsound, but in its practical potentialities shortsighted. Opponents of state antidiscrimination statutes are now in a position to argue that such legislation should be defeated because, if enacted, it may be unrepealable. More fundamentally, the doctrine underlying this decision may hamper, if not preclude, attempts to deal with the delicate and troublesome problems of race relations through the legislative process. The lines that have been and must be drawn in this area, fraught as it is with human sensibilities and frailties of whatever race or creed, are difficult ones. The drawing of them requires understanding, patience, and compromise, and is best done by legislatures rather than by courts. When legislation in this field is unsuccessful there should be wide opportunities for legislative amendment, as well as for change through such processes as the popular initiative and referendum. This decision, I fear, may inhibit such flexibility. Here the electorate itself overwhelmingly wished to overrule and check its own legislature on a matter left open by the Federal Constitution. By refusing to accept the decision of the people of California, and by contriving a new and ill-defined constitutional concept to allow federal judicial interference, I think the Court has taken to itself powers and responsibilities left elsewhere by the Constitution.

I believe the Supreme Court of California misapplied the Fourteenth Amendment, and would reverse its judgment, and remand the case for further appropriate proceedings.

Richard Perry Loving et ux. v. Virginia
388 U.S. 1 (1967)

The "equal protection" clause of the Fourteenth Amendment has been applied to eradicate inequality in public education, voting rights, employment, and use of public accommodations and recreation facilities. In the improving climate of interracial relationships and the increasing freedom of sexual expression, it appeared to be just a matter of time until impediments to a person's right to cohabit with a person of another race would be eliminated.

Anti-miscegenation statutes have been in existence since 1661. The intent of a Maryland statute of 1661 was to prevent a shortage of slave labor. There were insufficient numbers of Negro women, and white men of the same class as the white female indentured servants were few in number. Proximity at work in the fields and in the tenant housing provided for Negro slaves and indentured servants resulted in intermingling and eventually in intermarriage. The prevailing custom was that a child born of such a union became a free man since the child acquired the mother's status. The Maryland statute changed this by making the female miscegenator a slave during her husband's life and by declaring the children of such a union slaves as their fathers were.

Anti-miscegenation statutes have provided the rule in thirty-eight states at one time or another. Although most statutes were intended to prevent Negro-white unions, they were also directed against Indians, Orientals, and other minority groups. Rulings on anti-miscegenation in some cases were so intricate that it was virtually impossible for certain groups, particularly mulattoes, to marry, even within their own race.

The Supreme Court first reviewed anti-miscegenation statutes in *Pace v. Alabama*, 106 U.S. 583 (1882). It upheld an Alabama law against interracial sexual relations because punishment fell equally upon the white and non-white participants and therefore did not violate the Equal Protection Clause of the Fourteenth Amendment. In 1955 the subject came up again in the case of *Naim v. Naim*, 76 Sup. Ct. 151, but no ruling resulted. The U.S. Supreme Court wished to have the case returned to the trial court in order to obtain more facts, but the Virginia Supreme Court of Appeals stated that such action would be contrary to Virginia procedure. Thus the Virginia ruling upholding the anti-miscegenation law remained valid.

In *McLaughlin v. Florida*, 379 U.S. 184 (1964), an anti-miscegenation case was brought to the Supreme Court on appeal on the grounds that the defendants had been deprived of the Fourteenth Amendment's guarantee of equal protection of the laws. Dewey McLaughlin, a Honduran, and Connie Hoffman, a white woman, lived as common-law husband and wife. Florida does not prohibit cohabitation by persons of the *same* race, and the defendants were unable to plead common-law marriage because another Florida law forbids interracial marriage. The Court found it unnecessary to consider the basic statute because it was possible to dispose of it on the grounds of the cohabitation statute. Although the majority ruling did not extend to invalidate state laws that made interracial marriages a crime, Justices Stewart and Douglas in a concurring opinion indicated their readiness to further legal equality of the races.

The opportunity arrived as a result of the marriage in June, 1958, in Washington, D.C., of Mildred Jeter, a Negro woman, and Richard Loving, a white man; residents of Virginia. Five weeks after their return and establishment of a home in their native Caroline County, where little commotion had resulted from their marriage, the Lovings were charged with violating Virginia's ban on interracial marriages. On January 6, 1959, the Lovings pleaded guilty to the charge and were sentenced to one year in jail. The sentence, however, was suspended for a twenty-five year period on the condition that the Lovings leave Virginia and not return together for twenty-five years. Frightened and unaware of their rights, the Lovings moved to Washington, D.C., where they lived in financial difficulty for five years. Returning to Virginia to visit Mrs. Loving's parents they were arrested again. While released on bail they wrote Attorney-General Robert F. Kennedy, appealing for help. With assistance from the American Civil Liberties Union, the Loving's case appeared before the Supreme Court of Appeals of Virginia. There the constitutionality of the anti-miscegenation statutes were upheld, and with modified sentence, the conviction was affirmed. The Lovings then appealed their case to the United States Supreme Court.

MR. CHIEF JUSTICE WARREN delivered the opinion of the Court.

This case presents a constitutional question never addressed by this

Court: whether a statutory scheme adopted by the State of Virginia to prevent marriages between persons solely on the basis of racial classifications violates the Equal Protection and Due Process Clauses of the Fourteenth Amendment. For reasons which seem to us to reflect the central meaning of those constitutional commands, we conclude that these statutes cannot stand consistently with the Fourteenth Amendment.

. . . The two statutes under which appellants were convicted and sentenced are part of a comprehensive statutory scheme aimed at prohibiting and punishing interracial marriages. The Lovings were convicted of violating Sec. 20-58 of the Virginia Code:

> *Leaving State to evade law.*—If any white person and colored person shall go out of this State, for the purpose of being married, and with the intention of returning, and be married out of it, and afterwards return to and reside in it, cohabiting as man and wife, they shall be punished as provided in Sec. 20-59, and the marriage shall be governed as if it had been solemnized in this State. The fact of their cohabitation here as man and wife shall be evidence of their marriage.

Section 20-59, which defines the penalty for miscegenation, provides

> *Punishment for marriage.*—If any white person intermarry with a colored person, or any colored person intermarry with a white person, he shall be guilty of a felony and shall be punished by confinement in the penitentiary for not less than one nor more than five years.

Other central provisions in the Virginia statutory scheme are Sec. 20-57, which automatically voids all marriages between "a white person and a colored person" without any judicial proceeding, and Secs. 20-54 and 1-14 which, respectively, define "white persons" and "colored persons and Indians" for purposes of the statutory prohibitions. . . .

. . . The present statutory scheme dates from the adoption of the Racial Integrity Act of 1924, . . . The central features of this Act, and current Virginia law, are the absolute prohibition of a "white person" marrying other than another "white person," a prohibition against issuing marriage licenses until the issuing official is satisfied that the applicants' statements as to their race are correct, certificates of "racial composition" to be kept by both local and state registrars, and the carrying forward of earlier prohibitions against racial intermarriage.

I.

In upholding the constitutionality of these provisions in the decision below, the Supreme Court of Appeals of Virginia referred to its 1955 decision in *Naim v. Naim*, 87 SE2d 749, as stating the reasons supporting the validity of these laws. In Naim, the state court concluded that the State's legitimate purposes were "to preserve the racial integrity of its citizens," and to prevent "the corruption of blood," "a mongrel breed of citizens," and "the obliteration of racial pride," obviously an endorsement of the doctrine of White Supremacy. . . . The court also reasoned that marriage has traditionally been subject to state regulation without federal intervention, and, consequently, the regulation of marriage should be left to exclusive state control by the Tenth Amendment.

[2] While the state court is no doubt correct in asserting that marriage is a social relation subject to the State's police power, . . . the State does not contend in its argument before this Court that its powers to regulate marriage are unlimited notwithstanding the commands of the Fourteenth Amendment. . . . Instead, the State argues that the meaning of the Equal Protection Clause, as illuminated by the statements of the Framers, is only that state penal laws containing an interracial element as part of the definition of the offense must apply equally to whites and Negroes in the sense that members of each race are punished to the same degree. Thus, the State contends that, because its miscegenation statutes punish equally both the white and the Negro participants in an interracial marriage, these statutes, despite their reliance on racial classifications, do not constitute an invidious discrimination based upon race. The second argument advanced by the State assumes the validity of its equal application theory. The argument is that, if the Equal Protection clause does not outlaw miscegenation statutes because of their reliance on racial classifications, the question of constitutionality would thus become whether there was any rational basis for a State to treat interracial marriages differently from other marriages. On this question, the State argues, the scientific evidence is substantially in doubt and, consequently, this Court should defer to the wisdom of the state legislature in adopting its policy of discouraging interracial marriages.

[3] Because we reject the notion that the mere "equal application" of a statute containing racial classifications is enough to remove the classifications from the Fourteenth Amendment's proscription of all invidious racial discriminations, we do not accept the State's contention that these statutes should be upheld if there is any possible basis for concluding that they serve a rational purpose. . . . [Here] we deal with statutes containing racial classifications, and the fact of equal application does not immunize the statute from the very heavy burden of justification which the Fourteenth Amendment has traditionally required of state statutes drawn according to race.

[4] The State argues that statements in the Thirty-ninth Congress

about the time of the passage of the Fourteenth Amendment indicate that the Framers did not intend the Amendment to make unconstitutional state miscegenation laws. . . . [W]e have said in connection with a related problem, that although these historical sources "cast some light" they are not sufficient to resolve the problem; "[a]t best they are inconclusive. The most avid proponents of the post-War Amendments undoubtedly intended them to remove all legal distinctions among 'all persons born or naturalized in the United States.' Their opponents, just as certainly, were antagonistic to both the letter and the spirit of the Amendments and wished them to have the most limited effect." *Brown et al. v. Board of Education of Topeka et al.*, 347 U.S. 483 (1954). . . . We have rejected the proposition that the debates in the Thirty-ninth Congress or in the state legislatures which ratified the Fourteenth Amendment supported the theory advanced by the State, that the requirement of equal protection of the laws is satisfied by penal laws defining offenses based on racial classification so long as white and Negro participants in the offense were similarly punished. *McLaughlin et al. v. Florida*, 379 U.S. 184 (1964).

[5, 6] The State finds support for its "equal application" theory in the decision of the Court in *Pace v. Alabama*, 106 U.S. 583 (1882). In that case, the Court upheld a conviction under an Alabama statute forbidding adultery or fornication between a white person and a Negro which imposed a greater penalty than that of a statute proscribing similar conduct by members of the same race. The Court reasoned that the statute could not be said to discriminate against Negroes because the punishment for each participant in the offense was the same. However, as recently as the 1964 Term, in rejecting the reasoning of that case, we stated "Pace represents a limited view of the Equal Protection Clause which has not withstood analysis in the subsequent decisions of this Court." *McLaughlin et al. v. Florida*, supra. . . . As we there demonstrated, the Equal Protection Clause requires the consideration of whether the classifications drawn by any statute constitute an arbitrary and invidious discrimination. The clear and central purpose of the Fourteenth Amendment was to eliminate all official state sources of invidious racial discrimination in the States. . . .

[7, 8] There can be no question but that Virginia's miscegenation statutes rest solely upon distinctions drawn according to race. The statutes proscribe generally accepted conduct if engaged in by members of different races. . . . [I]f they are ever to be upheld, they must be shown to be necessary to the accomplishment of some permissible state objective, independent of the racial discrimination which it was the object of the Fourteenth Amendment to eliminate. Indeed, two members of this Court have already stated that they "cannot conceive of a valid legislative purpose which makes the color of a person's skin the test of whether his

conduct is a criminal offense." *McLaughlin v. Florida,* (Justice Stewart, joined by Justice Douglas, concurring).

[9] There is patently no legitimate overriding purpose independent of invidious racial discrimination which justifies this classification. The fact that Virginia only prohibits interracial marriages involving white persons demonstrates that the racial classifications must stand on their own justification, as measures designed to maintain White Supremacy. We have consistently denied the constitutionality of measures which restrict the rights of citizens on account of race. There can be no doubt that restricting the freedom to marry solely because of racial classifications violates the central meaning of the Equal Protection Clause.

II.

[10] These statutes also deprive the Lovings of liberty without due process of law in violation of the Due Process Clause of the Fourteenth Amendment. The freedom to marry has long been recognized as one of the vital personal rights essential to the orderly pursuit of happiness by free men.

[1, 11, 12] Marriage is one of the "basic civil rights of man," fundamental to our very existence and survival. *Skinner v. Oklahoma,* 316 U.S. 535 (1942). . . . To deny this fundamental freedom on so unsupportable a basis as the racial classifications embodied in these statutes, classifications so directly subversive of the principle of equality at the heart of the Fourteenth Amendment, is surely to deprive all the State's citizens of liberty without due process of law. The Fourteenth Amendment requires that the freedom of choice to marry not be restricted by invidious racial discriminations. Under our Constitution, the freedom to marry, or not marry, a person of another race resides with the individual and cannot be infringed by the State.

These convictions must be reversed.

It is so ordered.

MR. JUSTICE STEWART, concurring.

I have previously expressed the belief that "it is simply not possible for a state law to be valid under our Constitution which makes the criminality of an act depend upon the race of the actor." *McLaughlin v. Florida* (concurring opinion). Because I adhere to that belief, I concur in the judgment of the Court.

IV FREEDOM OF EXPRESSION

Democratic self-government cannot endure without freedom; totalitarian government cannot endure with it. To destroy freedom for the purpose of preserving democracy is like cutting out a man's heart to reduce his blood pressure.

. . . . .

Freedom either is a growing thing or it is not freedom. The world did not come to a standstill in 1787, or 1789, or 1791, or 1868. Principles remain unchanged while the understanding of them grows and their application enlarges.

> Irving Brant, The Bill of Rights, Its Origin and Meaning, *Indianapolis, The Bobbs-Merrill Co., 1965, pp. 52, 78.*

Terminiello v. Chicago
337 U.S. 1 (1949)

THE FIRST AMENDMENT TO the Constitution states, in part, that "Congress shall make no law . . . abridging the freedom of speech, or of the press; or the right of the people peaceably to assemble, and to petition the Government for a redress of grievances." Thus, in these few words is embodied perhaps the most important of American freedoms.

It must be remembered that since the first ten amendments were originally limitations on the federal government alone, the First Amendment restrictions applied only to Congress. However, in 1925, the Supreme Court announced that freedom of speech, press and assembly are among the fundamental personal rights and liberties which are protected *against state action* by the Due Process clause of the Fourteenth Amendment. Therefore, today *both* the states and the federal government are limited by the First Amendment guarantee of freedom of expression. But the freedom of expression, like other freedoms, is not an absolute right. It is relative in the sense that it is limited by co-existing other rights and by the need for public peace and order. But in actual cases it is not always easy to draw the line. This is demonstrated well by the various opinions of the *Terminiello* case and of those that follow in this chapter.

Arthur Terminiello, a rabble rousing Catholic priest under suspension by his bishop, was brought from Birmingham, Alabama, to Chicago to deliver an address under the auspices of the Christian Veterans of America, a right wing, anti-semitic group. The auditorium was filled to capacity with over eight hundred people. Many others who had hoped to hear the controversial priest were turned away. Outside the auditorium an "angry and turbulent" crowd of about one thousand persons gathered to protest the meeting. A cordon of policemen surrounded the building and tried to maintain order with little success. Terminiello himself had to be escorted into the building through the jeering, howling crowd. Police officers were stationed near the stage and doors as Terminiello began to speak. In his long, provocative address Terminiello referred to the crowd outside as "scum" and made insulting comments concerning the Jewish people, President Roosevelt, and others. Additional facts concerning the speech and the conditions under which Terminiello spoke are contained in Justice Robert H. Jackson's vigorous dissenting opinion.

Terminiello was arrested and charged with breach of peace in violation of a Chicago ordinance. He was found guilty and fined $100.00. Two higher courts in Illinois affirmed the judgment. Terminiello then brought his case to the Supreme Court on a writ of certiorari.

The majority opinion is a good example of the kind that can be expected from Justice William O. Douglas in civil liberties cases. He usually sides with the claimed rights of an individual as against the claims of the government. Justice Douglas was appointed to the Court by President Franklin D. Roosevelt after a spectacular rags-to-riches success story as a law school professor and vigorous governmental administrator. As a Supreme Court justice he is best known as a staunch defender of individual freedoms. Justice Robert H. Jackson was also deeply committed to the enlargement of American freedoms. But, as his dissenting opinion shows, he was often as deeply concerned with the problems of maintaining a stable society.

MR. JUSTICE DOUGLAS delivered the opinion of the Court.

The trial court charged that "breach of the peace" consists of any "misbehavior which violates the public peace and decorum"; and that the "misbehavior may constitute a breach of the peace if it stirs the public to anger, invites dispute, brings about a condition of unrest, or creates a disturbance, or if it molests the inhabitants in the enjoyment of peace and quiet by arousing alarm." Petitioner did not take exception to that instruction. But he maintained at all times that the ordinance as applied to his conduct violated his right of free speech under the Federal Constitution. . . .

As we have noted, the statutory words "breach of the peace" were defined in instructions to the jury to include speech which "stirs the public to anger, invites dispute, brings about a condition of unrest, or creates a disturbance. . . ." That construction of the ordinance is a ruling on a question of state law that is as binding on us as though the precise words had been written into the ordinance. . . .

The vitality of civil and political institutions in our society depends on free discussion. . . . [I]t is only through free debate and free exchange of ideas that government remains responsive to the will of the people and peaceful change is effected. The right to speak freely and to promote diversity of ideas and programs is therefore one of the chief distinctions that sets us apart from totalitarian regimes.

Accordingly a function of free speech under our system of government is to invite dispute. It may indeed best serve its high purpose when it induces a condition of unrest, creates dissatisfaction with conditions as they are, or even stirs people to anger. Speech is often provocative and challenging. It may strike at prejudices and preconceptions and have profound unsettling effects as it presses for acceptance of an idea. That is why freedom of speech, though not absolute, . . . is nevertheless protected against censorship or punishment, unless shown likely to produce a clear and present danger of a serious substantive evil that rises far above public inconvenience, annoyance, or unrest. . . . There is no room under our Constitution for a more restrictive view. For the alternative would lead to standardization of ideas either by legislatures, courts, or dominant political or community groups.

The ordinance as construed by the trial court seriously invaded this province. It permitted conviction of petitioner if his speech stirred people to anger, invited public dispute, or brought about a condition of unrest. A conviction resting on any of those grounds may not stand. . . .

Reversed.

MR. JUSTICE JACKSON, dissenting:

. . . [T]he local court that tried Terminiello . . . was dealing with a riot and with a speech that provoked a hostile mob and incited a friendly one, and threatened violence between the two. When the trial judge instructed the jury that it might find Terminiello guilty of inducing a breach of the peace if his behavior stirred the public to anger, invited dispute, brought about unrest, created a disturbance or molested peace and quiet by arousing alarm, he was not speaking of these as harmless or abstract conditions. He was addressing his words to the concrete behavior and specific consequences disclosed by the evidence. He was saying to the jury, in effect, that if this particular speech added fuel to the situation already so inflamed as to threaten to get beyond police control, it could be punished as inducing a breach of peace. . . .

Terminiello's own testimony shows the conditions under which he spoke. . . .

. . . We got there (the meeting place) approximately fifteen or twenty minutes past eight. The car stopped at the front entrance. There was a crowd of three or four hundred congregated there shouting and cursing and picketing. . . .

When we got there the pickets were not marching; they were body to body and covered the sidewalk completely, some on the steps so that we had to form a flying wedge to get through. Police escorted us to the building, and I noticed four or five others there.

They called us "God damned Fascists, Nazis, out to hang the so-and-sos." When I entered the building I heard the howls of the people outside. . . . There were four or five plain-clothes officers standing at the entrance to the stage and three or four at the entrance to the back door.

The officers threatened that if they broke the door again they would arrest them, and every time they opened the door a little to look out something was thrown at the officers, including ice-picks and rocks.

A number of times the door was broken, was partly broken through. There were doors open this way and they partly opened and the officers looked out two or three times and each time ice-picks, stones, and bottles were thrown at the police at the door. I took my place on the stage, before this I was about ten or fifteen minutes in the body of the hall.

I saw a number of windows broken by stones or missiles. I saw the back door being forced open, pushed open.

The front door was broken partly open after the doors were closed. There were about seven people seated on the stage. Smith opened the meeting with prayer, the Pledge of Allegiance to the Flag, and singing of America. There were other speakers who spoke before me and before I spoke I heard things happening in the hall and coming from the outside.

I saw rocks being thrown through windows and that continued throughout at least the first half of the meeting, probably longer, and again attempts were made to force the front door, rather the front door was forced partly. The howling continued on the outside, cursing could be heard audibly in the hall at times. Police were rushing in and out of the front door protecting the front door, and there was a general commotion, all kinds of noises and violence—all from the outside.

Between the time the first speaker spoke and I spoke, stones and bricks were thrown in all the time. I started to speak about 35 or 40 minutes after the meeting started, a little later than nine o'clock. . . .

The court below, in addition to this recital, heard other evidence, that the crowd reached an estimated number of 1,500. Picket lines obstructed and interfered with access to the building. The crowd constituted "a surging, howling mob hurling epithets" at those who would enter and "tried to tear their clothes off." One young woman's coat was torn off and she had to be assisted into the meeting by policemen. Those inside the hall could hear the loud noises and hear those on the outside yell, "Fascists," "Hitlers," and curse words like "damn Fascists." Bricks were thrown through the windowpanes before and during the speaking. About twenty-eight windows were broken. The street was black with people on both sides for at least a block either way; bottles, stink bombs, and brickbats were thrown. Police were unable to control the mob, which kept breaking the windows at the meeting hall, drowning out the speaker's voice at times and breaking in through the back door of the auditorium. About seventeen of the group outside were arrested by the police.

Knowing of this environment, Terminiello made a long speech. . . .

. . . Evidence showed that it stirred the audience not only to cheer and applaud but to expressions of immediate anger, unrest, and alarm. [The stenographic record of the speech, portions of which were quoted by Justice Jackson, was extremely provocative. Terminiello bitterly attacked the Jewish people and others, using abusive language.] . . .

Terminiello, of course, disclaims being a Fascist. Doubtless many of the indoor audience were not consciously such. His speech, however, followed, with fidelity that is more than coincidental, the pattern of European fascist leaders. . . .

I am unable to see that the local authorities have transgressed the Federal Constitution. Illinois imposed no prior censorship or suppression upon Terminiello. On the contrary, its sufferance and protection was all that enabled him to speak. It does not appear that the motive in punishing him is to silence the ideology he expressed as offensive to the State's policy or as untrue, or has any purpose of controlling his thought or its peaceful communication to others. There is no claim that the proceedings against Terminiello are designed to discriminate against him or the faction he represents or the ideas that he bespeaks. There is no indication that the charge against him is a mere pretext to give the semblance of legality to a covert effort to silence him or to prevent his followers or the public from hearing any truth that is in him.

A trial court and jury has found only that in the context of violence and disorder in which it was made, this speech was a provocation to immediate breach of the peace and therefore cannot claim constitutional immunity from punishment. Under the Constitution as it has been understood and applied, at least until most recently, the State was within its powers in taking this action.

Rioting is a substantive evil, which I take it no one will deny that the State and the City have the right and the duty to prevent and punish. Where an offense is induced by speech, the Court has laid down and often reiterated a test of the power of the authorities to deal with the speaking as also an offense. "The question in every case is whether the words *used are used in such circumstances* and are of *such a nature as* to create a *clear and present danger* that they will bring about the substantive evils that Congress (or the State or City) has a right to prevent." . . . No one ventures to contend that the State on the basis of this test, for whatever it may be worth, was not justified in punishing Terminiello. In this case the evidence proves beyond dispute that danger of rioting and violence in response to the speech was clear, present, and immediate. If this Court has not silently abandoned this long-standing test and substituted for the purposes of this case an unexpressed but more stringent test, the action of the State would have to be sustained. . . .

. . . [I]f we maintain a general policy of free speaking, we must recognize that its inevitable consequence will be sporadic local outbreaks of violence, for it is the nature of men to be intolerant of attacks upon institutions, personalities, and ideas for which they really care. In the long run, maintenance of free speech will be more endangered if the population can have no protection from the abuses which lead to violence. No liberty is made more secure by holding that its abuses are inseparable from its enjoyment. . . .

This Court has gone far toward accepting the doctrine that civil liberty means the removal of all restraints from these crowds and that all local attempts to maintain order are impairments of the liberty of the citizen. The choice is not between order and liberty. It is between liberty with order and anarchy without either. There is danger that, if the Court does not temper its doctrinaire logic with a little practical wisdom, it will convert the constitutional Bill of Rights into a suicide pact.

I would affirm the conviction.

MR. JUSTICE BURTON joins in this opinion.

[Separate dissenting opinions were also written by CHIEF JUSTICE VINSON and JUSTICE FRANKFURTER who was joined by JUSTICE JACKSON and JUSTICE BURTON.]

Feiner v. New York
340 U.S. 315 (1951)

Irving Feiner, an articulate young Syracuse University student, addressed a crowd on a street corner in Syracuse, New York, several blocks from the campus. Standing on a large wooden box on the sidewalk and speaking over a loud-speaker, Feiner, in a loud, high-pitched voice, urged his audience of some seventy-five to eighty whites and Negroes to attend a meeting that evening on racial discrimination and civil rights. In the course of his speech Feiner called the then President Harry S. Truman a "bum" and referred to the Mayor of Syracuse as a "champagne sipping bum." He remarked that the "American Legion is a Nazi Gestapo," and that the colored people should "rise up in arms" and fight for their rights. After about twenty minutes of listening to Feiner, the crowd became somewhat restless and there was some shoving, pushing, and milling around. There were two policemen at the scene, but they seemed more concerned with the movement of traffic and the fact that pedestrians were forced to walk in the road around the crowd than in Feiner's speech. But the crowd became more restless. "Angry mutterings" were heard, and a man in the audience accompanied by his wife and two small children told the policemen to get Feiner off the wooden box or he would pull him off himself. Thereupon one of the officers asked Feiner to get down off the box so that the crowd could be dispersed but Feiner refused. After he refused a second and third time to step down and stop speaking, the officer arrested him for disorderly conduct.

Feiner was convicted in the local trial court and sentenced to thirty days imprisonment. After the conviction was sustained by a county court and the highest state court, Feiner brought his case to the Supreme Court on a writ of certiorari.

As indicated in the opinion below, Chief Justice Fred M. Vinson was generally more likely to support the government against the claimed rights of an individual. He did write several landmark opinions in the course of equal rights for Negroes which paved the way for the famous school desegregation case of *Brown v. Board of Education* discussed in Chapter 3. Vinson was named Chief Justice by President Truman after serving as a Democratic Congressman from Kentucky, federal court of appeals judge, World War II Administrator and Secretary of the Treasury.

MR. CHIEF JUSTICE VINSON delivered the opinion of the Court.

. . . We are not faced here with blind condonation by a state court of arbitrary police action. Petitioner was accorded a full, fair trial. The trial judge heard testimony supporting and contradicting the judgment of the police officers that a clear danger of disorder was threatened. After weighing this contradictory evidence, the trial judge reached the conclusion that the police officers were justified in taking action to prevent a breach of the peace. The exercise of the police officers' proper discretionary power to prevent a breach of the peace was thus approved by the trial court and later by two courts on review. The courts below recognized petitioner's right to hold a street meeting at this locality, to make use of loud-speaking equipment in giving his speech, and to make derogatory remarks concerning public officials and the American Legion. They found that the officers in making the arrest were motivated solely by a proper concern for the preservation of order and protection of the general welfare and that there was no evidence which could lend color to a claim that the acts of the police were a cover for suppression of petitioner's views and opinions. Petitioner was thus neither arrested nor convicted for the making or the content of his speech. Rather it was the reaction which it actually engendered.

The language of *Cantwell v. Connecticut*, 310 U.S. 296 . . . is appropriate here. "The offense known as breach of the peace embraces a great variety of conduct destroying or menacing public order and tranquility. It includes not only violent acts and words likely to produce violence in others. No one would have the hardihood to suggest that the principle of freedom of speech sanctions incitement to riot or that religious liberty connotes the privilege to exhort others to physical attack upon those belonging to another sect. When clear and present danger of riot, disorder, interference with traffic upon the public streets, or other immediate threat to public safety, peace, or order, appears the power of the State to prevent or punish is obvious." . . . The findings of the New York courts as to the condition of the crowd and the refusal of petitioner to obey the police requests, supported as they are by the record of this case, are persuasive that the conviction of petitioner for violation of public peace, order and authority does not exceed the bounds of proper state police action. This Court respects, as it must, the interest of the community in maintaining peace and order on its streets. . . . We cannot say that the preservation of that interest here encroaches on the constitutional rights of this peti-tioner.

We are well aware that the ordinary murmurings and objections of a hostile audience cannot be allowed to silence a speaker, and are also mindful of the possible danger of giving overzealous police officials com-plete discretion to break up otherwise lawful public meetings. "A State may not unduly suppress free communication of views, religious or other, under the guise of conserving desirable conditions." . . . But we are not faced here with such a situation. It is one thing to say that the police cannot be used as an instrument for the oppression of unpopular views, and another to say that, when as here the speaker passes the bounds of argument or persuasion and, undertakes incitement to riot, they are power-less to prevent a breach of the peace. Nor in this case can we condemn the considered judgment of three New York courts approving the means which the police, faced with a crisis, used in the exercise of their power and duty to preserve peace and order. The findings of the state courts as to the existing situation and the imminence of greater disorder coupled with petitioner's deliberate defiance of the police officers convince us that we should not reverse this conviction in the name of free speech.

Affirmed.

MR. JUSTICE BLACK, dissenting.

. . . I think this conviction makes a mockery of the free speech guaran-tees of the First and Fourteenth Amendments. The end result of the affirmance here is to approve a simple and readily available technique by which cities and states can with impunity subject all speeches, political or otherwise, on streets or elsewhere, to the supervision and censorship of the local police. . . .

The Court's opinion apparently rests on this reasoning: The policeman, under the circumstances detailed, could reasonably conclude that serious fighting or even riot was imminent; therefore he could stop petitioner's speech to prevent a breach of peace; accordingly, it was "disorderly con-duct" for petitioner to continue speaking in disobedience of the officer's request. As to the existence of a dangerous situation on the street corner, it seems far-fetched to suggest that the "facts" show any imminent threat of riot or uncontrollable disorder. It is neither unusual nor unexpected that some people at public street meetings mutter, mill about, push, shove, or disagree, even violently, with the speaker. Indeed, it is rare where contro-versial topics are discussed that an outdoor crowd does not do some or all of these things. Nor does one isolated threat to assault the speaker forbode disorder. Especially should the danger be discounted where, as here, the person threatening was a man whose wife and two small children accompanied him and who, so far as the record shows, was never close enough to petitioner to carry out the threat.

Moreover, assuming that the "facts" did indicate a critical situation, I reject the implication of the Court's opinion that the police had no obligation to protect petitioner's constitutional right to talk. The police of course have power to prevent breaches of the peace. But if, in the name of preserving order, they ever can interfere with a lawful public speaker, they first must make all reasonable efforts to protect him. Here the policeman did not even pretend to try to protect petitioner. According to the officers' testimony, the crowd was restless but there is no showing of any attempt to quiet it, pedestrians were forced to walk into the street, but there was no effort to clear a path on the sidewalk; one person threatened to assault petitioner but the officers did nothing to discourage this when even a word might have sufficed. Their duty was to protect petitioner's right to talk, even to the extent of arresting the man who threatened to interfere. Instead, they shirked that duty and acted only to suppress the right to speak. . . .

I would reverse the conviction, thereby adhering to the great principles of the First and Fourteenth Amendments.

[JUSTICE DOUGLAS, joined by JUSTICE MINTON, also wrote a separate dissenting opinion.]

Aftermath

On February 17, 1951, almost two years after his conviction in the trial court, Feiner began serving his thirty day prison term. He was not allowed to return to the university and when last heard from he was working as a writer for several left wing publications.

It is difficult to reconcile the Court's position in this case with the Terminiello holding since Feiner's remarks seemed to stir up much less excitement and disorder than that evoked by Terminiello's provocative speech. Yet there are some important differences in the two cases. Terminiello was speaking in a hall to an audience which was there voluntarily to hear him while Feiner, through the use of his loudspeaker, could reach passers-by in the street who had little, if any, interest in what he was saying. Terminiello was convicted in the trial court of breach of the peace because of the alleged condition of disorder brought about by his speech while Feiner was charged with disorderly conduct. Nevertheless, it seems clear that the Chicago police tried much harder to protect Terminiello's right to speak than did the two Syracuse policemen in the *Feiner* case. As one writer has well noted, it is difficult to justify the majority opinion in the *Feiner* case "unless 'the interest of the community in maintaining peace and order on its streets' wipes out the interest of the community in maintaining freedom of speech. If the 'threat' of one member of an audience can effectively silence a speaker, then there is no such thing as free speech." But at the same time, Justice Douglas' majority opinion in the *Terminiello* case seemed to seriously restrict the power of the community to maintain public order.

Edwards v. South Carolina
372 U.S. 229 (1963)

As young American Negroes took to the streets in the 1960's in protest against discrimination in a number of states, the clashing claims of freedom of expression and public order were presented to the Supreme Court in a new and different context. These cases forced the Court to rethink the Terminiello and Feiner decisions.

One such typical case originated in Columbia, South Carolina, when Edwards and eighty-six other Negro students met late one morning in March, 1961, at the Zion Baptist Church. At about noon they left the church and walked in separate groups of about fifteen strong to the South Carolina State House grounds—an area encompassing two city blocks which had long been open to the public. Their purpose was to submit a protest to the people of South Carolina and to the state legislature against continued racial discrimination and to ask that discriminating state laws be repealed. The police had received advance notice of the demonstration; and, when the students reached the State House grounds, thirty or more policemen were on hand. As the students entered the grounds each group was told by the police that they had a right to be there "as long as they were peaceful." For the next thirty to forty-five minutes the students remained in their respective groups and walked in an orderly fashion displaying placards bearing slogans such as "I am proud to be a Negro," "Down with Segregation," and "You may jail our bodies but not our souls." Some of them were singing as they walked.

A crowd of some two hundred to three hundred onlookers soon gathered in the area and the adjacent sidewalks to see what was going on, but no threatening remarks or hostile gestures of any kind were made. Neither was pedestrian or vehicular traffic obstructed on the state grounds. But the police officers, fearing violence because some "possible troublemakers" were recognized in the crowd of on-lookers, told the students they would have to disperse in fifteen minutes or be arrested. Instead of leaving, the students listened to a religious talk by one of their leaders, sang "The Star Spangled Banner" and other patriotic and religious songs, and stamped their feet or clapped their hands. After fifteen minutes the police arrested all eighty-seven students and marched them off to jail.

All of the students were convicted of breach of the peace and sentences were imposed ranging from a $10.00 fine or five days in jail to a $100 fine or thirty days in jail. After the convictions were affirmed by the highest state court, Edwards brought the case to the Supreme Court on a writ of certiorari. Justice Potter Stewart's lucid opinion demonstrates well why he has gained a reputation for clear, concise writing. Though Justice Stewart, like many other justices, does not like to be labeled, he has voted rather consistently (but with some notable exceptions) with the "judicial self-restraint" bloc on the Court. When appointed by President Eisenhower, Justice Stewart was one of the youngest men (forty-three) ever named to the Court. An Ohio Republican who earned his law degree at Yale, he served on the Cincinnati City Council, was active in Republican circles and served as a federal court of appeals judge before his elevation to the Supreme Court.

MR. JUSTICE STEWART delivered the opinion of the Court.

. . . It is clear to us that in arresting, convicting, and punishing the petitioners under the circumstances disclosed by this record, South Carolina infringed the petitioners' constitutionally protected rights of free speech, free assembly, and freedom to petition for redress of their grievances.

It has long been established that these First Amendment freedoms are protected by the Fourteenth Amendment from invasion by the States. . . . The circumstances in this case reflect an exercise of these basic constitutional rights in their most pristine and classic form. The petitioners felt aggrieved by laws of South Carolina which allegedly "prohibited Negro privileges in this State." They peaceably assembled at the site of the State Government and there peaceably expressed their grievances "to the citizens of South Carolina, along with the Legislative Bodies of South

Carolina." Not until they were told by police officials that they must disperse on pain of arrest did they do more. Even then, they but sang patriotic and religious songs after one of their leaders had delivered a "religious harangue." There was no violence or threat of violence on their part, or on the part of any member of the crowd watching them. Police protection was "ample."

This, therefore, was a far cry from the situation in *Feiner v. New York*, . . . where two policemen were faced with a crowd which was "pushing, shoving, and milling around," . . . where at least one member of the crowd "threatened violence if the police did not act," . . . where "the crowd was pressing closer around petitioner and the officer," . . . and where "the speaker passes the bounds of argument or persuasion and undertakes incitement to riot." . . . And the record is barren of any evidence of "fighting words." . . .

We do not review in this case criminal convictions resulting from the even-handed application of a precise and narrowly drawn regulatory statute evincing a legislative judgment that certain specific conduct be limited or proscribed. If, for example, the petitioners had been convicted upon evidence that they had violated a law regulating traffic, or had disobeyed a law reasonably limiting the periods during which the State House grounds were open to the public, this would be a different case. . . . These petitioners were convicted of an offense so generalized as to be, in the words of the South Carolina Supreme Court, "not susceptible of exact definition." And they were convicted upon evidence which showed no more than that the opinions which they were peaceably expressing were sufficiently opposed to the views of the majority of the community to attract a crowd and necessitate police protection.

The Fourteenth Amendment does not permit a State to make criminal the peaceful expression of unpopular views. "[A] function of free speech under our system of government is to invite dispute. It may indeed best serve its high purpose when it induces a condition of unrest, creates dissatisfaction with conditions as they are, or even stirs people to anger. Speech is often provocative and challenging. It may strike at prejudices and preconceptions and have profound unsettling effects as it presses for acceptance of an idea. That is why freedom of speech . . . is . . . protected against censorship or punishment, unless shown likely to produce a clear and present danger of a serious substantive evil that rises far above public inconvenience, annoyance, or unrest. . . . There is no room under our Constitution for a more restrictive view. For the alternative would lead to standardization of ideas either by legislatures, courts, or dominant political or community groups." *Terminiello v. Chicago*. . . . As in the Terminiello Case, the courts of South Carolina have defined a criminal offense so as to permit conviction of the petitioners if their speech "stirred people to anger, invited public dispute, or brought about a condition of unrest. A conviction resting on any of those grounds may not stand." . . .

As Chief Justice Hughes wrote in *Stromberg v. California*, "The maintenance of the opportunity for free political discussion to the end that government may be responsive to the will of the people and that changes may be obtained by lawful means, an opportunity essential to the security of the Republic, is a fundamental principle of our constitutional system. A statute which upon its face and as authoritatively construed is so vague and indefinite as to permit the punishment of the fair use of this opportunity is repugnant to the guaranty of liberty contained in the Fourteenth Amendment. . . ."

For these reasons we conclude that these criminal convictions cannot stand.

Reversed.

[JUSTICE CLARK wrote a dissenting opinion.]

AFTERMATH

In several cases after the *Edwards* decision the Court continued to reverse convictions of demonstrators gathering peacefully to protest racial discrimination. The first setback did not come until 1966 when in a close five to four decision *Adderley v. Florida*, 385 U.S. 39 (1967), the Court upheld the trespass convictions of 32 young Negroes who demonstrated against segregation by gathering peacefully in front of the local, segregated jail where other demonstrators had previously been placed after being arrested for protesting against segregation in theatres. Foreshadowed by his surprising opinions in several recent cases, Justice Black's majority opinion sought to distinguish the *Edwards* case on the grounds that: 1) the Adderley defendants demonstrated on jail grounds, property under control of the State, rather than on the public streets; 2) the charge in Adderley was trespass rather than breach of the peace. It is not certain that these distinctions will stand the test of time.

Nevertheless, generalizations in all such cases are extremely dangerous for in addition to the justice's own interpretation of the factual situation of a particular case, time and place and circumstances are also important factors influencing the Court's decisions. The difficulties are revealed well by the Court's references in Edwards to the *Feiner* case. In his majority opinion Justice Stewart, as indicated above, tried to distinguish the *Edwards* case by claiming that the Feiner situation was much more likely to erupt into violence. But Justice Clark pointed out aptly in his lone Edwards dissenting opinion that in the *Feiner* case the Court "upheld a conviction for breach of the peace in a situation no more dangerous than found here. There the demonstration was conducted by only one person and the crowd was limited to approximately 80, as compared with the present lineup of some two hundred demonstrators and three hundred onlookers. There the petitioner was 'endeavoring to arouse the Negro people against the whites, urging that they rise up in arms and fight for equal rights.' . . . Only one person—in a city having an entirely different historical background—was exhorting adults. Here two hundred youthful Negro demonstrators were being aroused to a fever pitch before a crowd of some three hundred people who undoubtedly were hostile. . . . It is my belief that anyone conversant with the almost spontaneous combustion in some Southern communities in such a situation will agree that [the arrests] may well have averted a major catastrophe."

Jacobellis v. Ohio
378 U.S. 184 (1964)

Since deciding its first obscenity case in 1957, the Supreme Court has been plagued with controversial cases calling for the clarification of the issue of free expression versus obscenity. "It is an issue that not only taxes human ingenuity but teases human patience. So sensitive and complicated is the problem that a simple solution, however extreme, becomes a delicious alternative, even to many otherwise judicious people. Should there be any censorship of obscenity? If so, where should it start? And stop?" That there are no easy answers to these questions is revealed clearly by the varied and sometimes bitter opinions in this and the next case. In reading these opinions it is well to remember, in the words of Irving Brant, a distinguished commentator on American liberties, that "in obscenity cases juries often agree, witnesses never do and judges almost never. The reasons are not far to seek. First, obscenity is a matter of taste and social custom, not of fact. Secondly, the restraint of obscenity inevitably infringes upon freedom of speech and of the press."

Nico Jacobellis, manager of a motion picture theater in Cleveland Heights, Ohio, was convicted in a state court of violating the Ohio obscenity statute for possessing and showing a French film entitled *The Lovers*. Jacobellis was fined $2,500 and ordered to jail if the fines were not paid. His conviction was sustained by an intermediate state court and by the Ohio Supreme Court. Jacobellis then brought his case to the Supreme Court on appeal.

The Lovers tells the story of an ill-matched and unhappy marriage —the husband happy and content in his work, family and home in the country; the wife bored with husband and home and aching for new adventures. On her return home from a trip the wife meets a young archaeologist with whom she falls suddenly in love. She abandons her husband and child to go off into a new life with the archaeologist. The most controversial part of the film was in the last reel where some explicit but fragmentary and fleeting love scenes involving the wife and newly found lover are depicted.

The Lovers had previously been shown in about one hundred cities in the United States including Columbus and Toledo, Ohio. It had been admitted by the Customs Bureau after an express ruling that the film was not obscene. Favorably reviewed by film critics in a number of national publications, *The Lovers* was rated by two critics as one of the best films of the year it was produced.

MR. JUSTICE BRENNAN announced the judgment of the Court and delivered an opinion in which MR. JUSTICE GOLDBERG joins. . . .

Motion pictures are within the ambit of the constitutional guarantees of freedom of speech and of the press. *Joseph Burstyn, Inc., v. Wilson,* 343 U.S. 495. But in *Roth v. United States* and *Alberts v. California,* 354 U.S. 476, we upheld that obscenity is not subject to those guarantees. Application of an obscenity law to suppress a motion picture thus requires ascertainment of the "dim and uncertain line" that often separates obscenity from constitutionally protected expression. . . .

[W]e reaffirm the principle that, in "obscenity" cases as in all others involving rights derived from the First Amendment guarantees of free expression, this Court cannot avoid making an independent constitutional judgment on the facts of the case as to whether the material involved is constitutionally protected.

The question of the proper standard for making this determination has been the subject of much discussion and controversy since our decision in *Roth-Alberts* seven years ago. Recognizing that the test for obscenity enunciated there—"whether to the average person, applying contemporary community standards, the dominant theme of the material taken as a whole appeals to prurient interest," . . . —is not perfect, we think any substitute would raise equally difficult problems, and we therefore adhere to that standard. . . .

It has been suggested that the "contemporary community standards" aspects of the *Roth* test implies a determination of the constitutional question of obscenity in each case by the standards of the particular local community from which the case arises. This is an incorrect reading of *Roth.* . . .

We do not see how any "local" definition of the "community" could properly be employed in delineating the area of expression that is protected by the Federal Constitution. MR. JUSTICE HARLAN pointed out in *Manual Enterprises, Inc., v. Day* . . . that a standard based on a particular local community would have "the intolerable consequence of denying some sections of the country access to material, there deemed acceptable, which in others might be considered offensive to prevailing community standards of decency. . . . Furthermore, to sustain the suppression of a particular book or film in one locality would deter its dissemination in other localities where it might be held not obscene, since sellers and exhibitors would be reluctant to risk criminal conviction in testing the variation between the two places. It would be a hardy person who would sell a book or exhibit a film anywhere in the land after this Court had sustained the judgment of one "community" holding it to be outside the constitutional protection. The result would thus be "to restrict the public's access to forms of the printed word which the State could not constitutionally suppress directly." . . .

It is true that local communities throughout the land are in fact diverse, and that in cases such as this one the Court is confronted with the task of reconciling the rights of such communities with the rights of individuals. Communities vary, however, in many respects other than their toleration of alleged obscenity, and such variances have never been considered to require or justify a varying standard for application of the Federal Constitution. The Court has regularly been compelled, in reviewing criminal convictions challenged under the Due Process Clause of the Fourteenth Amendment, to reconcile the conflicting rights of the local community which brought the prosecution and of the individual defendant. Such a task is admittedly difficult and delicate, but it is inherent in the Court's duty of determining whether a particular conviction worked a deprivation of rights guaranteed by the Federal Constitution. The Court has not shrunk from discharging that duty in other areas, and we see no reason why it should do so here. The Court has explicitly refused to tolerate a result whereby "the constitutional limits of free expression in the Nation would vary with state lines," . . . we see even less justification for allowing such limits to vary with town or county lines. We thus reaffirm the position taken in *Roth* to the effect that the constitutional status of an allegedly obscene work must be determined on the basis of a national standard. It is, after all, a national Constitution we are expounding.

We recognize the legitimate and indeed exigent interest of States and localities throughout the Nation in preventing the dissemination of material deemed harmful to children. But that interest does not justify a total suppression of such material, the effect of which would be to "reduce the adult population . . . to reading only what is fit for children." . . . State and local authorities might well consider whether their objectives in this area would be better served by laws aimed specifically at preventing distribution of objectionable material to children, rather than at totally prohibiting its dissemination. Since the present conviction is based upon exhibition of the film to the public at large and not upon its exhibition to children, the judgment must be reviewed under the strict standard applicable in determining the scope of the expression that is protected by Constitution.

We have applied that standard to the motion picture in question. . . . We have viewed the film, in the light of the record made in the trial court, and we conclude that it is not obscene within the standards enunciated in *Alberts v. California* and *Roth v. United States*, which we reaffirm here.

Reversed.

[JUSTICES WHITE, BLACK (joined by JUSTICE DOUGLAS), STEWART, and GOLDBERG concurred in the judgment of the Court.]

The CHIEF JUSTICE, with whom MR. JUSTICE CLARK joins, dissenting.

In this and other cases in this area of the law, which are coming to us in ever-increasing numbers, we are faced with the resolution of rights basic both to individuals and to society as a whole. Specifically, we are called upon to reconcile the right of the Nation and of the States to maintain a decent society and, on the other hand, the right of individuals to express themselves freely in accordance with the guarantees of the First and Fourteenth Amendments. Although the Federal Government and virtually every State has had laws proscribing obscenity since the Union was formed, and although this Court has recently decided that obscenity is not within the protection of the First Amendment, neither courts nor legislatures have been able to evolve a truly satisfactory definition of obscenity. . . .

It is my belief that when the Court said in *Roth* that obscenity is to be defined by reference to "community standards," it meant community standards—not a national standard, as is sometimes argued. I believe that there is no provable "national standard," and perhaps there should be none. At all events, this Court has not been able to enunciate one, and it would be unreasonable to expect local courts to divine one. It is said that such a "community" approach may well result in material being proscribed as obscene in one community but not in another, and, in all probability, that is true. But communities throughout the Nation are in fact diverse, and it must be remembered that, in cases such as this one the Court is confronted with the task of reconciling conflicting rights of the diverse communities within our society and of individuals. . . .

In my opinion, the use to which various materials are put—not just the words and pictures themselves—must be considered in determining whether or not the materials are obscene. A technical or legal treatise on pornography may well be inoffensive under most circumstances but, at the same time, "obscene" in the extreme when sold or displayed to children.

Finally, material which is in fact obscene under the *Roth* test may be proscribed in a number of ways—for instance, by confiscation of the material or by prosecution of those who disseminate it—provided always that the proscription, whatever it may be, is imposed in accordance with constitutional standards. If the proceeding involved is criminal, there must be a right to a jury trial, a right to counsel, and all the other safeguards necessary to assure due process of law. If the proceeding is civil in nature the constitutional requirements applicable in such a case must also be observed. There has been some tendency in dealing with this area of the law for enforcement agencies to do only that which is easy to do—for instance, to seize and destroy books with only a minimum of protection. As a result, courts are often presented with procedurely bad cases and, in dealing with them, appear to be acquiescing in the dissemination of obscenity. But if cases were well prepared and were conducted with the appropriate concern for constitutional safeguards, courts would not hesitate to enforce the laws against obscenity. Thus, enforcement agencies must realize that there is no royal road to enforcement; hard and conscientious work is required. . . .

While in this case, I do not subscribe to some of the State's extravagant contentions, neither can I say that the courts below acted with intemperance or without sufficient evidence in finding the moving picture obscene within the meaning of the *Roth* test. Therefore, I would affirm the judgment.

[JUSTICE HARLAN also wrote a dissenting opinion.]

Ginzburg v. United States
383 U.S. 463 (1966)

On June 14, 1963, Ralph Ginzburg was convicted in a federal district court in Pennsylvania for sending through the mails three allegedly obscene publications in violation of the federal obscenity statute. The three publications were:

1. EROS, a hard-cover, quarterly magazine of glossy, expensive format "devoted to the subjects of love and sex" with articles and photo-essays on sexual relations. A particularly controversial feature of one issue was a color portfolio of a white woman and Negro man, both naked, in various embraces. *Eros* had been sold to some 150,000 subscribers at $25 a year.

2. *Liaison,* a bi-weekly newsletter described as "cupid's chronicle" and dedicated to "keeping sex an art and preventing it from becoming a service." The newsletter featured articles on sex which had previously appeared in professional journals and argued in favor of the broadest possible license in sexual relations.

3. *The Housewife's Handbook on Selective Promiscuity,* a woman's sexual autobiography which contained explicit descriptions of the author's sexual experiences from early childhood to age thirty-six. The two hundred page book left nothing to the imagination and was condemned by the trial judge as a perfect example of "hard-core pornography."

The federal district judge, who was sitting without a jury, sentenced Ginzburg, who also published an exposé magazine called *Fact,* to five years imprisonment and fined him $28,000. A court of appeals affirmed the convictions and the Supreme Court granted certiorari.

On the same day that the Ginzburg ruling was announced, the Court rendered opinions in two related cases decided together with Ginzburg. In *A Book Named "John Cleland's Memoirs of a Woman of Pleasure" v. Attorney General of Massachusetts,* 383 U.S. 413, the Court reversed, by a six to three vote, a Massachusetts ruling that the eighteenth-century novel, known as "Fanny Hill," was obscene. In *Mishkin v. New York*, 383 U.S. 502, again by a six to three vote, the Court affirmed the conviction of a bookseller for publishing some fifty books found to be "sadistic and masochistic" and therefore obscene under the state's criminal obscenity statute.

MR. JUSTICE BRENNAN delivered the opinion of the Court.

In the cases in which this Court has decided obscenity questions since *Roth [Roth v. United States]* it has regarded the materials as sufficient in themselves for the determination of the question. In the present case, however, the prosecution charged the offense in the context of the circumstances of production, sale, and publicity and assumed that, standing alone, the publications themselves might not be obscene. We agree that the question of obscenity may include consideration of the setting in which the publications were presented as an aid to determining the question of obscenity, and assume without deciding that the prosecution could not have succeeded otherwise. . . . [W]e view the publications against a background of commercial exploitation of erotica solely for the sake of their prurient appeal. The record in that regard amply supports the decision of the trial judge that the mailing of all three publications offended the statute. . . .

Besides testimony as to the merit of the material, there was abundant evidence to show that each of the accused publications was originated or sold as stock in trade of the sordid business of pandering—"the business of purveying textual or graphic matter openly advertised to appeal to the erotic interest of their customers." EROS early sought mailing privileges from the postmasters of Intercourse and Blue Ball, Pennsylvania. The trial court found the obvious, that these hamlets were chosen only for the value their names would have in furthering petitioners' efforts to sell their publications on the basis of salacious appeal; the facilities of the post offices were inadequate to handle the anticipated volume of mail, and the privileges were denied. Mailing privileges were then obtained from the postmaster of Middlesex, New Jersey. EROS and *Liaison* thereafter mailed several million circulars soliciting subscriptions from that post office; over 5,500 copies of the *Handbook* were mailed.

The "leer of the sensualist" also permeates the advertising for the three publications. The circulars sent for EROS and *Liaison* stressed the sexual candor of the respective publications, and openly boasted that the publishers would take full advantage of what they regarded as an unrestricted license allowed by law in the expression of sex and sexual matters. The advertising for the *Handbook,* apparently mailed from New York, consisted almost entirely of a reproduction of the introduction of the book, written by one Dr. Albert Ellis. Although he alludes to the book's informational value and its putative therapeutic usefulness, his remarks are preoccupied with the book's sexual imagery. The solicitation was indiscriminate, not limited to those, such as physicians or psychiatrists, who might independently discern the book's therapeutic worth. Inserted in each advertisement was a slip labeled "GUARANTEE" and reading, "Documentary Books, Inc. unconditionally guarantees full refund of the price of THE HOUSEWIFE'S HANDBOOK ON SELECTIVE PROMIS-CUITY if the book fails to reach you because of U. S. Post Office censorship interference." Similar slips appeared in the advertising for EROS and *Liaison;* they highlighted the gloss petitioners put on the publications, eliminating any doubt what the purchaser was being asked to buy.

This evidence, in our view, was relevant in determining the ultimate question of obscenity and, in the context of this record, serves to resolve all ambiguity and doubt. The deliberate representation of petitioners' publications as erotically arousing, for example, stimulated the reader to accept them as prurient; he looks for titillation, not for saving intellectual content. Similarly, such representation would tend to force public confrontation with the potentially offensive aspects of the work; the brazenness of such an appeal heightens the offensiveness of the publications to those who are offended by such material. And the circumstances of presentation and dissemination of material are equally relevant to determining whether social importance claimed for material in the courtroom was, in the circumstances, pretense or reality—whether it was the basis upon which it was traded in the marketplace or a spurious claim for litigation purposes. Where the purveyor's sole emphasis is on the sexually provocative aspects of his publications, that fact may be decisive in the determination of obscenity. Certainly in a prosecution which, as here, does not necessarily imply suppression of the materials involved, the fact that they originate or are used as a subject of pandering is relevant to the application of the *Roth* case. . . . EROS was created, represented and sold solely as a claimed instrument of the sexual stimulation it would bring. Like the other publications, its pervasive treatment of sex and sexual matters rendered it available to exploitation by those who would make a business of pandering to "the widespread weakness for titillation by pornography." Petitioners' own expert agreed, correctly we think, that "[i]f the object [of a work] is material gain for the creator through an appeal to the sexual curiosity and appetite," the work is pornographic. In other words, by animating sensual detail to give the publication a salacious cast, petitioners reinforced what is conceded by the Government to be an otherwise debatable conclusion.

A similar analysis applies to the judgment regarding the *Handbook.* The bulk of the proofs directed to social importance concerned this publication. Before selling publication rights to petitioners, its author had printed it privately; she sent circulars to persons whose names appeared on membership lists of medical and psychiatric associations, asserting its value as an adjunct in therapy. Over 12,000 sales resulted from this solicitation, and a number of witnesses testified that they found the work useful in their professional practice. The Government does not seriously contest the claim that the book has worth in such a controlled, or even neutral, environment. Petitioners, however, did not sell the book to such a limited audience, or focus their claims for it on its supposed therapeutic or educational value; rather, they deliberately emphasized the sexually provocative aspects of the work, in order to catch the salaciously disposed. They proclaimed its obscenity; and we cannot conclude that the court below erred in taking their own evaluation at its face value and declaring the book as a whole obscene despite the other evidence. . . .

We perceive no threat to First Amendment guarantees in thus holding that in close cases evidence of pandering may be probative with respect to the nature of the material in question and thus satisfy the *Roth* test. No weight is ascribed to the fact that petitioners have profited from the sale of publications which we have assumed but do not hold cannot themselves be adjudged obscene in the abstract; to sanction consideration of this fact might indeed induce self-censorship, and offend the frequently stated principle that commercial activity, in itself, is no justification for narrowing the protection of expression secured by the First Amendment. Rather, the fact that each of these publications was created or exploited entirely on the basis of its appeal to prurient interests strengthens the conclusion that the transactions here were sales of illicit merchandise, not sale of constitutionally protected matter. A conviction for mailing obscene publications, but explained in part by the presence of this element, does not necessarily suppress the materials in question, nor chill their proper distribution for a proper use. Nor should it inhibit the enterprise of others seeking through serious endeavor to advance human knowledge or understanding in science, literature, or art. All that will have been determined is that questionable publications are obscene in a context which brands them as obscene as that term is defined in *Roth*—a use inconsistent with any claim to the shelter of the First Amendment. . . .

Where an exploitation of interests in titillation by pornography is shown with respect to material lending itself to such exploitation through pervasive treatment or description of sexual matters, such evidence may support the determination that the material is obscene even though in other contexts the material would escape such condemnation. . . .

Affirmed.

MR. JUSTICE BLACK, dissenting.

Only one stark fact emerges with clarity out of the confusing welter of opinions and thousands of words written in this and two other cases today. That fact is that Ginzburg, petitioner here, is now finally and authoritatively condemned to serve five years in prison for distributing printed matter about sex which neither Ginzburg nor anyone else could possibly have known to be criminal. Since, as I have said many times, I believe the Federal Government is without any power whatever under the Constitution to put any type of burden on speech and expression of ideas of any kind (as distinguished from conduct), . . . and I would reverse Ginzburg's conviction on this ground alone. . . .

Criminal punishment by government, although universally recognized as a necessity in limited areas of conduct, is an exercise of one of government's most awesome and dangerous powers. Consequently, wise and good governments make all possible efforts to hedge this dangerous power by restricting it within easily identifiable boundaries. Experience, and wisdom flowing out of that experience, long ago led to the belief that agents of government should not be vested with power and discretion to define and punish as criminal past conduct which had not been clearly defined as a crime in advance. . . .

I agree with my Brother Harlan that the Court has in effect rewritten the federal obscenity statute and thereby imposed on Ginzburg standards and criteria that Congress never thought about, or if it did think about them certainly did not adopt them. Consequently, Ginzburg is, as I see it, having his conviction and sentence affirmed upon the basis of a statute amended by this Court for violation of which amended statute he was not charged in the courts below. Such an affirmance we have said violates due process. . . . Quite apart from this vice in the affirmance, I think that the criteria declared by a majority of the Court today as guidelines for a court or jury to determine whether Ginzburg or anyone else can be punished as a common criminal for publishing or circulating obscene material are so vague and meaningless that they practically leave the fate of a person charged with violating censorship statutes to the unbridled discretion, whim and caprice of the judge or jury which tries him. I shall separately discuss the three elements which a majority of the Court seems to consider material in proving obscenity.

(a) The first element considered necessary for determining obscenity is that the dominant theme of the material taken as a whole must appeal to the prurient interest in sex. It seems quite apparent to me that human beings, serving either as judges or jurors, could not be expected to give any sort of decision on this element which would even remotely promise any kind of uniformity in the enforcement of this law. What conclusion an individual, be he judge or juror, would reach about whether the material appeals to "prurient interest in sex" would depend largely in the long run not upon testimony of witnesses such as can be given in ordinary criminal cases where conduct is under scrutiny, but would depend to a large extent upon the judge's or juror's personality, habits, inclinations, attitudes and other individual characteristics. In one community or in one courthouse a matter would be condemned as obscene under this so-called criterion but in another community, maybe only a few miles away, or in another court-house in the same community, the material could be given a clean bill of health. In the final analysis the submission of such an issue as this to a judge or jury amounts to practically nothing more than a request for the judge or juror to assert his own personal beliefs about whether the matter should be allowed to be legally distributed. Upon this subjective deter-mination the law becomes certain for the first and last time.

(b) The second element for determining obscenity . . . is that the material must be "patently offensive because it affronts contemporary community standards relating to the description or representation of sexual matters. . . ." Nothing that I see in any position adopted by a majority of the Court today and nothing that has been said in previous opinions for the Court leaves me with any kind of certainty as to whether the "community standards" referred to are world-wide, nation-wide, section-wide, state-wide, country-wide, precinct-wide or township-wide. But even if some definite areas were mentioned, who is capable of assess-ing "community standards" on such a subject? Could one expect the same application of standards by jurors in Mississippi as in New York City, in Vermont as in California? So here again the guilt or innocence of a de-fendant charged with obscenity must depend in the final analysis upon the personal judgment and attitudes of particular individuals and the place where the trial is held. And one must remember that the Federal Government has the power to try a man for mailing obscene matter in a court 3,000 miles from his home.

(c) A third element which three of my Brethren think is required to establish obscenity is that the material must be "utterly without redeem-ing social value." This element seems to me to be as uncertain, if not even more uncertain, than is the unknown substance of the Milky Way. If we are to have a free society as contemplated by the Bill of Rights, then I can find little defense for leaving the liberty of American individuals sub-ject to the judgment of a judge or jury as to whether material that pro-vokes thought or stimulates desire is "utterly without redeeming social value. . . ." Whether a particular treatment of a particular subject is with or without social value in this evolving, dynamic society of ours is a question upon which no uniform agreement could possibly be reached among politicians, statesmen, professors, philosophers, scientists, religious groups or any other type of group. A case-by-case assessment of social values by individual judges and jurors is, I think, a dangerous technique for government to utilize in determining whether a man stays in or out of the penitentiary.

My conclusion is that certainly after the fourteen separate opinions handed down in these three cases today no person, not even the most learned judge much less a layman, is capable of knowing in advance of an ultimate decision in his particular case by this Court whether certain material comes within the area of "obscenity" as that term is confused by the Court today. . . . I think the First Amendment forbids any kind or type or nature of governmental censorship over views as distinguished from conduct. . . .

It is obvious that the effect of the Court's decisions in the three obscenity cases handed down today is to make it exceedingly dangerous for people to discuss either orally or in writing anything about sex. Sex is a fact of life. Its pervasive influence is felt throughout the world and it cannot be ignored. Like all other facts of life it can lead to difficulty and trouble and sorrow and pain. But while it may lead to abuses, and has in many instances, no words need be spoken in order for people to know that the subject is one pleasantly interwoven in all human activities and involves the very substance of the creation of life itself. It is a subject which people are bound to consider and discuss whatever laws are passed by any government to try to suppress it. Though I do not suggest any way to solve the problems that may arise from sex or discussions about sex, of one thing I am confident, and that is that federal censorship is not the answer to these problems. I find it difficult to see how talk about sex can be placed under the kind of censorship the Court here approves without subjecting our society to more dangers than we can anticipate at the moment. It was to avoid exactly such dangers that the First Amendment was written and adopted. For myself I would follow the course which I believe is required by the First Amendment, that is, recognize that sex at least as any other aspect of life is so much a part of our society that its discussion should not be made a crime. . . .

MR. JUSTICE STEWART, dissenting.

Ralph Ginzburg has been sentenced to five years in prison for sending through the mail copies of a magazine, a pamphlet, and a book. There was testimony at his trial that these publications possess artistic and social merit. Personally, I have a hard time discerning any. Most of the material strikes me as both vulgar and unedifying. But if the First Amendment means anything, it means that a man cannot be sent to prison merely for distributing publications which offend a judge's esthetic sensibilities, mine or any other's.

Censorship reflects a society's lack of confidence in itself. It is a hallmark of an authoritarian regime. Long ago those who wrote our First Amendment charted a different course. They believed a society can be truly strong only when it is truly free. In the realm of expression they put their faith, for better or for worse, in the enlightened choice of the people, free from the interference of a policeman's intrusive thumb or a judge's heavy hand. So it is that the Constitution protects coarse expression as well as refined, and vulgarity no less than elegance. A book worthless to me may convey something of value to my neighbor. In the free society to which our Constitution has committed us, it is for each to choose for himself. . . .

The Court today appears to concede that the materials Ginzburg mailed were themselves protected by the First Amendment. But, the Court says, Ginzburg can still be sentenced to five years in prison for mailing them. Why? Because, says the Court, he was guilty of "commercial exploitation," of "pandering," and of "titillation." But Ginzburg was not charged with "commercial exploitation"; he was not charged with "pandering"; he was not charged with "titillation." Therefore to affirm his conviction now on any of those grounds, even if otherwise valid, is to deny him due process of law. . . . But those grounds are *not,* of course, otherwise valid. Neither the statute under which Ginzburg was convicted nor any other federal statute I know of makes "commercial exploitation" or "pandering" or "titillation" a criminal offense. And any criminal law that sought to do so in the terms so elusively defined by the Court would, of course, be unconstitutionally vague and therefore void. . . .

There is another aspect of the Court's opinion in this case that is even more regrettable. Today the Court assumes the power to deny Ralph Ginzburg the protection of the First Amendment because it disapproves of his "sordid business." That is a power the Court does not possess. For the First Amendment protects us all with an even hand. It applies to Ralph Ginzburg with no less completeness and force than to G. P. Putnam's Sons [publishers of Fanny Hill]. In upholding and enforcing the Bill of Rights, this Court has not power to pick or to choose. When we lose sight of that fixed star of constitutional adjudication, we lose our way. For then we forsake a government of law and are left with government by Big Brother.

[Separate dissenting opinions were also written by JUSTICES DOUGLAS and HARLAN.]

AFTERMATH

After the Supreme Court decision Ginzburg requested that the district court reduce the five-year prison term. This request was denied but more than a year after the Supreme Court's decision Ginzburg was still a free man because his lawyers continued to bring new appeals. Many liberal groups which had supported the Court in many other areas condemned the Ginzburg holding. Committees such as "The Committee to Protest Absurd Censorship" were formed to protest the Ginzburg conviction and fight censorship in general.

In enlarging the Roth-Alberts test for obscenity to include consideration of the setting in which the publications are presented or how they are advertised or peddled the Court followed the suggestion first made by Chief Justice Warren in his Jacobellis dissent. It will be recalled that Warren stated as follows: "In my opinion, the use to which various materials are put—not just the words and pictures themselves—must be considered in determining whether or not the materials are obscene." How long the Court will be able to apply this enlarged standard only time will tell. But is it not possible that the Ginzburg majority was reflecting some of the popular outrage and disgust with the deluge in recent years of sheer pornography in the form of magazines, plays, movies and books?

Keyishian v. Board of Regents of the State University of New York
385 U.S. 589 (1967)

Though generally considered ineffective and quite useless in ferreting out Communists, loyalty oaths and loyalty standards of some kind for teachers in public institutions have long been required by many states. Typical of this type of legislation was the Feinberg Law passed in 1949 in New York State which was designed to disqualify and remove employees and teachers in the public schools who advocated the overthrow of the government by unlawful means or who were members of organizations which had a like purpose. The Feinberg Law did not establish new policy. It was written to implement a 1939 civil service law which denied public employment to anyone advocating the overthrow of the government by force and violence. The Feinberg Law required the State Board of Regents which supervises and controls all public education in the state to: (1) promulgate rules for the removal of ineligible public-school employees; (2) draw up a list of "subversive" organizations; (3) make membership in any listed organization *prima-facie* evidence (evidence good and sufficient on its face) of disqualification to hold any position in the public school system. In *Adler v. Board of Education*, 342 U.S. 485 (1952), the Supreme Court upheld the Feinberg Law over the vigorous dissents of Justices Black and Douglas. Justice Frankfurter also dissented but on technical grounds alone.

In 1953 an amendment extended the application of the Feinberg Law to teachers in state colleges and universities. Three years later the Board of Regents began requiring that teachers in the state university system, as a condition of employment, sign "Feinberg certificates" stating that they were not members of the Communist Party and that if they had been members they had so informed the president of the state university. In 1962 when the University of Buffalo became a part of the state university, all staff members were required to sign "Feinberg certificates." Keyishian, an instructor in English at the university, and four other staff members refused to sign the certificates. Each was notified that continued refusal to sign the certificate would result in dismissal. Keyishian's one-year contract with the university was not renewed because of his failure to sign the certificate. Three other staff members were dismissed. The fifth resigned.

Keyishian and the three dismissed staff members brought an action in a federal district court challenging the constitutionality of the Feinberg Law and the entire complex plan of anti-subversive legislation and administrative regulations. The three judge district court upheld the legislation. Keyishian and his friends then brought the case to the Supreme Court on appeal.

MR. JUSTICE BRENNAN delivered the opinion of the Court. . . .

[The Feinberg Law] bars employment of any person who "by word of mouth or writing willfully and deliberately advocates, advises or teaches the doctrine" of forceful overthrow of government. This provision is plainly susceptible to sweeping and improper application. It may well prohibit the employment of one who merely advocates the doctrine in the abstract without any attempt to indoctrinate others, or incite others to action in furtherance of unlawful aims. . . . And in prohibiting "advising" the "doctrine" of unlawful overthrow does the statute prohibit mere "advising" of the existence of the doctrine, or advising another to support the doctrine? Since "advocacy" of the doctrine of forceful overthrow is separately prohibited, need the person "teaching" or "advising" this doctrine himself "advocate" it? Does the teacher who informs his class about the precepts of Marxism or the Declaration of Independence violate this prohibition? . . .

[The Feinberg Law also] requires the disqualification of an employee involved with the distribution of written material "containing or advocating, advising or teaching the doctrine" of forceful overthrow, and who himself "advocates, advises, teaches or embraces the duty, necessity or propriety of adopting the doctrine contained therein." Here again, mere advocacy of abstract doctrine is apparently included. And does the prohibition of distribution of matter "containing" the doctrine bar histories of the evolution of Marxist doctrine or tracing the background of the French, American, and Russian revolutions? The additional requirement, that the person participating in distribution of the material be one who "advocates, advises, teaches, or embraces the duty, necessity or propriety of adopting the doctrine" of forceful overthrow, does not alleviate the uncertainty . . . but exacerbates it. . . . [T]his language may reasonably be construed to cover mere expression of belief. For example, does the university librarian who recommends the reading of such materials thereby "advocate . . . the propriety of adopting the doctrine contained therein?"

We do not have the benefit of a judicial gloss by the New York courts enlightening us as to the scope of this complicated plan. In light of the intricate administrative machinery for its enforcement, this is not surprising. The very intricacy of the plan and the uncertainty as to the scope of its proscriptions make it a highly efficient *in terrorem* mechanism. It would be a bold teacher who would not stay as far as possible from utterance or acts which might jeopardize his living by enmeshing him in this intricate machinery. The uncertainty as to the utterances and acts proscribed increases that caution in "those who believe the written law means what it says." . . . The result must be to stifle "that free play of the spirit which all teachers ought especially to cultivate and practice. . . ." That probability is enhanced by the provisions requiring an annual review of every teacher to determine whether any utterance or act of his, inside the classroom or out, came within the sanctions of the laws. For a memorandum warns employees that under the statutes "subversive" activities may take the form of "the writing of articles, the distribution of pamphlets, the endorsement of speeches made or articles written or acts performed by others," and reminds them "that it is the primary duty of the school authorities in each school district to take positive action to eliminate from the school system any teacher in whose case there is evidence that he is guilty of subversive activity. School authorities are under obligation to proceed immediately and conclusively in every such case. . . .

There can be no doubt of the legitimacy of New York's interest in protecting its education system from subversion. But "even though the governmental purpose be legitimate and substantial, that purpose cannot be pursued by means that broadly stifle fundamental personal liberties when the end can be more narrowly achieved." . . . The principle is not inapplicable because the legislation is aimed at keeping subversives out of the teaching ranks. In *DeJonge v. Oregon,* 299 U.S. 353, 364, the Court said:

> The greater the importance of safeguarding the community from incitements to the overthrow of our institutions by force and violence, the more imperative is the need to preserve inviolate the constitutional rights of free speech, free press and free assembly in order to maintain the opportunity for free political discussion, to the end that government may be responsive to the will of the people and that changes, if desired, may be obtained by peaceful means. Therein lies the security of the Republic, the very foundation of constitutional government.

Our Nation is deeply committed to safeguarding academic freedom, which is of transcendent value to all of us and not merely to the teachers concerned. That freedom is therefore a special concern of the First Amendment, which does not tolerate laws that cast a pall of orthodoxy over the classroom. "The vigilant protection of constitutional freedoms is nowhere more vital than in the community of American schools." . . . The classroom is peculiarly the "marketplace of ideas." The Nation's future depends upon leaders trained through wide exposure to that robust exchange of ideas which discovers truth "out of a multitude of tongues, [rather] than through any kind of authoritative selection." . . . In *Sweezy v. New Hampshire,* 354 U.S. 234, 250, we said:

> The essentiality of freedom in the community of American universities is almost self-evident. No one should underestimate the vital role in a democracy that is played by those who guide and train our youth. To impose any strait-jacket upon the intellectual leaders in our colleges and universities would imperil the future of our Nation. No field of education is so thoroughly comprehended by man that new discoveries cannot yet be made. Particularly is that true in the social sciences, where few, if any, principles are accepted as absolutes. Scholarship cannot flourish in an atmosphere of suspicion and distrust. Teachers and students must always remain free to inquire, to study and to evaluate, to gain new maturity and understanding; otherwise our civilization will stagnate and die.

We emphasize once again that "precision of regulation must be the touchstone in an area so closely touching our most previous freedoms." . . . "For standards of permissible statutory vagueness are strict in the area of free expression. . . . Because First Amendment freedoms need breathing space to survive, government may regulate in the area only with narrow specificity." . . . New York's complicated and intricate scheme plainly violates that standard. When one must guess what conduct or utterance may lose him his position, one necessarily will "steer far wider of the unlawful zone. . . ." . . . For "The threat of sanctions may deter . . . almost as potently as the actual application of sanctions." . . . The danger of that chilling effect upon the exercise of vital First Amendment rights must be guarded against by sensitive tools which clearly inform teachers what is being sanctioned. . . .

The regulatory maze created by New York is wholly lacking in "terms susceptible of objective measurement." . . . It has the quality of "extraordinary ambiguity." . . . Vagueness of wording is aggravated by prolixity and profusion of statutes, regulations, and administrative machinery, and by manifold cross-references to interrelated enactments and rules. . . .

[C]onstitutional doctrine which has emerged since . . . [the *Adler* decision] has rejected its major premise. That premise was that public employment, including academic employment, may be conditioned upon the surrender of constitutional rights which could not be abridged by direct government action. Teachers, the Court said in *Adler*, "may work for the school system upon the reasonable terms laid down by the proper authorities of New York. If they do not choose to work on such terms, they are at liberty to retain their beliefs and associations and go elsewhere." . . . The Court also stated that a teacher denied employment because of membership in a listed organization "is not thereby denied the right of free speech and assembly. His freedom of choice between membership in the organization and employment in the school system might be limited, but not his freedom of speech or assembly, except in the remote sense that limitation is inherent in every choice." . . .

". . . [T]he theory that public employment which may be denied altogether may be subjected to any conditions, regardless of how unreasonable, has been uniformly rejected." . . . Indeed, that theory was expressly rejected in a series of decisions following *Adler*. . . .

We proceed then to the question of the validity of the provisions . . . barring employment to members of listed organizations. Here again constitutional doctrine has developed since *Adler*. Mere knowing membership without a specific intent to further the unlawful aims of an organization is not a constitutionally adequate basis for exclusion from such positions as those held by appellants.

In *Elfbrandt v. Russell*, 384 U.S. 11, we said, "Those who join an organization but do not share its unlawful purposes and who do not participate in its unlawful activities surely pose no threat, either as citizens or as public employees." We there struck down a statutorily required oath binding the state employees not to become a member of the Communist Party with knowledge of its unlawful purpose, on threat of discharge and perjury prosecution if the oath were violated. We found that "any lingering doubt that proscription of mere knowing membership, without any showing of 'specific intent,' would run afoul of the Constitution was set at rest by our decision in *Aptheker v. Secretary of State*." . . . As we said in *Schneiderman v. United States*, 320 U.S. 118, 136, "[U]nder our traditions beliefs are personal and not a matter of mere association, and . . . men in adhering to a political party or other organization do not subscribe unqualifiedly to all of its platforms or asserted principles." "A law which applies to membership without the 'specific intent' to further the illegal aims of the organization infringes unnecessarily on protected freedoms. It rests on the doctrine of 'guilt by association' which has no place here." . . . Thus mere Party membership, even with knowledge of the Party's unlawful goals, cannot suffice to justify criminal punishment. . . .

[L]egislation which sanctions membership unaccompanied by specific intent to further the unlawful goals of the organization or which is not active membership violates constitutional limitations. . . .

The judgment of the District Court is reversed and the case is remanded for further proceedings consistent with this opinion.

Reversed and remanded.

MR. JUSTICE CLARK, with whom MR. JUSTICE HARLAN, MR. JUSTICE STEWART and MR. JUSTICE WHITE join, dissenting.

The blunderbuss fashion in which the majority couches "its artillery of words" together with the morass of cases it cites as authority and the obscurity of their application to the question at hand makes it difficult to grasp the true thrust of its decision. . . .

It is clear that the Feinberg Law, in which this Court found "no constitutional infirmity" in 1952, has been given its death blow today. Just as the majority here finds that there "can be no doubt of the legitimacy of New York's interest in protecting its education system from subversion" there can also be no doubt that "the be-all and end-all" of New York's effort is here. And regardless of its correctness neither New York nor the several States that have followed the teaching of *Adler* for some fifteen years, can ever put the pieces together again. No court has ever reached out so far to destroy so much with so little. . . .

In view of [the] long list of decisions covering over fifteen years of this Court's history, in which no opinion of this Court even questioned the validity of the *Adler* line of cases, it is strange to me that the Court now finds that the "constitutional doctrine which has emerged since . . . has rejected [*Adler's*] major premise." With due respect, as I read them, our cases have done no such thing. . . .

I regret to say—and I do so with deference—that the majority has by its broadside swept away one of our most precious rights, namely, the right of self-preservation. Our public educational system is the genius of our democracy. The minds of our youths are developed there and the character of that development will determine the future of our land. Indeed, our very existence depends upon it. The issue here is a very narrow one. It is not freedom of speech, freedom of thought, freedom of press, freedom of assembly, or of association, even in the Communist Party. It is simply this: May the State provide that one who, ·after a hearing with full judicial review, is found to wilfully and deliberately advocate, advise, or teach that our Government should be overthrown by force or violence or other unlawful means; or who wilfully and deliberately prints, publishes, etc., any book or paper that so advocates *and who personally* advocates such doctrine himself; or who wilfully and deliberately becomes a member of an organization that advocates such doctrine, is prima facie disqualified from teaching in its university? My answer, in keeping with all of our cases up until today, is "Yes!"

I dissent.

Aftermath

That both the Supreme Court and the country had come a long way since the early days of the 1950's when the late Senator Joseph P. McCarthy had contributed to the hysteria-like fear of communism was indicated clearly both by the Court's Keyishian opinion and by the overall general reaction to the decision. Some of the immediate reaction to the decision was not far different from what might have been expected in the early 1950's. State Supreme Court Justice Michael A. Musmanno, for example, long a near-hysterical foe of communism, called for a constitutional convention to nullify the Court's decision and agreed with Justice Clark's statement in his dissenting opinion that "the majority has by its broadside swept away one of our most precious rights, namely, the right of self-preservation." It is interesting to note in this regard that Clark's statement was rebutted by Justice Brennan when the opinions were delivered.

Brennan remarked that "of course our decision today does no such thing."

Other comments in the Musmanno view included the suggestions made by a Philadelphia newspaper that the Court might welcome a traitor like Benedict Arnold as a dean of faculty and the unfortunate remark made by the *Wall Street Journal* that the Court "somehow never grasped the nature of the Communist party." Nevertheless, much of the editorial opinion acclaimed the Court's "ringing affirmation of academic freedom" and thereby revealed the country's confidence in a free society. The *St. Louis Post-Dispatch* remarked editorially, for example, that most schools "do not need the panoply of loyalty oaths and disclaimers and special inquisitorial procedures that frightened legislatures sometimes dream up. The schools are safer without them, not only from subversion but from political meddling."

V FREEDOM OF RELIGION

No chapter in human history has been so largely written in terms of persecution and intolerance as the one dealing with religious freedom. From ancient times to the present day, the ingenuity of man has known no limits in its ability to forge weapons of oppression for use against those who dare to express or practice unorthodox religious beliefs.

> Justice Frank Murphy, Prince v. Massachusetts, 321 U.S. 158 (1944).

A government that will coerce its citizens in the domain of the spiritual will hardly hesitate to coerce them in the domain of the temporal. If it will direct how they shall worship it will certainly direct how they shall vote. Certain it is that religious liberty is the progenitor of most other civil liberties. Out of victory in the struggle of freedom to worship as one's conscience dictates come victory in the struggle for freedom to speak as one's reason dictates. Freedom of the press comes from the struggle for freedom to print religious tracts, and freedom to assemble politically can be traced to the successful struggle for freedom to assemble religiously. Even procedural liberties incident to our concept of a fair trial grew largely out of the struggle for procedural fairness in heresy and other religious trials.

> Leo Pfeffer, The Liberties of An American, The Supreme Court Speaks, *Boston,* Beacon Press, p. 31, 1963.

Minersville School District v. Gobitis
310 U.S. 586 (1940)

THE OPENING CLAUSE OF the First Amendment states that "Congress shall make no law respecting an establishment of religion or prohibiting the free exercise thereof." It is readily apparent that this brief but extremely important provision contains not one, but two prohibitions: it forbids laws which prohibit freedom of religion as well as laws respecting state religion. Though in many instances the Supreme Court considers freedom of religion and the separation of church and state as parts of the same general principle, the distinction between the two prohibitions is important since many cases turn on only one or the other.

The brief First Amendment provision dealing with religion confirmed the feelings of the overwhelming majority of Americans who looked upon religion as a private, personal matter, of no concern to government. But it must be recalled that the First Amendment was originally a restriction upon Congress *alone*. It was only after the development of the doctrine that First Amendment restrictions applied to the states through the Fourteenth Amendment that state action affecting religion could be challenged in the federal courts. It was not until 1940, in *Cantwell v. Connecticut*, 310 U.S. 296, that the Supreme Court held, for the first time, that the freedom of religion provision of the First Amendment constituted a restriction upon the states through the Fourteenth Amendment. Seven years later the Court, in *Everson v. Board of Education*, 330 U.S. 1 (1947), held that the establishment of religion clause was also applicable to the states through the Fourteenth Amendment.

The conflict between freedom of religion and governmental authority was most dramatically presented to the Supreme Court by the refusal of Jehovah's Witnesses, a tightly organized and fanatically devoted religious sect, to salute the flag. The Witnesses interpret the Bible literally and look upon modern history as a struggle between Jesus and Satan. They see themselves as allies of Jesus in his battle to overcome Satan and usher in a new kingdom. The Witnesses' conflicts with the law in various communities stemmed largely from their violent attacks on other religious groups, particularly Roman Catholics, and from their sometimes aggressive and intolerant attitude toward prospective converts. But it was their continued refusal to salute the flag which contributed most to their widespread unpopularity. The Witnesses' refusal to salute the flag stemmed from the belief that the flag was a "graven image" as revealed to them from the Old Testament Book of Exodus, Chapter 20, verses 3 through 5 which state as follows:

3. Thou shalt have no other gods before me.
4. Thou shalt not make unto thee any graven image, or any

likeness of anything that is in heaven above, or that is in the earth beneath, or that is in the water under the earth.

5. Thou shalt not bow down thyself to them, nor serve them. . . .

In Minersville, Pennsylvania, a small community with a population of less than 10,000, the School Board had adopted a resolution requiring pupils to salute the flag as part of the daily school exercises and provided for the expulsion of students who refused to participate in the ceremony. Lillian Gobitis, aged 12, and her brother William, aged 10, following the instructions of their parents, both Jehovah's Witnesses, refused to salute the flag. The Gobitis case came into being when the two children wrote letters to Charles E. Roudabush, Superintendent of Schools, and the School Board explaining why they could not salute the flag. Lillian Gobitis wrote as follows:

These are my reasons for not saluting the flag.

1. The Lord clearly says in Exodus 20:3,5, that you should have no gods besides Him and that we should serve Him.

2. The Constitution of [the] United States is based upon religious freedom. According to the dictates of my conscience, based on the Bible, I must give full allegiance to Jehovah God.

3. Jehovah my God and the Bible is my creed. I try my best to obey the Creator.

In his letter of November 6, 1935, William Gobitis stated as follows:

I don't salute the flag because I have promised to do the will of God. That means that I must not worship anything out of harmony with God's commandments. In the twentieth chapter of Exodus it is stated, 'Thou shalt not make unto thee any given image, nor bow to them, nor serve them for I, thy God, am a jealous God visiting the iniquity of the fathers upon the children unto the third and fourth generation of them that hate me.' I am a true follower of Christ and must obey his commandment. I do not salute the flag because I do not like my country. I love my country but I love God more. Therefore I must obey his commandments.

The letter was signed "Your pupil, Billy Gobitis."

Superintendent Roudabush—who had little sympathy for Jehovah's

Witnesses, in general, and Walter Gobitis, father of the two children, in particular—was outraged by the students' refusal to salute the flag. He believed firmly that the flag salute was necessary to the promotion of patriotism and good citizenship. After the School Board voted unanimously that failure to salute the flag was an act of insubordination, Roudabush immediately expelled Lillian and William Gobitis from the Minersville school. As a result, Walter Gobitis was forced to send his children to a private school which he could barely afford. Later three more of his children were expelled from school for refusing to salute the flag. After consulting at length with members of his church and with the help of the American Civil Liberties Union, Walter Gobitis sued in a federal district court in Philadelphia for an injunction to restrain the School Board from continuing to require the flag salute as a condition of his children's attendance in the Minersville school. In a careful and thoughtful opinion the district court stated that "no man, even though he be a school director or a judge, is empowered to censor another's religious convictions or set bounds to the areas of human conduct in which these convictions should be permitted to control his actions, unless compelled to do so by an overriding public necessity." Accordingly, the court held that as applied to the Gobitis children, the School Board regulation violated the religious freedom guarantees of the Pennsylvania Constitution, and the religious freedom provision of the First Amendment as applied to the states through the Fourteenth Amendment. A court of appeals sustained the district court's ruling. The embittered Minersville School Board then brought the case to the Supreme Court on a writ of certiorari.

Perhaps no other of Justice Frankfurter's early opinions so well reveals his deep attachment to the doctrine of judicial self-restraint as his controversial Gobitis one. If he had been a member of the Minersville School Board, Frankfurter certainly would not have insisted that the Gobitis children salute the flag. In fact, he felt privately that the School Board had acted foolishly. But, as a Supreme Court justice, he also felt that the local authorities had a right to deal with the problem as they saw fit. It was their prime responsibility—not the Court's—to resolve the issue.

Born in Vienna, Frankfurter did not hear English spoken until he came to the United States at the age of twelve with his family. Yet he was to become a master of the English language and one of the most articulate champions of American legal institutions. Frankfurter graduated from City College of New York with highest honors and obtained his law degree in 1906 at the Harvard Law School where he subsequently became a professor and respected authority on American law. At Harvard he espoused liberal causes and sent a stream of his students—"happy hot dogs"—to Washington to work for his friend, Franklin D. Roosevelt, and the New Deal. Appointed to the Court by President Roosevelt in 1939, Frankfurter, much to the dismay of his liberal friends, stuck to the self-restraint notion that the Court should interfere with legislature enactments only as a last resort. He retired from the Court in 1962 after a long illness.

Justice Harlan F. Stone's lone dissenting opinion in the Gobitis case remains one of the classics in the literature of American liberties. Unlike Frankfurter, Stone was a native New Englander, born in New Hampshire so close to the Vermont line that it was said that he could be nothing but a Republican all of his life. Expelled from a state agricultural college for instigating a series of boisterous escapades, Stone entered Amherst College to prepare for a medical career but ended up graduating from Columbia University Law School. After teaching and serving as Dean at Columbia, Stone was named Attorney General of the United States by his old college friend, President Coolidge. He was later elevated to the Supreme Court by Coolidge and named Chief Justice by President Roosevelt in 1941 upon the retirement of Charles Evans Hughes. An independent Justice who looked upon the Constitution as a broad charter of government, Stone was said to look like a smoothed out version of Carl Sandburg. He was taken ill while presiding over the Court and died on April 22, 1946, at the age of seventy-three.

MR. JUSTICE FRANKFURTER delivered the opinion of the Court. . . .

The case before us must be viewed as though the legislature of Pennsylvania had itself formally directed the flag-salute for the children of Minersville; had made no exemption for children whose parents were possessed of conscientious scruples like those of the Gobitis family; and had indicated its belief in the desirable ends to be secured by having its public school children share a common experience at those periods of development when their minds are supposedly receptive to its assimilation, by an exercise appropriate in time and place and setting, and one designed to evoke in them appreciation of the nation's hopes and dreams, its sufferings and sacrifices. The precise issue, then, for us to decide is whether the legislatures of the various states and the authorities in a thousand counties and school districts of this country are barred from determining the appropriateness of various means to evoke that unifying sentiment without which there can ultimately be no liberties, civil or religious. To stigmatize legislative judgment in providing for this universal gesture of respect for the symbol of our national life in the setting of the common school as a lawless inroad on that freedom of conscience which the Constitution protects, would amount to no less than the pronouncement of pedagogical and psychological dogma in a field where courts possess no marked and certainly no controlling competence. The influences which help toward a common feeling for the common country are manifold. Some may seem harsh and others no doubt are foolish. Surely, however, the end is legitimate. And the effective means for its attainment are still so uncertain and so unauthenticated by science as to preclude us from putting the widely prevalent belief in flag-saluting beyond the pale of legislative power. . . .

The wisdom of training children in patriotic impulses by those compulsions which necessarily pervade so much of the educational process is not for our independent judgment. Even were we convinced of the folly of such a measure, such belief would be no proof of its unconstitutionality. For ourselves, we might be tempted to say that the deepest patriotism is best engendered by giving unfettered scope to the most crochety beliefs. Perhaps it is best, even from the standpoint of those interests which ordinances like the one under review seek to promote, to give to the least popular sect leave from conformities like those here in issue. But the courtroom is not the arena for debating issues of educational policy. It is not our province to choose among competing considerations in the subtle process of securing effective loyalty to the traditional ideals of democracy, while respecting at the same time individual idiosyncracies among a people so diversified in racial origins and religious allegiances. So to hold would, in effect, make us the school board for the country. That authority has not been given to this Court, nor should we assume it. . . .

Except where the transgression of constitutional liberty is too plain for argument, personal freedom is best maintained—so long as the remedial channels of the democratic process remain open and unobstructed—when it is ingrained in a people's habits and not enforced against popular policy by the coercion of adjudicated law. That the flag-salute is an allowable portion of a school program for those who do not invoke conscientious scruples is surely not debatable. But for us to insist that, though the ceremony may be required, exceptional immunity must be given to dissidents, is to maintain that there is no basis for a legislative judgment that such an exemption might introduce elements of difficulty into the school discipline, might cast doubts in the minds of the other children which would themselves weaken the effect of the exercise.

The preciousness of the family relation, the authority and independence which give dignity to parenthood, indeed the enjoyment of all freedom, presuppose the kind of ordered society which is summarized by our flag. A society which is dedicated to the preservation of these ultimate values of civilization may in self-protection utilize the educational process for inculcating those almost unconscious feelings which bind men together in a comprehending loyalty, whatever may be their lesser differences and difficulties. That is to say, the process may be utilized so long as men's right to believe as they please, to win others to their way of belief, and their right to assemble in their chosen places of worship for the devotional ceremonies of their faith, are all fully respected.

Judicial review, itself a limitation on popular government, is a fundamental part of our constitutional scheme. But to the legislature no less than to courts is committed the guardianship of deeply-cherished liberties. . . . Where all the effective means of inducing political changes are left free from interference, education in the abandonment of foolish legislation is itself a training in liberty. To fight out the wise use of legislative authority in the forum of public opinion and before legislative assemblies rather than to transfer such a contest to the judicial arena, serves to vindicate the self-confidence of a free people.

Reversed.

[MR. JUSTICE McREYNOLDS concurred without writing a separate opinion.]

MR. JUSTICE STONE, dissenting: . . .

The law which is . . . sustained is unique in the history of Anglo-American legislation. It does more than suppress freedom of speech and more than prohibit the free exercise of religion, which concededly are forbidden by the First Amendment and are violations of the liberty guaranteed by the Fourteenth. For by this law the state seeks to coerce these children to express a sentiment which, as they interpret it, they do not entertain, and which violates their deepest religious convictions. . . .

Concededly the constitutional guaranties of personal liberty are not always absolutes. Government has a right to survive and powers conferred upon it are not necessarily set at naught by the express prohibitions of the Bill of Rights. It may make war and raise armies. To that end it may compel citizens to give military service, . . . It may suppress religious practices dangerous to morals, and presumably those also which are inimical to public safety, health, and good order. . . . But it is a long step, and one which I am unable to take, to the position that government may, as a supposed educational measure and as a means of disciplining the young, compel public affirmations which violate their religious conscience. . . .

The guaranties of civil liberty are but guaranties of freedom of the human mind and spirit and of reasonable freedom and opportunity to express them. They presuppose the right of the individual to hold such opinions as he will and to give them reasonably free expression, and his freedom, and that of the state as well, to teach and persuade others by the communication of ideas. The very essence of the liberty which they guarantee is the freedom of the individual from compulsion as to what he shall think and what he shall say, at least where the compulsion is to bear false witness to his religion. If these guaranties are to have any meaning they must, I think, be deemed to withhold from the state any authority to compel belief or the expression of it where that expression violates religious convictions, whatever may be the legislative view of the desirability of such compulsion.

History teaches us that there have been but few infringements of personal liberty by the state which have not been justified, as they are here, in the name of righteousness and the public good, and few which have not been directed, as they are now, at politically helpless minorities. The framers were not unaware that under the system which they created most governmental curtailments of personal liberty would have the support of a legislative judgment that the public interest would be better served by its curtailment than by its constitutional protection. I cannot conceive that in prescribing, as limitations upon the powers of government, the freedom of the mind and spirit secured by the explicit guaranties of freedom of speech and religion, they intended or rightly could have left any latitude for a legislative judgment that the compulsory expression of belief which violates religious convictions would better serve the public interest than their protection. The Constitution may well elicit expressions of loyalty to it and to the government which it created, but it does not command such expressions or otherwise give any indication that compulsory expressions of loyalty play any such part in our scheme of government as to override the constitutional protection of freedom of speech and religion. And while such expressions of loyalty, when voluntarily given, may promote national unity, it is quite another matter to say that their compulsory expression by children in violation of their own and their parents' religious convictions can be regarded as playing so important a part in our national unity as to leave school boards free to exact it despite the constitutional guaranty of freedom of religion. The very terms of the Bill of Rights preclude, it seems to me, any reconciliation of such compulsions with the constitutional guaranties by a legislative declaration that they are more important to the public welfare than the Bill of Rights.

But even if this view be rejected and it is considered that there is some scope for the determination by legislatures whether the citizen shall be compelled to give public expression of such sentiments contrary to his religion, I am not persuaded that we should refrain from passing upon the legislative judgment "as long as the remedial channels of the democratic process remain open and unobstructed." This seems to me no more than the surrender of the constitutional protection of the liberty of small minorities to the popular will. . . . Here we have such a small minority entertaining in good faith a religious belief, which is such a departure from the usual course of human conduct, that most persons are disposed to regard it with little toleration or concern. In such circumstances careful scrutiny of legislative efforts to secure conformity of belief and opinion by a compulsory affirmation of the desired belief, is especially needful if civil rights are to receive any protection. Tested by this standard, I am not prepared to say that the right of this small and helpless minority, including children having a strong religious conviction, whether they understand its nature or not, to refrain from an expression obnoxious to their religion, is to be overborne by the interest of the state in maintaining discipline in the schools.

The Constitution expresses more than the conviction of the people that democratic processes must be preserved at all costs. It is also an expression of faith and a command that freedom of mind and spirit must be preserved, which government must obey, if it is to adhere to that justice and moderation without which no free government can exist. . . .

I cannot say that the inconveniences which may attend some sensible adjustment of school discipline in order that the religious convictions of these children may be spared, present a problem so momentous or pressing as to outweigh the freedom from compulsory violation of religious faith which has been thought worthy of constitutional protection.

AFTERMATH

The *Gobitis* decision was handed down on June 3, 1940—a time when German victories in Europe appeared to be decisive. Hitler's armies had swept through the Netherlands, Belgium and Luxembourg almost without opposition. Dunkirk had been evacuated by the British; Norway had been invaded and then, early in June, France had collapsed. Hitler's seemingly invincible army, still all but intact, appeared ready for an assault on England and perhaps eventually the United States. Worried and deeply concerned about the success of the Nazis in Europe, Americans were caught up in a wave of near fanatical patriotism. And even though the *Gobitis* decision was widely criticized throughout the country, Jehovah's Witnesses were a natural target for many Americans.

Hundreds of attacks upon the Witnesses were made throughout the United States. In Maine an enraged mob of 2,500 burned down a meeting hall after two Witnesses refused to salute the flag. In Maryland the police assisted a mob in dispersing a Bible meeting. In Illinois almost an entire town mobbed a group of Witnesses, and state troopers had to be called out to protect them. A lawyer who attempted to defend several Witnesses in Indiana was beaten and driven out of town. Members of veterans' organizations in several states forcibly removed a number of Witnesses from various communities. Finally, in several states children who refused to salute the flag were classified as delinquents by the courts and committed to reformatories. Thus, "ironically enough, the flag, intended as a symbol of freedom, had become for many persons an instrument of oppression of a religious minority."

The persecution of the Witnesses disturbed many Americans. Many responsible commentators argued vehemently that the *Gobitis* decision had contributed significantly to the outburst of violence and contended that Stone's dissenting opinion should be supported. On this point it is interesting to note that Justice Frankfurter had been surprised and dismayed by Stone's dissenting opinion and had tried to persuade him to join with the majority. One writer has maintained that due to the "rush of work at the close of the term, in June, 1940, Justice Stone's dissenting opinion was not read by other justices until after the decision was announced. Justices Black, Douglas and Murphy at once told Justice Stone that they agreed with him and would stand with him at the first opportunity." (Irving Brant, *The Bill of Rights, Its Origin and Meaning*, Indianapolis, The Bobbs-Merrill Co., 1965)

In June, 1942, still deeply disturbed by the nation's reaction to the *Gobitis* decision, Justices Black, Douglas and Murphy, in a dissenting opinion in another case (*Jones v. Opelika*, 316 U.S. 584) jointly stated that they had become convinced that the *Gobitis* case was "wrongly decided." In the meantime, there had also been some important changes on the Court. Chief Justice Hughes retired in 1941 and Justice Stone was elevated to the top post. Robert H. Jackson of New York was named to the vacancy created by the appointment of Stone. In 1941 the embittered ultra-conservative, James C. McReynolds, also retired from the Court and James F. Byrnes of South Carolina was named to replace him. But Byrnes resigned from the Court after one year and was succeeded by Wiley B. Rutledge, an outstanding exponent of the doctrine that the protection of individual freedom was the Court's most vital responsibility. Thus, by 1943, the stage was set for the second flag salute case—*West Virginia State Board of Education v. Barnette.*

West Virginia Board of Education v. Barnette
319 U.S. 624 (1943)

Largely inspired by Justice Frankfurter's opinion in the *Gobitis* case, the West Virginia legislature amended its laws in 1941 so as to require all the schools in the state to teach, foster and perpetuate the "ideals, principles and spirit of Americanism." Acting under this law, the West Virginia Board of Education adopted a resolution requiring all public school teachers and pupils to salute the flag as a "regular part of the program of activities." Refusal to salute the flag was made an act of insubordination which was punishable by expulsion. Readmission was possible only if the expelled child agreed to render the salute. Meanwhile, the expelled child was considered unlawfully absent, and therefore subject to proceedings as a "delinquent." Parents or guardians could be prosecuted, and, if convicted, could be fined $50 and jailed for thirty days.

A number of the Witnesses' children were expelled from various public schools in West Virginia for refusal to salute the flag. State officials threatened to send these children to reformatories and to prosecute their parents for causing delinquency. Walter Barnette and two other families with strong Witness ties brought suit in a federal district court to enjoin the enforcement of the Board's regulation against their children who had already been expelled. Noting that Justices Black, Douglas and Murphy had recanted their support of the *Gobitis* holding in *Jones v. Opelika,* the district court granted the injunction. The Board of Education then brought the case to the Supreme Court by direct appeal. Friend-of-the-court briefs were filed before the Court in support of Barnette by the American Civil Liberties Union and a committee of the American Bar Association. One of the members of the Bar Association committee was Abe Fortas who was named to the Supreme Court by President Johnson in 1965. These briefs contended that the compulsory flag salute violated religious freedom as protected against state impairment by the Fourteenth Amendment. A brief in support of the flag salute filed by the American Legion argued that it was necessary to the promotion of national security.

Justice Robert H. Jackson's majority opinion is one of the strongest and most eloquent in Supreme Court history. Some of its moving paragraphs should be read several times slowly and savoured. Though his writing style sometimes stole attention from the substance of an opinion (as in the *Barnette* case), Jackson's verbal brilliance is remarkable for a man who went to the Court without a college education and with only one year of formal legal education. Jackson was one of the last well-known public figures to have entered law by way of the old apprenticeship system in a law office. After a successful career as a country lawyer in Jamestown, N.Y., Jackson, a strongly partisan New Dealer, held a number of important posts in Washington, including that of Attorney General of the United States. He was named to the Court in 1941 by President Roosevelt. In 1945 Jackson took a leave of absence to serve as chief prosecutor for the United States in the trials of Nazi war criminals in Nuremberg.

MR. JUSTICE JACKSON delivered the opinion of the Court.

. . . The freedom asserted by these appellees does not bring them into collision with rights asserted by any other individual. It is such conflicts which most frequently require intervention of the State to determine where the rights of one end and those of another begin. But the refusal of these persons to participate in the ceremony does not interfere with or deny rights of others to do so. Nor is there any question in this case that their behavior is peaceable and orderly. The sole conflict is between authority and rights of the individual. The State asserts power to condition access to public education on making a prescribed sign and profession and at the same time to coerce attendance by punishing both parent and child. The latter stand on a right of self-determination in matters that touch individual opinion and personal attitude.

There is no doubt that, in connection with the pledges, the flag salute is a form of utterance. Symbolism is a primitive but effective way of communicating ideas. The use of an emblem or flag to symbolize some system, idea, institution, or personality, is a short cut from mind to mind. Causes and nations, political parties, lodges, and ecclesiastical groups seek to knit the loyalty of their followings to a flag or banner, a color or design. The State announces rank, function, and authority through crowns and maces, uniforms and black robes; the church speaks through the Cross, the Crucifix, the altar and shrine, and clerical raiment. Symbols of State often convey political ideas just as religious symbols come to convey theological ones. Associated with many of these symbols are appropriate gestures of acceptance or respect: a salute, a bowed or bared head, a bended knee. A person gets from a symbol the meaning he puts into it, and what is one man's comfort and inspiration is another's jest and scorn.

Over a decade ago Chief Justice Hughes led this Court in holding that the display of a red flag as a symbol of opposition by peaceful and legal means to organize government was protected by the free-speech guaranties of the Constitution. *Stromberg v. California*, 283 U.S. 359. Here it is the State that employs a flag as a symbol of adherence to government as presently organized. It requires the individual to communicate by word and sign his acceptance of the political ideas it thus bespeaks. Objection to this form of communication when coerced is an old one, well-known to the framers of the Bill of Rights.

It is also to be noted that the compulsory flag salute and pledge requires affirmation of a belief and an attitude of mind. It is not clear whether the regulation contemplates that pupils forego any contrary convictions of their own and become unwilling converts to the prescribed ceremony, or whether it will be acceptable if they simulate assent by words without belief and by a gesture barren of meaning. It is now a commonplace that censorship or suppression of expression of opinion is tolerated by our Constitution only when the expression presents a clear and present danger of action of a kind the State is empowered to prevent and punish. It would seem that involuntary affirmation could be commanded only on even more immediate and urgent grounds than silence. But here the power of compulsion is invoked without any allegation that remaining passive during a flag-salute ritual creates a clear and present danger that would justify an effort even to muffle expression. To sustain the compulsory flag salute we are required to say that a Bill of Rights which guards the individual's right to speak his own mind, left it open to public authorities to compel him to utter what is not in his mind.

Whether the First Amendment to the Constitution will permit officials to order observance of ritual of this nature does not depend upon whether as a voluntary exercise we would think it to be good, bad, or merely innocuous. Any credo of nationalism is likely to include what some disapprove or to omit what others think essential, and to give off different overtones as it takes on different accents or interpretations. If official power exists to coerce acceptance of any patriotic creed, what it shall contain cannot be decided by courts, but must be largely discretionary with the ordaining authority, whose power to prescribe would no doubt include power to amend. Hence validity of the asserted power to force an American citizen publicly to profess any statement of belief or to engage in any ceremony of assent to one, presents questions of power that must be considered independently of any idea we may have as to the utility of the ceremony in question.

Nor does the issue as we see it turn on one's possession of particular religious views or the sincerity with which they are held. While religion supplies appellees' motive for enduring the discomforts of making the issue in this case, many citizens who do not share these religious views hold such a compulsory rite to infringe constitutional liberty of the individual. It is not necessary to inquire whether nonconformist beliefs will exempt from the duty to salute unless we first find power to make the salute a legal duty.

The *Gobitis* decision, however, *assumed,* as did the argument in that case and in this, that power exists in the State to impose the flag-salute discipline upon school children in general. The Court only examined and rejected a claim based on religious beliefs of immunity from an unquestioned general rule. The question which underlies the flag-salute controversy is whether such a ceremony so touching matters of opinion and political attitude may be imposed upon the individual by official authority under powers committed to any political organization under our Constitution. We examine rather than assume existence of this power and, against this broader definition of issues in this case, reexamine specific grounds assigned for the *Gobitis* decision.

1. It was said that the flag-salute controversy confronted the Court with "the problem which Lincoln cast in memorable dilemma: 'Must a government of necessity be too *strong* for the liberties of its people, or too *weak* to maintain its own existence?'" and that the answer must be in favor of strength. . . .

We think these issues may be examined free of pressure or restraint growing out of such considerations.

It may be doubted whether Mr. Lincoln would have thought that the strength of government to maintain itself would be impressively vindicated by our confirming power of the State to expel a handful of children from school. Such oversimplification, so handy in political debate, often lacks the precision necessary to postulates of judicial reasoning. If validly applied to this problem, the utterance cited would resolve every issue of power in favor of those in authority and would require us to override every liberty thought to weaken or delay execution of their policies.

Government of limited power need not be anemic government. Assurance that rights are secure tends to diminish fear and jealousy of strong government, and by making us feel safe to live under it makes for its better support. Without promise of a limiting Bill of Rights it is doubtful if our Constitution could have mustered enough strength to enable its ratification. To enforce those rights today is not to choose weak government over strong government. It is only to adhere as a means of strength to individual freedom of mind in preference to officially disciplined uniformity, for which history indicates a disappointing and disastrous end.

The subject now before us exemplifies this principle. Free public education, if faithful to the ideal of secular instruction and political neutrality, will not be partisan or enemy of any class, creed, party, or faction. If it is to impose any ideological discipline, however, each party or denomination must seek to control, or failing that, to weaken the influence of the educational system. Observance of the limitations of the Constitution will not weaken government in the field appropriate for its exercise.

2. It was also considered in the *Gobitis* case that functions of educational officers in States, counties, and school districts were such that to interfere with their authority "would in effect make us the school board for the country." . . .

The Fourteenth Amendment, as now applied to the States, protects the citizen against the State itself and all of its creatures—Boards of Education not excepted. These have, of course, important, delicate, and highly discretionary functions, but none that they may not perform within the limits of the Bill of Rights. That they are educating the young for citizenship is reason for scrupulous protection of constitutional freedoms of the individual, if we are not to strangle the free mind at its source and teach youth to discount important principles of our government as mere platitudes.

Such Boards are numerous and their territorial jurisdiction often small. But small and local authority may feel less sense of responsibility to the Constitution, and agencies of publicity may be less vigilant in calling it to account. The action of Congress in making flag observance voluntary and respecting the conscience of the objector in a matter so vital as raising the Army contrasts sharply with these local regulations in matters relatively trivial to the welfare of the nation. . . .

3. The *Gobitis* opinion reasoned that this is a field "where courts possess no marked and certainly no controlling competence," that it is committed to the legislatures as well as the courts to guard cherished liberties and that it is constitutionally appropriate to "fight out the wise use of legisla-

tive authority in the forum of public opinion and before legislative assemblies rather than to transfer such a contest to the judicial arena," since all the "effective means of inducing political changes are left free." . . .

The very purpose of a Bill of Rights was to withdraw certain subjects from the vicissitudes of political controversy, to place them beyond the reach of majorities and officials and to establish them as legal principles to be applied by the Courts. One's right to life, liberty, and property, to free speech, a free press, freedom of worship and assembly, and other fundamental rights may not be submitted to vote; they depend on the outcome of no elections.

In weighing arguments of the parties it is important to distinguish between the due process clause of the Fourteenth Amendment as an instrument for transmitting the principles of the First Amendment and those cases in which it is applied for its own sake. The test of legislation which collides with the Fourteenth, because it also collides with the principles of the First, is much more definitive than the test when only the Fourteenth is involved. Much of the vagueness of the due process clause disappears when the specific prohibitions of the First become its standard. The right of a State to regulate, for example, a public utility may well include, so far as the due process test is concerned, power to impose all of the restrictions which a legislature may have a "rational basis" for adopting. But freedoms of speech and of press, of assembly, and of worship may not be infringed on such slender grounds. They are susceptible of restriction only to prevent grave and immediate danger to interests which the State may lawfully protect. It is important to note that while it is the Fourteenth Amendment which bears directly upon the State, it is the more specific limiting principles of the First Amendment that finally govern this case.

Nor does our duty to apply the Bill of Rights to assertions of official authority depend upon our possession of marked competence in the field where the invasion of rights occurs. True, the task of translating the majestic generalities of the Bill of Rights, conceived as part of the pattern of liberal government in the eighteenth century, into concrete restraints on officials dealing with the problems of the twentieth century, is one to disturb self-confidence. These principles grew in soil which also produced a philosophy that the individual was the center of society, that his liberty was attainable through mere absence of governmental restraints, and that government should be entrusted with few controls and only the mildest supervision over men's affairs. We must transplant these rights to a soil in which the *laissez-faire* concept or principle of noninterference has withered at least as to economic affairs, and social advancements are increasingly sought through closer integration of society and through expanded and strengthened governmental controls. These changed conditions often deprive precedents of reliability and cost us more than we would choose upon our own judgment. But we act in these matters not only by authority of our competence but by force of our commissions. We cannot, because of modest estimates of our competence in such specialties as public education, withhold the judgment that history authenticates as the function of this Court when liberty is infringed.

4. Lastly, and this is the very heart of the *Gobitis* opinion, it reasons that "National unity is the basis of national security," that the authorities have "the right to select appropriate means for its attainment," and hence reaches the conclusion that such compulsory measures toward "national unity" are constitutional. . . . Upon the verity of this assumption depends our answer in this case.

National unity as an end which officials may foster by persuasion and example is not in question. The problem is whether under our Constitution compulsion as here employed is a permissible means for its achievement.

Struggles to coerce uniformity of sentiment in support of some end thought essential to their time and country have been waged by many good as well as by evil men. Nationalism is a relatively recent phenomenon, but at other times and places the ends have been racial or territorial security, support of a dynasty or regime, and particular plans for saving souls. As first and moderate methods to attain unity have failed, those bent on its accomplishment must resort to an ever-increasing severity. . . . Ultimate futility of such attempts to compel coherence is the lesson of every such effort from the Roman drive to stamp out Christianity as a disturber of its pagan unity, the Inquisition, as a means to religious and dynastic unity, the Siberian exiles as a means to Russian unity, down to the fast failing efforts of our present totalitarian enemies. Those who begin coercive elimination of dissent soon find themselves exterminating dissenters. Compulsory unification of opinion achieves only the unanimity of the graveyard.

It seems trite but necessary to say that the First Amendment to our Constitution was designed to avoid these ends by avoiding these beginnings. There is no mysticism in the American concept of the State or of the nature or origin of its authority. We set up government by consent of the governed, and the Bill of Rights denies those in power any legal opportunity to coerce that consent. Authority here is to be controlled by public opinion, not public opinion by authority.

The case is made difficult not because the principles of its decision are obscure but because the flag involved is our own. Nevertheless, we apply the limitations of the Constitution with no fear that freedom to be intellectually and spiritually diverse or even contrary will disintegrate the social organization. To believe that patriotism will not flourish if patriotic ceremonies are voluntary and spontaneous instead of a compulsory routine is to make an unflattering estimate of the appeal of our institutions to free minds. We can have intellectual individualism and the rich cultural diversities that we owe to exceptional minds only at the price of occasional eccentricity and abnormal attitudes. When they are so harmless to others or to the State as those we deal with here, the price is not too great. But freedom to differ is not limited to things that do not matter much. That would be a mere shadow of freedom. The test of its substance is the right to differ as to things that touch the heart of the existing order.

If there is any fixed star in our constitutional constellation, it is that no official, high or petty, can prescribe what shall be orthodox in politics, nationalism, religion, or other matters of opinion or force citizens to confess by word or act their faith therein. If there are any circumstances which permit an exception, they do not now occur to us.

We think the action of the local authorities in compelling the flag salute and pledge transcends constitutional limitations on their power and invades the sphere of intellect and spirit which it is the purpose of the First Amendment to our Constitution to reserve from all official control.

The decision of this Court in *Minersville School District v. Gobitis* [is] overruled, and the judgment enjoining enforcement of the West Virginia Regulation is

Affirmed.

[MR. JUSTICE BLACK, MR. JUSTICE DOUGLAS, and MR. JUSTICE MURPHY concurred.]

MR. JUSTICE FRANKFURTER, dissenting:

One who belongs to the most vilified and persecuted minority in history is not likely to be insensible to the freedoms guaranteed by our Constitution. Were my purely personal attitude relevant I should wholeheartedly associate myself with the general libertarian views in the Court's opinion, representing as they do the thought and action of a lifetime. But as judges we are neither Jew nor Gentile, neither Catholic nor agnostic. We owe equal attachment to the Constitution and are equally bound by our judicial obligations whether we derive our citizenship from the earliest or the latest immigrants to these shores. As a member of this Court I am not justified in writing my private notions of policy into the Constitution, no matter how deeply I may cherish them or how mischievous I may deem their disregard. The duty of a judge who must decide which of two claims before the Court shall prevail, that of a State to enact and enforce laws within its general competence or that of an individual to refuse obedience because of the demands of his conscience, is not that of the ordinary person. It can never be emphasized too much that one's own opinion about the wisdom or evil of a law should be excluded altogether when one is doing one's duty on the bench. The only opinion of our own even looking in that direction that is material is our opinion whether legislators could in reason have enacted such a law. In the light of all the circumstances, including the history of this question in this Court, it would require more daring than I possess to deny that reasonable legislators could have taken the action which is before us for review. Most unwillingly, therefore, I must differ from my brethren with regard to legislation like this. I cannot bring my mind to believe that the "liberty" secured by the Due Process Clause gives this Court authority to deny to the State of West Virginia the attainment of that which we all recognize as a legitimate legislative end, namely, the promotion of good citizenship, by employment of the means here chosen.

. . . When Mr. Justice Holmes, speaking for this Court, wrote that "it must be remembered that legislatures are ultimate guardians of the liberties and welfare of the people in quite as great a degree as the courts," . . . he went to the very essence of our constitutional system and the democratic conception of our society. He did not mean that for only some phases of civil government this Court was not to supplant legislatures and sit in judgment upon the right or wrong of a challenged measure. He was stating the comprehensive judicial duty and role of this Court in our constitutional scheme whenever legislation is sought to be nullified on any ground, namely, that responsibility for legislation lies with legislatures, answerable as they are directly to the people, and this Court's only and very narrow function is to determine whether within the broad grant of authority vested in legislatures they have exercised a judgment for which reasonable justification can be offered.

. . . The reason why from the beginning even the narrow judicial authority to nullify legislation has been viewed with a jealous eye is that it serves to prevent the full play of the democratic process. The fact that it may be an undemocratic aspect of our scheme of government does not call for its rejection or its disuse. But it is the best of reasons, as this Court has frequently recognized, for the greatest caution in its use.

. . . If the function of this Court is to be essentially no different from that of a legislature, if the considerations governing constitutional construction are to be substantially those that underlie legislation, then indeed judges should not have life tenure and they should be made directly responsible to the electorate. . . .

[MR. JUSTICE ROBERTS and MR. JUSTICE REED also dissented

announcing simply that they adhered to the views expressed in the *Gobitis* case.]

AFTERMATH

The *Barnette* decision was delivered, appropriately enough, on Flag Day—June 14, 1943—just three years and ten days after the *Gobitis* case. Seldom has the Supreme Court so completely reversed itself in so short a time! Though the *Barnette* case had no effect on Lillian and William Gobitis since, by 1943, they had already left school, the Minersville School was finally forced to admit the three younger Gobitis children who had been expelled between 1940 and 1943. The two Barnette children had been readmitted right after the federal district court's decision in their case.

Justice Frankfurter's opening sentence in his dissenting opinion—"One who belongs to the most vilified and persecuted minority in history is not likely to be insensible to the freedom guaranteed by our Constitution"—is one of the most personal and poignant in judicial literature. It reveals the difficult, soul-searching questions posed for him by the flag salute controversy.

Justice Stone's lone dissenting opinion in the *Gobitis* case was truly vindicated by the *Barnette* decision. Replying to a close friend who had written him a congratulatory note after the *Barnette* decision, Stone wrote: "All's well that ends well, but I should like to have seen the case end well in the first place without following such a devious route to the desired end." (Quoted in Alpheus T. Mason, *Harlan Fiske Stone: Pillar of the Law*, N.Y., The Viking Press, 1956, p. 601.)

Zorach v. Clauson
343 U.S. 306 (1952)

During most of our history the establishment of the religion clause of the First Amendment was all but forgotten. But in more recent years the Court's interpretation of the establishment clause has provoked bitter controversy. This is revealed well by the so called "released time" cases. The term "released time" refers simply to a program under which clergymen of the various faiths—Protestant, Catholic and Jewish—provide religious instruction for public school children during school hours.

A typical "released time" program was that conducted in the public school system of Champaign, Illinois, where religious instruction was provided by the three denominations in the regular class-rooms of the school building. Attendance was compulsory for students released from secular activities for religious instruction. Students who did not wish to take religious instruction were not re-leased from school, but rather left their classrooms for some other room in the building to pursue their non-religious activities. The Protestant, Catholic and Jewish teachers were not paid by the school but were under the supervision of the school authorities. In *McCollum v. Board of Education*, 333 U.S. 203 (1948), the Supreme Court, in a decision by Justice Black, held that tax-supported property in Champaign was being used for religious instruction in violation of the establishment clause of the First Amendment as made applicable to the states by the Fourteenth Amendment. Justice Black stated that in Champaign "not only are the State's tax-supported public school buildings used for the dissemination of religious doctrines. The State also affords sectarian groups an invaluable aid in that it helps to provide pupils for their religious classes through the use of the State's compulsory public school machinery. This is not separation of Church and State." Justice Stanley F. Reed was the lone dissenter in the *McCollum* case.

The *McCollum* decision created a wave of bitter criticism since similar released-time programs were being conducted throughout the country. Moreover, the *McCollum* decision "was announced when the nation was on the threshold or in the early stages of a period of religious revival. Periods of great fear drive men toward religion, and the steadily advancing threat of atomic destruction made the mid-century a period of great fear. Religion, moreover, had become a staunch ally of nationalism, for in the eyes of many the major difference between Americanism and Communism was acceptance or rejection of God. It was thus scarcely surprising that the *McCollum* decision, which in effect held that the public schools must be not only nonsectarian but secular or godless, should evoke a storm of acrimonious criticism." The voices of many who supported the Court's decision were "drowned in the strident chorus of disapproval."

It was against this background that the Court again considered the released time issue—this time the New York City program—in

Zorach v. Clauson. The only significant difference between the New York and Illinois programs was that in New York students were released to take religious education in centers set up *outside* the school grounds. Students were released on written request of their parents and left the school buildings for the religious centers at specified times. Students not released simply stayed in their classrooms. Tessim Zorach, a taxpayer and resident of New York City whose children attended its public schools, and another resident challenged the constitutionality of New York's released-time program. They contended that the program violated both the free exercise and establishment clauses of the First Amendment by reason of the Fourteenth Amendment. The highest state court upheld the released-time program. Zorach then brought the case to the Supreme Court on appeal. Clauson was a member of the New York City Board of Education against whom Zorach had brought his case.

MR. JUSTICE DOUGLAS delivered the opinion of the Court. . . .

This "released-time" program [New York City] involves neither religious instruction in public-school classrooms nor the expenditure of public funds. All costs, including the application blanks, are paid by the religious organizations. The case is therefore unlike *McCollum v. Board of Education.* . . . In that case the classrooms were turned over to religious instructors. We accordingly held that the program violated the First Amendment which (by reason of the Fourteenth Amendment) prohibits the states from establishing religion or prohibiting its free exercise. . . .

[O]ur problem reduces itself to whether New York by this system has either prohibited the "free exercise" of religion or has made a law "respecting an establishment of religion" within the meaning of the First Amendment.

It takes obtuse reasoning to inject any issue of the "free exercise" of religion to the present case. No one is forced to go to the religious classroom and no religious exercise or instruction is brought to the classrooms of the public schools. A student need not take religious instruction. He is left to his own desires as to the manner or time of his religious devotions, if any.

There is a suggestion that the system involves the use of coercion to get public-school students into religious classrooms. There is no evidence in the record before us that supports that conclusion. The present record indeed tells us that the school authorities are neutral in this regard and do no more than release students whose parents so request. If in fact coercion were used, if it were established that any one or more teachers were

using their office to persuade or force students to take the religious instruction, a wholly different case would be presented. Hence we put aside
that claim of coercion both as respects the "free exercise" of religion and
"an establishment of religion" within the meaning of the First Amendment.

Moreover, apart from that claim of coercion, we do not see how New
York by this type of "released-time" program has made a law respecting
an establishment of religion within the meaning of the First Amendment.
There is much talk of the separation of Church and State in the history of
the Bill of Rights and in the decisions clustering around the First Amendment. . . . There cannot be the slighest doubt that the First Amendment
reflects the philosophy that Church and State should be separated. And
so far as interference with the "free exercise" of religion and an "establishment" of religion are concerned, the separation must be complete and
unequivocal. The First Amendment within the scope of its coverage permits no exception; the prohibition is absolute. The First Amendment,
however, does not say that in every and all respects there shall be a
separation of Church and State. Rather, it studiously defines the manner,
the specific ways, in which there shall be no concert or union or dependency one on the other. That is the common sense of the matter.
Otherwise the state and religion would be aliens to each other—hostile,
suspicious, and even unfriendly. Churches could not be required to pay
even property taxes. Municipalities would not be permitted to render
police or fire protection to religious groups. Policemen who helped pari-
shioners into their places of worship would violate the Constitution.
Prayers in our legislative halls; the appeals to the Almighty in the
messages of the Chief Executive; the proclamations making Thanksgiving
Day a holiday; "so help me God" in our courtroom oaths—these and all
other references to the Almighty that run through our laws, our public
rituals, our ceremonies would be flouting the First Amendment. A fastidi-
ous atheist or agnostic could even object to the supplication with which
the Court opens each session: "God save the United States and this
Honorable Court."

We would have to press the concept of separation of Church and
State to these extremes to condemn the present law on constitutional
grounds. . . .

We are a religious people whose institutions presuppose a Supreme
Being. We guarantee the freedom to worship as one chooses. We make
room for as wide a variety of beliefs and creeds as the spiritual needs of
man deem necessary. We sponsor an attitude on the part of government
that shows no partiality to any one group and that lets each flourish according to the zeal of its adherents and the appeal of its dogma. When

the state encourages religious instruction or cooperates with religious authorities by adjusting the schedule of public events to sectarian needs, it follows the best of our traditions. For it then respects the religious nature of our people and accommodates the public service to their spiritual needs. To hold that it may not would be to find in the Constitution a requirement that the government show a callous indifference to religious groups. That would be preferring those who believe in no religion over those who do believe. Government may not finance religious groups nor undertake religious instruction nor blend secular and sectarian education nor use secular institutions to force one or some religion on any person. But we find no constitutional requirement which makes it necessary for government to be hostile to religion and to throw its weight against efforts to widen the effective scope of religious influence. The government must be neutral when it comes to competition between sects. It may not thrust any sect on any person. It may not make a religious observance compulsory. It may not coerce anyone to attend church, to observe a religious holiday, or to take religious instruction. But it can close its doors or suspend its operations as to those who want to repair to their religious sanctuary for worship or instruction. No more than that is undertaken here. . . .

In the *McCollum* case [Illinois] the classrooms were used for religious instruction and the force of the public school was used to promote that instruction. Here, as we have said, the public schools do no more than accommodate their schedules to a program of outside religious instruction. We follow the McCollum case. But we cannot expand it to cover the present released-time program unless separation of Church and State means that public institutions can make no adjustments of their schedules to accommodate the religious needs of the people. We cannot read into the Bill of Rights such a philosophy of hostility to religion.

Affirmed.

MR. JUSTICE BLACK, dissenting:

. . . I see no significant difference between the invalid Illinois system and that of New York here sustained. Except for the use of the school buildings in Illinois, there is no difference between the systems which I consider even worthy of mention. In the New York program, as in that of Illinois, the school authorities release some of the children on the condition that they attend the religious classes, get reports on whether they attend, and hold the other children in the school building until the religious hour is over. As we attempted to make categorically clear, the *McCollum* decision would have been the same if the religious classes had not been held in the school buildings. . . .

I am aware that our *McCollum* decision on separation of Church and State has been subjected to a most searching examination throughout the country. . . . Our insistence on "a wall between Church and State which must be kept high and impregnable" has seemed to some a correct exposition of the philosophy and a true interpretation of the language of the First Amendment to which we should strictly adhere. With equal conviction and sincerity, others have thought the *McCollum* decision fundamentally wrong and have pledged continuous warfare against it.

Here the sole question is whether New York can use its compulsory education laws to help religious sects get attendants presumably too unenthusiastic to go unless moved to do so by the pressure of this state machinery. That this is the plan, purpose, design, and consequence of the New York program cannot be denied. The state thus makes religious sects beneficiaries of its power to compel children to attend secular schools. Any use of such coercive power by the state to help or hinder some religious sects or to prefer all religious sects over non-believers or vice versa is just what I think the First Amendment forbids. In considering whether a state has entered this forbidden field the question is not whether it has entered too far but whether it has entered at all. New York is manipulating its compulsory education laws to help religious sects get pupils. This is not separation but combination of Church and State.

The Court's validation of the New York system rests in part on its statement that Americans are "a religious people whose institutions presuppose a Supreme Being." This was at least true when the First Amendment was adopted; and it was just as true when eight Justices of this Court invalidated the released-time system in *McCollum* on the premise that a state can no more "aid all religions" than it can aid one. It was precisely because eighteenth-century Americans were a religious people divided into many fighting sects that we were given the constitutional mandate to keep Church and State completely separate. . . .

Under our system of religious freedom, people have gone to their religious sanctuaries not because they feared the law but because they loved their God. The choice of all has been as free as the choice of those who answered the call to worship moved only by the music of the old Sunday-morning church bells. The spiritual mind of man has thus been free to believe, disbelieve, or doubt, without repression, great or small, by the heavy hand of government. Statutes authorizing such repression have been stricken. Before today, our judicial opinions have refrained from drawing invidious distinctions between those who believe in no religion and those who do believe. The First Amendment has lost much if the religious follower and the atheist are no longer to be judicially regarded as entitled to equal justice under the law.

State help to religion injects political and party prejudices into a holy field. It too often substitutes force for prayer, hate for love, and persecution for persuasion. Government should not be allowed, under cover of the soft euphemism of "cooperation," to steal into the sacred area of religious choice. . . .

MR. JUSTICE JACKSON, dissenting:

This released time program is founded upon a use of the State's power of coercion, which, for me, determines its unconstitutionality. Stripped to its essentials, the plan has two stages: first, that the State compel each student to yield a large part of his time for public secular education; and, second, that some of it be "released" to him on condition that he devote it to sectarian religious purposes.

No one suggests that the Constitution would permit the State directly to require this "released" time to be spent "under the control of a duly constituted religious body." This program accomplishes that forbidden result by indirection. If public education were taking so much of the pupil's time as to injure the public or the students' welfare by encroaching upon their religious opportunity, simply shortening everyone's school day would facilitate voluntary and optional attendance at Church classes. But that suggestion is rejected upon the ground that if they are made free many students will not go to the Church. Hence, they must be deprived of freedom for this period, with Church attendance put to them as one of the two permissible ways of using it.

The greater effectiveness of this system over voluntary attendance after school hours is due to the truant officer who, if the youngster fails to go to the Church school, dogs him back to the public schoolroom. Here schooling is more or less suspended during the "released time" so the non-religious attendants will not forge ahead of the churchgoing absentees. But it serves as a temporary jail for a pupil who will not go to Church. It takes more subtlety of mind than I possess to deny that this is governmental constraint in support of religion. It is as unconstitutional, in my view, when exerted by indirection as when exercised forthrightly.

As one whose children, as a matter of free choice, have been sent to privately supported Church schools, I may challenge the Court's suggestion that opposition to this plan can only be antireligious, atheistic. or agnostic. My evangelistic brethren confuse an objection to compulsion with an objection to religion. It is possible to hold a faith with enough confidence to believe that what should be rendered to God does not need to be decided and collected by Caesar.

The day that this country ceases to be free for irreligion it will cease to be free for religion—except for the sect that can win political power. The same epithetical jurisprudence used by the Court today to beat down those who oppose pressuring children into some religion can devise as good epithets tomorrow against those who object to pressuring them into a favored religion. And, after all, if we concede to the State power and wisdom to single out "duly constituted religious" bodies as exclusive alternatives for compulsory secular instruction, it would be logical to also uphold the power and wisdom to choose the true faith among those "duly constituted." We start down a rough road when we begin to mix compulsory public education with compulsory godliness.

A number of Justices just short of a majority of the majority that promulgates today's passionate dialectics joined in answering them in *Illinois* ex rel. *McCollum v. Board of Education,* . . . The distinction attempted between that case and this is trivial, almost to the point of cynicism, magnifying its non-essential details and disparaging compulsion which was the underlying reason for invalidity. A reading of the Court's opinion in that case along with its opinion in this case will show such difference of overtones and undertones as to make clear that the *McCollum* case has passed like a storm in a teacup. The wall which the Court was professing to erect between Church and State has become even more warped and twisted than I expected. Today's judgment will be more interesting to students of psychology and of the judicial processes than to students of constitutional law.

[JUSTICE FRANKFURTER also wrote a dissenting opinion.]

Engel et al. v. Vitale
370 U.S. 421 (1962)

Ten years after the furor over the released-time cases the Supreme Court was presented with an even more controversial and difficult religious issue—the use of prayers in the public schools. In November, 1951, the New York State Board of Regents, which controls and supervises the State's public school system, proposed a prayer for daily recitation in the public schools. The brief prayer was regarded by the Board of Regents as non-sectarian and read as follows: "Almighty God, we acknowledge our dependence upon Thee, and we beg Thy blessings upon us, our parents, our teachers and our country." The Regents proposal was by no means mandatory; it was simply a recommendation which local school boards were free to adopt or not as they saw fit, and only about 10 per cent of the local boards did adopt the prayer.

In 1958 the school board of New Hyde Park, a Long Island suburb of New York City, adopted the Regent's prayer and directed the
school district principal to cause the prayer "to be said aloud by each
class in the presence of a teacher at the beginning of each school
day." Steven Engel, who had two children enrolled in the Hyde Park
schools, and a group of other parents in the community, brought
suit in a state court with the help of the New York chapter of the
American Civil Liberties Union. The parents argued that the use of
the official prayer "was contrary to the beliefs, religions and religious
practices of both themselves and their children" and hence constituted a violation of the First and Fourteenth Amendments. Specifically, Engel and the other parents asked the trial court for a
mandamus [order] to compel the school board to discontinue the
use of the prayer, but it was denied. The trial court remanded the
case to the school board so that measures could be taken, if necessary, to eliminate any possible coercion and "to protect those who
objected to reciting the prayer." The trial court decision was affirmed
by the Appellate Division. Upon appeal the New York Court of Appeals (New York's highest court) also affirmed by a vote of five to
two, holding that the noncompulsory daily recitation of the prayer
did not violate the constitutional guaranties concerning freedom of
religion. The Supreme Court then granted certiorari.

The respondents are the members of the New Hyde Park school
board. William J. Vitale, Jr., was the presiding officer of the board.

MR. JUSTICE BLACK delivered the opinion of the Court.

. . . We think that by using its public school system to encourage recitation of the Regents' prayer, the State of New York has adopted a practice wholly inconsistent with the Establishment Clause. There can, of
course, be no doubt that New York's program of daily classroom invocation
of God's blessings as prescribed in the Regents' prayer is a religious activity. It is a solemn avowal of divine faith and supplication for the blessings
of the Almighty. . . .

The petitioners contend among other things that the state laws requiring or permitting use of the Regents' prayer must be struck down as a
violation of the Establishment Clause because that prayer was composed
by governmental officials as a part of a governmental program to further
religious beliefs. For this reason, petitioners argue, the State's use of the
Regents' prayer in its public school system breaches the constitutional
wall of separation between Church and State. We agree with that conten-

tion since we think that the constitutional prohibition against laws respecting an establishment of religion must at least mean that in this country it
is no part of the business of government to compose official prayers for
any group of the American people to recite as a part of a religious program carried on by government.

It is a matter of history that this very practice of establishing governmentally composed prayers for religious services was one of the reasons
which caused many of our early colonists to leave England and seek religious freedom in America. The Book of Common Prayer, which was
created under governmental direction and which was approved by Acts
of Parliament in 1548 and 1549, set out in minute detail the accepted
form and content of prayer and other religious ceremonies to be used in
the established, tax-supported Church of England. The controversies over
the Book and what should be its content repeatedly threatened to disrupt
the peace of that country as the accepted forms of prayer in the established church changed with the views of the particular ruler that happened to be in control at the time. Powerful groups representing some
of the varying religious views of the people struggled among themselves
to impress their particular views upon the Government and obtain amendments of the Book more suitable to their respective notions of how religious services should be conducted in order that the official religious
establishment would advance their particular religious beliefs. Other
groups, lacking the necessary political power to influence the Government on the matter, decided to leave England and its established church
and seek freedom in America from England's governmentally ordained
and supported religion.

It is an unfortunate fact of history that when some of the very groups
which had most strenuously opposed the established Church of England
found themselves sufficiently in control of colonial governments in this
country to write their own prayers into law, they passed laws making their
own religion the official religion of their respective colonies. Indeed, as
late as the time of the Revolutionary War, there were established churches
in at least eight of the thirteen former colonies and established religions
in at least four of the other five. But the successful Revolution against
English political domination was shortly followed by intense opposition
to the practice of establishing religion by law. This opposition crystallized
rapidly into an effective political force in Virginia where the minority
religious groups such as Presbyterians, Lutherans, Quakers and Baptists
had gained such strength that the adherents to the established Episcopal
Church were actually a minority themselves. In 1785-1786, those opposed
to the established Church, led by James Madison and Thomas Jefferson,
who, though themselves not members of any of these dissenting religious

groups, opposed all religious establishments by law on grounds of principle, obtained the enactment of the famous "Virginia Bill for Religious Liberty" by which all religious groups were placed on an equal footing so far as the State was concerned. Similar though less far-reaching legislation was being considered and passed in other States.

By the time of the adoption of the Constitution, our history shows that there was a widespread awareness among many Americans of the dangers of a union of Church and State. These people knew, some of them from bitter personal experience, that one of the greatest dangers to the freedom of the individual to worship in his own way lay in the Government's placing its official stamp of approval upon one particular kind of prayer or one particular form of religious services. They knew the anguish, hardship and bitter strife that could come when zealous religious groups struggled with one another to obtain the Government's stamp of approval from each King, Queen, or Protector that came to temporary power. The Constitution was intended to avert a part of this danger by leaving the government of this country in the hands of the people rather than in the hands of any monarch. But this safeguard was not enough. Our Founders were no more willing to let the content of their prayers and their privilege of praying whenever they pleased be influenced by the ballot box than they were to let these vital matters of personal conscience depend upon the succession of monarchs. The First Amendment was added to the Constitution to stand as a guaranty that neither the power nor the prestige of the Federal Government would be used to control, support or influence the kinds of prayer the American people can say—that the people's religions must not be subjected to the pressures of government for change each time a new political administration is elected to office. Under that Amendment's prohibition against governmental establishment of religion, as reinforced by the provisions of the Fourteenth Amendment, government in this country, be it state or federal, is without power to prescribe by law any particular form of prayer which is to be used as an official prayer in carrying on any program of governmentally sponsored religious activity.

There can be no doubt that New York's state prayer program officially establishes the religious beliefs embodied in the Regents' prayer. . . . Neither the fact that the prayer may be denominationally neutral, nor the fact that its observance on the part of the students is voluntary can serve to free it from the limitations of the Establishment Clause, as it might from the Free Exercise Clause, of the First Amendment, both of which are operative against the States by virtue of the Fourteenth Amendment. Although these two clauses may in certain instances overlap, they forbid two quite different kinds of governmental encroachment upon religious freedom. The Establishment Clause, unlike the Free Exercise Clause, does not depend upon any showing of direct governmental compulsion and is violated by the enactment of laws which establish an official religion whether those laws operate directly to coerce non-observing individuals or not. This is not to say, of course, that laws officially prescribing a particular form of religious worship do not involve coercion of such individuals. When the power, prestige and financial support of government is placed behind a particular religious belief, the indirect coercive pressure upon religious minorities to conform to the prevailing officially approved religion is plain. But the purposes underlying the Establishment Clause go much further than that. Its first and most immediate purpose rested on the belief that a union of government and religion tends to destroy government and to degrade religion. The history of governmentally established religion, both in England and in this country, showed that whenever government had allied itself with one particular form of religion, the inevitable result had been that it had incurred the hatred, disrespect and even contempt of those who held contrary beliefs. That same history showed that many people had lost their respect for any religion that had relied upon the support of government to spread its faith. The Establishment Clause thus stands as an expression of principle on the part of the Founders of our Constitution that religion is too personal, too sacred, too holy, to permit its "unhallowed perversion" by a civil magistrate. Another purpose of the Establishment Clause rested upon an awareness of the historical fact that governmentally established religions and religious persecutions go hand in hand. The Founders knew that only a few years after the Book of Common Prayer became the only accepted form of religious services in the established Church of England, an Act of Uniformity was passed to compel all Englishmen to attend those services and to make it a criminal offense to conduct or attend religious gatherings of any other kind—a law which was consistently flouted by dissenting religious groups in England and which contributed to widespread persecutions of people like John Bunyan who persisted in holding "unlawful [religious] meetings . . . to the great disturbance and distraction of the good subjects of this kingdom. . . ." And they knew that similar persecutions had received the sanction of law in several of the colonies in this country soon after the establishment of official religions in those colonies. It was in large part to get completely away from this sort of systematic religious persecution that the Founders brought into being our Nation, our Constitution, and our Bill of Rights with its prohibition against any governmental establishment of religion. The New York laws officially prescribing the Regents' prayer are inconsistent with both the purposes of the Establishment Clause and with the Establishment Clause itself.

It has been argued that to apply the Constitution in such a way as to prohibit state laws respecting an establishment of religious services in public schools is to indicate a hostility toward religion or toward prayer. Nothing, of course, could be more wrong. The history of man is inseparable from the history of religion. And perhaps it is not too much to say that since the beginning of that history many people have devoutly believed that "More things are wrought by prayer than this world dreams of." It was doubtless largely due to men who believed this that there grew up a sentiment that caused men to leave the cross-currents of officially established state religions and religious persecution in Europe and come to this country filled with hope that they could find a place in which they could pray when they pleased to the God of their faith in the language they chose. And there were men of this same faith in the power of prayer who led the fight for adoption of our constitution and also for our Bill of Rights with the very guaranties of religious freedom that forbid the sort of governmental activity which New York has attempted here. These men knew that the First Amendment, which tried to put an end to governmental control of religion and of prayer, was not written to destroy either. They knew rather that it was written to quiet well-justified fears which nearly all of them felt arising out of an awareness that governments of the past had shackled men's tongues to make them speak only the religious thoughts that government wanted them to speak and to pray only to the God that government wanted them to pray to. It is neither sacrilegious nor antireligious to say that each separate government in this country should stay out of the business of writing or sanctioning official prayers and leave that purely religious function to the people themselves and to those the people choose to look to for religious guidance.

It is true that New York's establishment of its Regents' prayer as an officially approved religious doctrine of that State does not amount to a total establishment of one particular religious sect to the exclusion of all others—that, indeed, the governmental endorsement of that prayer seems relatively insignificant when compared to the governmental encroachments upon religion which were commonplace 200 years ago. To those who may subscribe to the view that because the Regents' official prayer is so brief and general there can be no danger to religious freedom in its governmental establishment, however, it may be appropriate to say in the words of James Madison, the author of the First Amendment:

> [I]t is proper to take alarm at the first experiment on our liberties. . . . Who does not see that the same authority which can establish Christianity, in exclusion of all other Religions, may establish with the same ease any particular sect of Christians, in exclusion of all other Sects? That the same authority which can

force a citizen to contribute three pence only of his property for the support of any one establishment, may force him to conform to any other establishment in all cases whatsoever?

The judgment of the Court of Appeals of New York is reversed and the cause remanded for further proceedings not inconsistent with this opinion.

Reversed and remanded.

MR. JUSTICE FRANKFURTER took no part in the decision of this case. MR. JUSTICE WHITE took no part in the consideration or decision of this case.

[JUSTICE DOUGLAS wrote a concurring opinion.]

MR. JUSTICE STEWART, dissenting.

. . . The Court does not hold, nor could it, that New York has interfered with the free exercise of anybody's religion. For the state courts have made clear that those who object to reciting the prayer must be entirely free of any compulsion to do so, including any "embarrassments and pressures." . . . But the Court says that in permitting school children to say this simple prayer, the New York authorities have established "an official religion."

With all respect, I think the Court has misapplied a great constitutional principle. I cannot see how an "official religion" is established by letting those who want to say a prayer say it. On the contrary, I think that to deny the wish of these school children to join in reciting this prayer is to deny them the opportunity of sharing in the spiritual heritage of our Nation.

The Court's historical review of the quarrels over the Book of Common Prayer in England throws no light for me on the issue before us in this case. England had then and has now an established church. Equally unenlightening, I think, is the history of the early establishment and later rejection of an official church in our own States. For we deal here not with the establishment of a state church, which would, of course, be constitutionally impermissible, but with whether school children who want to begin their day by joining in prayer must be prohibited from doing so. . . . What is relevant to the issue here is not the history of an established church in sixteenth-century England or in eighteenth-century America, but the history of the religious traditions of our people, reflected in countless practices of the institutions and officials of our government.

At the opening of each day's Session of this Court we stand, while one of our officials invokes the protection of God. Since the days of John Marshall our Crier has said, "God save the United States and this Honorable Court." Both the Senate and the House of Representatives open their daily Sessions with prayer. Each of our Presidents, from George

Washington to John F. Kennedy, has upon assuming his Office asked the protection and help of God.

The Court today says that the state and federal governments are without constitutional power to prescribe any particular form of words to be recited by any group of the American people on any subject touching religion. The third stanza of "The Star-Spangled Banner," made our National Anthem by Act of Congress in 1931, contains these verses:

> Blest with victory and peace, may the heav'n rescued land
> Praise the Pow'r that hath made and preserved us a nation!
> Then conquer we must, when our cause it is just,
> And this be our motto, "In God is our Trust."

In 1954 Congress added a phrase to the Pledge of Allegiance to the Flag so that it now contains the words "one Nation under God, indivisible, with liberty and justice for all." In 1952 Congress enacted legislation calling upon the President each year to proclaim a National Day of Prayer. Since 1865 the words "In God We Trust" have been impressed on our coins.

Countless similar examples could be listed, but there is no need to belabor the obvious. . . .

I do not believe that this Court, or the Congress, or the President has by the actions and practices I have mentioned established an "official religion" in violation of the Constitution. And I do not believe the State of New York has done so in this case. What each has done has been to recognize and to follow the deeply entrenched and highly cherished spiritual traditions of our Nation—traditions which come down to us from those who almost 200 years ago avowed their "firm reliance on the Protection of Divine Providence" when they proclaimed the freedom and independence of this brave new world.

I dissent.

Aftermath

A storm of protest greeted the Court's decision in the *Engel* case. In fact, few decisions in American history have aroused so much controversy and public antagonism.

Though the *Engel v. Vitale* ruling had some powerful supporters, it was loudly condemned by newspapers, politicians, many Roman Catholics, a good proportion of Protestants, the American Legion, and even former Presidents Hoover and Eisenhower. For example, Representative George W. Andrews, a Democrat from Alabama who had previously launched bitter attacks on *Brown v. Board of Educa-*

tion and subsequent cases against segregation, remarked that the justices "put the Negroes in the schools and now they've driven God out." Cardinal Spellman said: "I am shocked and frightened that the Supreme Court has declared unconstitutional a simple and voluntary declaration of belief in God by public school children. The decision strikes at the very heart of the Godly tradition in which America's children have for so long been raised." Evangelist Billy Graham also attacked the decision arguing that the Constitution "meant that we were to have freedom *of* religion, not freedom *from* religion." *Engel v. Vitale* was deplored and damned on the floor of Congress, where more than a hundred proposals for a constitutional amendment nullifying the decision were introduced. One writer has aptly remarked that "the halls of Congress resounded with denunciation, some of it from members who had not prayed in fifty years." At its annual meeting the Governors' Conference adopted a resolution, with only the Governor of New York abstaining, condemning the decision and calling for a constitutional amendment which would allow the use of voluntary prayers in public classrooms.

Given this response to the *Engel* decision, many commentators demanded that the ruling be ignored. Gradually, however, the realization grew that many of the more extreme statements had been made by politicians and others who had never bothered to read the Court's opinion and by those who were using the *Engel* decision to attack the Court because they had been angered by other opinions principally in the areas of school segregation, criminal procedure and national security. Under the leadership of more enlightened church organizations calmer voices began to prevail and the furor died down. But already winding their way to the Court were two more potentially explosive cases involving Bible reading and the recitation of the Lord's Prayer in the public schools, to which we now turn.

Abington School District v. Schempp
Murray v. Curlett
374 U.S. 203 (1963)

On some occasions, when two or more cases coming from different states raise similar issues, the Supreme Court decides them together as in these two companion cases dealing with Bible reading and the recitation of the Lord's Prayer in public schools. The *Schempp* case originated in Pennsylvania, where a state law required that "at least ten verses from the Holy Bible shall be read, without comments, at the opening of each public school on each day." The statute further provided that any child could be excused from attending the Bible reading upon the written request of his parent or guardian. The Schempp family—husband, wife and two children who attended one of the Abington district schools—were devoted Unitarians, a Christian denomination which emphasizes freedom in religious belief. They brought suit to enjoin the practice of daily Bible readings, contending that it violated their rights under the establishment clause of the First Amendment as applied to the states by the due process clause of the First Amendment. A three judge district court in Pennsylvania found the statute unconstitutional. The case then went to the Supreme Court on appeal.

The *Murray* case originated in Baltimore, where the Board of School Commissioners, relying on an appropriate state statute, adopted a rule providing for opening exercises in the Baltimore public schools consisting primarily of the "reading, without comment, of a chapter in the Holy Bible and/or the use of the Lord's Prayer." Unlike the Schempps, the flamboyant Mrs. Murray and her son, a student in one of the city schools, were both professed atheists who found the Bible "nauseating, historically inaccurate, replete with the ravings of madness." They argued that the public schools should "prepare children to face the problems on earth, not to prepare for heaven—which is a delusional dream of the unsophisticated minds of the ill-educated clergy." The Murrays filed for an order to compel Curlett, the President of the Board of School Commissioners, to rescind the rule requiring Bible reading or the recitation of the Lord's Prayer. The trial court ruled against the Murrays. The state's highest court affirmed the judgment by a close four to three vote. The case then went to the Supreme Court on certiorari.

MR. JUSTICE CLARK delivered the opinion of the Court.

Once again we are called upon to consider the scope of the provision of the First Amendment to the United States Constitution which declares that "Congress shall make no law respecting an establishment of religion or prohibiting the free exercise thereof. . . ." These companion cases present the issues in the context of state action requiring that schools begin each day with readings from the Bible. While raising the basic questions under slightly different factual situations, the cases permit of joint treatment. In light of the history of the First Amendment and of our cases interpreting and applying its requirements, we hold that the practices at issue and the laws requiring them are unconstitutional under the Establishment Clause, as applied to the states through the Fourteenth Amendment. . . .

It is true that religion has been closely identified with our history and government. As we said in *Engel v. Vitale* . . . "The history of man is inseparable from the history of religion. And . . . since the beginning of that history many people have devoutly believed that 'More things are wrought by prayer than this world dreams of.'" In *Zorach v. Clauson* . . . we gave specific recognition to the proposition that "we are a religious people whose institutions presuppose a Supreme Being." The fact that the Founding Fathers believed devotedly that there was a God and that the unalienable rights of man were rooted in Him is clearly evidenced in their writings, from the Mayflower Compact to the Constitution itself. This background is evidenced today in our public life through the continuance in our oaths of office from the Presidency to the Alderman of the final supplication, "So help me God." Likewise each House of the Congress provides through its Chaplain an opening prayer, and the sessions of this Court are declared open by the crier in a short ceremony, the final phrase of which invokes the grace of God. Again, there are such manifestations in our military forces, where those of our citizens who are under the restrictions of military service wish to engage in voluntary worship. Indeed, only last year an official survey of the country indicated that 64 per cent of our people have church membership . . . while less than three per cent profess no religion whatever. . . . It can be truly said, therefore, that today, as in the beginning, our national life reflects a religious people. . . .

This is not to say, however, that religion has been so identified with our history and government that religious freedom is not likewise as strongly imbedded in our public and private life. Nothing but the most telling of personal experiences in religious persecution suffered by our forebears . . . could have planted our belief in liberty of religious opinion any more deeply in our heritage. It is true that this liberty frequently was not realized by the colonists, but this is readily accountable to their close ties to the Mother Country. However, the views of Madison and Jefferson, preceded by Roger Williams, came to be incorporated not only in the Federal Constitution but likewise in those of most of our States. This freedom to worship was indispensable in a country whose people came from the four quarters of the earth and brought with them a diversity of religious bodies, each with memberships exceeding 50,000, existing among our people, as well as innumerable small groups. . . .

[T]his Court has decisively settled that the First Amendment's mandate that "Congress shall make no law respecting an establishment of religion, or prohibiting the free exercise thereof" has been made wholly applicable to the states by the Fourteenth Amendment. . . .

[T]his Court has rejected unequivocally the contention that the establishment clause forbids only governmental preference of one religion over another. Almost 20 years ago [in *Everson v. Board of Education*] . . . the Court said that "neither a state nor the Federal government can set up a church. Neither can pass laws which aid one religion, or prefer one religion over another." . . . Further, Mr. Justice Rutledge, joined by Justices Frankfurter, Jackson and Burton, declared:

> The [First] Amendment's purpose was not to strike merely at the official establishment of a single sect, creed or religion, outlawing only a formal relation such as had prevailed in England and some of the Colonies. Necessarily it was to uproot all such relationships. But the object was broader than a separating church and state in this narrow sense. It was to create a complete and permanent separation of the spheres of religious activity and civil authority by comprehensively forbidding every form of public aid or support for religion. . . .

The same conclusion has been firmly maintained ever since that time . . . and we reaffirm it now.

While none of the parties to either of these cases has questioned these basic conclusions of the Court, both of which have been long established, recognized and consistently reaffirmed, others continue to question their history, logic, and efficacy. Such contentions, in the light of the consistent interpretation in cases of this Court, seem entirely untenable and of value only as academic exercises. . . .

[I]n *Engel v. Vitale*, only last year, these principles were so universally recognized that the Court without the citation of a single case and over the sole dissent of Mr. Justice Stewart reaffirmed them. The Court found the 22-word prayer used in "New York's program of daily classroom invocation of God's blessings as prescribed in the Regents' prayer . . . [to be] a religious activity." . . . It held that "it is no part of the business of government to compose official prayers for any group of the American people to recite as a part of a religious program carried on by the government. . . . [T]he Court found that the "first and most immediate purpose [of the Establishment Clause] rested on a belief that a union of government and religion tends to destroy government and to degrade religion." . . . When government, the Court said, allies itself with one particular form of religion, the inevitable result is that it incurs "the hatred, disrespect and even contempt of those who held contrary beliefs."

. . . The wholesome "neutrality" of which this Court's cases speak thus stems from a recognition of the teachings of history that powerful sects or groups might bring about a fusion of governmental and religious functions or a concert or dependency of one upon the other to the end that official support of the State or Federal Government would be placed behind the tenets of one or of all orthodoxies. This the Establishment Clause prohibits. And a further reason for neutrality is found in the Free Exercise Clause, which recognizes the value of religious training, teaching and observance and, more particularly, the right of every person to freely choose his own course with reference thereto, free of any compulsion from the state. This the Free Exercise Clause guarantees. Thus . . . the two clauses may overlap. . . . [T]he Establishment Clause has been directly considered by this Court eight times in the past score of years and, with only one Justice dissenting on the point, it has consistently held that the clause withdrew all legislative power respecting religious belief or the expression thereof. The test may be stated as follows: what are the purpose and the primary effect of the enactment? If either is the advancement or inhibition of religion then the enactment exceeds the scope of legislative power as circumscribed by the Constitution. That is to say that to withstand the strictures of the Establishment Clause there must be a secular legislative purpose and a primary effect that neither advances nor inhibits religion. . . . The Free Exercise Clause, likewise considered many times here, withdraws from legislative power, state and federal, the exertion of any restraint on the free exercise of religion. Its purpose is to secure religious liberty in the individual by prohibiting any invasions thereof by civil authority. Hence it is necessary in a free exercise case for one to show the coercive effect of the enactment as it operates against him in the practice of his religion. The distinction between the two clauses is apparent—a violation of the Free Exercise Clause is predicated on coercion while the Establishment Clause violation need not be so attended.

Applying the Establishment Clause principles to the cases at bar we find that the States are requiring the selection and reading at the opening of the school day of verses from the Holy Bible and the recitation of the Lord's Prayer by the students in unison. These exercises are prescribed as part of the curricular activities of students who are required by law to attend school. They are held in the school buildings under the supervision and with the participation of teachers employed in those schools. None of these factors, other than compulsory school attendance, was present in the program upheld in *Zorach v. Clauson.*

The conclusion follows that in both cases the laws require religious exercises and such exercises are being conducted in direct violation of the rights of the appellees and petitioners. Nor are these required exercises mitigated by the fact that individual students may absent themselves upon parental request, for that fact furnishes no defense to a claim of unconstitutionality under the Establishment Clause. . . . Further, it is no defense to urge that the religious practices here may be relatively minor encroachments on the First Amendment. The breach of neutrality that is today a trickling stream may all too soon become a raging torrent and, in the words of Madison, "it is proper to take alarm at the first experiment on our liberties."

. . . It is insisted that unless these religious exercises are permitted a "religion of secularism" is established in the schools. We agree of course that the State may not establish a "religion of secularism" in the sense of affirmatively opposing or showing hostility to religion, thus "preferring those who believe in no religion over those who do believe." . . . We do not agree, however, that this decision in any sense has that effect. In addition, it might well be said that one's education is not complete without a study of comparative religion or the history of religion and its relationship to the advancement of civilization. It certainly may be said that the Bible is worthy of study for its literary and historic qualities. Nothing we have said here indicates that such study of the Bible or of religion, when presented objectively as part of a secular program of education, may not be effected consistent with the First Amendment. But the exercises here do not fall into those categories. They are religious exercises, required by the States in violation of the command of the First Amendment that the Government maintain strict neutrality, neither aiding nor opposing religion.

Finally, we cannot accept that the concept of neutrality, which does not permit a State to require a religious exercise even with the consent of the majority of those affected, collides with the majority's right to free exercise of religion. While the Free Exercise Clause clearly prohibits the use of state action to deny the rights of free exercise to anyone, it has never meant that a majority could use the machinery of the State to practice its beliefs. Such a contention was effectively answered by Mr. Justice Jackson for the Court in *West Virginia Board of Education v. Barnette*. . . .

> The very purpose of a Bill of Rights was to withdraw certain subjects from the vicissitudes of political controversy, to place them beyond the reach of majorities and officials and to establish them as legal principles to be applied by the courts. One's right to . . .

freedom of worship . . . and other fundamental rights may not be submitted to vote; they depend on the outcome of no elections.

The place of religion in our society is an exalted one, achieved through a long tradition of reliance on the home, the church and the inviolable citadel of the individual heart and mind. We have come to recognize through bitter experience that it is not within the power of government to invade that citadel, whether its purpose or effect be to aid or oppose, to advance or retard. In the relationship between man and religion, the State is firmly committed to a position of neutrality. Though the application of that rule requires interpretation of a delicate sort, the rule itself is clearly and concisely stated in the words of the First Amendment. Applying that rule to the facts of these cases, we affirm the judgment in [the *Schempp* case]. In [*Murray v. Curlett*] the judgment is reversed and the cause remanded to the Maryland Court of Appeals for further proceedings consistent with this opinion.

It is so ordered.

MR. JUSTICE BRENNAN, concurring.

. . . The Court's historic duty to expound the meaning of the Constitution has encountered few issues more intricate or more demanding than that of the relationship between religion and the public schools. . . .

When John Locke ventured in 1689, "I esteem it above all things necessary to distinguish exactly the business of civil government from that of religion and to settle the just bounds that lie between the one and the other," he anticipated the necessity which would be thought by the Framers to require adoption of a First Amendment, but not the difficulty that would be experienced in defining those "just bounds." The fact is that the line which separates the secular from the sectarian in American life is elusive. . . .

I see no escape from the conclusion that the exercises called in question in these two cases violate the constitutional mandate. . . .

The religious nature of the exercises here challenged seems plain. Unless *Engel v. Vitale* is to be overruled, or we are to engage in wholly disingenuous distinction, we cannot sustain these practices. Daily recital of the Lord's Prayer and the reading of the passages of Scripture are quite as clearly breaches of the command of the Establishment Clause as was the daily use of the rather bland Regents' Prayer in the New York public schools. Indeed, I would suppose that if anything the Lord's Prayer and the Holy Bible are more clearly sectarian, and the present violations of the First Amendment consequently more serious.

[In the next 27 pages of his opinion Justice Brennan reviews the long history of Bible reading and daily prayer in the public schools and con-

*cludes that "these practices standing by themselves constitute an imper-
missible breach of the Establishment Clause."]*

. . . These considerations bring me to a final contention of the school
officials in these cases: that the invalidation of the exercises at bar permits
this Court no alternative but to declare unconstitutional every vestige,
however slight, of cooperation or accommodation between religion and
government. I cannot accept that contention. While it is not, of course,
appropriate for this Court to decide questions not presently before it, I
venture to suggest that religious exercises in the public schools present a
unique problem. For not every involvement of religion in public life
violates the Establishment Clause. Our decision in these cases does not
clearly forecast anything about the constitutionality of other types of
interdependence between religious and other public institutions. . . .

I think a brief survey of certain of these forms of accommodation will
reveal that the First Amendment commands not official hostility toward
religion, but only a strict neutrality in matters of religion. Moreover, it
may serve to suggest that the scope of our holding today is to be measured by the special circumstances under which these cases have arisen,
and by the particular dangers to church and state which religious exercises in the public schools present. . . .

A. The Conflict Between Establishment and Free Exercise

—There are certain practices, conceivably violative of the Establishment
Clause, the striking down of which might seriously interfere with certain
religious liberties also protected by the First Amendment. Provisions for
churches and chaplains at military establishments for those in the armed
services may afford one such example. The like provision by state and
federal governments for chaplains in penal institutions may afford another
example. It is argued that such provisions may be assumed to contravene
the Establishment Clause, yet be sustained on constitutional grounds as
necessary to secure to the members of the Armed Forces and prisoners
those rights of worship guaranteed under the Free Exercise Clause. Since
government has deprived such persons of the opportunity to practice
their faith at places of their choice, the argument runs, government may,
in order to avoid infringing the free exercise guaranties, provide substitutes where it requires such persons to be. Such a principle might support,
for example, the constitutionality of draft exemptions for ministers and
divinity students . . . ; of the excusal of children from school on their
respective religious holidays; and of the allowance by government of
temporary use of public buildings by religious organizations when their

own churches have become unavailable because of a disaster or emergency.

Such activities and practices seem distinguishable from the sponsorship of daily Bible reading and prayer recital. For one thing, there is no element of coercion present in the appointment of military or prison chaplains; the soldier or convict who declines the opportunities for worship would not ordinarily subject himself to the suspicion or obloquy of his peers. Of special significance to this distinction is the fact that we are here usually dealing with adults, not with impressionable children as in the public schools. Moreover, the school exercises are not designed to provide the pupils with general opportunities for worship denied them by the legal obligation to attend school. The student's compelled presence in school for five days a week in no way renders the regular religious facilities of the community less accessible to him than they are to others. The situation of the school child is therefore plainly unlike that of the isolated soldier or the prisoner. . . .

B. Establishment and Exercises in Legislative Bodies

—The saying of invocational prayers in legislative chambers, state or federal, and the appointment of legislative chaplains, might well represent no involvements of the kind prohibited by the Establishment Clause. Legislators, federal and state, are mature adults who may presumably absent themselves from such public and ceremonial exercises without incurring any penalty, direct or indirect. It may also be significant that, at least in the case of the Congress, Art. I, Section 5, of the Constitution makes each House the monitor of the "Rules of its Proceedings" so that it is at least arguable whether such matters present "political questions" the resolution of which is exclusively confided to Congress. . . . Finally, there is the difficult question of who may be heard to challenge such practices. . . .

C. Non-Devotional Use of the Bible in the Public Schools

—The holding of the Court today plainly does not foreclose teaching about the Holy Scriptures or about the differences between religious sects in classes in literature or history. Indeed, whether or not the Bible is involved, it would be impossible to teach meaningfully many subjects in the social sciences or the humanities without some mention of religion. To what extent, and at what points in the curriculum religious materials should be cited, are matters which the courts ought to entrust very largely to the experienced officials who superintend our Nation's public schools. They are experts in such matters, and we are not. . . .

D. UNIFORM TAX EXEMPTIONS INCIDENTALLY AVAILABLE TO RELIGIOUS INSTITUTIONS

—Nothing we hold today questions the propriety of certain tax deductions or exemptions which incidentally benefit churches and religious institutions, along with many secular charities and nonprofit organizations. If religious institutions benefit, it is in spite of rather than because of their religious character. For religious institutions simply share benefits which government makes generally available to educational, charitable, and eleemosynary groups. There is no indication that taxing authorities have used such benefits in any way to subsidize worship or foster belief in God. And as among religious beneficiaries, the tax exemption or deduction can be truly nondiscriminatory, available on equal terms to small as well as large religious bodies, to popular and unpopular sects, and to those organizations which reject as well as those which accept a belief in God.

E. RELIGIOUS CONSIDERATIONS IN PUBLIC WELFARE PROGRAMS

—Since Government may not support or directly aid religious activities without violating the Establishment Clause, there might be some doubt whether nondiscriminatory programs of governmental aid may constitutionally include individuals who become eligible wholly or partially for religious reasons. For example, it might be suggested that where a State provides unemployment generally to those who are unable to find suitable work, it may not extend such benefits to persons who are unemployed by reason of religious beliefs or practices without thereby establishing the religion to which those persons belong. Therefore, the argument runs, the State may avoid an establishment only by singling out and excluding such persons on the ground that religious beliefs or practices have made them potential beneficiaries. Such a construction would, it seems to me, require government to impose religious discriminations and disabilities, thereby jeopardizing the free exercise of religion, in order to avoid what is thought to constitute an establishment.

The inescapable flaw in the argument, I suggest, is its quite unrealistic view of the aims of the Establishment Clause. The Framers were not concerned with the effects of certain incidental aids to individual worshippers which come about as by-products of general and nondiscriminatory welfare programs. If such benefits serve to make easier or less expensive the practice of a particular creed, or of all religions, it can hardly be said that the purpose of the program is in any way religious, or that the consequence of its nondiscriminatory application is to create the forbidden degree of interdependence between secular and sectarian institutions. I cannot therefore accept the suggestion, which seems to me implicit in the argument outlined here, that every judicial or administrative construction which is designed to prevent a public welfare program from abridging the free exercise of religious beliefs, is for that reason *ipso facto* an establishment of religion.

F. Activities Which, Though Religious in Origin, Have Ceased to Have Religious Meaning

— . . . [N]early every criminal law on the books can be traced to some religious principle or inspiration. But that does not make the present enforcement of the criminal law in any sense an establishment of religion, simply because it accords with widely-held religious principles. . . . This rationale suggests that the use of the motto "In God We Trust" on currency, on documents and public buildings and the like may not offend the cause. It is not that the use of those four words can be dismissed as "de minimis"—for I suspect there would be intense opposition to the abandonment of that motto. The truth is that we have simply interwoven the motto so deeply into the fabric of our civil polity that its present use may well not present that type of involvement which the First Amendment prohibits.

This general principle might also serve to insulate the various patriotic exercises and activities used in the public schools and elsewhere which, whatever may have been their origins, no longer have a religious purpose or meaning. The reference to divinity in the revised pledge of allegiance, for example, may merely recognize the historical fact that our Nation was believed to have been founded "under God." Thus reciting the pledge may be no more of a religious exercise than the reading aloud of Lincoln's Gettysburg Address, which contains an allusion to the historical fact. . . .

[Concurring opinions were also written by JUSTICE DOUGLAS and JUSTICE GOLDBERG, joined by JUSTICE HARLAN. JUSTICE STEWART wrote a dissenting opinion.]

Aftermath

The decision in the *Schempp* case bolstered the Court's bold stand made in *Engel v. Vitale,* and though the effect was to outlaw Bible reading in two dozen states and prohibit the recitation of the Lord's Prayer in another dozen, the reaction was much less violent than it had been after the *Engel* decision. This was due, in part, to the fact that many church leaders had anticipated the decision and had worked quietly to gain the approval of their respective congregations. Moreover, in the year since the *Engel* decision, many Protestant churchmen, in particular, had begun openly to support the Court's stand for a complete divorce between the public schools and religious devotions.

The popular reaction was also somewhat muffled by the fact that the Court in the *Schempp* case wrote a more careful series of opinions. In his long majority opinion Justice Clark, a Presbyterian, attempted to set at rest some of the public fears engendered by *Engel v. Vitale*. The explanatory concurring opinions by Justice Brennan, a Roman Catholic, and Justice Goldberg, a Jew, also helped obtain acceptance of the decision.

VI THE RIGHT TO VOTE AND POLITICAL EQUALITY

Every American citizen must have an equal right to vote. There is no reason which can excuse the denial of that right. There is no duty which weighs more heavily on us than the duty we have to ensure that right. Yet the harsh fact is that in many places in this country men and women are kept from voting simply because they are Negroes. . . . Their cause must be our cause too. It is not just Negroes, but it is all of us, who must overcome the crippling legacy of bigotry and injustice. And we shall *overcome.*

> President Lyndon B. Johnson, address to joint session of Congress requesting passage of Voting Rights Bill of 1965, March 15, 1965.

Today is a triumph for freedom as huge as any victory won on the battlefield. Today we strike away the last major shackle of those fierce and ancient bonds. Today the Negro story and the American story fuse and blend.

> President Johnson, on signing the Voting Rights Act of 1965, August 6, 1965.

Gomillion v. Lightfoot
364 U.S. 339 (1960)

THE MAJOR CASES PRESENTED to the Supreme Court on voting and political equality have involved two distinct but closely related problems which go to the heart of our democratic system of government: voting rights of American Negroes and dilution of a citizen's vote because of unequal and unfair apportionment of election districts. The first three cases in this chapter are concerned with the long-standing efforts to enfranchise American Negroes while the last two deal with the more recent and revolutionary attempts of the Court to bring about equality in voting for all Americans.

It will be recalled that the Thirteenth, Fourteenth, and Fifteenth Amendments freed the slaves, made them citizens of the United States and sought to secure them the right to vote. But, as seen in Chapter III, the American Negro has yet to achieve complete freedom. His struggle to secure the fundamental right to vote has been particularly violent and bitter. Despite the promise of the Civil War Amendments, Negroes in the South and other parts of the country were effectively disfranchised by the early 1880's.

Over the years a variety of legal devices such as the novel "grandfather clauses" adopted in several states were used to deny Negroes the right to vote. In general, the various "grandfather clauses" permitted certain classes of individuals other than Negroes to vote without meeting certain property and literacy tests. The 1910 Oklahoma grandfather clause, for example, required a literacy test (ability to read and write *any* section of the Oklahoma Constitution) for voting. However, it provided that the test need not be taken by persons or descendants of such persons who were entitled to vote under any form of government or who resided in a foreign nation prior to January 1, 1866. Since Negroes could not vote prior to 1866 in Oklahoma, as well as in most other states, the required literacy test was used to deny most of them the right to vote. In 1915 the Supreme Court in *Guinn v. United States,* 238 U.S. 347, struck down the Oklahoma grandfather clause as a violation of the Fifteenth Amendment and gradually through the years, held unconstitutional other methods designed to deprive Negroes of the right to vote. But there always seemed to be available other devices such as poll taxes (discussed in *Harper v. Virginia* below), more ingenious literacy tests (noted in *South Carolina v. Katzenbach* below) and the white primary which could prevent Negroes from voting. The white primary simply excluded Negroes from voting in the Democratic Party primary in a host of Southern states. For all practical purposes this action disfranchised the colored race because the dominance of the Democratic Party in the South still makes victory in the primary tantamount to election. In *Smith v. Allwright,* 321 U.S. 649 (1944), the Supreme Court held the Texas white primary unconstitutional after a long and tortuous process of litigation. But, as President Truman's Committee on Civil Rights noted in 1947, in addition to the "formal, legal methods of disfranchisement, there are the long-standing techniques of terror and intimidation, in the face of which great courage is required of the Negro who tries to vote. In the regions most characterized by generalized violence against Negroes, little more than 'advice' is often necessary to frighten them away from the polls. They have learned, through the years, to discover threats in mood and atmosphere."

A good example of an unusual and ingenious scheme designed to keep Negroes from voting is provided by *Gomillion v. Lightfoot*, which went to the Supreme Court from Tuskegee, Alabama, the seat of Macon County and the home of Tuskegee Institute, the famed Negro college founded by Booker T. Washington in 1881. Negroes have long outnumbered whites in Tuskegee by a margin of approximately four to one. After World War II Negroes in Tuskegee began to register and vote in greater numbers in municipal elections, and in 1954 a Negro ran for the school board and lost by a relatively small margin. This frightened the local white leaders, who decided to press for legislation which would keep the city under white control. Accordingly, in 1957, the Alabama legislature passed, unanimously and without debate, Local Act No. 140, which redefined the boundaries of Tuskegee. The statute altered the shape of the city from a simple square to an irregular 28-sided figure resembling a "stylized sea horse." The effect was to place Tuskegee Institute and all but four or five Negro voters outside the city limits without removing a single white voter. Professor Charles G. Gomillion of Tuskegee Institute and other Negroes whose homes had been placed outside the city brought an action in a federal district court seeking a declaratory judgment (a decision simply declaring the rights of the Negroes without ordering that anything else be done) that Local Act No. 140 was unconstitutional. At the same time they asked for an injunction to restrain Mayor Phil M. Lightfoot and other municipal officers from enforcing the Act. The Negroes argued that enforcement of the Act would deny them benefits of residence in Tuskegee in violation of the due process and equal protection clauses of the Fourteenth Amendment and also deny them the right to vote in municipal elections in violation of the Fifteenth Amendment. The district court dismissed the case, stating that it had no power to change municipal boundaries fixed by an elected legislative body, and a court of appeals affirmed, with one judge dissenting. The Supreme Court then granted certiorari. *Gomillion v. Lightfoot* was the first racial gerrymander case ever considered by the Court.

232 These Liberties: Case Studies In Civil Rights

(Gerrymandering means simply the drawing or redrawing of political boundaries to favor the group or political party in power.)

MR. JUSTICE FRANKFURTER delivered the opinion of the Court.

The complaint amply alleges a claim of racial discrimination. Against this claim the respondents have never suggested, either in their brief or in oral argument, any countervailing municipal function which Act 140 is designed to serve. The respondents invoke generalities expressing the State's unrestricted power—unlimited, that is, by the United States Constitution—to establish, destroy, or reorganize by contraction or expansion its political subdivisions, to wit, cities, counties, and other local units. We freely recognize the breadth and importance of this aspect of the State's political power. To exalt this power into an absolute is to misconceive the reach and rule of this Court's decisions. . . .

[T]he Court has never acknowledged that the States have power to do as they will with municipal corporations regardless of consequences. Legislative control of municipalities, no less than other state power, lies within the scope of relevant limitations imposed by the United States Constitution. . . .

A statute which is alleged to have worked unconstitutional deprivations of petitioners' rights is not immune to attack simply because the mechanism employed by the legislature is a redefinition of municipal boundaries. According to the allegations here made, the Alabama Legislature has not merely redrawn the Tuskegee city limits with incidental inconvenience to the petitioners; it is more accurate to say that it has deprived the petitioners of the municipal franchise and consequent rights and to that end it has incidentally changed the city's boundaries. While in form this is merely an act redefining metes and bounds, if the allegations are established, the inescapable human effect of this essay in geometry and geography is to despoil colored citizens, and only colored citizens, of their theretofore enjoyed voting rights. . . .

When a State exercises power wholly within the domain of state interest, it is insulated from federal judicial review. But such insulation is not carried over when state power is used as an instrument for circumventing a federally protected right. . . . "Acts generally lawful may become unlawful when done to accomplish an unlawful end . . . and a constitutional power cannot be used by way of condition to attain an unconstitutional result." . . .

For these reasons, the principal conclusions of the District Court and the Court of Appeals are clearly erroneous and the decision below must be

Reversed.

[JUSTICES DOUGLAS and WHITTAKER wrote separate concurring opinions.]

South Carolina v. Katzenbach
383 U.S. 301 (1966)

Despite the many favorable Supreme Court opinions on Negro voting and the efforts by Congress outlined in the opinion below to do away with racial discrimination, it soon became apparent that more stringent legislation was needed. This finally came in the form of the Voting Rights Act of 1965 which marked an important milestone in the American Negroes' struggle for equality. President Johnson remarked aptly upon signing the bill that it represented a "triumph for freedom as huge as any victory won on the battlefield. Today we strike away the last major shackle of the fierce and ancient bonds. Today the Negro story and the American story fuse and blend."

The Voting Rights Act contained several interrelated provisions designed to enforce the right of Negroes to vote as follows:

> 1. Literacy tests and other restrictions on voting are sus-pended for five years in any state or political subdivision in which less than 50% of the residents of voting age were regis-tered on November 1, 1964, or voted in the presidential election in that month. On the basis of this formula tests were immediately suspended in Alabama, Louisiana, Mississippi, Georgia, South Carolina, and North Carolina. Other areas were later brought within the coverage formula of the Act.
> 2. During the suspension of literacy tests and other similar voting qualifications no new voting standards or procedures may be adopted by the states without the prior approval of the Attorney General or the District Court for the District of Columbia.
> 3. The Attorney General is authorized to dispatch *federal* examiners to areas that attempt to evade the law. These fed-eral examiners are empowered to register qualified applicants who are then entitled to vote in all elections.

South Carolina challenged these basic provisions of the Act by invoking the rarely used original jurisdiction of the Supreme Court. This was done by the state's suit against Attorney General Katz-enbach, a citizen of another state. Article III of the Constitution provides that the Supreme Court has original jurisdiction in cases commenced by a state against citizens of another state. Specifically, South Carolina sought to have the key provisions of the Act declared unconstitutional and asked for an injunction against enforcement of these provisions by Katzenbach.

MR. CHIEF JUSTICE WARREN delivered the opinion of the Court.

The constitutional propriety of the Voting Rights Act of 1965 must be judged with reference to the historical experience which it reflects. Before enacting the measure, Congress explored with great care the problem of racial discrimination in voting. . . . At the close of these deliberations, the verdict of both chambers was overwhelming. The House approved the Act by a vote of 328-74, and the measure passed the Senate by a margin of 79-18.

Two points emerge vividly from the voluminous legislative history of the Act contained in the committee hearings and floor debates. First: Congress felt itself confronted by an insidious and pervasive evil which had been perpetuated in certain parts of our country through unremitting and ingenious defiance of the Constitution. Second: Congress concluded that the unsuccessful remedies which it had prescribed in the past would have to be replaced by sterner and more elaborate measures in order to satisfy the clear commands of the Fifteenth Amendment. . . .

The Fifteenth Amendment to the Constitution was ratified in 1870. Promptly thereafter Congress passed the first Enforcement Act, which made it a crime for public officers and private persons to obstruct exercise of the right to vote. The statute was amended in the following year, to provide for detailed federal supervision of the electoral process, from registration to the certification of returns. As the years passed and fervor for racial equality waned, enforcement of the laws became spotty and ineffective, and most of their provisions were repealed in 1894. The remnants have had little significance in the recently renewed battle against voting discrimination.

Meanwhile, beginning in 1890, the States of Alabama, Georgia, Lousiana, Mississippi, North Carolina, South Carolina, and Virginia enacted tests still in use which were specifically designed to prevent Negroes from voting. Typically, they made the ability to read and write a registration qualification and also required completion of a registration form. These laws were based on the fact that as of 1890 in each of the named States, more than two-thirds of the adult Negroes were illiterate while less than one-quarter of the adult whites were unable to read or write. At the same time, alternate tests were prescribed in all of the named States to assure that white illiterates would not be deprived of the franchise. These included grandfather clauses, property qualifications, "good character" tests, and the requirement that registrants "understand" or "interpret" certain matter.

The course of subsequent Fifteenth Amendment litigation in this Court demonstrates the variety and persistence of these and similar institutions designed to deprive Negroes of the right to vote. Grandfather clauses were invalidated in *Guinn v. United States*, 238 U.S. 347, and *Myers v. Anderson*, 238 U.S. 368. Procedural hurdles were struck down in *Lane v. Wilson*, 307 U.S. 268. The white primary was outlawed in *Smith v. Allwright*, 321 U.S. 649, and *Terry v. Adams*, 345 U.S. 461. Improper challenges were nullified in *United States v. Thomas*, 362 U.S. 58. Racial gerrymandering was forbidden by *Gomillion v. Lightfoot*, 364 U.S. 339. Finally, discriminatory application of voting tests was condemned in *Schnell v. Davis*, 336 U.S. 933; *Alabama v. United States*, 371 U.S. 37; and *Louisiana v. United States*, 380 U.S. 145.

According to the results of recent Justice Department voting suits, the latter strategem is now the principal method used to bar Negroes from the polls. . . . White applicants for registration have often been excused altogether from the literacy and understanding tests or have been given easy versions, have received extensive help from voting officials, and have been registered despite serious errors in their answers. Negroes, on the other hand, have typically been required to pass difficult versions of all the tests, without any outside assistance and without the slightest error. The good morals requirement is so vague and subjective that it has constituted an open invitation to abuse at the hands of voting officials. Negroes obliged to obtain vouchers from registered voters have found it virtually impossible to comply in areas where almost no Negroes are on the rolls.

In recent years, Congress has repeatedly tried to cope with the problem by facilitating case-by-case litigation against voting discrimination. The Civil Rights Act of 1957 authorized the Attorney General to seek injunctions against public and private interference with the right to vote on racial grounds. Perfecting amendments in the Civil Rights Act of 1960 permitted the joinder of States as party defendants, gave the Attorney General access to local voting records, and authorized courts to register voters in areas of systematic discrimination. Title I of the Civil Rights Act of 1964 expedited the hearing of voting cases before three-judge courts and outlawed some of the tactics used to disqualify Negroes from voting in federal elections.

Despite the earnest efforts of the Justice Department and of many federal judges, these new laws have done little to cure the problem of voting discrimination. According to estimates by the Attorney General during hearings on the Act, registration of voting age Negroes in Alabama rose only from 10.2% to 19.4% between 1958 and 1964; in Louisiana it barely inched ahead from 31.7% to 31.8% between 1956 and 1965; and in Mississippi it increased only from 4.4% to 6.4% between 1954 and 1964. In each instance, registration of voting age whites ran roughly 50 percentage points or more ahead of Negro registration.

The previous legislation has proved ineffective for a number of reasons. Voting suits are unusually onerous to prepare, sometimes requiring as many as 6,000 man-hours spent combing through registration records in preparation for trial. Litigation has been exceedingly slow, in part because of the ample opportunities for delay afforded voting officials and others involved in the proceedings. Even when favorable decisions have finally been obtained, some of the States affected have merely switched to discriminatory devices not covered by the federal decrees or have enacted difficult new tests designed to prolong the existing disparity between white and Negro registration. Alternatively, certain local officials have defied and evaded court orders or have simply closed their registration offices to freeze the voting rolls. The provision of the 1960 law authorizing registration by federal officers has had little impact on local maladministration because of its procedural complexities.

During the hearings and debates on the Act, Selma, Alabama, was repeatedly referred to as the pre-eminent example of the ineffectiveness of existing legislation. In Dallas County, of which Selma is the seat, there were four years of litigation by the Justice Department and two findings by the federal courts of widespread voting discrimination. Yet in those four years, Negro registration rose only from 156 to 383, although there are approximately 15,000 Negroes of voting age in the county. Any possibility that these figures were attributable to political apathy was dispelled by the protest demonstrations in Selma in the early months of 1965. . . .

The Voting Rights Act of 1965 reflects Congress' firm intention to rid the country of racial discrimination in voting. . . . [The Court then describes in detail the key provisions of the Voting Rights Act of 1965 noted in the introductory statement above.]

The basic question presented by the case [is]: Has Congress exercised its powers under the Fifteenth Amendment in an appropriate manner with relation to the States?

The ground rules for resolving this question are clear. The language and purpose of the Fifteenth Amendment, the prior decisions construing its several provisions, and the general doctrines of constitutional interpretation, all point to one fundamental principle. As against the reserved powers of the States, Congress may use any rational means to effectuate the constitutional prohibition of racial discrimination in voting. . . .

Section I of the Fifteenth Amendment declares that "the right of citizens of the United States to vote shall not be denied or abridged by the United States or by any State on account of race, color, or previous condition of servitude." This declaration has always been treated as self-executing and has repeatedly been construed, without further legislative specification, to invalidate state voting qualifications or procedures which are discriminatory on their face or in practice. . . . The gist of the matter is that the Fifteenth Amendment supersedes contrary exertions of state power. "When a State exercises power wholly within the domain of state interest, it is insulated from federal judicial review. But such insulation is not carried over when state power is used as an instrument for circumventing a federally protected right." *Gomillion v. Lightfoot*. . . .

[Section] 2 of the Fifteenth Amendment expressly declares that "Congress shall have the power to enforce this article by appropriate legislation." By adding this authorization, the Framers indicated that Congress was to be chiefly responsible for implementing the rights created in §1. "It is the power of Congress which has been enlarged. Congress is authorized to *enforce* the prohibitions by appropriate legislation. Some legislation is contemplated to make the [Civil War] amendments fully effective." . . . Accordingly, in addition to the courts, Congress has full remedial powers to effectuate the constitutional prohibition against racial discrimination in voting.

Congress has repeatedly exercised these powers in the past, and its enactments have repeatedly been upheld. . . . On the rare occasions when the Court has found an unconstitutional exercise of these powers, in its opinion Congress had attacked evils not comprehended by the Fifteenth Amendment. . . .

The basic test to be applied in a case involving §2 of the Fifteenth Amendment is the same as in all cases concerning the express powers of Congress with relation to the reserved powers of the States. Chief Justice Marshall laid down the classic formulation, 50 years before the Fifteenth Amendment was ratified:

> Let the end be legitimate, let it be within the scope of the constitution, and all means which are appropriate, which are plainly adapted to that end, which are not prohibited, but consist with the letter and spirit of the constitution, are constitutional. *McCulloch v. Maryland*. . . .

We therefore reject South Carolina's argument that Congress may appropriately do no more than to forbid violations of the Fifteenth

Amendment in general terms—that the task of fashioning specific remedies or of applying them to particular localities must necessarily be left entirely to the courts. Congress is not circumscribed by any such artificial rules under §2 of the Fifteenth Amendment. In the oft-repeated words of Chief Justice Marshall, referring to another specific legislative authorization in the Constitution, "This power, like all others vested in Congress, is complete in itself, may be exercised to its utmost extent, and acknowledges no limitations, other than are prescribed in the constitution." *Gibbons v. Ogden.* . . .

Congress exercised its authority under the Fifteenth Amendment in an inventive manner when it enacted the Voting Rights Act of 1965. First: The measure prescribes remedies for voting discrimination which go into effect without any need for prior adjudication. This was clearly a legitimate response to the problem, for which there is ample precedent under other constitutional provisions. . . . Congress had found that case-by-case litigation was inadequate to combat widespread and persistent discrimination in voting, because of the inordinate amount of time and energy required to overcome the obstructionist tactics invariably encountered in these lawsuits. After enduring nearly a century of systematic resistance to the Fifteenth Amendment, Congress might well decide to shift the advantage of time and inertia from the perpetrators of the evil to its victims. . . . Second: The Act intentionally confines these remedies to a small number of States and political subdivisions which in most instances were familiar to Congress by name. This, too, was a permissible method of dealing with the problem. Congress had learned that substantial voting discrimination presently occurs in certain sections of the country, and it knew no way of accurately forecasting whether the evil might spread elsewhere in the future. In acceptable legislative fashion, Congress chose to limit its attention to the geographic areas where immediate action seemed necessary. . . . The doctrine of the equality of States, invoked by South Carolina, does not bar this approach, for that doctrine applies only to the terms upon which States are admitted to the Union, and not to the remedies for local evils which have subsequently appeared. . . .

We now consider the related question of whether the specific States and political subdivisions . . . were an appropriate target for the new remedies. . . .

The areas [Alabama, Louisiana, Mississippi, Georgia, North Carolina, and South Carolina] for which there was evidence of actual voting discrimination, share two characteristics incorporated by Congress into the coverage formula: the use of tests and devices for voter registration, and a voting rate in the 1964 presidential election at least 12 points below the national average. Tests and devices are relevant to voting discrimination because of their long history as a tool for perpetrating the evil; a low voting rate is pertinent for the obvious reason that widespread disenfranchisement must inevitably affect the number of actual voters. Accordingly, the coverage formula is rational in both practice and theory. It was therefore permissible to impose the new remedies on the few remaining States and political subdivisions covered by the formula, at least in the absence of proof that they have been free of substantial voting discrimination in recent years. . . .

It is irrelevant that the coverage formula excludes certain localities which do not employ voting tests and devices but for which there is evidence of voting discrimination by other means. Congress had learned that widespread and persistent discrimination in voting during recent years has typically entailed the misuse of tests and devices, and this was the evil for which the new remedies were specifically designed. . . .

South Carolina assails the temporary suspension of existing voting qualifications, . . . [arguing] that literacy tests and related devices are not in themselves contrary to the Fifteenth Amendment. . . . The record shows that in most of the States covered by the Act, including South Carolina, various tests and devices have been instituted with the purpose of disenfranchising Negroes, have been framed in such a way as to facilitate this aim, and have been administered in a discriminatory fashion for many years. Under these circumstances, the Fifteenth Amendment has clearly been violated. . . .

The Act suspends literacy tests and similar devices for a period of five years from the last occurrence of substantial voting discrimination. This was a legitimate response to the problem, for which there is ample precedent in Fifteenth Amendment cases. . . .

The Act suspends new voting regulations pending scrutiny by federal authorities to determine whether their use would violate the Fifteenth Amendment. This may have been an uncommon exercise of congressional power, as South Carolina contends, but the Court has recognized that exceptional conditions can justify legislative measures not otherwise appropriate. . . . Congress knew that some of the States . . . had resorted to the extraordinary stratagem of contriving new rules of various kinds for the sole purpose of perpetuating voting discrimination in the face of adverse federal decrees. Congress had reason to suppose that these States might try similar maneuvers in the future, in order to evade the remedies for voting discrimination contained in the Act itself. Under the compulsion of these unique circumstances, Congress responded in a permissibly decisive manner. . . .

There was nothing inappropriate about limiting litigation under this provision to the District Court for the District of Columbia, and in putting the burden of proof on the areas seeking relief. . . .

The Act authorizes the appointment of federal examiners to list qualified applicants who are thereafter entitled to vote, subject to an expeditious challenge procedure. This was clearly an appropriate response to the problem, closely related to remedies authorized in prior cases. . . . In many of the political subdivisions . . . voting officials have persistently employed a variety of procedural tactics to deny Negroes the franchise, often in direct defiance or evasion of federal decrees. Congress realized that merely to suspend voting rules which have been misused or are subject to misuse might leave this localized evil undisturbed. . . .

In recognition of the fact that there were political subdivisions . . . in which the appointment of federal examiners might be unnecessary, Congress assigned the Attorney General the task of determining the localities to which examiners should be sent. . . .

After enduring nearly a century of widespread resistance to the Fifteenth Amendment, Congress has marshalled an array of potent weapons against the evil, with authority in the Attorney General to employ them effectively. Many of the areas directly affected by this development have indicated their willingness to abide by any restraints legitimately imposed upon them. We here hold that the portions of the Voting Rights Act properly before us are a valid means for carrying out the commands of the Fifteenth Amendment. Hopefully, millions of non-white Americans will now be able to participate for the first time on an equal basis in the government under which they live. We may finally look forward to the day when truly "the right of citizens of the United States to vote shall not be denied or abridged by the United States or by any State on account of race, color, or previous condition of servitude."

The bill of complaint is

Dismissed.

[Justice Black wrote a separate concurring and dissenting opinion agreeing with substantially all of the Court's opinion but *arguing* that the provision requiring the approval of the Attorney General or the District Court for the District of Columbia for any new state voting legislation was unconstitutional. Justice Black remarked that this provision "so distorts our constitutional structure of government as to render any distinction drawn in the Constitution between state and federal power almost meaningless."]

Harper v. Virginia Board of Elections
383 U.S. 663 (1966)

Like the white primary, literacy tests, the grandfather clauses and other devices, the poll tax was adopted in a number of Southern states principally to keep Negroes from voting. But, by the time the Harper case went to the Supreme Court, the poll tax, never as effective as other devices, was a dying institution. A section of the Voting Rights Act of 1965 condemned poll taxes and directed the Justice Department to challenge their constitutionality in the courts. The Twenty-Fourth Amendment, ratified in January, 1964, outlawed poll taxes in all *federal* elections. It did not apply to state and local elections, but, by early 1966 only four states—Alabama, Mississippi, Texas and Virginia—still required a poll tax as a condition for voting. Eight states had previously abolished all such poll tax requirements.

The Virginia poll tax was based on a section of the state constitution which directed the state legislature to levy an annual poll tax not to exceed $1.50 on every resident of the state twenty-one years of age and older. The tax was to be paid at least six months prior to the election in which the voter sought to vote. Annie E. Harper, a retired Negro citizen of Fairfax County, Virginia, who lived on social security and three other impoverished Negro citizens were denied the right to vote in state and local elections because they had never paid the poll tax. With the help of the American Civil Liberties Union they brought suits to declare the tax unconstitutional as a violation of the equal protection clause of the Fourteenth Amendment. Acting under the mandate of the Voting Rights Act of 1965, the Department of Justice filed a brief in *amicus curiae* (friend of the Court) in support of Annie E. Harper and her friends. A federal district court upheld the Virginia poll tax relying principally on *Breedlove v. Suttles*, 302 U.S. 277 (1937), where the Supreme Court unanimously upheld the Georgia poll tax. The case then went directly to the Supreme Court on appeal.

It is interesting to note that in the 1951 case of *Butler v. Thompson*, 341 U.S. 937, the Supreme Court upheld the Virginia poll tax law itself over the lone dissent of Justice Douglas who delivered the majority opinion below. It should also be noted that though Annie Harper and her friends were Negroes, the Court's holding is concerned with *economic* discrimination rather than with *racial* discrimination.

MR. JUSTICE DOUGLAS delivered the opinion of the Court. . . .

We conclude that a State violates the Equal Protection Clause of the Fourteenth Amendment whenever it makes the affluence of the voter or payment of any fee an electoral standard. Voter qualifications have no relation to wealth nor to paying or not paying this or any other tax. Our cases demonstrate that the Equal Protection Clause of the Fourteenth Amendment restrains the States from fixing voter qualifications which invidiously discriminate. . . .

Long ago in *Yick Wo v. Hopkins,* 118 U.S. 356 . . . the Court referred to "political franchise of voting" as a "fundamental political right, because preservative of all rights." Recently in *Reynolds v. Sims* . . . we said, "Undoubtedly, the right of suffrage is a fundamental matter in a free and democratic society. Especially since the right to exercise the franchise in a free and unimpaired manner is preservative of other basic civil and political rights, any alleged infringement of the right of citizens to vote must be carefully and meticulously scrutinized." . . .

We say the same whether the citizen, otherwise qualified to vote, has $1.50 in his pocket or nothing at all, pays the fee or fails to pay it. The principle that denies the State the right to dilute a citizen's vote on account of his economic status or other such factors by analogy bars a system which excludes those unable to pay a fee to vote or who fail to pay.

It is argued that a State may exact fees from citizens for many different kinds of licenses; that if it can demand from all an equal fee for a driver's license, it can demand from all an equal poll tax for voting. But we must remember that the interest of the State, when it comes to voting, is limited to the power to fix qualifications. Wealth, like race, creed, or color, is not germane to one's ability to participate intelligently in the electoral process. Lines drawn on the basis of wealth or property, like those of race . . . are traditionally disfavored. . . . To introduce wealth or payment of a fee as a measure of a voter's qualifications is to introduce a capricious or irrelevant factor. The degree of the discrimination is irrelevant. In this context—that is, as a condition of obtaining a ballot—the requirement of fee paying causes an "invidious" discrimination . . . that runs afoul of the Equal Protection Clause. Levy "by the poll," as stated in *Breedlove v. Suttles* [302 U.S. 277] . . . is an old familiar form of taxation; and we say nothing to impair its validity so long as it is not made a condition to the exercise of the franchise. *Breedlove v. Suttles* sanctioned its use as "a prerequisite of voting." . . . To that extent the *Breedlove* case is overruled.

We agree, of course, with Mr. Justice Holmes that the Due Process Clause of the Fourteenth Amendment "does not enact Mr. Herbert Spencer's Social Statics." . . . Likewise, the Equal Protection Clause is not shackled to the political theory of a particular era. In determining what lines are unconstitutionally discriminatory, we have never been confined to historic notions of equality, any more than we have restricted due process to a fixed catalogue of what was at a given time deemed to be the limits of fundamental rights. . . . Notions of what constitutes equal treatment for purposes of the Equal Protection Clause *do* change. This Court in 1896 held that laws providing for separate public facilities for white and Negro citizens did not deprive the latter of the equal protection and treatment that the Fourteenth Amendment commands. *Plessy v. Ferguson.* . . . Seven of the eight Justices then sitting subscribed to the Court's opinion, thus joining in expressions of what constituted unequal and discriminatory treatment that sound strange to a contemporary ear. When, in 1954—more than a half-century later—we repudiated the "separate-but-equal" doctrine of *Plessy* as respects public education we stated: "In approaching this problem, we cannot turn the clock back to 1868 when the Amendment was adopted, or even to 1896 when *Plessy v. Ferguson* was written." *Brown v. Board of Education.* . . .

In a recent searching re-examination of the Equal Protection Clause, we held, as already noted, that "the opportunity for equal participation by all voters in the election of state legislators" is required. *Reynolds v. Sims.* . . . We decline to qualify that principle by sustaining this poll tax. Our conclusion, like that in *Reynolds v. Sims,* is founded not on what we think governmental policy should be, but on what the Equal Protection Clause requires.

We have long been mindful that where fundamental rights and liberties are asserted under the Equal Protection Clause, classifications which might invade or restrain them must be closely scrutinized and carefully confined. . . .

Those principles apply here. For to repeat, wealth or fee paying has, in our view, no relation to voting qualifications; the right to vote is too precious, too fundamental to be so burdened or conditioned.

Reversed.

MR. JUSTICE HARLAN, whom MR. JUSTICE STEWART joins, dissenting.

The final demise of state poll taxes, already totally proscribed by the Twenty-Fourth Amendment with respect to federal elections and abolished by the States themselves in all but four States with respect to state elections, is perhaps in itself not of great moment. But the fact that the *coup de grace* has been administered by this Court instead of being left to the affected States or to the federal political process should be a matter of continuing concern to all interested in maintaining the proper role of this tribunal under our scheme of government. . . .

The Equal Protection Clause prevents States from arbitrarily treating people differently under their laws. Whether any such differing treatment is to be deemed arbitrary depends on whether or not it reflects an appropriate differentiating classification among those affected; the clause has never been thought to require equal treatment of all persons despite differing circumstances. The test evolved by this Court for determining whether an asserted justifying classification exists is whether such a classification can be deemed to be founded on some rational and otherwise constitutionally permissible state policy. . . .

In substance the Court's analysis of the equal protection issue goes no further than to say that the electoral franchise is "precious" and "fundamental," . . . and to conclude that "[t]o introduce wealth or payment of a fee as a measure of a voter's qualifications is to introduce a capricious or irrelevant factor," . . . These are, of course, captivating phrases, but they are wholly inadequate to satisfy the standard governing adjudication of the equal protection issue: Is there a rational basis for Virginia's poll tax as a voting qualification? I think the answer to that question is undoubtedly "yes."

Property qualifications and poll taxes have been a traditional part of our political structure. In the Colonies the franchise was generally a restricted one. Over the years these and other restrictions were gradually lifted, primarily because popular theories of political representation had changed. Often restrictions were lifted only after wide public debate. The issue of woman suffrage, for example, raised questions of family relationships, of participation in public affairs, of the very nature of the type of society in which Americans wished to live; eventually a consensus was reached, which culminated in the Nineteenth Amendment no more than 45 years ago.

Similarly with property qualifications, it is only by fiat that it can be said, especially in the context of American history, that there can be no rational debate as to their advisability. Most of the early Colonies had them; many of the States have had them during much of their histories; and, whether one agrees or not, arguments have been and still can be made in favor of them. For example, it is certainly a rational argument that payment of some minimal poll tax promotes civic responsibility, weeding out those who do not care enough about public affairs to pay

$1.50 or thereabouts a year for the exercise of the franchise. It is also arguable, indeed it was probably accepted as sound political theory by a large percentage of Americans through most of our history, that people with some property have a deeper stake in community affairs, and are consequently more responsible, more educated, more knowledgeable, more worthy of confidence, than those without means, and that the community and Nation would be better managed if the franchise were restricted to such citizens. Nondiscriminatory and fairly applied literacy tests, upheld by this Court . . . find justification on very similar grounds.

These viewpoints, to be sure, ring hollow on most contemporary ears. Their lack of acceptance today is evidenced by the fact that nearly all of the States, left to their own devices, have eliminated property or poll-tax qualifications; by the cognate fact that Congress and three-quarters of the States quickly ratified the Twenty-Fourth Amendment. . . .

Property and poll-tax qualifications, very simply, are not in accord with current egalitarian notions of how a modern democracy should be organized. It is, of course, entirely fitting that legislatures should modify the law to reflect such changes in popular attitudes. However, it is all wrong, in my view, for the Court to adopt the political doctrines popularly accepted at a particular moment of our history and to declare all others to be irrational and invidious, barring them from the range of choice by reasonably minded people acting through the political process. It was not too long ago that Mr. Justice Holmes felt impelled to remind the Court that the Due Process Clause of the Fourteenth Amendment does not enact the *laissez-faire* theory of society. . . . The times have changed, and perhaps it is appropriate to observe that neither does the Equal Protection Clause of that Amendment rigidly impose upon America an ideology of unrestrained egalitarianism.

I would affirm the decision of the District Court.

[JUSTICE BLACK also wrote a separate dissenting opinion.]

Wesberry v. Sanders
376 U.S. 1 (1964)

It is a well known fact that for many years state legislative and congressional districts were designed to favor rural interests even in the face of revolutionary migrations to urban centers. Over the years rurally dominated state legislatures simply refused to draw up state legislative or congressional districts which would give equal representation to urban voters. There are some dramatic examples. At one time some four hundred inhabitants of rural Union, Connecticut, sent as many representatives to the state legislature as did the 162,000 inhabitants of urban Hartford. In Michigan, a rural congressional district of some 177,000 voters sent one representative to Congress while an urban-suburban district of over 800,000 inhabitants also elected but one representative to Congress.

The Supreme Court's decisions on reapportionment are among the most important in American history for, unlike many great cases, they have deeply affected the governmental power structure. As a result of these cases the United States today is in the process of shifting legislative control from the more conservative rural areas to the cities and surrounding metropolitan areas where voters are more sympathetic toward social change. In a real sense the reapportionment cases were the logical outcome of the decisions on racial and other types of discrimination. If it is illegal under the Equal Protection Clause of the Fourteenth Amendment or other portions of the Constitution to deny anyone the right to vote on the basis of his race, sex or creed, is it not just as wrong to dilute a citizen's vote because he lives in a city or suburban area where his vote counts for less than his counterpart in a rural area? This was the difficult question posed by the reapportionment cases in a country that has, for all practical purposes, become urban.

For a long time questions involving reapportionment were deemed *political*—meaning simply that reapportionment problems were to be resolved by the state legislatures, Congress and executive officers rather than by the courts. In the most important case of *Colegrove v. Green*, 328 U.S. 549 (1946), for example, the Court in an opinion by Justice Frankfurter held that it was powerless to remedy the failure of the Illinois legislature to redistrict for Congressional representation. Frankfurter remarked that Courts ought not to enter the "political thicket" of reapportionment and that the "remedy for unfairness in districting is to secure state legislatures that will apportion properly, or to invoke the ample powers of Congress." But by 1962 it was readily apparent that neither the state legislatures nor Congress had taken any important steps toward securing fairness in reapportionment. Prodded by the swelling chorus of discontented urban voters, the Court in 1962 ruled, in the famous case of *Baker v. Carr*, 369 U.S. 186 (1962), that federal courts have jurisdiction to scrutinize the fairness of legislative apportionments under the Fourteenth Amendment and thereby overruled the *Colegrove* doctrine over the bitter dissents of Justices Frankfurter and Harlan. However, the Court did not give any guidance on the critical question of what constitutes a "fair" apportionment.

Baker v. Carr had an almost immediate impact. In fact, never before, after an assertion of expanded jurisdiction by the Court, has there been such a flurry of widespread political and judicial activity. Almost within hours of the decision litigation was begun in state and federal courts challenging the existing schemes of legislative representation. At present practically all of the states are involved in some form of litigation. Existing apportionment schemes in more than half the states have already been invalidated. In a number of states both regular and special sessions of the legislature are in the process of changing present arrangements. In Georgia, for example, the legislature acted under pressure to modify the "county unit" system to provide fewer inequities in party primaries. The Georgia "county unit" scheme assigned to each county electoral votes which went to the candidate receiving the highest popular votes. It was designed principally to disfranchise the urban Negro population. Relying heavily on *Baker v. Carr,* a federal district court held that Georgia's revised "county unit" system violated the equal protection clause of the Fourteenth Amendment. In *Gray v. Sanders,* 372 U.S. 368 (1963), the Supreme Court agreed with the lower court. Moreover, the highest Court held that the equal protection clause requires that every voter be equal to every other voter in the state when he casts his ballot in a state-wide election. Speaking for the Court over the lone dissent of Justice Harlan, Justice Douglas stated that the conception of political equality "can mean one thing—one person, one vote." Thus the Court established the standard for fairness in apportionment—namely that districts must be substantially equal in population. This is essentially the meaning of the "one person, one vote" standard.

These decisions culminated in two landmark decisions—*Wesberry v. Sanders,* dealing with congressional districts, and *Reynolds v. Sims,* which was concerned with representation in state legislatures.

The *Wesberry* case originated in Atlanta, Georgia, when a young accountant named James P. Wesberry, Jr., and another qualified voter brought a suit claiming that population disparities in congressional districts deprived them of a right under the Federal Constitution to have their votes for Congressmen given the same weight as the votes of other Georgians. The Atlanta congressional district had 823,680 persons as compared with the total population of 272,154 in the smallest district of the state. The average population of the ten Georgia districts was 394,312. Each district elected only one Congressman.

In his suit Wesberry asked that the Georgia districting statute be declared invalid and that Sanders, the Governor of Georgia and the state Secretary of State be enjoined from conducting elections under it. Wesberry contended that voters in the Atlanta district were deprived of the full benefit of their right to vote in violation of the following:

1. Article I, sec. 2 of the Constitution which provides that "The House of Representatives shall be composed of Members chosen every second Year by the People of the several States . . ."
2. The Due Process, Equal Protection, and Privileges and Immunities Clauses of the Fourteenth Amendment.
3. That part of Section 2 of the Fourteenth Amendment which provides that "Representatives shall be apportioned among the several States according to their respective numbers . . ."

In a 2 to 1 decision a federal district court dismissed the complaint on the ground that challenges to apportionment of congressional districts raised only "political" questions which are not justifiable. The district court relied on Justice Frankfurter's opinion in *Colegrove v. Green* in reaching its decision. The dissenting district judge relied on *Baker v. Carr*. The case then went to the Supreme Court on appeal. It is interesting to note that Justice Black, author of the majority opinion here, wrote a dissenting opinion in *Colegrove v. Green* in which he was joined by Justices Douglas and Murphy. Justice Harlan's impassioned dissenting opinion again reveals his deep commitment to the concept of judicial self-restraint.

MR. JUSTICE BLACK delivered the opinion of the Court.

. . . We hold that, construed in its historical context, the command of Art. I, Section 2, that Representatives be chosen "by the People of the several States" means that as nearly as is practicable one man's vote in a congressional election is to be worth as much as another's. This rule is followed automatically, of course, when Representatives are chosen as a group on a statewide basis, as was a widespread practice in the first 50 years of our Nation's history. It would be extraordinary to suggest that in such statewide elections the votes of inhabitants of some parts of a State . . . could be weighed at two or three times the value of the votes of people living in more populous parts of the State. . . . We do not believe that the Framers of the Constitution intended to permit the same vote-diluting discrimination to be accomplished through the device of districts containing widely varied numbers of inhabitants. To say that a vote is worth more in one district than in another would not only run counter to our fundamental ideas of democratic government, it would cast aside the principle of a House of Representatives elected "by the People," a principle tenaciously fought for and established at the Constitutional Convention. The history of the Constitution, particularly that part of it relating to the adoption of Art. I, Section 2, reveals that those who framed the Constitution meant that, no matter what the mechanics of an election, whether statewide or by districts, it was population which was to be the basis of the House of Representatives. . . . *[Justice Black then relies principally on the debates of the Constitutional Convention to show that the framers intended that every man's vote was "to count alike."]*

. . . It would defeat the principle solemnly embodied in the Great Compromise—equal representation in the House of equal numbers of people—for us to hold that, within the States, legislatures may draw the lines of congressional districts in such a way as to give some voters a greater voice in choosing a Congressman than others. The House of Representatives, the [Constitutional] Convention agreed, was to represent the people as individuals, and on a basis of complete equality for each voter. The delegates were quite aware of what Madison called the "vicious representation" in Great Britain whereby "rotten boroughs" with few inhabitants were represented in Parliament on or almost on a par with cities of greater population. [James] Wilson urged that people must escape the evils of the English system under which one man could send two members to Parliament to represent the borough of Old Sarum while London's million people sent but four. The delegates referred to rotten borough apportionments in some of the state legislatures as the kind of objectionable governmental action that the Constitution should not tolerate in the election of congressional representatives.

Madison in *The Federalist* described the system of division of States into congressional districts, the method which he and others assumed States probably would adopt: "The city of Philadelphia is supposed to contain between fifty and sixty thousand souls. It will therefore form nearly two districts for the choice of Federal Representatives." "[N]umbers," he said, not only are a suitable way to represent wealth but in any event "are the only proper scale of representation." In the state conventions, speakers urging ratification of the Constitution emphasized the theme of equal representation in the House which had permeated the debates in Philadelphia. . . . Speakers at the ratifying conventions emphasized that the House of Representatives was meant to be free of the malapportionment then existing in some of the state legislatures—such as those of Connecticut, Rhode Island, and South Carolina—and argued that the power given Congress in Art. I, Section 4, was meant to be used to vindicate the people's right to equality of representation in the House. Congress' power, said John Steele at the North Carolina convention, was not to be used to allow Congress to create rotten boroughs; in answer to another delegate's suggestion that Congress might use its power to favor people living near the seacoast, Steele said that Congress "most probably" would "lay the State off into districts," and if it made laws "inconsistent with the Constitution, independent judges will not uphold them, nor will the people obey them."

Soon after the Constitution was adopted, James Wilson of Pennsylvania, by then an Associate Justice of this Court, gave a series of lectures at Philadelphia in which, drawing on his experience as one of the most active members of the Constitutional Convention, he said:

> [A]ll elections ought to be equal. Elections are equal, when a given number of citizens, in one part of the state, choose as many representatives, as are chosen by the same number of citizens, in any part of the state. In this manner, the proportion of the representatives and of the constituents will remain invariably the same.

It is in the light of such history that we must construe Art. I, Section 2, of the Constitution, which, carrying out the ideas of Madison and those of like views, provides that Representatives shall be chosen "by the People of the several States" and shall be "apportioned among the several States . . . according to their respective numbers." It is not surprising that our Court has held that this Article gives persons qualified to vote a constitutional right to vote and to have their votes counted. . . . No right is more precious in a free country than that of having a voice in the election of those who make the laws under which, as good citizens, we must live. Other rights, even the most basic, are illusory if the right to vote is undermined. Our Constitution leaves no room for classification of people in a way that unnecessarily abridges this right. . . .

While it may not be possible to draw congressional districts with mathematical precision, that is no excuse for ignoring our Constitution's plain objective of making equal representation for equal numbers of people the fundamental goal for the House of Representatives. That is the high standard of justice and common sense which the Founders set for us.

Reversed and remanded.

... MR. JUSTICE HARLAN, dissenting.

I had not expected to witness the day when the Supreme Court of the United States would render a decision which casts grave doubt on the constitutionality of the composition of the House of Representatives. It is not an exaggeration to say that such is the effect of today's decision. The Court's holding that the Constitution requires States to select Representatives either by elections at large or by elections in districts composed "as nearly as is practicable" of equal population places in jeopardy the seats of almost all the members of the present House of Representatives.

In the last congressional election, in 1962, Representatives from 42 States were elected from congressional districts. In all but five of those States, the difference between the populations of the largest and smallest districts exceeded 100,000 persons. A difference of this magnitude in the size of districts the average population of which in each State is less than 500,000 is presumably not equality among districts "as nearly as is practicable," although the Court does not reveal its definition of that phrase. Thus, today's decision impugns the validity of the election of 398 Representatives from 37 States, leaving a "constitutional" House of 37 members now sitting.

Only a demonstration which could not be avoided would justify this Court in rendering a decision the effect of which, inescapably as I see it, is to declare constitutionally defective the very composition of a coordinate branch of the Federal Government. The Court's opinion not only fails to make such a demonstration. It is unsound logically on its face and demonstrably unsound historically. . . .

[T]he language of Art. I, Sections 2 and 4, the surrounding text, and the revelant history are all in strong and consistent direct contradiction of the Court's holding. The constitutional scheme vests in the States plenary power to regulate the conduct of elections for Representatives, and, in order to protect the Federal Government, provides for congressional supervision of the States' exercise of their power. . . .

The unstated premise of the Court's conclusion quite obviously is that the Congress has not dealt, and the Court believes it will not deal, with the problem of congressional apportionment in accordance with what the Court believes to be sound political principles. . . .

Today's decision has portents for our society and the Court itself which should be recognized. This is not a case in which the Court vindicates the kind of individual rights that are assured by the Due Process Clause of the Fourteenth Amendment, whose "vague contours," . . . of course leave much room for constitutional developments necessitated by changing conditions in a dynamic society. Nor is this a case in which an emergent set of facts requires the Court to frame new principles to protect recognized constitutional rights. The claim for judicial relief in this case strikes at one of the fundamental doctrines of our system of government, the separation of powers. In upholding that claim, the Court attempts to effect reforms in a field which the Constitution, as plainly as can be, has committed exclusively to the political process.

This Court, no less than all other branches of the Government, is bound by the Constitution. The Constitution does not confer on the Court blanket authority to step into every situation where the political branch may be thought to have fallen short. The stability of this institution ultimately depends not only upon its being alert to keep the other branches of government within constitutional bounds but equally upon recognition of the limitations on the Court's own functions in the constitutional system.

What is done today saps the political process. The promise of judicial intervention in matters of this sort cannot but encourage popular inertia in efforts for political reform through the political process, with the inevitable result that the process itself weakened. By yielding to the demand for a judicial remedy in this instance, the Court in my view does a disservice both to itself and to the broader values of our system of government.

[JUSTICE CLARK wrote a separate opinion concurring in part and dissenting in part. JUSTICE STEWART joined JUSTICE HARLAN'S dissent with a single qualification.]

AFTERMATH

Four days after the *Wesberry* decision, the Georgia legislature, in a wild and tumultuous session, divided the heavily populated Atlanta district in two, each with its own Congressman, and redrew the lines of other districts to provide units of near-equal size in terms of population. Thus, for the first time since 1931, a reapportionment bill was passed which gave Atlanta the representation in Congress to which it was entitled by population.

One writer has aptly noted that the swift reaction to the *Wesberry* decision reveals how wrong Justice Harlan was in the last paragraph of his dissenting opinion where he argues that judicial intervention in reapportionment cases "saps the political process." "My response," says Professor C. Herman Pritchett, "is that it is a naive, static view of politics which holds that if courts do more, the legislature and executive will do less. If the courts act, it is quite possible that they will stimulate others to act." ("Equal Protection and the Urban Majority," *American Political Science Review,* Vol. 58, p. 874, 1964)

Reynolds v. Sims
377 U.S. 533 (1964)

Reynolds v. Sims is the leading case in a series of six dealing with reapportionment coming from Alabama, New York, Maryland, Virginia, Delaware, and Colorado. Justice Harlan dissented in all six cases while Justice Stewart, joined by Justice Clark, dissented in the Colorado and New York cases.

M. O. Sims and other qualified voters living in highly urbanized Alabama counties brought suit in a federal district court against Reynolds, a probate judge and other officials responsible for the administration of the state election laws, challenging the apportionment of the Alabama legislature. Though the 1901 Alabama Constitution required reapportionment of the legislature every ten years, no substantial reapportionment had taken place for over sixty years. During that period the population of the state was almost doubled with virtually all the gains occurring in urban counties. Sims contended that he and others were victims of serious discrimination. For example, Sims' own Jefferson county, with a population of over 600,000, and rural Lowndes county, with a population of 15,416, *each* elected *one* senator. At the same time, Jefferson county had only seven seats in the Alabama House of Representatives while Bullock county, with a population of 13,462, was allocated two seats. Thus, at issue in the case were the existing apportionment provisions and two new plans noted in the case below neither of which provided for apportionment on a population basis.

The three-judge district court held that all three apportionment schemes were unconstitutional. The case then went to the Supreme Court on direct appeal.

MR. CHIEF JUSTICE WARREN delivered the opinion of the Court.

. . . [T]he right of suffrage is a fundamental matter in a free and democratic society. Especially since the right to exercise the franchise in a free and unimpaired manner is preservative of other basic civil and political rights, any alleged infringement of the right of citizens to vote must be carefully and meticulously scrutinized. . . .

Legislators represent people, not trees or acres. Legislators are elected by voters, not farms or cities or economic interests. As long as ours is a representative form of government, and our legislatures are those instruments of government elected directly by and directly representative of the people, the right to elect legislators in a free and unimpaired fashion is a bedrock of our political system. It could hardly be gainsaid that a constitutional claim had been asserted by an allegation that certain otherwise qualified voters had been entirely prohibited from voting for members of their state legislature. And, if a State should provide that the votes of citizens in one part of the State should be given two times, or five times, or ten times the weight of votes of citizens in another part of the State, it could hardly be contended that the right to vote of those residing in the disfavored areas had not been effectively diluted. It would appear extraordinary to suggest that a state could be constitutionally permitted to enact a law providing that certain of the state's voters could vote two, five or ten times for their legislative representatives, while voters living elsewhere could vote only once. And it is inconceivable that a state law to the effect that, in counting votes for legislators, the votes of citizens in one part of the State would be multiplied by two, five or ten, while the votes of persons in another area would be counted only at face value, could be constitutionally sustainable. Of course, the effect of state legislative districting schemes which give the same number of representatives to unequal numbers of constituents is identical. Overweighting and overvaluation of the votes of those living here has the certain effect of dilution and undervaluation of the votes of those living there. The resulting discrimination against those individual voters living in disfavored areas is easily demonstrable mathematically. Their right to vote is simply not the same right to vote as that of those living in a favored part of the State. Two, five, or ten of them must vote before the effect of their voting is equivalent to that of their favored neighbor. Weighting the votes of citizens differently, by any method or means, merely because of where they happen to reside, hardly seems justifiable. One must be ever aware that the Constitution forbids "sophisticated as well as simple-minded modes of discrimination." . . .

State legislatures are, historically, the fountainhead of representative government in this country. A number of them have their roots in colonial times, and substantially antedate the creation of our Nation and our Federal Government. In fact, the first formal stirrings of American political independence are to be found, in large part, in the views and actions of several of the colonial legislative bodies. With the birth of our National Government, and the adoption and ratification of the Federal Constitution, state legislatures retained a most important place in our Nation's governmental structure. But representative government is in essence self-government through the medium of elected representatives of the people, and each and every citizen has an inalienable right to full and effective participation in the political processes of his State's legislative bodies. Most citizens can achieve this participation only as qualified voters through the election of legislators to represent them. Full and effective participation by all citizens in state government requires, therefore, that each citizen has an equally effective voice in the election of members of his state legislature. Modern and viable state government needs, and the Constitution demands, no less.

Logically, in a society ostensibly grounded on representative government, it would seem reasonable that a majority of the people of a State could elect a majority of that State's legislators. To conclude differently, and to sanction minority control of state legislative bodies, would appear to deny majority rights in a way that far surpasses any possible denial of minority rights that might otherwise be thought to result. Since legislatures are responsible for enacting laws by which all citizens are to be governed, they should be bodies which are collectively responsive to the popular will. And the concept of equal protection has been traditionally viewed as requiring the uniform treatment of persons standing in the same relation to the governmental action questioned or challenged. With respect to the allocation of legislative representation, all voters, as citizens of a State, stand in the same relation regardless of where they live. Any suggested criteria for the differentiation of citizens are insufficient to justify any discrimination, as to the weight of their votes, unless relevant to the permissible purposes of legislative apportionment. Since the achieving of fair and effective representation for all citizens is concededly the basic aim of legislative apportionment, we conclude that the Equal Protection Clause guarantees the opportunity for equal participation by all voters in the election of state legislators. Diluting the weight of votes because of place of residence impairs basic constitutional rights under the Fourteenth Amendment just as much as invidious discriminations based upon factors such as race, . . . or economic status. . . . Our constitutional system amply provides for the protection of minorities by means other than giving them majority control of state legislatures. And the democratic ideals of equality and majority rule, which have served this Nation so well in the past, are hardly of any less significance for the present and the future.

We are told that the matter of apportioning representation in a state legislature is a complex and many-faceted one. We are advised that States can rationally consider factors other than population in apportioning legislative representation. We are admonished not to restrict the power of the States to impose differing views as to political philosophy on their citizens. We are cautioned about the dangers of entering into political thickets and mathematical quagmires. Our answer is this: a denial of constitutionally protected rights demands judicial protection; our oath and our office require no less of us. As stated in *Gomillion v. Lightfoot:* . . .

> When a State exercises power wholly within the domain of state interest, it is insulated from federal judicial review. But such insulation is not carried over when state power is used as an instrument for circumventing a federally protected right.

To the extent that a citizen's right to vote is debased, he is that much less a citizen. The fact that an individual lives here or there is not a legitimate reason for overweighting or diluting the efficacy of his vote. The complexions of societies and civilizations change, often with amazing rapidity. A nation once primarily rural in character becomes predominantly urban. Representation schemes once fair and equitable become archaic and outdated. But the basic principle of representative government remains, and must remain, unchanged—the weight of a citizen's vote cannot be made to depend on where he lives. Population is, of necessity, the starting point for consideration and the controlling criterion for judgment in legislative apportionment controversies. A citizen, a qualified voter, is no more nor no less so because he lives in the city or on the farm. This is the clear and strong command of our Constitution's Equal Protection Clause. This is an essential part of the concept of a government of laws and not men. This is at the heart of Lincoln's vision of "government of the people, by the people, [and] for the people." The Equal Protection Clause demands no less than substantially equal state legislative representation for all citizens, of all places as well as of all races. . . .

We hold that, as a basic constitutional standard, the Equal Protection Clause requires that the seats in both houses of a bicameral state legislature must be apportioned on a population basis. Simply stated, an individual's right to vote for state legislators is unconstitutionally impaired when its weight is in a substantial fashion diluted when compared with votes of citizens living in other parts of the State. Since, under neither the existing apportionment provisions nor under either of the proposed plans was either of the houses of the Alabama Legislature apportioned on a population basis, the District Court correctly held that all three of these schemes were constitutionally invalid. Furthermore, the existing apportionment . . . presented little more than crazy-quilts, completely lacking in rationality and could be found invalid on that basis alone. . . .

Legislative apportionment in Alabama is signally illustrative and symptomatic of the seriousness of this problem in a number of the States. At the time this litigation was commenced, there had been no reapportionment of seats in the Alabama Legislature for over 60 years. Legislative inaction, coupled with the unavailability of any political or judicial remedy, had resulted, with the passage of years, in the perpetuated scheme becoming little more than an irrational anachronism. Consistent failure by the Alabama Legislature to comply with state constitutional requirements as to the frequency of reapportionment and the bases of legislative representation resulted in a minority strangle-hold on the State Legislature. Inequality of representation in one house added to the inequality in the other. With the crazy-quilt existing apportionment virtually conceded to be invalid, the Alabama Legislature offered two proposed plans for consideration by the District Court, neither of which was to be effective until 1966 and neither of which provided for the apportionment of even one of the two houses on a population basis. We find that the court below did not err in holding that neither of these proposed reapportionment schemes, considered as a whole, "meets the necessary constitutional requirements." . . .

Since neither of the houses of the Alabama Legislature, under any of the three plans considered by the District Court, was apportioned on a population basis, we would be justified in proceeding no further. However, one of the proposed plans, that contained in the so-called 67-Senator Amendment, at least superficially resembles the scheme of legislative representation followed in the Federal Congress. Under this plan, each of Alabama's 67 counties is allotted one senator, and no counties are given more than one Senate seat. Arguably, this is analogous to the allocation of two Senate seats, in the Federal Congress, to each of the 50 States, regardless of population. Seats in the Alabama House, under the proposed constitutional amendment, are distributed by giving each of the 67 counties at least one, with the remaining 39 seats being allotted among the more populous counties on a population basis. This scheme, at least at first glance, appears to resemble that prescribed for the Federal House of Representatives, where the 435 seats are distributed among the States on a population basis, although each State, regardless of its population, is given at least one Congressman. Thus, although there are substantial differences in underlying rationale and result, the 67-Senator Amendment, as proposed by the Alabama Legislature, at least arguably presents for consideration a scheme analogous to that used for apportioning seats in Congress.

Much has been written since our decision in *Baker v. Carr* about the applicability of the so-called federal analogy to state legislative apportionment arrangements. After considering the matter, the court below concluded that no conceivable analogy could be drawn between the federal scheme and the apportionment of seats in the Alabama Legislature under the proposed constitutional amendment. We agree with the District Court, and find the federal analogy inapposite and irrelevant to state legislative districting schemes. Attempted reliance on the federal analogy appears often to be little more than an after-the-fact rationalization offered in defense of maladjusted state apportionment arrangements. The original constitutions of 36 of our States provided that representation in both houses of the state legislatures would be based completely, or predominantly, on population. And the Founding Fathers clearly had no intention of establishing a pattern or model for the apportionment of seats in state legislatures when the system of representation in the Federal Congress was adopted. Demonstrative of this is the fact that the Northwest Ordinance, adopted in the same year, 1787, as the Federal Constitution, provided for the apportionment of seats in territorial legislatures solely on the basis of population.

The system of representation in the two Houses of the Federal Congress is one ingrained in our Constitution, as part of the law of the land. It is one conceived out of compromise and concession indispensable to the establishment of our federal republic. Arising from unique historical circumstances, it is based on the consideration that in establishing our type of federalism a group of formerly independent States bound themselves together under one national government. Admittedly, the original 13 States surrendered some of their sovereignty in agreeing to join together "to form a more perfect Union." But at the heart of our constitutional system remains the concept of separate and distinct governmental entities which have delegated some, but not all, of their formerly held powers to the single national government. The fact that almost three-fourths of our present States were never in fact independently sovereign does not detract from our view that the so-called federal analogy is inapplicable as a sustaining precedent for state legislative apportionments. The developing history and growth of our republic cannot cloud the fact that, at the time of the inception of the system of representation in the Federal Congress, a compromise between the larger and smaller States on this matter averted a deadlock in the constitutional convention which had threatened to abort the birth of our Nation. . . .

Political subdivisions of States—counties, cities, or whatever—never were and never have been considered as sovereign entities. Rather, they have been traditionally regarded as subordinate governmental instrumentalities created by the State to assist in the carrying out of state governmental functions. . . . [T]hese governmental units are "created as convenient agencies for exercising such of the governmental powers of the State as may be entrusted to them," and the "number, nature and duration of the powers conferred upon [them] . . . and the territory over which they shall be exercised rests in the absolute discretion of the State."

The relationship of the States to the Federal Government could hardly be less analogous.

Thus, we conclude that the plan contained in the 67-Senator Amendment for apportioning seats in the Alabama Legislature cannot be sustained by recourse to the so-called federal analogy. Nor can any other inequitable state legislative apportionment scheme be justified on such an asserted basis. This does not necessarily mean that such a plan is irrational or involves something other than a "republican form of government." We conclude simply that such a plan is impermissible for the States under the Equal Protection Clause, since perforce resulting, in virtually every case, in submergence of the equal-population principle in at least one house of a state legislature.

Since we find the so-called federal analogy inapposite to a consideration of the constitutional validity of state legislative apportionment schemes, we necessarily hold that the Equal Protection Clause requires both houses of a state legislature to be apportioned on a population basis. The right of a citizen to equal representation and to have his vote weighted equally with those of all other citizens in the election of members of one house of a bicameral state legislature would amount to little if States could effectively submerge the equal-population principle in the apportionment of seats in the other house. If such a scheme were permissible, an individual citizen's ability to exercise an effective voice in the only instrument of state government directly representative of the people might be almost as effectively thwarted as if neither house were apportioned on a population basis. Deadlock between the two bodies might result in compromise and concession on some issues. But in all too many cases the more probable result would be frustration of the majority will through minority veto in the house not apportioned on a population basis, stemming directly from the failure to accord adequate overall legislative representation to all of the State's citizens on a nondiscriminatory basis. . . .

We do not believe that the concept of bicameralism is rendered anachronistic and meaningless when the predominant basis of representation in the two state legislative bodies is required to be the same—population. A prime reason for bicameralism, modernly considered, is to insure mature and deliberate consideration of, and to prevent precipitate action on, proposed legislative measures. Simply because the controlling criterion for apportioning representation is required to be the same in both houses does not mean that there will be no differences in the composition and complexion of the two bodies. Different constituencies can be represented in the two houses. One body could be composed of single-member districts while the other could have at least some multi-member districts. The length of terms of the legislators in the separate bodies could differ. The numerical size of the two bodies could be made to differ, even significantly, and the geographical size of districts from which legislators are elected could also be made to differ. And apportionment in one house could be arranged so as to balance off minor inequities in the representation of certain areas in the other house. In summary, these and other factors could be, and are presently in many States, utilized to engender differing complexions and collective attitudes in the two bodies of a state legislature, although both are apportioned substantially on a population basis. . . .

By holding that as a federal constitutional requisite both houses of a state legislature must be apportioned on a population basis, we mean that the Equal Protection Clause requires that a State make an honest and good faith effort to construct districts, in both houses of its legislature, as nearly of equal population as is practicable. We realize that it is a practical impossibility to arrange legislative districts so that each one has an identical number of residents, or citizens, or voters. Mathematical exactness or precision is hardly a workable constitutional requirement.

In *Wesberry v. Sanders*, . . . the Court stated that congressional representation must be based on population as nearly as is practicable. In implementing the basic constitutional principle of representative government as enunciated by the Court in *Wesberry*—equality of population among districts—some distinctions may well be made between congressional and state legislative representation. Since, almost invariably, there is a significantly larger number of seats in state legislative bodies to be distributed within a State than congressional seats, it may be feasible to use political subdivision lines to a greater extent in establishing state legislative districts than in congressional districting while still affording adequate representation to all parts of the State. To do so would be constitutionally valid, so long as the resulting apportionment was one based substantially on population and the equal-population principle was not diluted in any significant way. Somewhat more flexibility may therefore be constitutionally permissible with respect to state legislative apportionment than in congressional districting. Lower courts can and assuredly will work out more concrete and specific standards for evaluating state legislative apportionment schemes in the context of actual litigation. For the present, we deem it expedient not to attempt to spell out any precise constitutional tests. What is marginally permissible in one State may be unsatisfactory in another, depending on the particular circumstances of the case. Developing a body of doctrine on a case-by-case basis appears to us to provide the most satisfactory means of arriving at detailed constitutional requirements in the area of state legislative apportionment. . . .

Whatever the means of accomplishment, the overriding objective must be substantial equality of population among the various districts, so that the vote of any citizen is approximately equal in weight to that of any other citizen in the State.

History indicates, however, that many States have deviated, to a greater or lesser degree, from equal-population principle in the apportionment of seats in at least one house of their legislatures. So long as the divergences from a strict population standard are based on legitimate considerations incident to the effectuation of a rational state policy, some deviations from the equal-population principle are constitutionally permissible with respect to the apportionment of seats in either or both of the two houses of a bicameral state legislature. But neither history alone, nor economic or other sorts of group interests, are permissible factors in attempting to justify disparities from population-based representation. Citizens, not history or economic interests, cast votes. Considerations of area alone provide an insufficient justification for deviations from the equal-population principle. Again, people, not land or trees or pastures, vote. Modern developments and improvements in transportation and communications make rather hollow, in the mid-1960's, most claims that deviations from population-based representation can validly be based solely on geographical considerations. Arguments for allowing such deviations in order to insure effective representation for sparsely settled areas and to prevent legislative districts from becoming so large that the availability of access of citizens to their representatives is impaired are today, for the most part, unconvincing.

A consideration that appears to be of more substance in justifying some deviations from population-based representation in state legislatures is that of insuring some voice to political subdivisions, as political subdivisions. Several factors make more than insubstantial claims that a State can rationally consider according political subdivisions some independent representation in at least one body of the state legislature, as long as the basic standard of equality of population among districts is maintained. Local governmental entities are frequently charged with various responsibilities incident to the operation of state government. In many States much of the legislature's activity involves the enactment of so-called local legislation, directed only to the concerns of particular political subdivisions. And a State may legitimately desire to construct districts along political subdivision lines to deter the possibilities of gerrymandering. However, permitting deviations from population-based representation does not mean that each local governmental unit or political subdivision can be given separate representation, regardless of population. Carried too far, a scheme of giving at least one seat in one house to each political subdivision (for example, to each county) could easily result, in many States, in a total subversion of the equal-population principle in that legislative body. This would be especially true in a State where the number of counties is large and many of them are sparsely populated, and the number of seats in the legislative body being apportioned does not significantly exceed the number of counties. Such a result, we conclude, would be constitutionally impermissible. And careful judicial scrutiny must of course be given, in evaluating state apportionment schemes, to the character as well as the degree of deviations from a strict population basis. But if, even as a result of a clearly rational state policy of according some legislative representation to political subdivisions, population is submerged as the controlling consideration in the apportionment of seats in the particular legislative body, then the right of all of the State's citizens to cast an effective and adequately weighted vote would be unconstitutionally impaired. . . .

One of the arguments frequently offered as a basis for upholding a State's legislative apportionment arrangement, despite substantial disparities from a population basis in either or both houses, is grounded on congressional approval, incident to admitting States into the Union, of state apportionment plans containing deviations from the equal-population principle. Proponents of this argument contend that congressional approval of such schemes, despite their disparities from population-based representation, indicate that such arrangements are plainly sufficient as establishing a "republican form of government." As we stated in *Baker v. Carr*, some questions raised under the Guaranty Clause are nonjusticiable, where "political" in nature and where there is a clear absence of judicially manageable standards. Nevertheless, it is not inconsistent with this view to hold that, despite congressional approval of state legislative apportionment plans at the time of admission into the Union, even though deviating from the equal-population principle here enunciated, the Equal Protection Clause can and does require more. And an apportionment scheme in which both houses are based on population can hardly be considered as failing to satisfy the Guaranty Clause requirement. Congress presumably does not assume, in admitting States into the Union, to pass on all constitutional questions relating to the character of state governmental organization. In any event, congressional approval, however well-considered, could hardly validate an unconstitutional state legislative apportionment. Congress simply lacks the constitutional power to insulate States from attack with respect to alleged deprivations of individual constitutional rights. . . .

That the Equal Protection Clause requires that both houses of a state legislature be apportioned on a population basis does not mean that States cannot adopt some reasonable plan for periodic revision of their apportionment schemes. Decennial reapportionment appears to be a rational approach to readjustment of legislative representation in order to take into account population shifts and growth. Reallocation of legislative seats every 10 years coincides with the prescribed practice in 41 of the States, often honored more in the breach than the observance, however. . . .

Although general provisions of the Alabama Constitution provide that the apportionment of seats in both houses of the Alabama Legislature should be on a population basis, other more detailed provisions clearly make compliance with both sets of requirements impossible. With respect to the operation of the Equal Protection Clause, it makes no difference whether a State's apportionment scheme is embodied in its constitution or in statutory provisions. . . .

[W]e affirm the judgment below and remand the cases for further proceedings consistent with the views stated in this opinion.

It is so ordered.

[JUSTICE CLARK wrote a separate concurring opinion. In a brief separate opinion JUSTICE STEWART also voted to affirm the judgment of the District Court.]

MR. JUSTICE HARLAN, dissenting. . . .

Today's holding is that the Equal Protection Clause of the Fourteenth Amendment requires every State to structure its legislature so that all the members of each house represent substantially the same number of people; other factors may be given play only to the extent that they do not significantly encroach on this basic "population" principle. Whatever may be thought of this holding as a piece of political ideology—and even on that score the political history and practices of this country from its earliest beginnings leave wide room for debate. . . . I think it demonstrable that the Fourteenth Amendment does not impose this political tenet on the States or authorize this Court to do so. . . .

Had the Court paused to probe more deeply into the matter, it would have found that the Equal Protection Clause was never intended to inhibit the States in choosing any democratic method they pleased for the apportionment of their legislature. This is shown by the language of the Fourteenth Amendment taken as a whole, by the understanding of those who proposed and ratified it, and by the political practices of the States at the time the Amendment was adopted. It is confirmed by numerous state and congressional actions since the adoption of the Fourteenth Amendment, and by the common understanding of the Amendment as evidenced by subsequent constitutional amendments and decisions of this Court before *Baker v. Carr* . . . made an abrupt break with the past in 1962.

The failure of the Court to consider any of these matters cannot be excused or explained by any concept of "developing" constitutionalism. It is meaningless to speak of constitutional "development" when both the language and history of the controlling provisions of the Constitution are wholly ignored. Since it can, I think be shown beyond doubt that state legislative apportionments, as such, are wholly free of constitutional limitations, save such as may be imposed by the Republican Form of Government Clause (Const., Art. IV, §4), the Court's action now bringing them within the purview of the Fourteenth Amendment amounts to nothing less than an exercise of the amending power by this Court.

So far as the Federal Constitution is concerned, the complaints in these cases should all have been dismissed below for failure to state a cause of action, because what has been alleged or proved shows no violation of any constitutional right. . . .

[Justice Harlan then provides a detailed history of the Fourteenth Amendment designed to show that it was never intended as a limitation on state legislative apportionments.]

With these cases the Court approaches the end of the third round set in motion by the complaint filed in *Baker v. Carr*. What is done today deepens my conviction that judicial entry into this realm is profoundly ill-advised and constitutionally impermissible. . . . I believe that the vitality of our political system, on which in the last analysis all else depends, is weakened by reliance on the judiciary for political reform; in time a complacent body politic may result.

These decisions also cut deeply into the fabric of our federalism. What must follow from them may eventually appear to be the product of State Legislatures. Nevertheless, no thinking person can fail to recognize that the aftermath of these cases, however desirable it may be thought in itself, will have been achieved at the cost of a radical alteration in the relationship between the States and the Federal Government, more particularly the Federal Judiciary. Only one who has an overbearing impatience with the federal system and its political processes will believe that that cost was not too high or was inevitable.

Finally, these decisions give support to a current mistaken view of the Constitution and the constitutional function of this Court. This view, in a nutshell, is that every major social ill in this country can find its cure in some constitutional "principle," and that this Court should "take the lead" in promoting reform when other branches of government fail to act. The Constitution is not a panacea for every blot upon the public welfare, nor should this Court, ordained as a judicial body, be thought of as a general haven for reform movements. The Constitution is an instrument of government, fundamental to which is the premise that in a diffusion of governmental authority lies the greatest promise that this Nation will realize liberty for all its citizens. This Court, limited in function in accordance with that premise, does not serve its high purpose when it exceeds its authority, even to satisfy justified impatience with the slow workings of the political process. For when, in the name of constitutional interpretation, the Court *adds* something to the Constitution that was deliberately excluded from it, the Court in reality substitutes its view of what should be so for the amending process.

I dissent in each of these cases, believing that in none of them have the plaintiffs stated a cause of action. To the extent that *Baker v. Carr*, expressly or by implication, went beyond a discussion of jurisdictional doctrines independent of the substantive issues involved here, it should be limited to what it in fact was: an experiment in venturesome constitutionalism.

AFTERMATH

Reynolds v. Sims and the other apportionment cases came under heavy fire in many parts of the country and brought the Court into the most serious direct conflict with Congress in recent years. In fact, not since the 1937 attempt by President Roosevelt to pack the Court has a more serious attack been mounted against the nine justices. Actually, *Reynolds v. Sims* did not arouse as much large scale opposition among the general public as that engendered by the school prayer cases considered in Chapter 5. But many politicians were deeply disturbed because their own seats might well be in jeopardy and because many of them saw clearly that the doctrine of the *Reynolds* case would result in a massive shift of power from the rural areas to the urban metropolitan centers. Moreover, many critics agreed generally with the views of Justice Harlan and felt that the Court had overstepped its bounds.

These pressures were soon felt in Congress where more than seventy measures were introduced to curb the power of the Court by either constitutional amendment or statutory enactment. The most serious challenge came from the House of Representatives where a drastic bill to nullify the reapportionment rulings by *revoking* the jurisdiction of all federal courts in redistricting cases was passed by a vote of 218–175 in 1964. But the Senate was not prepared to follow so drastic a course. Instead, the Senate seriously considered a proposal by Republican minority leader Everett M. Dirksen that would have postponed all federal court proceedings on redistricting until January 1, 1966. This was designed to give states time to ratify a constitutional amendment allowing them to elect one legislative house on a basis other than population. However, the Dirksen proposal failed to win the support of the Senate and instead a meaningless, toothless compromise resolution was passed simply requesting that federal courts give the states at least one legislative session, plus an additional thirty days, to meet the Supreme Court's one man—one vote requirement. All additional attempts to curb the Court's power have also thus far failed.

It now seems clear that the "goal of equal votes for equal citizens, far from being a radical departure in our political tradition, is consistent with this nation's efforts to extend a full franchise to all citizens. Reapportionment, insuring ballots of the same weight for all voters, is not only long overdue but will also lay the groundwork for an updating of our fifty state legislatures." (Andrew Hacker, "One Man, One Vote—Yes or No," *New York Times Magazine,* reprinted by the *American Civil Liberties Union,* January 1965.)

VII THE RIGHT OF PRIVACY

The proper posture of democratic man is surely not that of a snooper crouching over a recording device listening to the intimate and private conversations of two individuals. When we recognize fully the moral degradation created by our own involvement in these practices, our courts will exclude this type of evidence once and for all.

> Norman Redlich, Introduction to Lenore L. Cahn (editor), Confronting Injustice, The Edmond Cahn Reader, *Boston, Little, Brown and Co., p. XIX, 1966.*

I believe that, [U]nder the [Fourth] Amendment, the "sanctity of a man's house and the privacies of life" still remain protected from the uninvited intrusion of physical means by which words within the house are secretly communicated to a person on the outside. A man can still control a small part of his environment, his house; he can retreat thence from outsiders, secure in the knowledge that they cannot get at him without disobeying the Constitution. That is still a sizeable hunk of liberty—worth protecting from encroachment. A sane, decent, civilized society must provide some such oasis, some shelter from public scrutiny, some insulated enclosure, some enclave, some inviolate place which is a man's castle.

> Circuit Judge Jerome Frank, dissenting opinion, United States v. On Lee, *193 F (2d) 306 (1951)*

Olmstead v. United States
277 U.S. 438 (1928)

THOUGH THE RIGHT OF privacy is not specifically mentioned in the Constitution, it constitutes one of the most cherished rights of a civilized people. To Americans the right of privacy has generally meant, in the famous phrase of Justice Louis D. Brandeis, "the right to be left alone"—to be free from intrusion by government officials, employers and others at home, in church, at work, and at play. When the right of privacy is eroded or no longer exists, a society simply cannot be a democratic one. In Germany under Hitler and the Nazis, for example, "destruction of the individual's sense of his own privacy was one of the principal methods used to gain total state control over the German people. Wiretapping and electronic eavesdropping were high on the list of techniques used by the Gestapo; no one was safe from the listening ears of secret police. Visitors to a German home were sometimes taken into the bathroom to exchange comments in whispers, because this was the most difficult room to tap. Diplomats and officials—and private citizens as well—met in public parks to escape eavesdroppers. Even after World War II had started, Berliners steered clear of telephones when they wanted to talk freely. Another routine Gestapo technique was the predawn arrest. There was the unannounced bang on the door, the invasion of the home, and the dragging or driving of people in their night clothes into the streets. This kind of brutal invasion of privacy was designed to achieve the maximum in intimidation and fear. Mass raids were conducted regularly in this manner in Germany and later, all over conquered Europe. . . . Nazi Germany was a society in which privacy was, for all practical purposes, nonexistent. When the individual was not actually under surveillance, he was always possessed by the fear that he might be. Along with this was the fear that the secret police might descend on him at any time." (Senator Edward V. Long, *The Intruders, The Invasion of Privacy by Government and Industry*, pp. 21-22, Frederick A. Braeger, N.Y., 1967.)

Traditionally in the United States the private life of the individual citizen has been protected by specific guarantees in the Bill of Rights —particularly the Third, Fourth and Fifth Amendments. The Third Amendment prohibits the quartering of soldiers "in any house" in time of peace without the consent of the owner. This Amendment is of little practical importance today but, nevertheless, reveals the early American abhorrence of invasion of privacy. The search and seizure clause of the Fourth Amendment is the most important in any discussion of privacy for it positively recognizes the "right of the people to be secure in their persons, houses, papers, and effects, against unreasonable searches and seizures." The self-incrimination clause of the Fifth Amendment providing that no person "shall be compelled in any criminal case to be a witness against himself" as well as the due process clause of the Fifth Amendment stating that no person in criminal prosecution "shall be deprived of life, liberty, or property without due process of law" have also been relied upon to protect the private life of Americans. As will be seen in the cases that follow, particularly *Griswold v. Connecticut,* other specific guarantees of the Bill of Rights are also said to protect the right of privacy.

Despite the constitutional prohibitions, however, technological advancements which are in the process of creating a computerized society have made available sophisticated methods for the invasion of privacy which go far beyond the crude Nazi techniques of a generation ago. These developments have recently been vividly described by Justice Douglas, who has long been deeply troubled by increasing invasions of our privacy. In his dissenting opinion in *Osborn v. United States,* 385 U.S. 323 (1967), Justice Douglas remarked that "we are rapidly entering the age of no privacy, where everyone is open to surveillance at all times; where there are no secrets from the government. The aggressive breaches of privacy by the Government increase with geometric proportion. Wiretapping and 'bugging' run rampant, without effective judicial or legislative control. Secret observation booths in government offices and closed television circuits in industry, extending even to rest rooms, are common. Offices, conference rooms, hotel rooms and even bedrooms . . . are 'bugged' for the convenience of government. Peepholes in men's rooms are there to catch homosexuals. . . . Personality tests seek to ferret out a man's innermost thoughts on family life, religion, racial attitudes, national origin, politics, atheism, ideology, sex, and the like. Federal agents are often 'wired' so that their conversations are either recorded on their person . . . or transmitted to tape recorders some blocks away. The Food and Drug Administration recently put a spy in a church organization. Revenue agents have gone in the disguise of Coast Guard officers. They have broken or entered homes to obtain evidence. Polygraph tests (lie-detectors) of government employees and of employees in industry are rampant. The dossiers on all citizens mount in number and increase in size. Now they are being put on computers so that by pressing one button all the miserable, the sick, the suspect, the unpopular, the off-beat people of the nation can be instantly identified. These examples and many others demonstrate an alarming trend whereby the privacy and dignity of our citizens is being whittled away by sometimes imperceptible steps. Taken individually each step may be of little consequence. But when viewed as a whole, there begins to emerge a society quite unlike any we have seen—a society in which government may intrude into the secret regions of man's life at will."

It is in this emerging climate that the Supreme Court will be increasingly called upon to fashion new guidelines on the right of privacy. In so doing it must look to a number of previous decisions. Some of the fundamental problems currently raised by wiretapping and electronic devices were presented to the Court in the classic case of *Olmstead v. United States*. The *Olmstead* case was a direct outgrowth of the Eighteenth Amendment ratified in 1919 which prohibited the "manufacture, sale or transportation" of intoxicating liquors and the Volstead Act (National Prohibition Act) passed by Congress to enforce the prohibition amendment. Doomed to failure from the beginning, the Eighteenth Amendment was finally repealed in 1933 by the Twenty-First Amendment after more than a decade of frustrating attempts to enforce it.

Roy Olmstead, a former lieutenant on the Seattle police force, ran a profitable bootlegging business in the state of Washington with the help of eleven partners, some fifty employees and the unofficial cooperation of certain police officers. Olmstead had available two seagoing vessels and other smaller craft for the transportation of liquor from England and Canada. A number of underground caches in and around Seattle were used by the organization for storing the illegal liquor. The annual income from the smuggling business was more than two million dollars. Over a period of several months four federal prohibition agents obtained evidence on the bootlegging operation by tapping the telephone wires of Olmstead and his associates. The taps were made without trespassing on the property of the conspirators but in violation of a state statute of Washington adopted in 1909 which made wiretapping a crime. Olmstead and a number of his associates were convicted in a federal district court in the state of Washington of conspiring to violate the Volstead Act by unlawfully possessing, transporting, and importing intoxicating liquors. As ringleader, Olmstead drew the heaviest penalty—four years at hard labor plus an $8000 fine and partial costs of the prosecution. After the convictions were sustained by a federal court of appeals, Olmstead and his friends brought the case to the Supreme Court on a writ of certiorari.

It was no surprise to find the majority opinion written by Chief Justice William Howard Taft, for he had long been determined to enforce prohibition. Taft was the only man in American history who served as both President and Chief Justice. He always felt that the Chief Justiceship was the more important and prestigious post, and he fulfilled a lifelong ambition when President Harding named him to lead the Court in 1921 after considerable pressure from both Taft and Taft's political friends in Washington. The jovial appearing Taft was a conservative, property minded Republican justice who did much to improve the administration of the federal courts. Taft was suspicious of Justice Louis D. Brandeis whom he regarded as an enemy of private property and though much fonder of Justice Oliver W. Holmes, Jr., he felt that Holmes was unduly influenced by Brandeis. Nevertheless, particular note should be made of the dissenting opinions of Justices Holmes and Brandeis, below, for they state the arguments against wiretapping in eloquent terms which have not been surpassed to this day.

Unlike Taft, Holmes and Brandeis belong in the company of a handful of truly great Supreme Court justices. Brandeis, born of an immigrant Jewish family in Kentucky, and Holmes, a product of the New England literary and intellectual establishment, voted together on many crucial issues. Both educated at the Harvard Law School, they arrived at the same conclusions by different paths. Brandeis used social science data meticulously to reason logically from particulars to conclusions. He was a zealous, pragmatic crusader, sensitive to the needs of the poor and underprivileged, who could not stand aloof from the conflicts of his day. Holmes, on the other hand, was the detached Olympian philosopher who was essentially a skeptical conservative with little interest in social reform, yet he aligned himself with Brandeis in a number of great opinions because he felt that Supreme Court justices should not write their own economic notions into the Constitution or interfere with social experiments demanded by the American people. Moreover, both men were deeply committed to the protection and enlargement of American freedoms.

MR. CHIEF JUSTICE TAFT delivered the opinion of the Court.

. . . The Fourth Amendment provides: "The right of the people to be secure in their persons, houses, papers, and effects, against unreasonable searches and seizures, shall not be violated, and no warrants shall issue, but upon probable cause, supported by oath or affirmation, and particularly describing the place to be searched, and the persons or things to be seized." And the 5th: "No person . . . shall be compelled, in any criminal case, to be a witness against himself." . . .

There is no room in the present case for applying the Fifth Amendment unless the Fourth Amendment was first violated. There was no evidence of compulsion to induce the defendants to talk over their many telephones. They were continually and voluntarily transacting business without knowledge of the interception. Our consideration must be confined to the Fourth Amendment. . . .

The well-known historical purpose of the Fourth Amendment, directed against general warrants and writs of assistance, was to prevent the use of governmental force to search a man's house, his person, his papers, and his effects, and to prevent their seizure against his will. . . .

The Amendment itself shows that the search is to be of material things —the persons, the house, his papers, or his effects. The description of the warrant necessary to make the proceeding lawful is that it must specify the place to be searched and the person or *things* to be seized. . . .

The Fourth Amendment may have proper application to a sealed letter in the mail because of the constitutional provision for the Post Office Department and the relations between the government and those who pay to secure protection of their sealed letters. See Revised Statutes, §3978 to 3988, . . . whereby Congress monopolizes the carriage of letters and excludes from that business everyone else, and §3929, . . . which forbids any postmaster or other person to open any letter not addressed to himself. It is plainly within the words of the Amendment to say that the unlawful rifling by a government agent of a sealed letter is a search and seizure of the sender's papers or effects. The letter is a paper, an effect, and in the custody of a government that forbids carriage except under its protection.

The United States takes no such care of telegraph or telephone messages as of mailed sealed letters. The Amendment does not forbid what was done here. There was no searching. There was no seizure. The evidence was secured by the use of the sense of hearing and that only. There was no entry of the houses or offices of the defendants.

By the invention of the telephone fifty years ago, and its application for the purpose of extending communications, one can talk with another at a far distant place.

The language of the Amendment cannot be extended and expanded to include telephone wires reaching to the whole world from the defendant's house or office. The intervening wires are not part of his house or office, any more than are the highways along which they are stretched. . . .

Congress may, of course, protect the secrecy of telephone messages by making them, when intercepted, inadmissible in evidence in Federal criminal trials, by direct legislation, and thus depart from the common law of evidence. But the courts may not adopt such a policy by attributing an enlarged and unusual meaning to the Fourth Amendment. The reasonable view is that one who installs in his house a telephone instrument with connecting wires intends to project his voice to those outside, and that the wires beyond his house and messages while passing over them are not within the protection of the Fourth Amendment. Here those who intercepted the projected voices were not in the house of either party to the conversation.

Neither the cases we have cited nor any of the many Federal decisions brought to our attention hold the Fourth Amendment to have been violated as against a defendant unless there has been an official search and seizure of his person or such a seizure of his papers or his tangible material effects or an actual physical invasion of his house "or curtilage" [courtyard] for the purpose of making a seizure.

We think, therefore, that the wiretapping here disclosed did not amount to a search or seizure within the meaning of the Fourth Amendment.

. . . But some of our number . . . have concluded that there is merit in the twofold objection overruled in both courts below that evidence obtained through intercepting of telephone messages by government agents was inadmissible because the mode of obtaining it was unethical and a misdemeanor under the law of Washington. To avoid any misapprehension of our views of that objection, we shall deal with it in both of its phases. . . .

The common-law rule is that the admissibility of evidence is not affected by the illegality of the means by which it was obtained. . . .

The rule is supported by many English and American cases. . . .

Nor can we, without the sanction of congressional enactment, subscribe to the suggestion that the courts have a discretion to exclude evidence, the admission of which is not unconstitutional, because unethically secured. This would be at variance with the common-law doctrine generally supported by authority. There is no case that sustains, nor any recognized textbook that gives color to such a view. Our general experience shows that much evidence has always been receivable although not obtained by conformity to the highest ethics. The history of criminal trials shows numerous cases of prosecutions of oath-bound conspiracies for murder, robbery, and other crimes where officers of the law have disguised themselves and joined the organizations, taken the oaths, and given themselves every appearance of active members engaged in the promotion of crime for the purpose of securing evidence. Evidence secured by such means has always been received.

A standard which would forbid the reception of evidence if obtained by other than nice ethical conduct by government officials would make society suffer and give criminals greater immunity than has been known heretofore. In the absence of controlling legislation by Congress, those who realize the difficulties in bringing offenders to justice may well deem it wise that the exclusion of evidence should be confined to cases where rights under the Constitution would be violated by admitting it.

The statute of Washington . . . does not declare that evidence obtained by such interception shall be inadmissible, and by the common law, already referred to, it would not be. . . . (C)learly a statute, passed twenty years after the admission of the state into the Union, cannot affect the rules of evidence applicable in courts of the United States. . . .

Affirmed.

MR. JUSTICE HOLMES, dissenting:

. . . (T)he government ought not to use evidence obtained, and only obtainable, by a criminal act. There is no body of precedents by which we are bound, and which confines us to logical deduction from established rules. Therefore, we must consider the two objects of desire, both of which we cannot have, and make up our minds which to choose. It is desirable that criminals should be detected, and to that end that all available evidence should be used. It also is desirable that the government should not itself foster and pay for other crimes, when they are the means by which the evidence is to be obtained. If it pays its officers for having got evidence by crime I do not see why it may not as well pay them for getting it in the same way, and I can attach no importance to protestations of disapproval if it knowingly accepts and pays and announces that in future it will pay for the fruits. We have to choose, and for my part I think it a less evil that some criminals should escape than that the government should play an ignoble part.

For those who agree with me, no distinction can be taken between the government as prosecutor and the government as judge. If the existing code does not permit district attorneys to have a hand in such dirty business, it does not permit the judge to allow such iniquities to succeed. . . . And if all that I have said so far be accepted, it makes no difference that in this case wiretapping is made a crime by the law of the state, not by the law of the United States. It is true that a state cannot make rules of evidence for the courts of the United States, but the state has authority over the conduct in question, and I hardly think that the United States would appear to greater advantage when paying for an odious crime against state law than when inciting to the disregard of its own. . . . I have said that we are free to choose between two principles of policy. But if we are to confine ourselves to precedent and logic, the reason for excluding evidence obtained by violating the Constitution seems to me logically to lead to excluding evidence obtained by a crime of the officers of the law.

MR. JUSTICE BRANDEIS, dissenting:

. . . The government makes no attempt to defend the methods employed by its officers. Indeed, it concedes that if wiretapping can be deemed a search and seizure within the Fourth Amendment, such wiretapping as was practised in the case at bar was an unreasonable search and seizure, and that the evidence thus obtained was inadmissible. But it relies on the language of the Amendment; and it claims that the protection given thereby cannot properly be held to include a telephone conversation. . . .

When the Fourth and Fifth Amendments were adopted, "the form that evil had theretofore taken" had been necessarily simple. Force and violence were then the only means known to man by which a government could directly effect self-incrimination. It could compel the individual to testify—a compulsion effected, if need be, by torture. It could secure possession of his papers and other articles incident to his private life—a seizure effected, if need be, by breaking and entry. Protection against such invasion of "the sanctities of a man's home and the privacies of life" was provided in the Fourth and Fifth Amendments, by specific language. . . . But "time works changes, brings into existence new conditions and purposes." Subtler and more far-reaching means of invading privacy have become available to the government. Discovery and invention have made it possible for the government, by means far more effective than stretching upon the rack, to obtain disclosure in court of what is whispered in the closet.

Moreover, "in the application of a constitution, our contemplation cannot be only of what has been, but of what may be." The progress of science in furnishing the government with means of espionage is not likely to stop with wiretapping. Ways may some day be developed by which the government, without removing papers from secret drawers, can reproduce them in court, and by which it will be enabled to expose to a jury the most intimate occurrences of the home. Advances in the psychic and related sciences may bring means of exploring unexpressed beliefs, thoughts, and emotions. . . . Can it be that the Constitution affords no protection against such invasions of individual security? . . .

Applying to the Fourth and Fifth Amendments the established rule of construction, the defendants' objections to the evidence obtained by a wire-tapping must, in my opinion, be sustained. It is, of course, immaterial where the physical connection with the telephone wires leading into the defendants' premises was made. And it is also immaterial that the intrusion was in aid of law enforcement. Experience should teach us to be most on our guard to protect liberty when the government's purposes are beneficent. Men born to freedom are naturally alert to repel invasion of their liberty by evil-minded rulers. The greatest dangers to liberty lurk in insidious encroachment by men of zeal, well-meaning, but without understanding.

Independently of the constitutional question, I am of opinion that the judgment should be reversed. By the laws of Washington, wiretapping is a crime. . . . To prove its case, the government was obliged to lay bare the crimes committed by its officers on its behalf. A federal court should not permit such a prosecution to continue. . . .

Decency, security, and liberty alike demand that government officials shall be subjected to the same rules of conduct that are commands to the citizen. In a government of laws, existence of the government will be imperilled if it fails to observe the law scrupulously. Our government is the potent, the omnipresent, teacher. For good or for ill, it teaches the whole people by its example. Crime is contagious. If the government becomes a lawbreaker, it breeds contempt for law; it invites anarchy. To declare that in the administration of the criminal law the end justifies the means—to declare that the government may commit crimes in order to secure the conviction of a private criminal—would bring terrible retribution. Against that pernicious doctrine this court should resolutely set its face.

[JUSTICES BUTLER and STONE also wrote separate dissenting opinions.]

Aftermath

After the Supreme Court's decision, Roy Olmstead, who had been free on bail, was returned to the federal prison at McNeil Island, Washington, to complete his four year term. He was a "model prisoner, served his full sentence, and returned to Seattle, where he became a respected member of the community. Some years later he received a full pardon from the President." Walter F. Murphy, *Wire-*

tapping on Trial, a Case Study in the Judicial Process, N.Y., Random House, p. 123, (1965).

But the *Olmstead* case had repercussions far beyond the fate of the principals involved. The case has been aptly termed "the great retreat" for "the theory of Brandeis, rejected by all but one of his brethren (Stone; though Holmes and Butler also dissented they did not advocate a broad interpretation of the Fourth Amendment), would have made the Fourth Amendment a guaranty of a broad right of privacy. Had the Brandeis analysis prevailed, all government intrusions on a person's privacy at home, in his papers, and effects, and on his free movement would have had to be justified, with the government forced to bear the burden of showing why a particular form of interference was reasonable. Privacy, though not an absolute, would have a high place in the hierarchy of protected values. It was the position of Taft and the majority, however, and their opposition to any enlarged theory of the Fourth Amendment that was to prevail in the decades ahead." William M. Beaney, "The Constitutional Right to Privacy in the Supreme Court," *The Supreme Court Review,* p. 227, (1962).

Justice Brandeis' prophecy that new and more subtle ways of invading privacy would be developed by science and technology certainly has come to pass. But the *Olmstead* case has never been directly overruled. A number of bills to outlaw wiretapping by federal officers were introduced in Congress after the decision but none were enacted. However, a provision inserted in the Federal Communication Act of 1934 was designed to outlaw wiretapping by federal officers. Section 605 of that Act provided that "no person not being authorized by the sender shall intercept any communication and divulge or publish the existence, contents, substance, purport, effect, or meaning of such intercepted communication to any person." In its early decisions the Supreme Court interpreted Section 605 strictly to ban wiretapping by federal officers but it gradually retreated from this position and refused to extend the judicial ban on wiretapping to electronic eavesdropping. At the same time Section 605 has been enforced only on very rare occasions. The result is that wiretapping which is supposedly outlawed by Section 605 and electronic eavesdropping which is still "beyond the pale of federal law" are widely practiced throughout the nation at all levels of both private and public life.

Lopez v. United States
373 U.S. 427 (1963)

German S. Lopez operated an inn under lease in North Falmouth, Massachusetts. In August, 1961, Roger S. Davis, an internal revenue agent, visited the inn in connection with his investigation of possible evasion of excise taxes in the area. Davis found that though the inn provided dancing, singing, and entertainment in the evenings, Lopez had never filed the required cabaret tax return. On a subsequent visit to the inn on October 21, 1961, Lopez urged Davis to drop the case. In addition Lopez gave Davis $420 in cash, urged him to bring his wife and family to the inn for a weekend "as my guest," and asked him to return in three days. Upon returning to his office, Davis gave an account of the incident to his superiors and turned over the $420. Davis, equipped with a pocket wire recorder (Minifon) and a battery operated transmitter, was instructed by his superiors to meet Lopez again as agreed and "to pretend to go along with the scheme." At the October 24th meeting Lopez again sought Davis' assistance in concealing any cabaret tax liability for past and present periods. At the same time he gave Davis another $200 in cash and said he should "come in every so often and I'll give you a couple hundred dollars every time you come in."

The entire conversation between Lopez and Davis was recorded on the concealed Minifon and admitted in evidence at the trial in a federal district court. Lopez was found guilty of attempted bribery and sentenced to a year in jail. After his conviction was sustained by a federal court of appeals, Lopez brought the case to the Supreme Court on a writ of certiorari. Hence, he is the petitioner in the case. Careful note should be made of Justice Brennan's raging dissent and his view of the current status of the *Olmstead* case.

MR. JUSTICE HARLAN delivered the opinion of the Court. . . .

Petitioner's . . . argument is primarily addressed to the recording of the conversation, which he claims was obtained in violation of his rights under the Fourth Amendment. Recognizing the weakness of this position if Davis was properly permitted to testify about the same conversation, petitioner now challenges that testimony as well, although he failed to do so at the trial. His theory is that, in view of Davis' alleged falsification of his mission, he gained access to petitioner's office by misrepresentation and all evidence obtained in the office, *i.e.,* his conversation with petitioner, was illegally "seized." . . .

We need not be long detained by the belated claim that Davis should not have been permitted to testify about the conversation of October 24. Davis was not guilty of an unlawful invasion of petitioner's office simply because his apparent willingness to accept a bribe was not real. . . . He was in the office with petitioner's consent, and while there he did not violate the privacy of the office by seizing something surreptitiously without petitioner's knowledge. . . . The only evidence obtained consisted of statements made by Lopez to Davis, statements which Lopez knew full well could be used against him by Davis if he wished. We decline to hold that whenever the offer of a bribe is made in private, and the offeree does not intend to accept, that offer is a constitutionally protected communication.

Once it is plain that Davis could properly testify about his conversation with Lopez, the constitutional claim relating to the recording of that conversation emerges in proper perspective. The Court has in the past sustained instances of "electronic eavesdropping" against constitutional challenge, when devices have been used to enable government agents to overhear conversations which would have been beyond the reach of the human ear. . . . It has been insisted only that the electronic device not be planted by an unlawful physical invasion of a constitutionally protected area. . . . The validity of these decisions is not in question here. Indeed this case involves no "eavesdropping" whatever in any proper sense of that term. The Government did not use an electronic device to listen in on conversations it could not otherwise have heard. Instead, the device was used only to obtain the most reliable evidence possible of a conversation in which the Government's own agent was a participant and which that agent was fully entitled to disclose. And the device was not planted by means of an unlawful physical invasion of petitioner's premises under circumstances which would violate the Fourth Amendment. It was carried in and out by an agent who was there with petitioner's assent, and it neither saw nor heard more than the agent himself. . . .

Stripped to its essentials, petitioner's argument amounts to saying that he has a constitutional right to rely on possible flaws in the agent's memory, or to challenge the agent's credibility without being beset by corroborating evidence that is not susceptible of impeachment. For no other argument can justify excluding an accurate version of a conversation that the agent could testify to from memory. We think the risk that petitioner took in offering a bribe to Davis fairly included the risk that the offer would be accurately reproduced in court, whether by faultless memory or mechanical recording. . . .

The function of a criminal trial is to seek out and determine the truth or falsity of the charges brought against the defendant. Proper fulfillment of this function requires that, constitutional limitations aside, all relevant, competent evidence be admissible, unless the manner in which it has been obtained—for example, by violating some statute or rule of procedure—compels the formulation of a rule excluding its introduction in a federal court. . . .

When we look for the overriding considerations that might require the exclusion of the highly useful evidence involved here, we find nothing. There has been no invasion of constitutionally protected rights, and no violation of federal law or rules of procedure. Indeed, there has not even been any electronic eavesdropping on a private conversation which government agents could not otherwise have overheard. There has, in short, been no act of any kind which could justify the creation of an exclusionary rule. We therefore conclude that the judgment of the Court of Appeals must be

Affirmed.

[CHIEF JUSTICE WARREN wrote a concurring opinion.]

MR. JUSTICE BRENNAN, with whom MR. JUSTICE DOUGLAS and MR. JUSTICE GOLDBERG join, dissenting. . . .

The question before us comes down to whether there is a legal basis, either in the Fourth Amendment or in the supervisory power, for excluding from federal criminal trials the fruits of surreptitious electronic surveillance by federal agents.

History and the text of the Constitution point the true path to the answer. [The Court then reviews the leading Fourth Amendment cases on the subject to *Olmstead v. United States.*] . . .

It is against this background that we must appraise *Olmstead v. United States* . . . where the Court, over the dissents of Justices Holmes, Brandeis, Stone and Butler, held that the fruits of wiretapping by federal officers were admissible as evidence in federal criminal trials. The Court's holding, which is fully pertinent here, rested on the propositions that there had been no search because no trespass had been committed against the petitioners and no seizure because no physical evidence had been obtained, thus making the Fourth Amendment inapplicable; and that evidence was not inadmissible in federal criminal trials merely because obtained by federal officers by methods violative of state law or otherwise unethical. . . . I think it is demonstrable that *Olmstead* was erroneously decided, that its authority has been steadily sapped by subsequent decisions of the Court, and that it and the cases following it are sports in our jurisprudence which ought to be eliminated.

(1) *Olmstead's* illiberal interpretation of the Fourth Amendment as limited to the tangible fruits of actual trespasses was a departure from the Court's previous decisions, notably *Boyd* [*Boyd v. United States,* 116 U.S. 616], and a misreading of the history and purpose of the Amendment. Such a limitation cannot be squared with a meaningful right to inviolate personal liberty. . . .

(2) As constitutional exposition, moreover, the *Olmstead* decision is insupportable. The Constitution would be an utterly impractical instrument of contemporary government if it were deemed to reach only problems familiar to the technology of the eighteenth century; yet the Court in *Olmstead* refused to apply the Fourth Amendment to wiretapping seemingly because the Framers of the Constitution had not been far-sighted enough to foresee the invention of the telephone.

(3) The Court's illiberal approach in *Olmstead* was a deviant in the law of the Fourth Amendment and not a harbinger of decisional revolution. . . .

(4) Specifically, the Court in the years since *Olmstead* has severed both supports for that decision's interpretation of the Fourth Amendment. We have held that the fruits of electronic surveillance, though intangible, nevertheless are within the reach of the Amendment. . . . Indeed, only the other day we reaffirmed that verbal fruits, equally with physical, are within the Fourth. . . . So too, the Court . . . has expressly held, in a case very close on its facts to that at bar, that an actual trespass need not be shown in order to support a violation of the Fourth Amendment. . . .

(5) Insofar as *Olmstead* rests on the notion that the federal courts may not exclude evidence, no matter how obtained, unless its admission is specifically made illegal by federal statute or by the Constitution, the decision is manifestly inconsistent with what has come to be regarded as the scope of the supervisory power over federal law enforcement. . . . We are empowered to fashion rules of evidence for federal criminal trials in conformity with "the principles of the common law as they may be interpreted . . . in the light of reason and experience." . . . Even if electronic surveillance as here involved does not violate the letter of the Fourth Amendment, which I do not concede, it violates its spirit and we ought to devise an appropriate prophylactic rule. . . .

(6) The *Olmstead* decision caused such widespread dissatisfaction that Congress in effect overruled it by enacting §605 of the Federal Communications Act, which made wiretapping a federal crime. We have consistently given §605 a generous construction, . . . recognizing that Congress had been concerned to prevent "resort to methods deemed inconsistent with ethical standards and destructive of personal liberty." . . .

To be sure, §605, being directed to the specific practice sanctioned by *Olmstead*, wiretapping, does not of its own force forbid the admission in evidence of the fruits of other techniques of electronic surveillance. But a congressional enactment is a source of judicial policy as well as a specific mandate to be enforced, and the same "broad considerations of morality and public well-being" . . . which make wiretap evidence inadmissible in the federal courts equally justify a court-made rule excluding the fruits of such devices as the Minifon. It is anomalous that the federal courts, while enforcing the right to privacy with respect to telephone communications, recognize no such right with respect to communications wholly within the sanctuaries of home and office. . . .

The comprehensive study [The Eavesdroppers, 1959] by Samuel Dash and his associates as well as a number of legislative inquiries reveal these truly terrifying facts: (1) Electronic eavesdropping by means of concealed microphones and recording devices of various kinds has become as large a problem as wiretapping, and is pervasively employed by private detectives, police, labor spies, employers and others for a variety of purposes, some downright disreputable. (2) These devices go far beyond simple "bugging," and permit a degree of invasion of privacy that can only be described as frightening. (3) Far from providing unimpeachable evidence the devices lend themselves to diabolical fakery. (4) A number of States have been impelled to enact regulatory legislation. (5) The legitimate law enforcement need for such techniques is not clear, and it surely has not been established that a stiff warrant requirement for electronic surveillance would destroy effective law enforcement.

But even without empirical studies, it must be plain that electronic surveillance imports a peculiarly severe danger to the liberties of the person. To be secure against police officers' breaking and entering to search for physical objects is worth very little if there is no security against the officers' using secret recording devices to purloin words spoken in confidence within the four walls of home or office. Our possessions are of little value compared to our personalities. And we must bear in mind that historically the search and seizure power was used to suppress freedom of speech and of the press, . . . and that today, also, the liberties of the person are indivisible. "Under Hitler, when it became known that the secret police planted dictaphones in houses, members of families often gathered in bathrooms to conduct whispered discussions of intimate affairs, hoping thus to escape the reach of the sending apparatus." . . . Electronic surveillance strikes deeper than at the ancient feeling that a man's home is his castle; it strikes at freedom of communication, a postulate of our kind of society. Lopez' words to Agent Davis captured by the Minifon were not constitutionally privileged by force of the First Amendment. But

freedom of speech is undermined where people fear to speak unconstrainedly in what they suppose to be the privacy of home and office.
... The right to privacy is the obverse of freedom of speech in another sense. This Court has lately recognized that the First Amendment freedoms may include the right, under certain circumstances, to anonymity.
... The passive and the quiet, equally with the active and the aggressive, are entitled to protection when engaged in the precious activity of expressing ideas or beliefs. Electronic surveillance destroys all anonymity and all privacy; it makes government privy to everything that goes on.

In light of these circumstances I think it is an intolerable anomaly that while conventional searches and seizures are regulated by the Fourth and Fourteenth Amendments and wiretapping is prohibited by federal statute, electronic surveillance as involved in the instant case, which poses the greatest danger to the right of private freedom, is wholly beyond the pale of federal law.

This Court has by and large steadfastly enforced the Fourth Amendment against physical intrusions into person, home, and property by law enforcement officers. But our course of decisions, it now seems, has been outflanked by the technological advances of the very recent past. I cannot but believe that if we continue to condone electronic surveillance by federal agents by permitting the fruits to be used in evidence in the federal courts, we shall be contributing to a climate of official lawlessness and conceding the helplessness of the Constitution and this Court to protect rights "fundamental to a free society."

Frank v. Maryland
360 U.S. 914 (1959)

The growth of services at all levels of government has led to increased dependency on administrative bureaucracies. As a result administrative searches which may invade privacy have increased in both size and scope. It is this kind of search rather than a search for evidence for criminal prosecution which is involved in this case.

After a resident complained of rats in her basement, a health inspector in Baltimore, Maryland, began an investigation of houses in the vicinity to find out where the rats were coming from. He went to Aaron D. Frank's home one afternoon in the course of his investigation but no one responded to his knock on the door. Thereupon the inspector looked around outside the house and found that it was "in an extreme state of decay." In the back of the house he found nearly a half ton pile of "rodent feces" mixed with straw, trash and other debris. At this point Frank emerged from the house and asked the health officer what he was doing on his property. The inspector explained his mission and requested permission to inspect the house even though he did not have a search warrant. Frank refused to let the inspector into the house without a search warrant.

The next morning the health inspector returned to Frank's house with two police officers and again received no response to his knock on the door. He then swore out a warrant for Frank's arrest for violation of a Baltimore ordinance requiring the opening of one's house to daytime inspection by city health officers having cause to suspect the existence of a nuisance. Frank was found guilty and fined $20. After his conviction was sustained by two Maryland courts, Frank brought his case to the Supreme Court on appeal. The Frankfurter and Douglas opinions below reveal clearly the differences in outlook between the activist and self-restraint justices.

MR. JUSTICE FRANKFURTER delivered the opinion of the Court. . . .

We have said that "[t]he security of one's privacy against arbitrary intrusion by the police" is fundamental to a free society and as such protected by the Fourteenth Amendment. . . . Application of the broad restraints of due process compels inquiry into the nature of the demand being made upon individual freedom in a particular context and the justification of social need on which the demand rests.

The history of the constitutional protection against official invasion of the citizen's home makes explicit the human concerns which it was meant to respect. In years prior to the Revolution leading voices in England and the Colonies protested against the ransacking by Crown officers of the homes of citizens in search of evidence of crime or of illegally imported goods. The vivid memory by the newly independent Americans of these abuses produced the Fourth Amendment as a safeguard against such arbitrary official action by officers of the new Union, as like provisions had already found their way into State Constitutions.

. . . [T]wo protections emerge from the broad constitutional proscription of official invasion. The first of these is the right to be secure from intrusion into personal privacy, the right to shut the door on officials of the state unless their entry is under proper authority of law. The second, and intimately related protection, is self-protection: the right to resist unauthorized entry which has as its design the securing of information to fortify the coercive power of the state against the individual, information which may be used to effect a further deprivation of life or liberty or property. Thus, evidence of criminal action may not, save in very limited and closely confined situations, be seized without a judicially issued search warrant. . . . Certainly it is not necessary to accept any particular theory of the interrelationship of the Fourth and Fifth Amendments to realize what history makes plain, that it was on the issue of the right to be secure from searches for evidence to be used in criminal prosecutions or for forfeitures that the great battle for fundamental liberty was fought. While these concerns for individual rights were the historic impulses behind the Fourth Amendment and its analogues in state constitutions, the application of the Fourth Amendment and the extent to which the essential right of privacy is protected by the Due Process Clause of the Fourteenth Amendment are of course not restricted within these historic bounds.

But giving the fullest scope to this constitutional right to privacy, its protection cannot be here invoked. The attempted inspection of appellant's home is merely to determine whether conditions exist which the Baltimore Health Code proscribes. If they do appellant is notified to remedy the infringing conditions. No evidence for criminal prosecution is sought to be seized. Appellant is simply directed to do what he could have been ordered to do without any inspection, and what he cannot properly resist, namely, act in a manner consistent with the maintenance of minimum community standards of health and well-being, including his own. Appellant's resistance can only be based, not on admissible self-protection, but on a rarely voiced denial of any official justification for seeking to enter his home. The constitutional "liberty" that is asserted is the absolute right to refuse consent for an inspection designed and pushed solely for the protection of the community's health, even when the inspection is conducted with due regard for every convenience of time and place.

The power of inspection granted by the Baltimore City Code is strictly limited, more exacting than the analogous provisions of many other municipal codes. Valid grounds for suspicion of the existence of a nuisance must exist. Certainly, the presence of a pile of filth in the back yard combined with the run-down condition of the house gave adequate grounds for such suspicion. The inspection must be made in the day time. Here was no midnight knock on the door, but an orderly visit in the middle of the afternoon with no suggestion that the hour was inconvenient. Moreover, the inspector has no power to force entry and did not attempt it. A fine is imposed for resistance, but officials are not authorized to break past the unwilling occupant.

Thus, not only does the inspection touch at most upon the periphery of the important interests safeguarded by the Fourteenth Amendment's protection against official intrusion, but it is hedged about with safeguards designed to make the least possible demand on the individual occupant, and to cause only the slightest restriction on his claims of privacy. . . .

The need to maintain basic, minimal standards of housing, to prevent the spread of disease and of that pervasive breakdown in the fiber of a people which is produced by slums and the absence of the barest essentials of civilized living, has mounted to a major concern of American government. The growth of cities, the crowding of populations, the increased awareness of the responsibility of the state for the living conditions of its citizens, all have combined to create problems of the enforcement of minimum standards of far greater magnitude than the writers of . . . ancient inspection laws ever dreamed. Time and experience have forcefully taught the power to inspect dwelling places, either as a matter of systematic area-by-area search or, as here, to treat a specific problem, is of indispensable importance to the maintenance of community health; a power that would be greatly hobbled by the blanket requirement of the safeguards necessary for a search of evidence of criminal acts. The need for preventive action is great, and city after city has seen this need and granted the power of inspection to its health officials; and these inspections are apparently welcomed by all but an insignificant few. Certainly, the nature of our society has not vitiated the need for inspections first thought necessary 158 years ago, nor has experience revealed any abuse or inroad on freedom in meeting this need by means that history and dominant public opinion have sanctioned. . . .

In light of the long history of this kind of inspection and of modern needs, we cannot say that the carefully circumscribed demand which Maryland here makes on appellant's freedom has deprived him of due process of law.

Affirmed.

[JUSTICE WHITTAKER wrote a brief concurring opinion.]
MR. JUSTICE DOUGLAS, with whom THE CHIEF JUSTICE, MR. JUSTICE BLACK and MR. JUSTICE BRENNAN concur, dissenting.

The decision today greatly dilutes the right of privacy which every homeowner had the right to believe was part of our American heritage. We witness, indeed, an inquest over a substantial part of the Fourth Amendment.

The question in this case is whether a search warrant is needed to enter a citizen's home to investigate sanitary conditions. The Court holds that no search warrant is needed, that a knock on the door is all that is required, that for failure of the citizen to open the door he can be punished. From these conclusions I am forced to dissent.

The Due Process Clause of the Fourteenth Amendment enjoins upon the States the guarantee of privacy embodied in the Fourth Amendment . . . —whatever may be the means established under the Fourth Amendment to enforce that guarantee. The Court now casts a shadow over that guarantee as respects searches and seizures in civil cases. Any such conclusion would require considerable editing and revision of the Fourth Amendment. For by its terms it protects the citizen against unreasonable searches and seizures by government, whatever may be the complaint. . . .

The Court said in *Wolf v. Colorado* . . . that "The security of one's privacy against arbitrary intrusion by the police—which is at the core of the Fourth Amendment—is basic to a free society." Now that resounding phrase is watered down to embrace only certain invasions of one's privacy. If officials come to inspect sanitary conditions, they may come without a warrant and demand entry as of right. This is a strange deletion to make from the Fourth Amendment. In some States the health inspectors are none other than the police themselves. In some States the presence of unsanitary conditions gives rise to criminal prosecutions. . . . The knock on the door in any health inspection case may thus lay the groundwork for a criminal prosecution. The resistance of the citizen in the present case led to the imposition of a fine. If a fine may be imposed, why not a prison term?

It is said, however, that this fine is so small as to amount only to an assessment to cover the costs of the inspection. Yet if this fine can be imposed, the premises can be revisited without a warrant and repeated fines imposed. The truth is that the amount of the fine is not the measure of the right. The right is the guarantee against invasion of the home by officers without a warrant. No officer of government is authorized to penalize the citizen because he invokes his constitutional protection.

Moreover, the protection of the Fourth Amendment has heretofore been thought to protect privacy when civil litigation, as well as criminal prosecutions, were in the offing. . . . The Court misreads history when it relates the Fourth Amendment primarily to searches for evidence to be used in criminal prosecutions. . . .

The philosophy of the Fourth Amendment was well expressed by Mr. Justice Butler speaking for the Court in *Agnello v. United States,* 269 U.S. 20, 32. "The search of a private dwelling without a warrant is in itself unreasonable and abhorrent to our laws." We have emphasized over and again that a search without a warrant can be made only in exceptional circumstances. If a house is on fire or if the police see a fugitive enter a building, entry without a search warrant can of course be made. Yet absent such extraordinary situations, the right of privacy must yield only when a judicial officer issues a warrant for a search on a showing of probable cause. . . .

In the present case, the homeowner agreed to let the inspector in, if he got a search warrant. But none was ever sought. No excuse exists here for not getting a search warrant. A whole day elapsed between the first inspection and the arrest. . . .

[T]he Fourth Amendment . . . was designed to protect the citizen against uncontrolled invasion of his privacy. It does not make the home a place of refuge from the law. It only requires the sanction of the judiciary rather than the executive before that privacy may be invaded. History shows that all officers tend to be officious; and health inspectors, making out a case for criminal prosecution of the citizen, are no exception.

We live in an era "when politically controlled officials have grown powerful through an ever increasing series of minor infractions of civil liberties." . . . One invasion of privacy by an official of government can be as oppressive as another. Health inspections are important. But they are hardly more important than the search for narcotic peddlers, rapists, kidnappers, murderers, and other criminal elements. . . . Many today would think that the search for subversives was even more important than the search for unsanitary conditions. It would seem that the public interest in protecting privacy is equally as great in one case as in another. The fear that health inspections will suffer if constitutional safeguards are applied is strongly held by some. Like notions obtain by some law enforcement officials who take shortcuts in pursuit of criminals. The same pattern appears over and again whenever government seeks to use its compulsive force against the citizen. Legislative Committees . . . , one-man grand juries . . . , fire marshalls . . . , police . . . , sometimes seek to place their requirements above the Constitution. The official's measure of his own need often does not square with the Bill of Rights.

Certainly this is a poor case for dispensing with the need for a search warrant. Evidence to obtain one was abundant. The house was in a state of extreme decay; and in the rear of the house was a pile of "rodent feces mixed with straw and debris to approximately half a ton."

. . . Figures submitted by the Baltimore Health Department show that citizens are mostly cooperative in granting entrance to inspectors. There were 28,081 inspections in 1954; 25,021 in 1955; 35,120 in 1956; 33,573 in 1957; and 36,119 in 1958. *And in all these instances the number of prosecutions was estimated to average one a year.* Submission by the overwhelming majority of the populace indicates there is no peril to the health program. One rebel a year . . . is not too great a price to pay for maintaining our guarantee of civil rights in full vigor.

England—a nation no less mindful of public health than we and keenly conscious of civil liberties—has long proceeded on the basis that where the citizen denies entrance to a health inspector, a search warrant is needed. . . .

We cannot do less and still be true to the command of the Fourth Amendment which protects even the lowliest home in the land from intrusion on the mere say-so of an official.

AFTERMATH

In 1967 the decision in *Frank v. Maryland* was overruled. Appointments to the Court following the retirement of Justices Frankfurter and Whittaker resulted in a shift to an activist majority. In *Camara v. Municipal Court of the City and County of San Francisco*, the majority opinion, delivered by Justice White, held that under the Fourth Amendment Camara had a constitutional right to insist that building inspectors obtain a search warrant. Consequently, he could not be convicted for withholding consent to a warrantless inspection of his residence. The majority opinion in *See v. City of Seattle*, delivered the same day, also by Justice White, ruled that the Fourth Amendment in this context applies equally to business premises.

Griswold et al. v. Connecticut
381 U.S. 479 (1965)

In response to a widespread movement to suppress sin and vice, Connecticut, in 1879, enacted a stringent law which made it a crime for *anyone*, including married people, to use contraceptives. The statute, characterized by one of the justices as an "uncommonly silly law," further provided that any person who "assists, abets, counsels, causes, hires, or commands another to use contraceptives" may also be prosecuted and punished.

Mrs. Estelle T. Griswold, executive director of a birth control clinic in New Haven, Connecticut, and Dr. C. Lee Buxton, a professor at the Yale Medical School, who served as medical director of the clinic, were arrested and fined $100 each for giving information and advice on birth control measures to married persons in violation of the statute. The defendants admitted that they gave physical examinations to married women, advised them on what kind of contraceptive devices or medicines would be most satisfactory, and then supplied the devices for a graduated scale of fees, based on family income. The convictions were affirmed by an intermediate appellate court and by the State's highest court. The case was then brought to the Supreme Court on appeal. It is interesting to note that among the several briefs in *amici curiae* urging reversal of the convictions was one filed by the Catholic Council on Civil Liberties, proclaiming that the Connecticut law constituted a "profane interference" with the "feelings most close to the expression of man and woman." This action was taken despite the fact that the Roman Catholic hierarchy in Connecticut, where nearly half the population is Catholic, stoutly supported the statute.

Justice Douglas' majority opinion represents the Court's first major attempt to clearly map out a broad constitutional right of privacy. In his dissenting opinion which is briefly noted at the end of the case, Justice Black surprisingly seems to have repudiated judicial activism in favor of judicial self-restraint.

MR. JUSTICE DOUGLAS delivered the opinion of the Court.

The association of people is not mentioned in the Constitution nor in the Bill of Rights. The right to educate a child in a school of the parent's choice—whether public or private or parochial—is also not mentioned. Nor is the right to study any particular subject or any foreign language. Yet the First Amendment has been construed to include certain of those rights.

By *Pierce v. Society of Sisters,* the right to educate one's children as one chooses is made applicable to the States by the force of the First and Fourteenth Amendments. By *Meyer v. Nebraska,* the same dignity is given the right to study the German language in a private school. In other words, the State may not, consistently with the spirit of the First Amendment, contract the spectrum of available knowledge. The right of freedom of speech and press includes not only the right to utter or to print, but the right to distribute, the right to receive, the right to read, . . . and freedom of inquiry, freedom of thought, and freedom to teach . . . indeed the freedom of the entire university community. . . . Without those peripheral rights the specific rights would be less secure. And so we re-affirm the principle of the *Pierce* and the *Meyer* case.

In *NAACP v. Alabama,* . . . we protected the "freedom to associate and privacy in one's association," noting that freedom of association was a peripheral First Amendment right. Disclosure of membership lists of a constitutionally valid association, we held, was invalid "as entailing the likelihood of a substantial restraint upon the exercise by petitioner's members of their right to freedom of association." In other words, the First Amendment has a penumbra where privacy is protected from governmental intrusion. In like context, we have protected forms of "association" that are not political in the customary sense but pertain to the social, legal, and economic benefit of the members. . . . In *Schware v. Board of Bar Examiners*, 353 U.S. 232, we held it not permissible to bar a lawyer from practice, because he had once been a member of the Communist Party. The man's "association with the Party" was not shown to be "anything more than a political faith in a political party" . . . and not action of a kind proving bad moral character. . . .

Those cases involved more than the "right of assembly—a right that extends to all, irrespective of their race or ideology. . . . The right of "association," like the right to believe, is more than the right to attend a meeting; it includes the right to express one's attitudes or philosophies by membership in a group or by affiliation with it or by other lawful means. Association in that context is a form of expression of opinion; and while it is not expressly included in the First Amendment its existence is necessary in making the express guarantees fully meaningful.

The foregoing cases suggest that specific guarantees in the Bill of Rights have penumbras, formed by emanations from those guarantees that help give them life and substance. . . . Various guarantees create zones of privacy. The right of association contained in the penumbra of the First Amendment is one, as we have seen. The Third Amendment in its prohibition against the quartering of soldiers "in any house" in time of peace without the consent of the owner is another facet of that privacy. The Fourth Amendment explicitly affirms the "right of the people to be secure in their persons, houses, papers, and effects against unreasonable searches and seizures." The Fifth Amendment in its Self-Incrimination Clause enables the citizen to create a zone of privacy which government may not force him to surrender to his detriment. The Ninth Amendment provides: "The enumeration in the Constitution, of certain rights, shall not be construed to deny or disparage others retained by the people." The Fourth and Fifth Amendments were described in *Boyd v. United States*, . . . as protection against all governmental invasions "of the sanctity of a man's home and the privacies of life. We recently referred in *Mapp v. Ohio*, . . . to the Fourth Amendment as creating a "right of privacy, no less important than any other right carefully and particularly reserved to the people." . . .

We have had many controversies over these penumbral rights of "privacy and repose." . . . These cases bear witness that the right of privacy which presses for recognition here is a legitimate one.

The present case, then, concerns a relationship lying within the zone of privacy created by several fundamental constitutional guarantees. And it concerns a law which, in forbidding the *use* of contraceptives rather than regulating their manufacture or sale, seeks to achieve its goals by means having a maximum destructive impact upon that relationship. Such a law cannot stand in light of the familiar principle, so often applied by this Court, that a "governmental purpose to control or prevent activities constitutionally subject to state regulation may not be achieved by means which sweep unnecessarily broadly and thereby invade the area of protected freedom. . . . Would we allow the police to search the sacred precincts of marital bedrooms for tell-tale signs of the use of contraceptives? The very idea is repulsive to the notions of privacy surrounding the marriage relationship.

We deal with a right of privacy older than the Bill of Rights—older than our political parties, older than our school system. Marriage is a coming together for better or for worse, hopefully enduring, and intimate to the degree of being sacred. It is an association that promotes a way of life, not causes; a harmony in living, not political faiths; a bilateral loyalty, not commercial or social projects. Yet it is an association for as noble a purpose as any involved in our prior decisions.

Reversed.

[Separate concurring opinions were written by JUSTICES GOLDBERG (joined by CHIEF JUSTICE WARREN and JUSTICE BRENNAN), JUSTICE HARLAN and JUSTICE WHITE.

JUSTICES BLACK and STEWART wrote separate dissenting opinions. JUSTICE BLACK remarked as follows: "I like my privacy as well as the next one, but I am nevertheless compelled to admit that government has a right to invade it unless prohibited by some *specific* constitutional provision." Emphasis supplied.]

APPENDIXES

APPENDIX I

FIRST TEN AMENDMENTS (ADOPTED IN 1791)

Amendment I

Congress shall make no law respecting an establishment of religion, or prohibiting the free exercise thereof; or abridging the freedom of speech, or of the press; or the right of the people peaceably to assemble and to petition the Government for a redress of grievances.

Amendment II

A well-regulated militia being necessary to the security of a free State, the right of the people to keep and bear arms, shall not be infringed.

Amendment III

No soldier shall, in time of peace, be quartered in any house without the consent of the owner, nor in time of war but in a manner to be prescribed by law.

Amendment IV

The right of the people to be secure in their persons, houses, papers, and effects, against unreasonable searches and seizures, shall not be violated, and no warrants shall issue but upon probable cause, supported by oath or affirmation, and particularly describing the place to be searched, and the persons or things to be seized.

Amendment V

No person shall be held to answer for a capital, or otherwise infamous crime, unless on a presentment or indictment of a Grand Jury, except in cases arising in the land or naval forces, or in the militia, when in actual service in time of war or public danger; nor shall any person be subjected for the same offense to be twice put in jeopardy of life or limb; nor shall be compelled in any criminal case to be a witness against himself, nor be deprived of life, liberty, or property, without due process of law; nor shall private property be taken for public use, without just compensation.

Amendment VI

In all criminal prosecutions, the accused shall enjoy the right to a speedy and public trial, by an impartial jury of the State and district wherein the crime shall have been committed, which districts shall have been previously ascertained by law, and to be informed of the nature and cause of the accusation; to be confronted with the witnesses against him; to have compulsory process for obtaining witnesses in his favor, and to have the assistance of counsel for his defense.

Amendment VII

In suits at common law, where the value in controversy shall exceed twenty dollars, the right of trial by jury shall be preserved, and no fact tried by a jury, shall be otherwise re-examined in any court of the United States, than according to the rules of the common law.

Amendment VIII

Excessive bail shall not be required, nor excessive fines imposed, nor cruel and unusual punishments inflicted.

Amendment IX

The enumeration in the Constitution of certain rights shall not be construed to deny or disparage others retained by the people.

Amendment X

The powers not delegated to the United States by the Constitution, nor prohibited by it to the States, are reserved to the States respectively, or to the people.

OTHER AMENDMENTS

Amendment XIII

1. Neither slavery nor involuntary servitude, except as a punishment for crime whereof the party shall have been duly convicted, shall exist within the United States, or any place subject to their jurisdiction.

2. Congress shall have power by appropriate legislation, to enforce the provisions of this article.

Amendment XIV

1. All persons born or naturalized in the United States, and subject to the jurisdiction thereof, are citizens of the United States and of the State wherein they reside. No State shall make or enforce any law which shall abridge the privileges or immunities of citizens of the United States, nor shall any State deprive any person of life, liberty, or property, without due process of law, nor deny to any person within its jurisdiction the equal protection of the laws. . . .

5. The Congress shall have power to enforce by appropriate legislation the provisions of this article.

Amendment XV

1. The right of citizens of the United States to vote shall not be denied or abridged by the United States or by any State on account of race, color, or previous condition of servitude.
2. The Congress shall have power to enforce this article by appropriate legislation.

Amendment XIX

1. The right of citizens of the United States to vote shall not be denied or abridged by the United States or by any State on account of sex.
2. Congress shall have power to enforce this article by appropriate legislation.

Amendment XXIV

1. The right of citizens of the United States to vote in any primary or other election for President or Vice President, for electors for President or Vice President, or for Senator or Representative in Congress, shall not be denied or abridged by the United States or any State by reason of failure to pay any poll tax or other tax.
2. The Congress shall have power to enforce this article by appropriate legislation.

PROVISIONS FROM ORIGINAL CONSTITUTION

Article I

Section 9. . . .
2. The privilege of the writ of habeas corpus shall not be suspended, unless when in cases of rebellion or invasion the public safety may require it.
3. No bill of attainder or ex post facto law shall be passed.
Section 10.
1. No State shall . . . pass any bill of attainder, ex post facto law, or law impairing the obligation of contracts. . . .

Article III

Section 2. . . .
3. The trial of all crimes, except in cases of impeachment, shall be by jury. . . .
Section 3.

1. Treason against the United States shall consist only in levying war against them, or in adhering to their enemies, giving them aid and comfort. No Person shall be convicted of treason unless on the testimony of two witnesses to the same overt act, or on confession in open court.

Article IV

Section 2.

1. The citizens of each State shall be entitled to all privileges and immunities of citizens in the several States.

Article VI

3. . . . . no religious test shall ever be required as a qualification to any office or public trust under the United States.

APPENDIX II

(Capital letters indicate Chief Justices)

NAME	Term of Office
JOHN JAY	1780-1795
John Rutledge	1789-1791
William Cushing	1789-1810
James Wilson	1789-1798
John Blair	1789-1796
James Iredell	1790-1799
Thomas Johnson	1791-1793
William Paterson	1793-1806
JOHN RUTLEDGE	1795[1]
Samuel Chase	1796-1811
OLIVER ELLSWORTH	1796-1799
Bushrod Washington	1798-1829
Alfred Moore	1799-1804
JOHN MARSHALL	1801-1835
William Johnson	1804-1834
Brockholst Livingston	1806-1823
Thomas Todd	1807-1826
Joseph Story	1811-1845
Gabriel Duval	1812-1835
Smith Thompson	1823-1843
Robert Trimble	1826-1828
John McLean	1829-1861
Henry Baldwin	1830-1844
James M. Wayne	1835-1867
ROGER B. TANEY	1836-1864
Philip P. Barbour	1836-1841
John Catron	1837-1865
John McKinley	1837-1852
Peter V. Daniel	1841-1860
Samuel Nelson	1845-1872
Levi Woodbury	1845-1851
Robert C. Grier	1846-1870

[1] John Rutledge's appointment as Chief Justice in 1795 was not confirmed by Congress.

NAME	Term of Office
Benj R. Curtis	1851-1857
John A. Campbell	1853-1861
Nathan Clifford	1858-1881
Noah H. Swayne	1862-1881
Samuel F. Miller	1862-1890
David Davis	1862-1877
Stephen J. Field	1863-1897
SALMON P. CHASE	1864-1873
William Strong	1870-1880
Joseph P. Bradley	1870-1892
Ward Hunt	1873-1882
MORRISON R. WAITE	1874-1888
John M. Harlan	1877-1911
William B. Woods	1881-1887
Stanley Matthews	1881-1889
Horace Gray	1882-1902
Samuel Blatchford	1882-1893
Lucius Q. C. Lamar	1888-1893
MELVILLE W. FULLER	1888-1910
David J. Brewer	1890-1910
Henry B. Brown	1891-1906
George Shiras, Jr.	1892-1903
Howell E. Jackson	1893-1895
Edward D. White	1894-1910
Rufus W. Peckham	1896-1909
Joseph McKenna	1898-1925
Oliver W. Holmes, Jr.	1902-1932
William R. Day	1903-1922
William H. Moody	1906-1910
Horace H. Lurton	1910-1914
Charles E. Hughes	1910-1916
Willis Van Devanter	1911-1937
Joseph R. Lamar	1911-1916
EDWARD D. WHITE	1910-1921
Mahlon Pitney	1912-1922
James C. McReynolds	1914-1941
Louis D. Brandeis	1916-1939
John H. Clarke	1916-1922
WILLIAM H. TAFT	1921-1930
George Sutherland	1922-1938
Pierce Butler	1923-1939

NAME	Term of Office
Edward T. Sanford	1923-1930
Harlan F. Stone	1925-1941
CHARLES E. HUGHES	1930-1941
Owen J. Roberts	1930-1945
Benjamin N. Cardozo	1932-1938
Hugo L. Black	1937-
Stanley F. Reed	1938-1957
Felix Frankfurter	1939-1962
William O. Douglas	1939-
Frank Murphy	1940-1949
HARLAN F. STONE	1941-1946
James F. Byrnes	1941-1942
Robert H. Jackson	1941-1954
Wiley B. Rutledge	1943-1949
Harold H. Burton	1945-1958
FREDERICK M. VINSON	1946-1953
Tom C. Clark	1949-1967
Shermon Minton	1949-1956
EARL WARREN	1953-
John M. Harlan	1955-
William J. Brennan, Jr.	1956-
Charles E. Whittaker	1957-1962
Potter Stewart	1958-
Byron R. White	1962-
Arthur J. Goldberg	1962-1965
Abe Fortas	1965-
Thurgood Marshall	1967-

APPENDIX III

SELECTED SUGGESTIONS FOR FURTHER READING

ABRAHAM, HENRY J., *Freedom and the Court,* Oxford University Press, 1967.

BERMAN, DANIEL M., *It is so Ordered,* Norton, 1966.

CAHN, EDMOND, (ed), *The Great Rights,* Macmillan, 1963.

DI SALLE, MICHAEL with LAWRENCE BLOCHMAN, *The Power of Life or Death,* Random House, 1965.

FRANK, JOHN P., *Marble Palace; the Supreme Court in American Life,* Knopf, 1961.

FRANK, JOHN P., *The Warren Court,* Macmillan, 1964.

LEWIS, ANTHONY, *Gideon's Trumpet,* Random House, 1964.

LEWIS, ANTHONY and the New York Times, *Portrait of a Decade,* Random House, 1964.

LONG, EDWARD V., *The Intruders,* Praeger, 1967.

MILLER, LOREN, *The Petitioners,* Pantheon Books, 1966.

PRETTYMAN, BARRETT, JR., *Death and the Supreme Court,* Harcourt, Brace and World, 1961.

ROCHE, JOHN P., *The Quest for the Dream,* Macmillan, 1963.

WILLIAMS, EDWARD BENNETT, *One Man's Freedom,* Atheneum, 1962.

Report of the Williamstown Workshop, Civil Liberties Educational Foundation, 1962.

INDEX OF CASES

(Titles of cases in capitals and figures which are italicized indicate opinions reprinted in this book. Other titles listed indicate cases cited or discussed in opinions and accompanying material.)

GENERAL INDEX